Front cover
Zawiya Sidi Nasr, cupolas, one whitewashed and the other entirely covered with green tiles, 11th/17th century, Testour.

Museum With No Frontiers *Exhibition Trails*

ISLAMIC ART IN THE MEDITERRANEAN | **TUNISIA**

Ifriqiya
Thirteen Centuries of Art and Architecture in Tunisia

Museum With No Frontiers

EUROPEAN UNION
Euromed Heritage

The realisation of the MWNF Exhibition Trail
IFRIQIYA: Thirteen Centuries of Islamic Art and Architecture
has been co-financed by the **European Union** within the framework
of the **Euromed Heritage** programme
and has received the support of the following Tunisian institutions:

NATIONAL INSTITUTE OF HERITAGE

Ministry of Culture, the National Institute of Heritage (INP)

AGENCY FOR THE DEVELOPMENT OF
THE HERITAGE AND PROMOTION OF CULTURE

Agency for the Development of the Heritage and Promotion of Culture
of the Tunisian Republic (AMVPPC)

Ministry of Tourism of the Tunisian Republic

First edition
© 2002 Ministry of Culture, the National Institute of Heritage, Tunis, Tunisia & Museum With No Frontiers
  (texts and illustrations)
© 2002 Electa (Grijalbo Mondadori S.A.), Madrid, Spain & Museum With No Frontiers

Second edition
© 2010 Ministry of Culture, the National Institute of Heritage, Tunis, Tunisia & Museum With No Frontiers
  (texts and illustrations)
© 2010 Museum With No Frontiers

ISBN: 978-3-902782-18-2

All rights reserved.

Information
www.museumwnf.org
www.mwnfbooks.net

Museum With No Frontiers
Idea and overall concept
Eva Schubert

Heads of Project
Boubaker Ben Fraj, Tunis
Moncef Guellaty, Tunis

Curatorial Committee
Jamila Binous, Tunis
Naceur Baklouti, Sfax
Aziza Ben Tanfous, Jerba
Kadri Bouteraa, Tunis
Mourad Rammah, Kairouan
Ali Zouari, Sfax

Catalogue

Introductions
Jamila Binous, Tunis
Mounira Chapoutot-Remadi, Tunis

Presentation of the Itineraries
Curatorial Committee

With the collaboration of
Ahmed Saadaoui, Tunis
Mohamed Tlili, Al-Kef

Technical Texts
Selim Benattia, Tunis

Photography
Salah Jabeur, Tunis
Guillermo Maestro Casado, Madrid
Selim Benattia, Tunis

General Map
Marie-Charlotte Saaiden, Tunis

Sketches
Riadh Fakhfakh, Tunis
Sergio Viguera, Madrid

General Introduction
Islamic Art in the Mediterranean
Jamila Binous, Tunis
Mahmoud Hawari, East Jerusalem
Manuela Marin, Madrid
Gönül Öney, Izmir

Plans
Şakir Çakmak, Izmir
Ertan Daş, Izmir
Yekta Demiralp, Izmir

Translation
Maria Leonidas Vlotides, London

Copy editor
Mandi Gomez, London

Layout and design
Augustina Fernández,
Electa España, Madrid
Christian Eckart,
MWNF, Vienna (2nd edition)

Local coordination

Production Managers
Selim Benattia, Tunis
Sophie Errais, Tunis

International coordination
Overall coordination
Eva Schubert

Curatorial committees, translations, editing and production of the catalogues (1st edition)
Sakina Missoum, Madrid

Acknowledgements

We thank the following institutions for their support:

The Alumni of the School in rue du Pasha
The Association for the Safeguarding of the Medina (A. S. M.) of Ghar el-Melh
The Association for the Safeguarding of the Medina (A. S. M.) of Bizerte
M. Habib Belhedi, Tataouine
M. Lazhar Cherif, Gafsa
Label Communication, Tunis
M. Mnouchi (Café Mnouchi), Tunis
The town halls as well as the proprietors and caretakers of the monuments of the Museum With No Frontiers Exhibition.

And special thanks to M. Mohamed Benani, who placed his private collection of illustrations at our disposal.

We would also like to thank:

The Spanish Ministry of Foreign Affairs and Cooperation, Spanish Agency for International Development Cooperation
The Spanish Ministry of Culture

The Federal Ministry of Foreign and European Affairs, Austria
The Ministry of Cultural Heritage and Cultural Activities (National Museum for Oriental Arts, Rome), Italy
The Secretary of State for Tourism, Portugal
The Museum of Mediterranean and Near-Eastern Antiquities, Stockholm, Sweden

as well as:

the Regional Government of Tyrol (Austria), where the MWNF Exhibition Trails pilot project was set up

Photographic references

See page 5, and
Ann & Peter Jousiffe (London), page 20 (Aleppo)
Archivos Oronoz Fotógrafos (Madrid), page 23 (Alhambra, Granada)

The opinions expressed in this work do not necessarily reflect the position either of the European Union or of its Member States.

Preface

In 1996 Museum With No Frontiers (MWNF) initiated a comprehensive programme to research, document and increase knowledge and public awareness of the history and cultural legacy of Islam in the countries surrounding the Mediterranean basin. This book is one of the outcomes of this programme, which involves hundreds of scholars and is carried out in cooperation with institutions from all the countries concerned. Important initial funding from the European Union made it possible to set the basis for a sustainable network of public and private partners implementing attractive projects in the field of culture, education and tourism.

When the MWNF programme was first launched, the topic of Islamic art and architecture was familiar only to experts and there was an implicit understanding that cultural heritage in the Mediterranean meant the legacy of the classical civilisations. Thanks to the launch coinciding with the establishment at the end of 1995 of the Euro-Mediterranean Partnership, a joint initiative of the European Union and its Mediterranean neighbours, the MWNF programme took off quickly and became a pioneering venture to disseminate knowledge about the world contribution of Islam.

The initial focus on the Mediterranean region was determined by its place at the centre stage of Islamic history and the economic and cultural interdependence of its shores throughout that history. However, we look forward to extending the programme to other areas of the Islamic and Arab world.

In connection with our Exhibition Trails and related thematic guides, MWNF also offers the possibility to participate in themed tours organised in cooperation with specialised local travel agencies in each country. For further details and virtual tours to the Exhibition Trails please visit *www.mwnftravels.net*.

Our Virtual Museum – *www.discoverislamicart.org* – offers access to a large collection of Islamic artefacts and monuments, with descriptions for all items regularly updated in Arabic, English, French and Spanish. A series of Virtual Exhibitions enables visitors to locate the topics of the Exhibition Trails within the relevant regional context.

All MWNF publications are compiled, written and illustrated by scholars and photographers from the country concerned and convey the cultural and historical context of the featured sites from a local perspective. 'We appreciate only what we see and we understand only what we know.' It was with this idea in mind that our Egyptian colleagues who designed the visit and wrote the text for this book paid particular attention to providing information that usually remains undisclosed to tourists.

On behalf of the whole MWNF team I wish you an enjoyable visit to *Ifriqiya* and look forward to meeting you soon in another part of our Euro-Mediterranean museum with no frontiers.

Eva Schubert
Chairperson and CEO
Museum With No Frontiers

Advice

Transliteration of the Arabic

We have retained standard spelling for Arabic words in common use and accepted by the English dictionary. We have used phonetic spellings for the various dialects spoken within different regions of Tunisia as provided by the authors themselves, as well as the French spelling of the localities. For all other words, we have simplified the transcription. We do not transcribe the initial *hamza* nor do we distinguish between long and short vowels, which have been transcribed as *a, i, u*. The *ta' marbuta* has been transcribed as *a* (in its absolute), and as *at* (when followed by a genitive). The transcription for the 28 Arabic consonants is as follows:

ء	'	ح	h	ز	z	ط	t	ق	q	ه	h
ب	b	خ	kh	س	s	ظ	z	ك	k	و	u/w
ت	t	د	d	ش	sh	ع	'	ل	l	ي	y/i
ث	th	ذ	(dh)	ص	s	غ	(gh)	م	m		
ج	j	ر	r	ض	d	ف	f	ن	n		

Words in italic in the text without an accompanying translation or explanation can be found in the glossary.

The Muslim Era

The Muslim era began with the exodus of the Prophet Muhammad from Mecca to Yathrib. Then the name was changed to Madina, "The City" or "the town of the Prophet". With his small community of followers (70 people including members of his family) recently converted to Islam, the Prophet undertook the *al-hijra* (literally "the emigration") and the new era began.

The date of the emigration is the first of the month of *Muharram* in year 1 of the *Hijra*, which corresponds to the 16th July of the year 622 of the Christian era. The Muslim year is made up of twelve lunar months, each month having 29 or 30 days. Thirty years form a cycle in which the 2nd, 5th, 7th, 10th, 13th, 16th, 18th, 21st, 24th, 26th and 29th are leap years having 355 days; the others are normal years with 354 days. The Muslim lunar year is 10 or 11 days shorter than the Christian solar year. Each day begins immediately after sunset, i.e. at dusk rather than after midnight. Most Muslim countries use both the *Hijra* Calendar (which marks all the religious events) and the Christian Calendar.

Dates

Dates are given according to the *Hijra* calendar followed by their equivalent date in the Christian calendar after an oblique stroke. The *Hijra* date is not indicated in references derived from Christian sources, European historical events or those that have occurred in Europe, Christian dynasties, or dates proceeding the Muslim era or subsequent to the establishment of the French Protectorate in Tunisia in 1881.
Exact correspondence between years in one calendar and another is only possible when the day and month are given. To facilitate reading, we have chosen to avoid intermediate years and, in the case of *Hijra* dates falling between the beginning and end of a century, both centuries are mentioned.
Dates before the Christian era are denoted by the abbreviation BC.

Abbreviations
AD = Anno Domini, BC = before Christ b. = born, d. = died, r. = reigned.

Practical Advice

The *Ifriqiya* Exhibition Trail, which extends from the north to the south of the country, consists of eleven itineraries that spread out between one or two days.

The use of a route map or town plan is recommended. Nonetheless, on the plaques attached to the monuments, the stages (indicated in Arabic numerals) of each itinerary (Roman numerals) are preceded by directions which relate to the choice of the proposed routes (italic texts).

The itineraries consist of main visits and other optional visits, which are distinguished within the catalogue text by their different tone and layout. The monuments whose visits require a lengthy detour, as well as those, which form part of a particularly lavish and meaty itinerary, belong to this latter category.

The paragraphs directly following on from the titles of the monuments offer technical information (for instance how to reach the monument, opening times, etc.), accurate at the time of this catalogue going to press. Museum With No Frontiers holds no responsibility with regard to any future changes liable to occur with respect to such information.

The paragraphs printed on a grey background are descriptions of landscapes and countryside areas chosen for their rich and abundant wildlife, flora and fauna and natural beauty.

A certain number of the monuments included in the itineraries cannot in fact be visited, or were not open to visitors at the time of going to press. Please inform yourselves on the current developments concerning visitor access.

We would like to remind visitors to behave discreetly and respectfully within the religious monuments, which are open to them. The visit to these latter monuments can only be undertaken in the morning, before midday prayers (*salat el-dhohr*). It is important to make sure that clothing is worn that is appropriate to the place and its function. Furthermore, most National Museums are closed on Mondays.

Museum With No Frontiers declines all responsibility with regard to accidents and incidents which could occur during a visit to the Exhibition Trail.

Selim Benattia
Sophie Errais
Production Managers

INDEX

15 **Islamic Art in the Mediterranean**
    Jamila Binous, Mahmoud Hawari, Manuela Marin, Gönül Öney

35 **Historical Overview**
    Mounira Chapoutot-Remadi

51 **Ifriqiya: Thirteen Centuries of Art and Architecture in Tunisia**
    Jamila Binous

64 **Itinerary I**
    The Medina
    Tunisian Ceramics
    Jamila Binous

98 **Itinerary II**
    The Summer Palaces
    Jamila Binous

112 **Itinerary III** (two days)
    The Andalusians
    Ahmed Saadaoui

136 **Itinerary IV**
    Sufism
    Mohamed Tlili

150 **Itinerary V**
    Architecture and Spirituality
    The Rugs of Kairouan
    Mourad Rammah

170 **Itinerary VI**
    The Towns of the Princes
    Tunisian Manuscripts
    Mourad Rammah

184 **Itinerary VII**
    The *Ribat* Towns
    Mourad Rammah

202 **Itinerary VIII**
    The Gate of the Levant
    Ali Zouari
    The Burj
    Ali Zouari

224 **Itinerary IX** (two days)
    The Caravan Staging Posts
    Kadri Bouteraa, Ali Zouari
    Weaving
    Naceur Baklouti
    The Mountain Oases in the Jerid
    Ali Zouari

250 **Itinerary X** (two days)
    Towards the Land of the *Qsur*
    Naceur Baklouti

278 **Itinerary XI**
    Ibadite Architecture
    The Pottery of Jerba
    Aziza Ben Tanfous

294 **Glossary**
299 **Historical Personalities**
303 **Further Reading**
304 **Authors**

ISLAMIC DYNASTIES IN THE MEDITERRANEAN

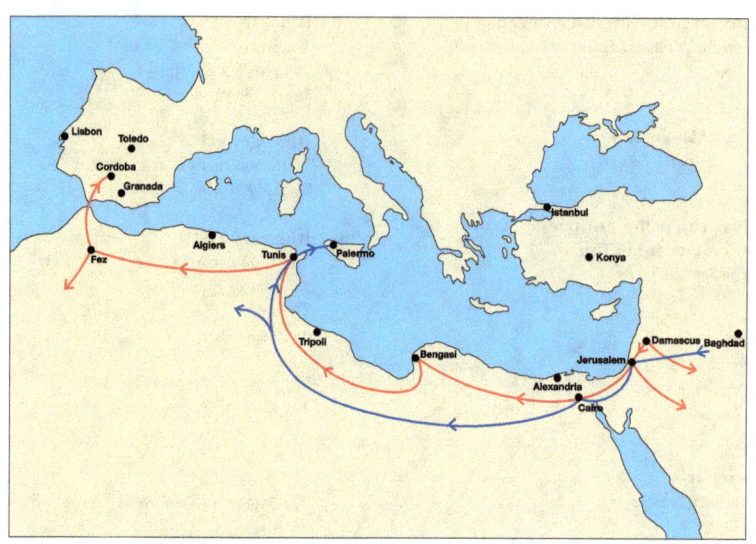

← The Umayyads (41/661-132/750)   Capital: Damascus
← The Abbasids (132/750-656/1258)   Capital: Baghdad

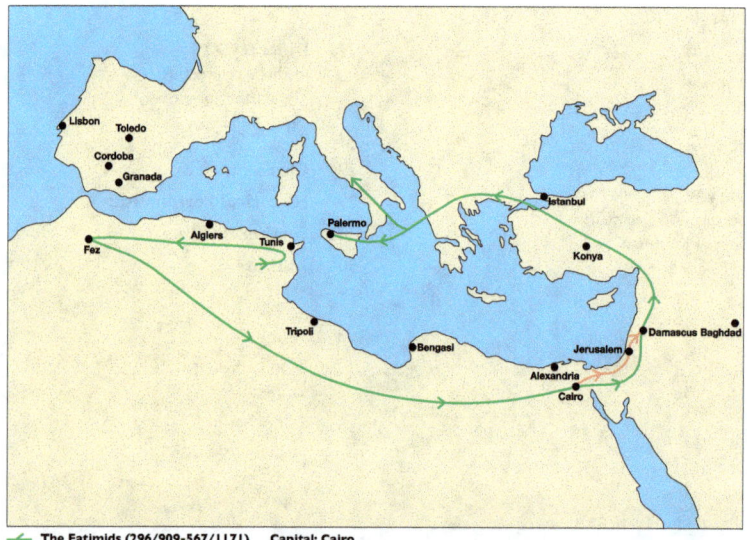

← The Fatimids (296/909-567/1171)   Capital: Cairo
← The Mamluks (648/1250-923/1517)   Capital: Cairo

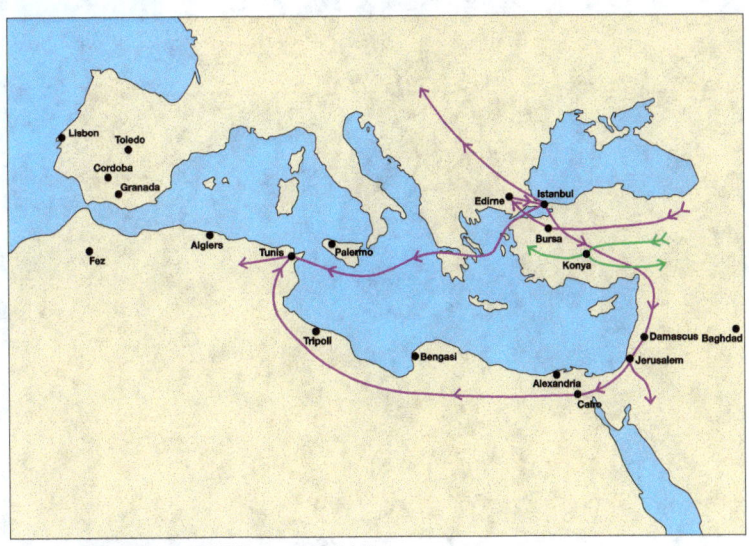

← The Seljuqs (571/1075-718/1318) Capital: Konya
← The Ottomans (699/1299-1340/1922) Capital: Istanbul

← The Almoravids (427/1036-541/1147) Capital: Marrakesh
← The Almohads (515/1121-667/1269) Capital: Marrakesh

Qusayr 'Amra, mural in the Audience Hall, Badiya of Jordan.

ISLAMIC ART IN THE MEDITERRANEAN

Jamila Binous
Mahmoud Hawari
Manuela Marín
Gönül Öney

The Legacy of Islam in the Mediterranean

Since the first half of the $1^{st}/7^{th}$ century, the history of the Mediterranean Basin has belonged, in remarkably similar proportion, to two cultures, Islam and the Christian West. This extensive history of conflict and contact has created a mythology that is widely diffused in the collective imagination, a mythology based on the image of the other as the unyielding enemy, strange and alien, and as such, incomprehensible. It is of course true that battles punctuated those centuries from the time when the Muslims spilled forth from the Arabian Peninsula and took possession of the Fertile Crescent, Egypt, and later, North Africa, Sicily, and the Iberian Peninsula, penetrating into Western Europe as far as the south of France. At the beginning of the $2^{nd}/8^{th}$ century, the Mediterranean came under Islamic control.

This drive to expand, of an intensity seldom equalled in human history, was carried out in the name of a religion that considered itself then heir to its two immediate antecedents: Judaism and Christianity. It would be a gross oversimplification to explain the Islamic expansion exclusively in religious terms. One widespread image in the West presents Islam as a religion of simple dogmas adapted to the needs of the common people, spread by vulgar warriors who poured out from the desert bearing the *Qur'an* on the blades of their swords. This coarse image does away with the intellectual complexity of a religious message that transformed the world from the moment of its inception. It identifies this message with a military threat, and thus justifies a response on the same terms. Finally, it reduces an entire culture to only one of its elements, religion, and in doing so, deprives it of the potential for evolution and change.

The Mediterranean countries that were progressively incorporated into the Muslim world began their journeys from very different starting points. Forms of Islamic life that began to develop in each were quite logically different within the unity that resulted from their shared adhesion to the new religious dogma. It is precisely the capacity to assimilate elements of previous cultures (Hellenistic, Roman, etc.), which has been one of the defining characteristics of Islamic societies. If one restricts one's observations to the geographical area of the Mediterranean, which was extremely diverse culturally at the time of the emergence of Islam, one will discern quickly that this initial moment does not represent a break with previous history in the least. One comes to realise that it is impossible to imagine a monolithic and immutable Islamic world, blindly following an inalterable religious message.

If anything can be singled out as the *leitmotiv* running through the area of the Mediterranean, it is diversity of expression combined with harmony of sentiment, a sentiment more cultural than religious. In the Iberian Peninsula – to begin with the western perimeter of the Mediterranean – the presence of Islam, initially brought about by military conquest, produced a society clearly differentiated from, but in permanent contact with Christian society. The importance of the cultural expression of this Islamic society was felt even after it ceased to exist as such, and gave rise to perhaps one of the most original components of Spanish culture, Mudejar art. Portugal maintained strong Mozarab traditions throughout the Islamic period and there are many imprints from this time that are still clearly visible today. In Morocco and Tunisia, the legacy of al-Andalus was assimilated into the local forms and continues to be evident to this day. The western Mediterranean produced original forms of expression that reflected its conflicting and plural historical evolution.

Lodged between East and West, the Mediterranean Sea is endowed with terrestrial enclaves, such as Sicily, that represent centuries-old key historical locations. Conquered by the Arabs established in Tunisia, Sicily has continued to perpetuate the cultural and historical memory of Islam long after the Muslims ceased to have any political presence on the island. The presence of Sicilian-Norman aesthetic forms preserved in architectural monuments clearly demonstrates that the history of these regions cannot be explained without an understanding of the diversity of social, economic and cultural experiences that flourished on their soil.

In sharp contrast, then, to the immutable and constant image alluded to at the outset, the history of Mediterranean Islam is characterised by surprising diversity. It is made up of a mixture of peoples and ethnicities, deserts and fertile lands. As the major religion has been Islam since the early Middle Ages, it is also true that religious minorities have maintained a presence historically. The Classical Arabic language of the *Qur'an,* has coexisted side-by-side with other languages, as well as with other dialects of Arabic. Within a setting of undeniable unity (Muslim religion, Arabic language and culture), each society has evolved and responded to the challenges of history in its own characteristic manner.

The Emergence and Development of Islamic Art

Throughout these countries, with ancient and diverse civilisations, a new art permeated with images from the Islamic faith emerged at the end of the $2^{nd}/8^{th}$ century, which successfully imposed itself in a period of less than 100 years. This art, in its own particular manner, gave rise to creations and innovations based on unifying regional formulas and architectural and decorative processes, and was simultaneously inspired by the artistic traditions that proceeded it: Greco-Roman and Byzantine, Sasanian, Visigothic, Berber or even Central Asian.

The initial aim of Islamic art was to serve the needs of religion and various aspects of socio-economic life. New buildings appeared for religious purposes such as mosques and sanctuaries. For this reason, architecture played a central role in Islamic art because a whole series of other arts are dependent on it. Apart from architecture a whole range of complimentary minor arts found their artistic expressions in a variety of materials, such as wood, pottery, metal, glass, textiles and paper. In pottery, a great variety of glaze techniques were employed and among these distinguished groups are the lustre and polychrome painted wares. Glass of great beauty was manufactured, reaching excellence with the type adorned with gold and bright enamel colours. In metal work, the most sophisticated technique is inlaying bronze with silver or copper. High-quality textiles and carpets, with geometric, animal and human designs, were made. Illuminated manuscripts with miniature paintings represent a spectacular achievement in the arts of the book. These types of minor arts serve to attest the brilliance of Islamic art.

Figurative art, however, is excluded from the Islamic liturgical domain, which means it is ostracised from the central core of Islamic civilisation and that it is tolerated only at its periphery. Relief work is rare in the decoration of monuments and sculptures are almost flat. This deficit is compensated with a richness in ornamentation on the lavish carved plaster panelling, sculpted wooden panelling, wall tiling and glazed mosaics, as well as on the stalactite friezes, or *muqarnas*. Decorative elements taken from nature, such as leaves, flowers and branches, are generally stylised to the extreme and are so complicated that they rarely call to mind their sources of origin. The intertwining and combining of geometric motifs such as rhombus and etiolated polygons, form interlacing networks that completely cover the surface, resulting in shapes often called arabesques. One innovation within the decorative repertoire is the introduction of epigraphic elements

Dome of the Rock, Jerusalem.

in the ornamentation of monuments, furniture and various other objects. Muslim craftsmen made use of the beauty of Arabic calligraphy, the language of the sacred book, the *Qur'an*, not only for the transcription of the Qur'anic verses, but in all of its variations simply as a decorative motif for the ornamentation of stucco panelling and the edges of panels.

Art was also at the service of rulers. It was for patrons that architects built palaces, mosques, schools, hospitals, bathhouses, *caravanserais* and mausoleums, which would sometimes bear their names. Islamic art is, above all, dynastic art. Each one contributed tendencies that would bring about a partial or complete renewal of artistic forms, depending on historical conditions, the prosperity enjoyed by their states, and the traditions of each people. Islamic art, in spite of its relative unity, allowed for a diversity that gave rise to different styles, each one identified with a dynasty.

The Umayyad Dynasty (41/661-132/750), which transferred the capital of the caliphate to Damascus, represents a singular achievement in the history of Islam. It absorbed and incorporated the Hellenistic and Byzantine legacy in such a way that the classical tradition of the Mediterranean was recast in a new and innovative mould. Islamic art, thus, was formed in Syria, and the architecture, unmistakably Islamic due to the personality of the founders, would continue to bear a relation to Hellenistic and Byzantine art as well. The most important of these monuments are the Dome of the Rock in Jerusalem, the earliest existing monumental Islamic sanctuary, the Great Mosque of Damascus, which served as a model for later mosques, and the desert palaces of Syria, Jordan and Palestine.

When the Abbasid caliphate (132/750-656/1258) succeeded the Umayyads, the political centre of Islam was moved from the Mediterranean to Baghdad in Mesopotamia. This factor would influence the development of Islamic civilisation and the entire range of culture, and art would bear the mark of that change. Abbasid art and architecture were influenced by three major traditions: Sassanian, Central Asian and Seljuq. Central Asian influence was already present in Sassanian architecture, but at Samarra this influence is represented by the stucco style with its arabesque ornamentation that would rapidly spread throughout the Islamic world. The influence of Abbasid monuments can be observed in the buildings constructed during this period in the other regions of the empire, particularly Egypt and Ifriqiya. In Cairo, the Mosque of Ibn Tulun (262/876-265/879) is a masterpiece, remarkable for its plan and unity of conception. It was modelled after the Abbasid Great Mosque of Samarra, particularly its spiral minaret. In Kairouan, the capital of Ifriqiya, vassals of the Abbasid caliphs, the Aghlabids (184/800-296/909) expanded the Great Mosque of Kairouan, one of the most venerable congregational mosques in the Maghrib. Its *mihrab* was covered by ceramic tiles from Mesopotamia.

Kairouan Mosque, mihrab, Tunisia.

Kairouan Mosque, minaret, Tunisia.

Citadel of Aleppo, view of the entrance, Syria.

Complex of Qaluwun, Cairo, Egypt.

The reign of the Fatimids (297/909-567/1171) represents a remarkable period in the history of the Islamic countries of the Mediterranean: North Africa, Sicily, Egypt and Syria. Of their architectural constructions, a few examples remain that bear witness to their past glory. In the central Maghrib the Qal'a of the Bani Hammad and the Mosque of Mahdiya; in Sicily, the Cuba (*Qubba*) and the Zisa (*al-'Aziza*) in Palermo, constructed by Fatimid craftsmen under the Norman King William II; in Cairo, the Azhar Mosque is the most prominent example of Fatimid architecture in Egypt.

The Ayyubids (567/1171-648/1250), who overthrew the Fatimid Dynasty in Cairo, were important patrons of architecture. They established religious institutions (*madrasa*s, *khanqa*s) for the propagation of *Sunni* Islam, mausoleums and welfare projects, as well as awesome fortifications pertaining to the military conflict with the Crusaders. The Citadel of Aleppo in Syria is a remarkable example of their military architecture.

The Mamluks (648/1250-923/1517) successors of the Ayyubids, successfully resisted the Crusades and the Mongols, achieved the unity of Syria and Egypt and created a formidable empire. The wealth and luxury of the Mamluk Sultan's court in Cairo motivated artists and architects to achieve an extraordinarily elegant style of architecture. For the world of Islam, the Mamluk period marked a rebirth and renaissance. The enthusiasm for establishing religious foundations and reconstructing existing ones place the Mamluks among the greatest patrons of art and architecture in the history of Islam. The Mosque of Hassan (757/1356), a funerary mosque built with a cruciform plan in which the four arms of the cross were formed by four *iwan*s of the building around a central courtyard, was typical of the era.

Selimiye Mosque, general view, Edirne, Turkey.

Anatolia was the birthplace of two great Islamic dynasties: the Seljuqs (571/1075-718/1318), who introduced Islam to the region; and the Ottomans (699/1299-1340/1922), who brought about the end of the Byzantine Empire upon capturing Constantinople, and asserted their hegemony throughout the region.

A distinctive style of Seljuq art and architecture flourished with influences from Central Asia, Iran, Mesopotamia and Syria, which merged with elements deriving from Anatolian Christian and antiquity heritage. Konya, the new capital in Central Anatolia, as well as other cities, were enriched with buildings in the newly developed Seljuq style. Numerous mosques, *madrasa*s, *turbe*s and *caravanserais,* which were richly decorated by stucco and tiling with diverse figural representations, have survived to our day.

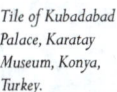

Tile of Kubadabad Palace, Karatay Museum, Konya, Turkey.

As the Seljuq Emirates disintegrated and Byzantium declined, the Ottomans expanded their territory swiftly changing their capital from Iznik to Bursa and then again to Edirne. The conquest of Constantinople in 858/1453 by Sultan Mehmet II provided the necessary impetus for the transition of an emerging state into a great empire. A superpower that extended its boundaries to Vienna including the Balkans in the West and to Iran in the East, as well

Great Mosque of Cordoba, mihrab, Spain.

Madinat al-Zahra', Dar al-Yund, Spain.

as North Africa from Egypt to Algeria, turning the Eastern Mediterranean into an Ottoman sea. The race to surpass the grandeur of the inherited Byzantine churches, exemplified by the Hagia Sophia, culminated in the construction of great mosques in Istanbul. The most significant one is the Mosque of Süleymaniye, built in the $10^{th}/16^{th}$ century by the famous Ottoman architect Sinan, it epitomises the climax in architectural harmony in domed buildings. Most major Ottoman mosques were part of a large building complex called *kulliye* that also consisted several *madrasa*s, a *Qur'an* school, a library, a hospital (*darussifa*), a hostel (*tabhane*), a public kitchen, a *caravanserai* and mausoleums (*turbes*). From the beginning of the $12^{th}/18^{th}$ century, during the so-called Tulip Period, Ottoman architecture and decorative style reflected the influence of French Baroque and Rococo, heralding the Westernisation period in arts and architecture.

Al-Andalus at the western part of the Islamic world became the cradle of a brilliant artistic and cultural expression. 'Abd al-Rahman I established an independent Umayyad caliphate (138/750-422/1031) with Cordoba as its capital. The Great Mosque of Cordoba would pioneer innovative artistic tendencies such as the double-tiered arches with two alternating colours and panels with vegetal ornamentation which would become part of the repertoire of al-Andalus artistic forms.

In the 5th/11th century, the caliphate of Cordoba broke up into a score of principalities incapable of preventing the progressive advance of the reconquest initiated by the Christian states of the Northwestern Iberian Peninsula. These petty kings, or Taifa Kings, summoned the Almoravids in 479/1086 and the Almohads in 540/1145 in order to repel the Christians and re-established partial unity in al-Andalus.

Tinmal Mosque, aerial view, Morocco.

Through their intervention in the Iberian Peninsula, the Almoravids (427/1036-541/1147) came into contact with a new civilisations and were captivated quickly by the refinement of al-Andalus art as reflected in their capital, Marrakesh, where they built a grand mosque and palaces. The influence of the architecture of Cordoba and other capitals such as Seville would be felt in all of the Almoravid monuments from Tlemcen, Algiers to Fez.

Under the rule of the Almohads (515/1121-667/1269), who expanded their hegemony as far as Tunisia, Western Islamic art reached its climax. During this period, artistic creativity that originated with the Almoravid rulers was renewed and masterpieces of Islamic art were created. The Great Mosque of Seville with its minaret the Giralda, the Kutubiya in Marrakesh, the Mosque of Hassan in Rabat and the Mosque of Tinmal high in the Atlas Mountains in Morocco are notable examples.

Ladies Tower and Gardens, Alhambra, Granada, Spain.

Upon the dissolution of the Almohad Empire, the Nasrid Dynasty (629/1232-897/1492) installed itself in Granada and was to experience a period of splendour in the 8th/14th century. The civilisation of Granada would become a cultural

Mertola, general view, Portugal.

Decoration detail, Abu Inan Madrasa, Meknes, Morocco.

model in future centuries in Spain (Mudejar Art) and particularly in Morocco, where this artistic tradition enjoyed great popularity and would be preserved until the present day in the areas of architecture and decoration, music and cuisine. The famous palace and fort of *al-Hamra'* (the Alhambra) in Granada marks the crowning achievement of al-Andalus art, with all features of its artistic repertoire.

At the same time in Morocco, the Merinids (641/1243-876/1471) replaced the Almohads, while in Algeria the 'Abd al-Wadid's reigned (633/1235-922/1516), as did the Hafsids (625/1228-941/1534) in Tunisia. The Merinids perpetuated al-Andalus art, enriching it with new features. They embellished their capital Fez with an abundance of mosques, palaces and *madrasa*s, with their clay mosaic and *zellij* panelling in the wall decorations, considered

Qal'a of the Bani Hammad, minaret, Algeria.

Sa'adian Tomb Marrakesh, Morocco.

to be the most perfect works of Islamic art. The later Moroccan dynasties, the Sa'adians (933/1527-1070/1659) and the 'Alawite (1077/1659 – until the present day), carried on the artistic tradition of al-Andalus that was exiled from its native soil in 897/1492. They continued to build and decorate their monuments using the same formulas and the same decorative themes as had the preceding dynasties, adding innovative touches characteristic of their creative genius. In the early 11th/17th century, emigrants from al-Andalus (the *Moriscos*), who took up residence in the northern cities of Morocco, introduced numerous features of al-Andalus art. Today, Morocco is one of the few countries that has kept traditions of al-Andalus alive in its architecture and furniture, at the same time modernising them as they incorporated the architectural techniques and styles of the 15th/20th century.

ARCHITECTURAL SUMMARY

In general terms, Islamic architecture can be classified into two categories: religious, such as mosques, *madrasas*, mausoleums, and secular, such as palaces, *caravanserais*, fortifications, etc.

Religious Architecture

Mosques

The mosque for obvious reasons lies at the very heart of Islamic architecture. It is an apt symbol of the faith that it serves. That symbolic role was understood by Muslims at a very early stage, and played an important part in the creation of suitable visual markers for the building: minaret, dome, *mihrab*, *minbar*, etc.

The first mosque in Islam was the courtyard of the Prophet's house in Medina, with no architectural refinements. Early mosques built by the Muslims as their empire was expanding were simple. From these buildings developed the congregational or Friday mosque (*jami'*), essential features of which remain today unchanged for nearly 1400 years. The general plan consists of a large courtyard surrounded by arched porticoes, with more aisles or arcades on the side facing Mecca (*qibla*) than the other sides. The Great Umayyad Mosque in Damascus, which followed the plan of the Prophet's Mosque, became the prototype for many mosques built in various parts of the Islamic world.

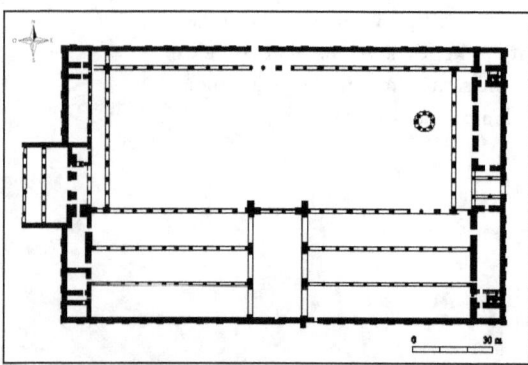

Umayyad Mosque of Damascus, Syria.

Two other types of mosques developed in Anatolia and afterwards in the Ottoman domains: the basilical and the dome types. The first type is a simple pillared hall or basilica that follows late Roman and Byzantine Syrian traditions, introduced with some modifications in the 5th/11th century. The second type, which developed during the Ottoman period, has its organisation of interior space under a single dome. The Ottoman architects in great imperial mosques created a new style of domed construction by merging the Islamic mosque tradition with that of dome building in Anatolia. The main dome rests on a hexagonal support system, while lateral bays are covered by smaller domes. This emphasis on an interior space dominated by a single dome became the starting point of a style that was to be introduced in the 10th/16th century. During this period, mosques became multipurpose social complexes consisting of a *zawiya*, a *madrasa*, a public kitchen, a bath, a *caravanserai* and a mausoleum of the founder. The supreme monument of this style is the Sülaymeniye Mosque in Istanbul built in 965/1557 by the great architect Sinan.

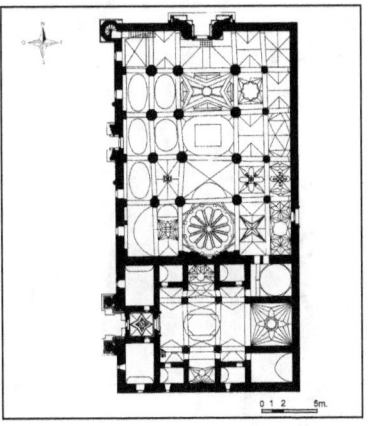

Great Mosque, Divriği, Turkey.

The minaret from the top of which the *muezzin* calls Muslims to prayer, is the most prominent marker of the mosque. In Syria the traditional minaret consists of a square-plan tower built of stone. In Mamluk Egypt minarets are each divided into three distinct zones: a square section at the bottom, an octagonal middle section and a circular section with a small dome on the top. Its shaft is richly decorated and the transition between each section is covered with a band of *muqarnas* decoration. Minarets in North Africa and Spain, that share the square-tower form with Syria, are decorated with panels of motifs around paired sets of windows. During the Ottoman period the octagonal or cylindrical minarets replaced the square tower. Often these are tall pointed minarets and although mosques generally have only one minaret, in major cities there are two, four or even six minarets.

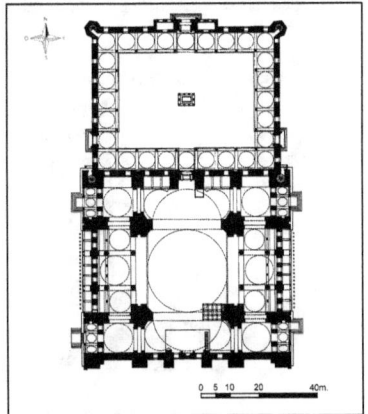

Sülaymeniye Mosque, Istanbul, Turkey.

Typology of minarets.

Madrasas

It seems likely that the Seljuqs built the first *madrasa*s in Persia in the early 5th/11th century when they were small structures with a domed courtyard and two lateral *iwan*s. A later type developed that has an open courtyard with a central *iwan* and which is surrounded by arcades. During the 6th/12th century in Anatolia, the *madrasa* became multifunctional and was intended to serve as a medical school, mental hospital, a hospice with a public kitchen (*imaret*) and a mausoleum. The promotion of *Sunni* (Orthodox) Islam reached a new zenith in Syria and Egypt under the Zengids and the Ayyubids (6th/12th–early 7th/13th centuries). This era witnessed the introduction of the *madrasa* established by a civic or political leader for the advancement of Islamic jurisprudence. The foundation was funded by an endowment in perpetuity (*waqf*), usually the revenues of land or property in the form of an orchard, shops in a market (*suq*), or a bathhouse (*hammam*). The *madrasa* traditionally followed a cruciform plan with a central court surrounded by four *iwan*s. Soon the *madrasa* became a dominant architectural form with mosques adopting a four-*iwan* plan. The *madrasa* gradually lost its sole religious and political function as a propaganda tool and tended to have a broader civic function, serving as a congregational mosque and a mausoleum for the benefactor.

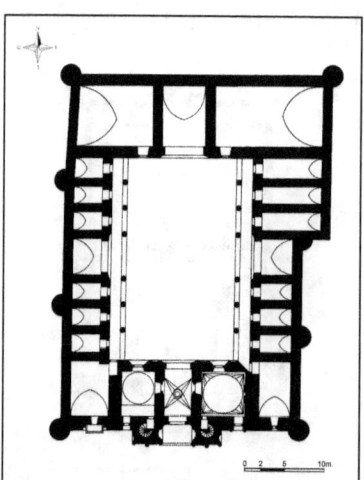

Sivas Gök Madrasa, Turkey.

The construction of m*adrasa*s in Egypt, and particularly in Cairo, gathered new momentum with the arrival of the Mamluks. The typical

Cairene *madrasa* of this era was a multifunctional gigantic four-*iwan* structure with a stalactite (*muqarnas*) portal and splendid façades. With the advent of the Ottomans in the 10th/16th century, the joint foundation, typically a mosque-*madrasa*, became a widespread, large complex that enjoyed imperial patronage. The *iwan* disappeared gradually and was replaced by a dominant dome chamber. A substantial increase in the number of domed cells used by students is a characteristic of Ottoman *madrasa*s.

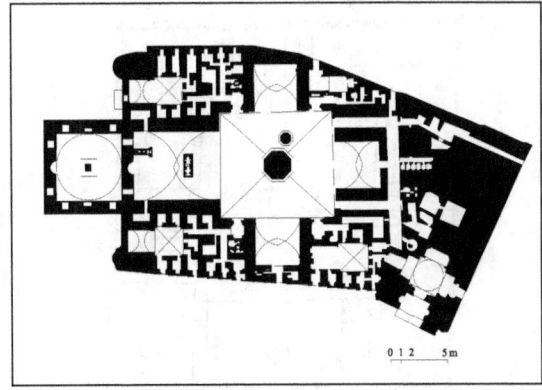

Mosque and Madrasa Sultan Hassan, Cairo, Egypt.

One of the various building types that by virtue of their function and of their form can be related to the *madrasa* is the *khanqa*. The term indicates an institution, rather than a particular kind of building, that houses members of a Muslim mystical (*sufi*) order. Several other words used by Muslim historians as synonyms for *khanqa* include: in the Maghrib, *zawiya*; in Ottoman domain, *tekke*; and in general, *ribat*. *Sufism* permanently dominated the *khanqa*, which originated in eastern Persia during the 4th/10th century. In its simplest form the *khanqa* was a house where a group of pupils gathered around a master (*shaykh*), and it had the facilities for assembly, prayer and communal living. The establishment of *khanqa*s flourished under the Seljuqs during the 5th/11th and the 6th/12th centuries and benefited from the close association between *Sufism* and the *Shafi'i madhhab* (doctrine) favoured by the ruling elite.

Mausoleums

The terminology of the building type of the mausoleum used in Islamic sources is varied. The standard descriptive term *turbe* refers to the function of the building as for burial. Another term is *qubba* that refers to the most identifiable, the dome, and often marks a structure commemorating Biblical prophets, companions of the Prophet Muhammad and religious or military notables. The function of mausoleums is not limited simply to a place of burial

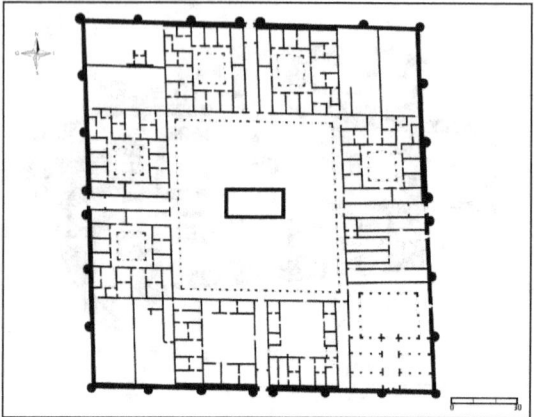

Qasr al-Khayr al-Sharqi, Syria.

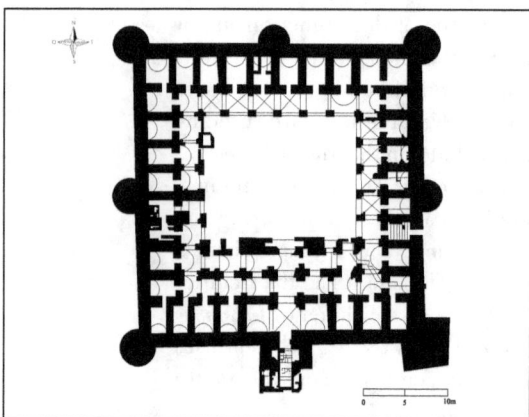

Ribat of Sousse, Tunisia.

and commemoration, but also plays an important role in "popular" religion. They are venerated as tombs of local saints and became places of pilgrimage. Often the structure of a mausoleum is embellished with Qur'anic quotations and contains a *mihrab* within it to render it a place of prayer. In some cases the mausoleum became part of a joint foundation. Forms of medieval Islamic mausoleums are varied, but the traditional one has a domed square plan.

Secular Architecture

Palaces

The Umayyad period is characterised by sumptuous palaces and bathhouses in remote desert regions. Their basic plan is largely derived from Roman military models. Although the decoration of these structures is eclectic, they constitute the best examples of the budding Islamic decorative style. Mosaics, mural paintings, stone or stucco sculpture were used for a remarkable variety of decorations and themes. Abbasid palaces in Iraq, such as those at Samarra and Ukhaidir, follow the same plan as their Umayyad forerunners, but are marked by an increase in size, the use of the great *iwan*, dome and courtyard, and the extensive use of stucco decorations. Palaces in the later Islamic period developed a distinctive style that was more decorative and less monumental. The most remarkable example of royal or princely palaces is the Alhambra. The vast area of the palace is broken up into a series of separate units: gardens, pavilions and courts. The most striking feature of Alhambra, however, is the decoration that provides an extraordinary effect in the interior of the building.

Aksaray Sultan Khan, Turkey.

Caravanserais

A *caravanserai* generally refers to a large structure that provides a lodging place for travellers and merchants. Normally, it has a square or rectangular floor plan, with a single projecting monumental entrance and towers in the exterior walls. A central courtyard is surrounded by porticoes and rooms for lodging travellers, storing merchandise and for the stabling of animals.

The characteristic type of building has a wide range of functions since it has been described as *khan, han, funduq, ribat*. These terms may imply no more than differences in regional vocabularies rather than being distinctive functions or types. The architectural sources of the various types of *caravanserais* are difficult to identify. Some are perhaps derived from the Roman *castrum* or military camp to which the Umayyad desert palaces are related. Other types, in Mesopotamia and Persia, are associated with domestic architecture.

Urban Organisation

From about the 3rd/10th century every town of any significance acquired fortified walls and towers, elaborate gates and a mighty citadel (*qal'a* or *qasba*) as the seat of power. These are massive constructions built in materials characteristic of the region in which they are found; stone in Syria, Palestine and Egypt, or brick, stone and rammed earth in the Iberian Peninsula and North Africa. A unique example of military architecture is the *ribat*. Technically, this is a fortified palace designated for the temporary or permanent warriors of Islam who committed themselves to the defence of frontiers. The *ribat* of Sousse in

Tunisia bears a resemblance to early Islamic palaces, but with a different interior arrangement of large halls, mosque and a minaret.

The division of the majority of Islamic cities into neighbourhoods is based on ethnic and religious affinity and it is also a system of urban organisation that facilitates the administration of the population. In the neighbourhood there is always a mosque. A bathhouse, a fountain, an oven and a group of stores are located either within or nearby. Its structure is formed by a network of streets, alleys and a collection of houses. Depending on the region and era, the home takes on diverse features governed by the historical and cultural traditions, climate and construction materials available.

The market (*suq*), which functions as the nerve-centre for local businesses, would be the most relevant characteristic of Islamic cities. Its distance from the mosque determines the spatial organisation of the markets by specialised guilds. For instance, the professions considered clean and honourable (bookmakers, perfume makers, tailors) are located in the mosque's immediate environs, and the noisy and foul-smelling crafts (blacksmiths, tanning, cloth dying) are situated progressively further from it. This geographic distribution responds to imperatives that rank on strictly technical grounds.

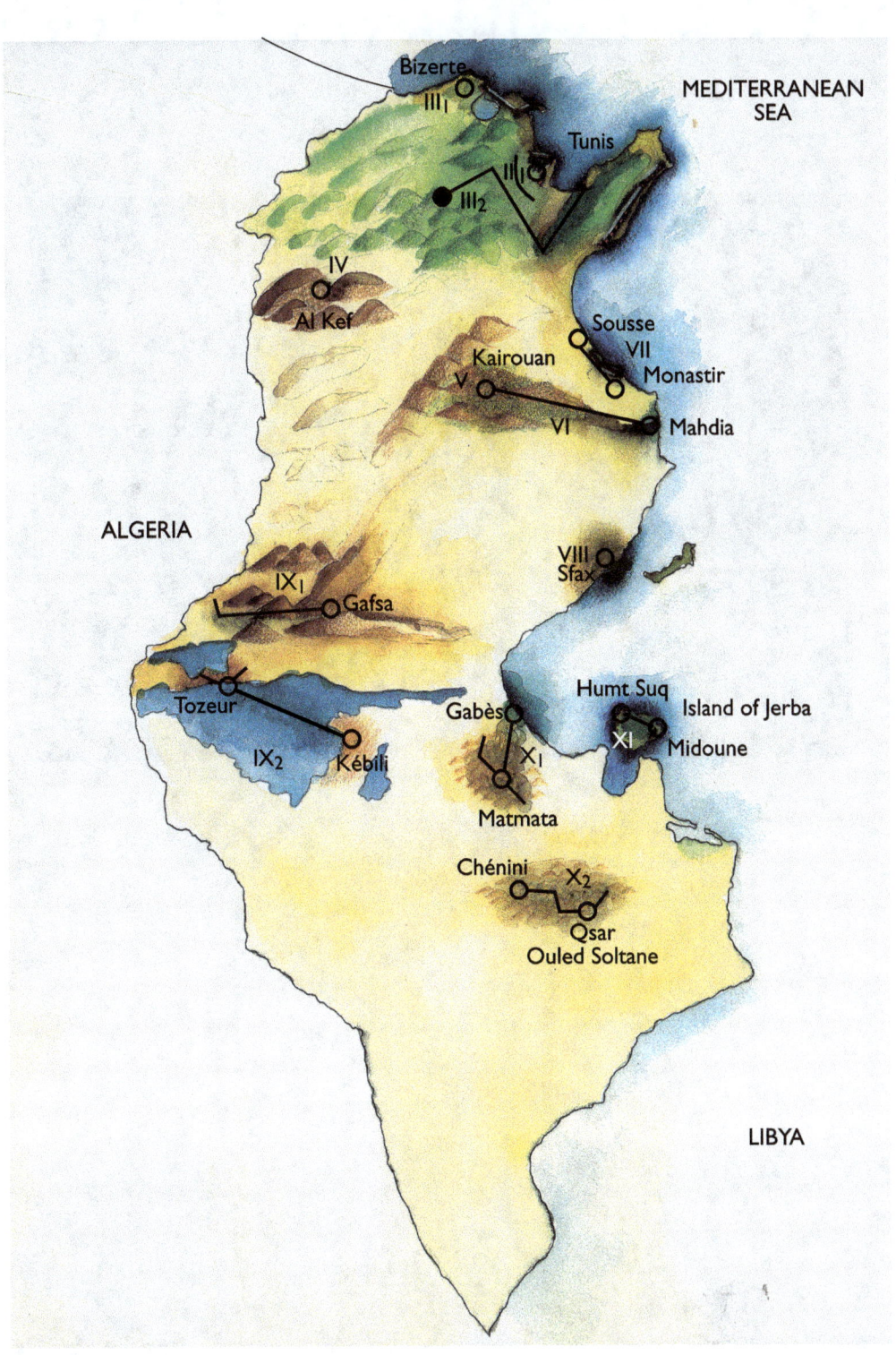

Sidi Tuati Mosque, entrance, Tamerza.

HISTORICAL OVERVIEW

Mounira Chapoutot-Remadi

Viewed on a map, Tunisia resembles a beautiful woman who, stretched out to face the sea, offers herself to the caresses of the waves and monotonous songs of the wind. But, just like Ulysses, who asked his sailors to strap him to the ship's mast so that he could enjoy the song of the sirens without succumbing or losing himself to them, she is built solidly onto the earth, anchored firmly to the continent, to the mountains, to the plains and to the desert.

Africa is a very ancient land occupied in the past by populations who went by the names of Libyans, Moors, Numids, Berbers from "barbarus", and who were foreign to Roman civilisation. In their native language they called themselves *Imazighen*, "Proud Men of the West", and lived in tribes which were regrouped into two main confederations: the Botr and the Baranis.

The eastern region of the Island of the Maghreb, she stood very close to Europe: Kelibia is 140 km. from Sicily and 200 km. from Sardinia. Her position, on the pivot of the two Mediterranean basins, reflects her dual fate, a destiny that is both Eastern and Western. The country lies between the 30th and 37th northern latitude; largely open to the sea with its 1,300 km. of coastline, it is bordered to the south by a sea of sand, the Sahara. Tunisia is both African and Mediterranean.

Its smooth landscape and pleasant climate, as well as the gulfs of Tunis, of Hammamet and of Gabes which irrigate vast plains, could not but attract navigators. The first, the Phoenicians, set up trading posts around 1100 BC, and founded Carthage in 814 BC. Kart Hadash, the "New Town" of Elyssa-Didon, soon overtook Tyr to become the capital of a maritime empire. Through its expansion, Carthage soon found itself confronting Rome and was subsequently destroyed by it in the course of three "Punic wars" (between 264 and 146 BC). Decreed as being a "beastly territory", the Romans burnt the town down and razed it to the ground; but, as the Phoenix rises from the ashes, so was Carthage rebuilt. During six centuries of Roman domination, the Mediterranean had become "Rome's lake", of which Tunisia was a part. After a century of Vandal occupation, the Byzantines, following the Phoenicians, secured onto the Africa Romana of the East in 533. Up until its conquest by the Arabs, she was appended twice to the West and twice to the East. From 24/645, her fate would take a decisive turn under the impetus of her new occupants, the Arabs, who had begun to march insuppressibly to the East and to the West following the death of the Prophet Muhammad in 10/632. The Arabs, more than any other population to land on its shores, would leave their mark on the country forever. Whilst the Phoenicians, Romans, and Byzantines had come from the sea, they had come overland, via an age-old route that linked Egypt to Tunisia. They shared the Berbers's way of life and, in contrast to their precursors, they settled at first inland, safe from the coast which was still in the hands of the Byzantines.

A Long and Difficult Conquest

The conquest of Ifriqiya – an Arabicised name from Roman Africa – was slow, full of pitfalls and setbacks. The Arabs found themselves far from their peninsula, and a chronicler reported that the Caliph, 'Umar, refused the temptation posed by adventure: *"It is not Ifriqiya",* he would say, *"it is a dangerous land which leads you astray and dupes you, and which no one will attack as long as I live."* Whilst it only took a few decades to capture Syria and Mesopotamia, followed by Iran and Egypt, it took nearly 50 years to

Historical Overview

Semi-troglodytic or cave-like habitat of Berber origin, village of Kesra.

instil peace and stability into the Ifriqiya region.

The Caliph 'Uthman decided to take up the advance to the west. He entrusted this mission to 'Abd Allah Ibn Abi Sarh who achieved a stunning victory at Sbeitla, Sufetula'in 26/647 against the patrician Gregory. The Byzantine leader died in battle, the Arabs amassed a sizable booty and negotiated the payment of 300 gold talents in tribute to themselves. But it was to be a short-lived victory. If Byzantium, like Syria and Egypt, had proved to be an idol with clay feet, the Berber resistance was on the other hand far more tenacious. The Arabs undertook several campaigns but each time withdrew further and further back towards Tripoli.

The "great discord" which divided the Muslims in the East, over the issue of the legitimate successor to the assassinated 'Uthman, slowed military operations down even further. 'Ali, cousin and son-in-law of the Prophet, who was the fourth *caliph* after him, was in confrontation with Mu'awiya, Governor of Syria and parent of 'Uthman. The civil war would have torn the young Muslim community apart, but the fighters called for arbitration in order to avoid blood spilling. 'Ali accepted and a few members of his party left in anger at his decision: they came to be called the *khawarij* (kharijite movment), the outcasts or outsiders. Mu'awiya gained the upper hand over his rival and went on to found the first Muslim dynasty: the Umayyads. 'Ali's party and its descendants, *shi'a*, in turn broke off from the *Umma*, the community. Two doctrines, Kharijite and Shi'ite, were thus born over the question of which direction the Muslims should legitimately take, and the conditions required to take it. The doctrines would spread across the whole Empire and would give rise to numerous sects.

In 44/665, Mu'awiyya Ibn Hodayj left Egypt with an army of 20,000 men; he joined up with the troops who had remained in Tripoli under the leadership of 'Uqba Ibn Nafi'. Neither the capture of Jalula in central Tunisia, nor the victorious offensives against Sousse (Hadrumete), Bizerte and Jerba sufficed to persuade the Arabs to stay put following battle. In 49/670, 'Uqba Ibn Nafi' took on a new campaign which resulted in the foundation of Kairouan. A first place in which to lay roots was finally chosen in this environment which remained hostile and uncertain. Called back to the East, 'Uqba was once again put in charge of conquering the "land of the West" in 61/681. 'Uqba seemed to have completed a victorious march which had brought him to the ocean, the neighbouring sea, the formidable liquid barrier which marked the vanishing point of the known world. But on the return to his basecamp, he was attacked and killed by Kosseila, leader of the powerful Awraba tribe, in Tahuda near Biskra in Algeria, in 63/683. Everything seemed to be thrown back into question. For several ensuing years, Kosseila held onto his advantageous position, until he himself was fought and killed by an army led by Zohayr Ibn Qays al-Balaui in 66/686. The Berbers, vanquished, had not however had their final say. The flame would be taken up by a woman, Dahia, or, as the Arabic sources call her, the Kahena, the priestess, of the Jarawa tribe, leader of the confederation of Berbers from the eastern Aures, who led the entire country into Revolt. The crises which were tearing the Eastern Caliphate apart delayed the Arabs's response to the situation, when they then sent Hassan Ibn Nu'man to the rescue. Despite several defeats, it was he who threw the Byzantines out of the country in 78/698 and who more importantly defeated the Kahena. From that time on, Ifriqiya and the Berbers were to become involved in the drive to conquer the rest of the Maghreb as well as Spain. Hassan Ibn Nu'man, master of Carthage, himself had a preference for Tunis, this small Numid city, close-by but protected more securely from the sea. He set up a town-camp there which for a while remained in the shadow of Kairouan, the undisputed capital of the new province gained by the Arab Empire.

In the space of half a century, the Byzantine empire was pushed back out of Syria, Egypt and the parts of Africa which had been taken over by the Arabs. When the Aghlabids took over Sicily, Byzantium only retained a fraction of its Western empire in southern Italy. The West was divided into small kingdoms which had arisen out of the first wave of Barbarian invasions. Of these, the most important kingdom was the Frank kingdom founded by Clovis, the first King of the Merovingian Dynasty (48-751).

Wullat Ifriqiya

As Ifriqiya was now a part of the empire, the Umayyad Caliphs of Damascus needed to designate governors to administer it on their behalf. Their mission was to spread and enforce the word of Islam and the Arab way of life: these were both done slowly and smoothly, in a climate of tolerance and coexistence, at the heart of a capital which was itself developing and evolving gradually. One has to view the foundation of the Kairouan in a wider context and be aware of certain facts. It was both the first Muslim town founded on Ifriqiyan and Maghrebi soil, and the fourth town – after Basra and Kufa in Iraq, and Fustat (ancient Cairo) in Egypt – founded by the Arabs on the same model as that of the Prophet in Medina. Through this gesture, undertaken each time by one of Muhammad's companions or their successors, the founders demonstrated to their people that they had found the home of the *hijra*, a place to which they could emigrate and in which they could observe, in all safety, the precepts of Islam. Like the Prophet, their first concern was to decide the location of the mosque and the residence for the leader of the community; then they proceeded in distributing plots of land for the housing of the different tribes which constituted their army. Temporary housing changed gradually in cities, these first settlements being known as town-camps. The difficulties which had been faced, as well as the suffering, perhaps explains why Kairouan quickly came to be seen as the fourth Holy City after Mecca, Medina and Jerusalem. According to the chroniclers,

Panoramic view of Tunis, 19th-century engraving.

the town housed a number of these famous successors of Muhammad's companions, a bonus which could only raise its profile and sanctity. The governors sent by the Umayyads had a difficult time in imposing their authority over the province. An administration based on the model of that in Damascus developed gradually, whilst its membership of the empire was reflected through it being sent an amount of land-tax and slaves, men and women who were very much appreciated by the Oriental Arabs.

Amongst the number of governors who administered the province in the name of the Umayyads and then on behalf of their successors, the Abbasids, certain ones stand out in particular: Hassan Ibn Nu'man, founder of Tunis, Musa Ibn Nosayr, the skilled orchestrater of the successful conquest of the Muslim West, his lieutenant Tariq Ibn Ziyad, who crossed the Strait and conquered Spain, giving his name to Gibraltar, mountain of Tariq, *jabal* Tariq. This first phase of Ifriqiya's history lasted nearly a century. Kharijism recruited partisans among the Berbers. The new faith served as a pretext for renewed fighting between 122/740 and 154/771, and these zelous believers, who advocated an egalitarian theory of government, and who were expelled from Kairouan, went on to found more-or-less solid dissident States in central and western Maghreb. One of the last governors, al-Aghlab Ibn Selim al-Tamimi, would found his own lineage and give birth to the first native dynasty, that of the Aghlabids.

In 132/750, pretenders claiming ancestral lineage to Muhammad took power. The Abbasid Caliphs founded a dynasty which would go on to reign for over five centuries, to the point at which they were being considered by the Sunnites as the only legitimate caliphate. A surviving Umayyad had been able to escape to Spain where he restored an Umayyad Dynasty, a dynasty of Cordoba, which was to reign over al-Andalus for a little under three centuries, but whose brilliance would rival that of the Eastern Caliphate.

The Aghlabid Emirate

The upheavals in the East could not have occurred without repercussions on Ifriqiya. In 183/800, Ibrahim Ibn al-Aghlab, nominated as Governor by Harun al-Rashid, established a viable autonomous government which took advantage of its distance from the central power base. In fact they were not the first: immediately before them, the Muhallabids had governed for about 30 years.

Western sources mention a delegation sent in 765-768 by Charlemagne to Baghdad. They brought with them Flemish cloth as an offering to the Caliph Harun al-Rashid who in turn sent back a clock. Among the Caliph's messengers was a Aghlabid representative. On the 25th December 800, Charlemagne, reunifying part of the West, crowned himself Emperor in Rome. He had unquestionably restored the empire, but not one that was centred around the Mediterranean. The Carolingian Empire was a Frank, continental and rural one whose capital was Aix-La-Chapelle.

The Aghlabid principality enjoyed a period of boom. The Amirs were enthusiastic builders; Kairouan grew and asserted itself as one of the most glorious capitals of the Muslim West. The town was in its "Baghdad" era; the Great Mosque of 'Uqba was enlarged and modified. The town was surrounded by ramparts; a fresh supply of water was facilitated by the construction of reservoirs which were admired by geographers and travellers alike. The Iraqi model was also employed in other areas. Ibrahim I

Historical Overview

founded al-'Abbasiya in 184/801, 3 km. from Kairouan, whose name reflects its loyalty to the caliphs. It had been preceded by the royal residence of al-'Askar, close to Fustat, which dated from 132/750. The governors of Egypt and Ifriqiya had followed the lead of the first Abbasids who had abandoned Damascus, which was not thought to be very safe, in favour of other places. They had erected several royal residences before founding Baghdad in 144/762. Perhaps it was also a case of needing or wanting to build a link between al-Qata'i', Egypt's royal residence founded in 254/868 by the Tulunids and based on the model of Samarra (221/836), whilst highlighting the same chronological coincidence with the foundation of the new Aghlabid residence of Raqqada near Kairouan in 262/876.

As the Abbasid Empire experienced a true urban explosion, the Barbaric West underwent the exact opposite, with the collapse and disappearance of towns. The Aghlabid Amir copied the institutions of the Caliphate: *vizier*, chamberlains, postmasters, and secretaries, all of whom were often Christian, to help administer the country and its revenues. He governed like a monarch, and whilst the caliph had Turkish guards, his guard was made up of black slaves. The towns were composed of a plural society, incorporating Berbers, those from ancient Byzantium *Rum*, who were bilingual natives, *Afariqa* Arabs from Syria and from Iraq, Yemenites, and Persians from Khurasan; Jews, Christians and Arabs lived together in harmony.

The Jews had arrived in Ifriqiya after the destruction of the Temple of Jerusalem in 70 BC, and Arab sources mention the existence of Judaicised Berber tribes who became Jewish. The Church of North Africa had its own prestigious personalities such as Saint Augustin, Saint Cyprian and Tertullian. Its communities, of which within towns there were many, played an important role within Ifriqiya's economy.

The Aghlabids attracted the educated and scholarly to Kairouan and founded a House of Wisdom, *Bayt al-Hikma*, like the one in Baghdad. Doctors from the East paid visit to the Aghlabid court and contributed to the establishment of a school of medicine for Kairouan. Malekism, which became the principal Sunnite sect knew its greatest scholars then, such as Asad Ibn al-Furat (141/759–213/829) and Sahnun (159/776–239/854). The latter, through his treaty, *Mudawwana*, defined *"the vulgate of North African Malekism"*.

The activities of the Aghlabids were not exclusive to Kairouan; they encompassed the whole of Ifriqiya. Towns like Tunis, Sousse, Monastir and Sfax also benefited according to their needs. The Great Mosque of Tunis was enlarged and embellished, the ramparts rebuilt, and palaces constructed

Intrados displaying Berber decorative work, Douiret.

Historical Overview

View of the town of Sousse, 19th-century watercolour.

outside the town walls, to the north and to the west of the town. The *amirs* protected the coastline with a series of fortresses called *ribats*, the most well-conserved of which were those in Monastir and in Sousse, all of which were guarded by warrior-monks. The Amir Abu Ibrahim Ahmed is attributed with the building of "ten thousand lime and stone fortresses furnished with iron gates". One can only measure accurately the Aghlabid effort through the impression it made on their contemporaries. Confident in their ruling position, they conquered Sicily (211/827–289/902), and Sardinia, a first step into the south of Italy, reaching Rome in 231/846. The Aghlabids ruled over Ifriqiya for close to a century (184/801–296/909) and contributed to its prosperity, but the country could no longer remain sheltered from the Shi'ite-Sunnite conflicts which were affecting and causing rifts along the entire Abbasid Empire.

The Fatimid Caliphate

A propagandist, Abu 'Abd Allah al-Sana'ani, succeeded in winning over the Kutama Berbers of Kabylia to support the cause of his master, 'Ubayd Allah al-Mahdi. A new Berber revolt broke out, this time in order to bring to power a man who claimed to be an *imam* in hiding and a descendant from the seventh *imam* who had given his name to the Isma'ili or Sevener Schism. In 296/909, he seized Kairouan, thus expelling the last of the Aghlabid Amirs, Ziyadat Allah III, whose reputation was tarnished with cruelty. Putting himself antagonistically against the Abbasids from the start, 'Ubayd Allah took the title of Amir of the Believers. He marked out his territory which went beyond that of the Aghlabids, stretching into the central Maghreb, and was in particular able to seize the gold routes of the Sahara. The Fatimids, who were not satisfied with stopping there, formed a strong army and possessed a large war booty which matched their imperial ambitions. They built up a strong navy and had an aggressive naval political policy.

In the 9th century, Europe was attacked by a second wave of "Barbaric" invasion. The Scandinavians from the north and the west, the Arabs along the length of the Mediterranean coastline, and the Hungarians from the east aggravated the situation and caused substantial damage. Since the feudal system had triumphed over the State, causing it to disappear, the counter-offensive could only be undertaken locally. The sea was dominated by the Arabs.

Two years after his accession, in 299/921, 'Ubayd Allah al-Mahdi founded a maritime capital which fitted in more closely with his ambitions for total domination of the Mediterranean, and to which he gave his name, Mahdia. During 24 years of rule, he managed to impose his power both within his own country as well as outside its borders, fighting relentlessly against the Byzantines and posing a threat to the two caliphates which rivalled his, that of Cordoba and Baghdad. A beautiful palace was built in the new capital of Ifriqiya, followed by a *suq*, a naval dockyard, and finally ramparts. The court of Mahdia in turn attracted scholars and doctors, writers and poets. However, the Shi'ite proselytism provoked resistance and renewed Kharijite revolts, the most serious of which was headed by Abu Yazid, nicknamed "the man on the donkey" because he led the insurgents perched on a donkey. A Kharijite extremist from the Nukkar sect, part of the Zenata Berber confederation, he originally came from the Jerid. The rebellion spread like wildfire from the Aures to Kairouan, beginning in 322/934 and lasting until 333/948. Once peace was restored, the Caliph Isma'il took the title of al-Mansur, the Victor, and returned to Kairouan, which then regained its role as the political and economic capital, and which was where he founded a new royal residence in 336/948, Sabra al-Mansuriya.

The Fatimids, faithful to their project of conquering the Abbasid East, were still not satisfied with what they had already acquired. Lead by al-Mu'izz, they made their presence felt all along the Mediterranean by threatening al-Andalus, Byzantium and Egypt. An army, having departed from Ifriqiya, succeeded in encroaching on the Fatimid Empire as far as Fez. In 358/969, al-Mu'izz sent a campaign under the leadership of his freed slave, Jawhar al-Siqilli, who was able to seize Egypt and found Cairo north of Fustat. Al-Mu'izz then left Ifriqiya, which he entrusted to his lieutenant, Bulughin Ibn Ziri, to govern in his name.

The 4th/10th century was called "the Isma'ili century of Islam": one has to remember that during the era of the Fatimid Caliphate, the Abbasid Caliphs had had to accept the protection of the Shi'ite Imam Amirs – the Buyids (333/945–441/1050) who had originally come from Daylam. The Zaydits from Tabaristan and Yemen, and the Karmats from Bahrain are also representative of Shi'ite sects that triumphed in that century but, divided as they were from one another, they were not able to triumph for good.

Zirid Ifriqiya

For the first time since the conquest, Ifriqiya was governed by Berbers. The Zirid Amirs were Sanhajas from central Maghreb who had helped the Fatimids quash the revolt lead by "the man on the donkey". They resided in their capital Achir for some time, before moving to Kairouan, and then to Mahdia. The country which had been left behind by the Fatimids, rose from the ruins it was left in following the great Kharijite revolt. Kairouan once again reappeared as the country's intellectual and economic Capital. However, the power of the Zirids was slowly being weakened by military campaigns in the centre and in the east against the pro-Umayyad Zenatas and pro-Fatimid Kutamas. Their cousins, the Banu Hammad, established an autonomous principality in

Berber mountain ridge village, Tamezret.

eastern Algeria, founding their own capital, the Qal'a. The Kairouanese, eager to reestablish Malikism, put pressure on the Zirids. Around 441/1050, the Amir al-Mu'izz Ibn Badis broke with Cairo and renewed links with Baghdad. At the same time, the arrival of the Turkish Seljuqs weakened Shi'ism in the East. The Caliph al-Mustansir responded to this situation by handing Ifriqiya over to the restless, wandering Arab tribes who swept through the country: the Hilalians.

The Hilalians: History and Epic

The Banu Hilal, *"Sons of the crescent moon"*, were Arab nomads who had a long time ago left their native *Najd* in the peninsula, some of whom had emigrated to Upper Egypt. In order to tempt them to move on again, a Fatimid *vizier* had told them: *"I give you the Maghreb and the kingdom of al-Mu'izz Ibn Badis, the rebel slave. Thus you will no longer be in need of anything"*. The treacherous land of Ifriqiya was thus made to seem like the promised land! That was how the sources described this fundamental turning point which the Muslim Empire underwent during the 5th/11th century, a century marked by a return to nomadic ways of living and a move away from urban life. Whilst the Hilalians emigrated to Ifriqiya, the Turkish Seljuqs, themselves also nomads, entered Baghdad, chasing away the Shi'ite guards of the caliph, putting themselves in their place.

Kairouan, pillaged and ruined by the Hilalians, lost its role as a capital city for good, and the countryside returned to a rural economy. The catastrophic consequences of Hilalian rule were described by all kinds of chroniclers and urban "civilised" eye-witnesses hostile to the Bedouins, who were seen as predators, as destroyers of culture and masters of ruin. In addition, the eternal conflict between the transhuman breeder and the sedentary peasant resurged. The presence of the Hilalians profoundly Arabicised the countryside, giving Tunisia very strong ethnic and cultural cohesion. Collective memory on the one hand recalls the arrival of these tribes, which represented a break in history, whilst also remembering mythical epic tales which recount their acts. Very long-sung poems tell of the long migration westward, the loves of Jazya and Abu Zayd al-Hilali, whilst paintings under glass naively depict a certain number of these episodes.

The towns which resisted the Hilalian invasion, such as Tunis, Sfax, Tozeur, Gabes, and Tripoli, handed themselves over to the leaders of Berber tribes who assured them protection. These small City-States were governed by autonomous dynasties like the Banu al-Ward in Bizerte, the Banu al-Rand in Gafsa, the Banu Malil in Sfax, and the Banu al-Jami in Gabes. Mahdia itself remained in the hands of the Zirids until the middle of the 6th/11th century. Tunis, in particular, was governed by the Banu Khurasan for nearly a century and thus experienced a relative amount of security. Not only was the town protected, but the suburban population increased, and Jews were allowed to settle inside the city walls. Its Amirs constructed a palace and a mosque, south-west of the Zituna Mosque, and in so doing displaced the town's centre of gravity, in preparation of it becoming the third capital city of Ifriqiya.

The situation was hardly better in Andalusia. The Umayyad caliphate was falling into decline whilst the Christian kingdoms in the north-west of Spain were arming themselves in order to start the Reconquest. Muslim Spain was politically divided up into tiny rival kingdoms, who often allied themselves with the Christians in order to fight each other.

Historical Overview

The West became offensive during the length of this, the $5^{th}/11^{th}$ century. The Normans were indisputably the most dynamic of the European counterparts. Having settled in Normandy in 911, some went on to conquer England in 1066 whilst others seized southern Italy and Sicily. Once they had reached the shores of the Mediterranean, they begun to dream of founding a vast maritime empire, encompassing Byzantium, Ifriqiya and Egypt. Their attacks were close to being successful, but, whilst they were not able to hold onto power in these three lands, they established a Sicilian-Norman monarchy which was both glorious and unique; they took part in the First Crusade at the end of this same century (490/1097) and it was one of them who founded the principality of Antioch. It was at the court of Roger II of Palermo that the Arab geographer al-Idrisi wrote his famous treaty "The pleasant character of he who is filled with the desire of discovering the horizons", also called the "Book of Roger" because he had dedicated it to the King.

During this period, the East was battling against the crusades. However, whilst the First Crusade brought about the creation of the four Latin States of the Holy Land – the principalities of Edesse, and Antioch, the earldom of Tripoli, and the kingdom of Jerusalem – the aim of the seven crusades that followed was to maintain these States whilst the spirit of Holy War encouraged the Zengids, followed by the Ayyubids and the Mamluks, to reconquer these lands.

Masters of the sea, the Italian, Frank and Catalan merchants flocked into the ports of the Maghreb and the East. They negotiated treaties that accorded them protection for themselves and their goods, as well as fiscal privileges and *funduqs*.

The profound transformations undergone by the Muslim world were reflected in attempts to react, in the East as in the West. While the Fatimids, followed by the Zirids, had attempted to unify the Maghreb starting with Ifriqiya, two Berber dynasties from the south of Morocco, the Almoravids and the Almohads, had tried in turn to reunite the Maghreb and al-Andalus. The latter succeeded, but it had not merely been a simple lust for power that had galvanised their troops. It was led by two men, the "Mahdi" Ibn Tumart and his disciple, 'Abd al-Mu'min, who claimed to be rigorous partisans of the uniqueness of God, hence the origin of their name, *Muwahhidun*, Almohads. Their leader was thus an infallible *imam*, assisted by a council of 10 of his closest disciples, and a council of 50 who represented the distinct populations. The Almohads defeated the Hilalians and called for a Holy War against the Normans who, having taken advantage of the chaos, had seized Sousse, Mahdia, Sfax and Jerba. A governor was nominated for Tunis, which had been chosen as the capital of the province, whilst they remained in Marrakesh.

Hafsid Ifriqiya

A great Almohad *shaykh*, 'Abd al-Wahid Ibn Abi Hafs, a member of the Hentata tribe of

A caravan stop, 19th- century watercolour.

Morocco, was chosen in 602/1206 to govern Ifriqiya. He had a difficult task to face as the country was being menaced by the princes of Mallorca as well as by Saladin's Lieutenant Karakush who was allied to the Hilalians. After a certain period, the distancing and estrangement of the Almohad capital, Marrakesh, allowed Governor Abu Zakariya Ibn Abi Hafs to seize the first opportunity to break away in 630/1233 and affirm his autonomy. A new dynasty had come to power in Ifriqiya and was to hold onto it for more than three centuries. Abu Zakariya had only taken the title of Amir; his son Abu 'Abd Allah took the title of Prince of the Worshipful, *Amir al-Mu'minin*, and the honorific title of al-Mustansir.

His ambitions can partly be explained by the situation in the East. The Mongols, who had begun to march westward under the leadership of Gengis Khan, entered Iraq in 655/1258. With the Abbasids assassinated and Baghdad destroyed, al-Mustansir thus laid claim to the caliphate. He was recognised as such by Mecca for a number of years, but things never went any further. The Abbasid Caliphate was restored in Cairo three years later by the Mamluks, who blow by blow seized power and saved Egypt through expelling the Franks of the Seventh Crusade and above all through having halted the Mongol invasion in 658/1260. A new power thus established itself in the East, possessing extraordinary prestige for having stopped the Mongol advance and saving Islam. Saint Louis, defeated in Egypt, turned his gaze towards Hafsid Ifriqiya in 668/1270. He wanted to cross the country and use the terrestrial route leading to Egypt, considered to be the only country capable of preventing the crusades, to keep themselves going in Syria-Palestine. But he was also being pushed into it by his brother, Charles of Anjou, King of Sicily, who himself wanted to resurrect Norman ambitions towards Ifriqiya. However, Saint Louis died in Tunis and was buried on the Hill of Carthage. The danger of war was avoided, and it was to be the final crusade ever organised in the West.

The Black Death of 748/1348 caused extreme chaos. Originating in Asia, it ravaged every European country as well as countries south of the Mediterranean, leaving behind considerable gaps in the populations. It then turned into an endemic disease which remained active until the $13^{th}/19^{th}$ century, and which was particularly common in ports.

In the middle of the $8^{th}/14^{th}$ century, the expansionist ambitions of a new force which had come to power in the west of the Maghreb posed a serious threat to Tunis and the Hafsid Dynasty: the force of the Merinids. Tunis was occupied twice, in 749/1349 and 756/1356, but despite these crises and grave dangers, the Hafsids managed to hold onto power. Ifriqiya experienced a renaissance during what was a glorious $9^{th}/15^{th}$ century, particularly under the reign of Abu Faris 'Abd al-'Aziz (796/1394–837/1494) and his son 'Uthman (838/1435–899/1494).

Tunis, which nevertheless was the intellectual and economic capital, adorned itself with finery. A number of monuments bearing witness to this time have remained. The Palace of the Kasbah, with its mosque, became the new centre of town. Monuments also include extensions to the Mosque of the Zituna, the construction of an ablutions fountain, *midha al-Sultan*, and the restoration and adaptation of the Roman aqueduct. But above all, the growing density of the population resulted not only in the expansion of the town's suburbs, but in the edification of a second city wall to enclose them. The expansion of the town coincided with the increase in great as well as neighbourhood mosques, *madrasas*, colleges and *zawiyas*. Ifriqiyan art reflects relatively well the dual influence of the East on the one hand and of al-Andalus on the other.

The invention of the printing press by Gutenberg is in itself a primordial moment in cultural history; progress in navigational technology would open European doors of discovery to the New World. The circumnavigation of Africa would allow the Portuguese to discover the route to India. The Mediterranean seemed to have lost its pulling power; Europe was turning itself towards the colonies across the Atlantic whilst it also experienced a new and very important period of civilisation. Both humanism and the Renaissance were expressed across the whole of Europe through the flourishing of the arts and literature which represented a break with past centuries.

Meanwhile, dark skies lay ahead for the Hafsid Dynasty whilst Europe got through the decisive stages which would lead it to modernity. After the fall of Granada in 897/1492, the African crusade undertaken by the Spanish threatened the Maghreb coast all the way up to Tunis. At the same time however, a new force rose to power in the East: the Turks conquered Constantinople in 856/1453 and were also themselves advancing into Europe and the Mediterranean, occupying Syria and Egypt in 922/1517. The Spanish and the Turks would from now on fight over who would be master of the Mediterranean. A couple of privateers or pirates, the brothers Baba 'Aruj and Khayr al-Din Barbarossa, who had occupied Algiers since 921/1516, seized Tunis in 940/1534 and expelled the Sultan Mulay al-Hassan, putting an end to the Hafsid Dynasty. However, a considerable fleet belonging to Charles Quint and his allies took the town back in 941/1535. The Spanish reinstated the deposed sultan and built a fort in la Goulette housing a garrison of 12,000 men to defend the entrance to the harbour and the Nova Arx Fort at the town's entrance, on the side of Bab al-Barh, the Gate of the Sea. The Spanish protectorate lasted until 981/1574, and consisted of a very troubled period in the history of Tunis and of the country. The pirates, in despair in trying to expel them with their own forces, called on the Turks to help, and the Ottoman fleet of Sinan Pasha seized the town for good in 981/1574.

Fernand Braudel noted correctly that the two powers would confront one another *"at the meeting of two seas"* at Tripoli (916/1511, 957/1551), at Jerba (915/1510, 926/1520, 967/1560), at Tunis (941/1535, 980/1573, 981/1574), at Malta (972/1565) and finally at Lepante (978/1571).

The Regency of Tunis

A new chapter in the history of Ifriqiya starts with the beginnings of the modern era. The country became a province of the Ottoman Empire, and remained so for three centuries. This time Ifriqiya found itself attached to the Ottoman East; Istanbul, a great Mediterranean capital, became the new empire's centre of gravity. But, given its distance from the metropolis, the Regency (*Iyala*) of Tunis was able to retain an autonomy of sorts as it was governed by local dynasties.

The expansion of European horizons after the discovery of the New World, the triumph of mercantile capitalism and the arrival of a "global economy", as well as the adoption of firearms, were among the factors which marked the ushering in of the modern age into Europe. The entire Maghreb had to adapt to these new circumstances. The country had been thrown into turmoil by the war and the resurgence of centrifugal forces like the forces of the tribes.

The *Pashas* nominated by the government in Istanbul, followed by the *deys*, were in charge of rebuilding the economy, of restoring law and order, and of establishing a political and military administration adapted to the new situation. A militia of janissaries, the *Ujak*, composed of 4,000 men divided into units of 100, each led by a *dey*, was stationed as a garrison in the coastal towns. Having been given firearms and taught the new techniques of war, it was put in charge of restoring the rule of law and order. The Pacha was deputised by the *Diwan*, an assembly of 40 *deys* from the militia, in governing the country. Turks, renegades and Andalusians held the highest administrative posts.

A heavy and complex fiscal system, based on the exploitation of local populations, required the biannual intervention of the army. In the towns and active regions, taxes were consolidated by rich local notables. Important revenues were also gained from commerce and privateering.

Power slowly transferred into the hands of the *deys* around the 10th-11th/end of 16th century. The rebel militia had in effect nominated one of the *deys*, Ibrahim Rodseli, to lead the country, confining the pacha to a merely honorary position. 'Uthman Dey (1002/1594–1018/1610) and Yussef Dey (1018/610–1046/1637) both played an important role in the reconstruction of the country. A new wave of Moorish emigration, following the expulsion edict of 1017/1609 promulgated by Philip III, bringing over an industrious population who would introduce the age-old practices of horticulture and a craft of fez – tarboosh making – which fed a prosperous maritime trade.

New *suqs* appeared, linked to the presence of the Turks: Suq *al-Truk*, Suq of the Turks, reunited the tailors specialised in the creation of Turkish outfits; the Suq of the *bashmaqiya*, where babouches were made; the Suq *al-Ghazl*, selling spun wool, the Suq *al-Bey*, and above all the Suq of the *Shawashis*. Mosques appeared belonging to the Hanifite sect subscribed to by the Turks. The first was the Mosque of the Kasbah, followed by one constructed by Yussef Dey at the heart of the *suqs*; Hammuda Pasha built another one, the Mosque of Sidi Ben 'Arus, in 1065/1655. The Bey Mohammed, in erecting the Mosque of the Domes of Sidi Mahrez in 1103/1692, endowed Tunis with a building similar to the monuments of Istanbul. The Madrasas of Murad II and of Yussef Dey should be added to this list of original architectural monuments.

At the beginning of the 11th/17th century, the *bey* in command of the army responsible for tax collection, the *mhalla*, gained greater and greater importance, at the expense of the *dey*. The Bey Usta Murad Corso, a renegade of Corsican origin, succeeded in imposing the principle of dynastic succession by order of offspring, and imposed it at the heart of his own family, thus passing his position onto his son Hammuda Pasha. The Muradids held onto a power of sorts for half a century. Tunis was renovated and embellished, as were other towns like Bizerte, Sousse and Sfax. The Andalusians founded agricultural villages like al-'Alya, Qal'at al-Andalus, Testur and Soliman. However, the rivalry between the *deys* and the *beys* lead to a period of trouble and instability which would last until 1116/1705.

The 16th and 17th centuries were the centuries of the Reformation, the Counter-Reformation, and of religious wars which took hold of Europe. It was also the century of Louis XIV, of Classicism and the Baroque in art, of Moliere, Racine, Corneille, Pascal and Descartes and many other great names.

Husaynite Tunisia

The Bey Husayn Ibn 'Ali came out of the crisis victorious and founded a dynasty which would rule over Tunisia until 1376/1957. In fact, the first few years of this dynasty were overshadowed by familial infighting between the *Husayniya* and their cousins the *Bashiya*, but the former ended up victorious in 1179/1766 with the help of the *deys* of Algiers. The Beylical monarchy consolidated itself progressively, whilst at its heart a cosmopolitan society – with its Turks, renegades, Andalusians, Leghornese' Jews, European merchants and natives – all blended harmoniously but very gradually together, due to their sharing activities.

Governmental activities were held by the Turkish aristocracy; originally composed of Ottomans, in particular from the Balkans and from the Levant – it was now made up of Mamluks or renegades of European origin, of men from Provence and of Italians captured at sea (taken as slaves, converted to Islam and then freed), and of *kulughlis*. These last were half-castes, the sons of Turks and native women. A commercial bourgeoisie emerged, linked to privateering, which was officially instituted in the 11th/17th century, and to export trading, whilst the *shawashi*s, the makers of tarbooshes or Fez hats, dominated the crafts, ahead of booksellers, perfume makers, saddle makers, goldsmiths, silk weavers and makers of babouches. The old *'ulema'* class, or educated minority, which played such a vital role under the Hafsids, resurfaced gradually in its former description as the keeper of knowledge, and filled the ranks of the administration and the judiciary. These large families allied themselves and formed the elite of Tunisian society. The Leghornese' Jews, *guerni*, were distinct from other local Jews, *twansa*, through their language, dress and activities. They dominated Mediterranean commerce and finances whilst the *twansa*s were, above all, jewellers and shop-owners and had no desire to mix, living in separate neighbourhoods with their own synagogues. In the rest of the country, local notables, *shaykh*s of tribes, marabout families and general farmers allied themselves to, and supported, the regime. The *Makhzen* tribes, allied to the government, pressurised the *mhalla* in the countryside for the collection of taxes.

Trade with Western Europe intensified, particularly from the second half of the 17th century onwards, with French merchants imposing themselves to the point of becoming intermediaries between the

Western fort, enclosure, Ghar al-Melh.

Regency and European countries. But things changed during the 18th century: the Spanish navy, which until then had been so formidable and terrifying, fell into decline; in 1798, on his way to Egypt, Bonaparte put an end to the State of Cavaliers of the Order of Saint John of Malta; the kingdoms of Naples and of the Two Sicilies found themselves isolated; and the Napoleonic Wars finally provoked the commercial decline of the French in the Mediterranean and put an end to the exclusivity they enjoyed in Tunisia.

The Husaynite *beys* abolished the titles of *deys* and *pashas*, becoming the sole representatives of the Ottoman Sultan, vesting to themselves the three dignitary positions with their attached responsibilities. While all in all enjoying *de facto* autonomy, the link to the Ottoman Gate was, in particular, highlighted by a certain imitation of their institutions. In fact, the positions of *sahib al-taba'a*, lord chancellor or keeper of the seals, of *bash-katib*, minister of writing, of *khaznadar*, minister of finance, of *agha*, *kahiya* and others were added to the already established posts of *dey* and *bey*. It is true that the currency and Friday prayers were reminders of the suzerainty of the Sultan of Istanbul, but this link was purely nominal. The Beylical army absorbed the old janissary militia and conscription via the drawing of lots, which secured the process of recruitment from then on. Hammuda Pasha (1195/1781–1228/1813) was responsible for the reorganisation of the military, and assured the country's defence. He reformed the fiscal system, improved the harbour network, and initiated the building of the Dar al-Bey in Tunis and the Palace of the Rose in his own neighbourhood.

It was a crucial period for Europe. Above all France put an end to its Bourbon monarchy with the Revolution of 1789. A Revolution whose slogan was "Liberty, Equality, Fraternity", which achieved "The Declaration of the Rights of Man and Citizen", whose theme tune was "the Marseillaise", and that dreamed of taking itself right across Europe. Following events characterised by bloody wars with neighbouring countries, the Revolution, which was essentially bourgeois in nature, came to a head in the form of a consulate led by a Corsican soldier, Napoleon Bonaparte, whose future held great promise as he later became Emperor in 1804. The adventure was a brilliant but relatively short lived one. At the Vienna Congress of 1815, the coalition of Europe put an end to the Napoleonic dream.

A radical transformation occurred after the Vienna Congress. Europe called for the suppression of privateering and an end to slavery, which caused a crisis. A series of catastrophic events then befell the country: privateering was abolished, the janissary militia revolted in 1230/1816, and two serious plague and cholera epidemics devastated the country in 1230/1816 and 1232/1818. The currency underwent a crucial devaluation in 1240/1825; the fleet was destroyed in the Battle of Navarin two years later; in 1244/1829, there was a drought. Worse still, the country's economy would henceforth suffer due to having to trade with Europe from a position in which it was no longer its equal: whereas the price of its exported raw materials decreased, European products flooded the market. Another even more serious hurdle in terms of its future arose with France's capture of Algiers in 1830. Shortly afterwards, France imposed a treaty on the *bey* which accorded it the privilege of coral fishing and which also guaranteed the commercial privileges of European nations.

The Husaynites were themselves also builders: they initiated the construction of several *madrasas* in Tunis, and several funerary monuments the most important of which, the Turbe al-Bey, holds the tombs of the Husaynite Beys. Meanwhile, the most original monument was built in the northern suburb of Bab Swiqa: it is a complex linking the mosque, a *turbe*, two *madrasas* and a *kuttab*, which was built by the Minister Yussef Sahib al-Taba'a in Halfaouine. In terms of their residence, they preferred the Palace of Bardo in the Dar al-Bey of the Muradids.

Great political and economic upheavals were affecting Europe. The Restoration, followed by the July Monarchy, tried but failed to pick up from where pre-Revolutionary France left off. In France the Second Republic of 1848 was accompanied by revolutions in Europe, but it did not last. Saint-Simon, Marx and Engels dominated the ideological movements of the century. In 1852, Napoleon III reinstated the Empire which lasted until 1870. The 19th century was the century of the industrial Revolution. The era of nationalities unfurled itself in Europe, in particular in Germany and Italy, but also in the Balkans.

The Husaynite Beys thus decided to put a chain of reforms into motion: at the same moment in which the Sultan Mahmoud II instituted the reforms, *Tanzimat*, Ahmed Bey (1252/1837–1271/1855) did likewise. He abolished slavery, founded the Polytechnic School of Bardo, reformed the military and education system, particularly that of the Zituna Mosque (1258/1842) and created modern teaching institutes. He founded a cloth factory in 1260/1844, as well as workshops and naval dockyards, and undertook the construction of the Palace of Mohammedia based on the model of Versailles. His successors, Mhamed Bey (1271/1855–1275/1859) and Sadok Bey (1276/1882) would pursue the same course of action: the Fundamental Pact promulgated in 1273/1857 proclaimed the equality of all before the law, and freedom of thought. The municipality of Tunis was created on the 9th *Muharram* 1274/30th August 1857. A government printing press was founded and an official Newspaper initiated. Mohamed Sadok Bey promulgated a Constitution, *Destur*, in 1277/1861.

Turbe al-Bey, Tunis, 19th-century watercolour.

All these reforms that contributed to the modernisation of the country came too late; they could not prevent the chain of events that followed from happening. There were renewed epidemics of cholera from 1264/1848–1266/1850, a bad harvest in 1268/1852, the sending of a Tunisian contingent to fight in the Crimean War – all of which helped to aggravate the situation. The growing weight of taxation, linked to the Beylical politics of renovation on the one hand and to the misappropriation of funds by Mustapha Khaznadar on the other, only resulted in burdening the State budget with debt. The introduction of poll tax unleashed the serious insurrection of 1280/1864 led by 'Ali Ben Ghedahem. It was bankruptcy which brought in European intervention, in the form of an international financial commission in 1285/1869. After about 30 years of bad management and tyranny, Mustapha Khaznadar was pushed out of the way in favour of Khayr al-Din, a man of great valour, who was thus given the responsibility of sorting out the situation. A Circasian Mamluk sold to the *bey*, he received a solid education and was sent on several occasions to Europe. He put into action a brave programme of reform aimed at cutting the tax which fell on the rural people and economy, at restoring the authority of the State over the whole of the country, at reforming the judiciary, and the management of *habus* and custom controls, at developing a modern system of education by reforming the teaching at the Zituna Mosque and opening Sadiki colleges, as well as advocating closer ties with the Sublime Gate. But all of his efforts were compromised by an alliance of Tunisian Conservatives and European businessmen.

At the Berlin Congress of 1878, "the Tunisian question" was part of "the Oriental question" which was dealt with by Europe; it authorised France to intervene in Tunisia. A border incident offered the French troops a pretext to invade the country. On May 12 1881, Ṣadok Bey signed the treaty of Bardo, followed by the Marsa Convention which established the French Protectorate in Tunisia.

The monumental Islamic history of Ifriqiya, followed by that of Tunisia, ended with the beginning of the Protectorate. A long history of colonialism unfolded over the first half of the 20th century for a good number of African and Asian countries. In the towns, new urban developments were added next to traditional buildings. At first these housing developments were occupied by the French and other non-Muslim foreigners; then, little by little, they were occupied by the Muslims themselves. Tunisian nationalism did not delay in rallying itself around the Party of the Constitution, *Destur*, in 1919, and the Tunisian Trade Union movement in 1920. It was brought to life by an enlightened elite who aimed to free the country from its colonial yolk. The Protectorate lasted until 1955; self-government, followed by Independence achieved on 20th March 1956, put an end to French domination. The Republic was proclaimed on 25th July 1957, terminating a monarchic regime whose existence was antiquated and outmoded. Tunisia as it is today is the fruit of 40 years of labour, of crucial choices, and of trial and error in the search for a better future, turning over a substantial new leaf; today, at the dawn of the 21st century, Tunisia is well aware of the wealth of its heritage and attends to it with all the care it can afford. It had, since a while back, taken note of the worth of its past, and established institutions for its conservation, its restoration and its study. These monuments, which mark so many moments in Tunisia's long history, beginning at the climax of antiquity, play as important a role in reminding every Tunisian of their heritage, and demonstrating to them how much their country consisted a crucible for many civilisations. They are also witness to 13 centuries of art and architecture, and it is of importance that the origins and different movements concerning these are explained.

IFRIQIYA: THIRTEEN CENTURIES OF ART AND ARCHITECTURE IN TUNISIA

Jamila Binous

In order to understand the birth of Islamic art, it is vital to study the extraordinary tale of the Arab Conquest. Within under a century, the area dominated by Arab tribes spanned from Turkestan as far as Spain, encompassing the Sassanid kingdom, heir to a thousand-year-old Persian culture, and the richest and most civilised provinces of the Byzantine kingdom including Syria and Palestine, the cradles of Holy Christian sites, Egypt which had Alexandria, the capital of Hellenic civilisation, as well as the Mediterranean coast of North Africa. This conquest, astonishing in its rapidity and immensity, can only be explained in terms of the driving force propelled by the new religion. It is certain that these divided Arab tribes had discovered a sense of cohesion through Islam, but they benefited just as greatly from the collapse of the great empires in order to accomplish their dazzling, high-speed achievement. The Sassanids were exhausted through warring against Byzantium, which itself had been undermined internally by the divisions between Christian Greeks and Christian Monophysites, who were composed of Armenians, Syrian Jacobites and Coptic Egyptians.

Right from the start, the Monophysites allied themselves to the Muslims, as Islam presented itself as respectful towards "the people of the Book", the Jews and Christians, assuring them of their freedom to religious belief and of the protection of their property. The "cohabitation" was one of the most fertile, resulting in the enrichment of Islam through the cultural contribution of these old civilisations. The undertaking of a considerable amount of work translating most of the writings by Greek scholars and philosophers was ordered by the caliphs themselves. The translation project was organised in true bureaucratic fashion within a specialised library, called the "House of Wisdom", *Bayt al-Hikma*, opened in Baghdad in 217/832. A short while later, the court of Kairouan got its own library, which was given the same name.

Of all the Greek philosophers, it was Plato who yielded the most influence on Islamic thought. His "theory of Ideas" was internalised without difficulty. Mankind can, thanks to its intelligence, find the eternal "Truths". The idea of absolute love was transposed into the *sufic* love of God. Al-Jahiz speaks of absolute "Beauty" in the same terms as Plato. *"Beauty, hosn"* he writes *"being synonymous with freedom, desert, nobility and the absolute, stands every test of time, and is neither withered by it nor altered by it; it cares not for amulets, precautions, secrets, brushes and make-up"*. Numbers, considered by Plato the purest and most essential forms of Reality, nourished the Arab passion for mathematics. The organic body which could be transformed into an abstract geometric formula possessed "metaphysical value". This innate evolution is certainly a Platonic one as it reveals the "mathematical forms" which underlie "organic matter".

Gradually, the idealisation of forms in nature, on which Greco-Roman art is based, gave way to a stylised and abstract form of expression. The abstract quality of Islamic art has nothing to do with Oriental abstract art. The latter defines itself as an attempt to escape from "the deformed world" and from "a reality which has become unbearable", towards the creation of a better world. The abstraction in Islamic art is not in the slightest an alternative "to the world of the senses and of reason", but is an attempt to access the essential nature and reality of things, a reality which suggests the omnipresence of God.

The Ribat, inscription in Kufic script, Monastir.

Here and there, the rhythmic repetitions of the same design or element, which can be extended and expanded at will, is a visual expression of the infinite.

"Each bay of the mosque, each unfurling of the arabesque, like each chapter of the Qur'an, is a vector of movement for our imagination and our life, throwing us onto a path of infinite stages, spiritual stages, or onto the reading of a frieze of architecture."

This specificity is the unifying element of Islamic art, despite the spread of its geographical area, and it allows us to qualify the analysis which accuses it of being a borrowed art form. It is true that the Arab leaders, through settling in ancient lands, imitated their predecessors in order to build houses, places of worship and public institutions. They called on native architects and craftsmen who were already on site in order to bring these initial works to life. These men inspired and expressed themselves through digging into their own stylistic repertoires and in putting to work their own ancestral knowledge, but not without following the ethics advocated by their new religion. One can thus witness the birth of a unique form of art, different from those that generated it, and one which is undeniably unified. Evolving within such a context as this, how did art in Ifriqiya make the transition from Antiquity to Islam?

Through this pursuit of the infinite, Islamic art is linked to the artistic tradition of the nomads, discerned not through works of architecture, as these are non-existent, but through other forms of expression such as weaving, embroidery, and the engraving and incrusting of metals. Sedentary art produced by a settled population portrays a static view of life: the line contours the object and contains it, whereas the line in nomadic art is a *"trail whose trajectory is one infinite movement like the infinity of the desert or of the steppe"*. Is not this infinite trail the exact principle which governs the arabesque, the basic element of Islamic decoration, just as the ramifications of the urban framework govern a *medina*?

Islamic Art in Ifriqiya

Ifriqiya occupies a predominant place in the history of art of the Muslim West, and by quite a long way. Heavily urbanised during the era of Antiquity, it was enriched by a number of monuments, and saw itself as the heir to an old architectural and urban tradition, whose transmission onto Islamic art it guaranteed. It possesses a wealth of architectural heritage, spread over 12 centuries of history, and presents itself as the Maghreb country which above all others has kept and conserved the greatest number of original works, notably those built by the Aghlabids in the $3^{rd}/9^{th}$ century.

Close examination of these monuments, propelled by archeological studies which have intensified in these last few years, has brought with it a greater understanding of this art.

Through looking at works of architecture, we will touch upon a variety of artistic expressions such as stonemasonry and sculpture, plaster moulding and carving, wood painting, calligraphy and many other forms of arts and crafts. Furthermore, personal belongings like furniture, dress, rugs and objects used in daily life will be looked at through the introduction of various specialised museums, as well as through the brackets or "windows" opened for the purpose of their study.

The works of Aghlabid architecture informs us of two important phenomenons of the $3^{rd}/9^{th}$ century: the first-rate role occupied by the Islamised Christians in the field of construction, and the large-scale use of material recycled from constructions of Antiquity. The skilled work of the Christians was recruited on site or "imported", as was the case at the end of the $1^{st}/7^{th}$ century, when the Governor of Egypt sent 1000 Coptic families to Tunis, who were employed for the construction of the first ship-building company to be set up in a Muslim country. An inscription, situated under the dome of the *mihrab* of the Zituna Mosque, tells us that the Caliph of Baghdad, al-Musta'in, ordered the construction of this new dome to be under the supervision of his freed slave Nacir and to be built "by the hand" of the architect, Fath. Freed slaves, or *mawali*, remained in the service of their old master. They were in charge of the supervision of buildings, among other important functions which they were employed to do. Their first names, featured in inscriptions, are not followed by patronymic ones, which attests to their Christian origin. Mansur, the freed slave of Ziyadet Allah, supervised the construction of the *ribat* tower of Sousse; Khalaf al-Fata gave his name to the signal tower which stands in the south-west corner of the town's enclosure walls. The Amir Abu al-'Abbas put forward his freed slave Mudam for the supervision of the building works for the Great Mosque of this same town.

The Ribat, viewed from the interior, Monastir.

Ifriqiya: Thirteen Centuries of Art and Architecture in Tunisia

Ramparts, viewed from the outside, Sousse.

The ruins of Roman Africa not only offered architectural models, but demonstrated the use of important kinds of materials, the most profuse being sculpted marble and clean-cut stone. These were very much sought after, and were acquired through means of buying, ordering, or through donation. Yazid Ibn Hatem (103/772) paid a lot for a green marble column. Al-Bakri reports that *"the Muslims rushed to snatch two splendid red columns covered in yellow marbling effect from the basilica, to take them to the Kairouan Mosque, as they had found out that the Emperor of Constantinople wanted to buy them for their weight in gold"*.

When Orientalist Europe discovered Islamic art at the end of the 19th century, a great polemic was initiated over the re-use of materials originating from Antiquity. Intellectual opinion swung from condemnation to fascination. Henry Bordeaux compared the columns of the Kairouan Mosque to *"women in captivity ... this indeed is the art of the Arabs, made of imitation and of rapture"* he added. As for George Duhamel, he recognised *"that all that is here is either Roman or Byzantine: columns, stone slabs, capitals."* However, *"the space itself is Arabic. The luminous void, created amongst all these remains, is Arabic. The spirit which has brought order to these sumptuous ruins is Arabic. You would not think yourself in Rome."*

Guy de Maupassant admired the Arabs who *"moved by sublime inspiration, erect a dwelling place for their God, a place made of pieces torn from crumbling towns, but one that is as perfect and as magnificent as the purest conceptions of the greatest stonemasons."*

Leandre Vaillant is astounded that one can feel anger towards the Muslim builders, *"whose only crime is having made a fire from firewood ... What are we complaining about? About the fact that the Arabs resurrected materials, the Roman columns which lay on the ground, thrown down by the Christians, by the Vandals, and who had the ingenious idea of using this inert debris, deprived of life, to build a beautiful and holy mosque? Can we not see that our anger is misplaced?"*

Islamic art in Ifriqiya, whose roots lie deep within the heritage of Antiquity, lay open to influences from the East, mainly those from Egypt and Mesopotamia. Despite being subject to the same historical and economic conditions, Ifriqiya witnessed, over the whole of the $3^{rd}/9^{th}$ century, the expansion of two schools of architecture that were distinctly different: that of Kairouan, and that of Sousse. The expression of the former can be seen through mosques like the 'Uqba Mosque and the Mosque of the Three Doors in Kairouan, as well as the Great Mosque of Sfax and that of Tunis. It makes exclusive use of antique marble columns as a means of support, employs the use of wooden ceilings and makes a feature of abundant decoration. The bringing into play of columns and antique capitals cannot but evoke Roman architecture. The capital does not directly support the fall of the arch. The abacus is surmounted by a superabacus or captial in the shape of a truncated pyramid, which is either moulded or sculpted. The superabacus supports a relatively slender, parallelepipedic-shaped impost, which compensates for the inequality of the column shafts as they are of different sizes, given that they come from different sources. The columns can, in each case, be placed either directly on the ground or on bases which can be raised in order to even out the inequality of the shafts. Thanks to these adaptations, these arches could flourish from one and the same level, endowing the architectural structure with an element of perfect harmony.

Filling up the space between the arch and the column was a procedure with which the Romans were certainly familiar, but it was one that soon gained classic status in Islamic art. It can be seen in the 'Amr Mosque in Fustat, rebuilt in 91/710. It is thus through Egypt that Ifriqiya rediscovered this process. Just as in the anatomy of its supporting structure, the use of wooden ceilings appears to be a trademark of the Kairouanese School in Egypt. The skullcap, a hemispherical dome, resting on shell corner squinches, is itself linked to local

The Kasbah, main gate al-Kef.

55

Al-'Abdelliya Palace, vault boss, the Marsa.

tradition. This kind of roof covering seems to have been the trend amongst Ifriqiyan architects, as is shown by the existence of the oratory of the Ribat of Sousse, built about 40 years earlier.

The Kairouanese School also distinguishes itself with its use of the "Moorish" arch, otherwise called the horseshoe arch, of which there are no pre-Islamic examples. It is an import from the East which in fact transited via Egypt. The semi-circular Roman arch, destined to have a great future within the Sousse school of architecture, is still used in the construction of windows and for small decorative arcatures. The existence of a segmented arch composed of circular foils is linked to the scalloped half-dome (the dome of the *mihrab* of the Great Mosques of Kairouan and of Tunis). It cannot be proved that they are of Mesopotamian origin.

As well as in terms of structure, the decoration of monuments displays a dual sense of belonging, to both the locality and to the East. The elaborate sculptures produced in marble or in stone (like the dome of the 'Uqba Mosque, the facade of the Mosque of the Three Doors, the dome of the *mihrab* of the Zituna Mosque) are of the same design, which is composed of two elements. One is the vegetal element, incorporating the leaf, the fruit and on rare occasions the flower, and in which the acanthus, the vineleaf, the pomegranate, and the grapeseed – each one inspired by the stylised hellenistic repertoire – can all be identified. The other is the supporting element of shafts or small branches which are of geometric design, giving rise to multiple web-like patterns. These interlaces constitute the framework and main body of decoration, and the floral design is there to fill the gaps within it.

Meanwhile, a particular ornamentation, characteristic of the Aghlabid period, deserves a special mention. It consists of both flora and geometry, and is composed of rosettes, spreading out their rounded or pointed petals which number between four and twelve, radiating out from the centre. These motifs are inscribed on diamond-shaped tiles, like the earthenware tiles which cover the wall of the *mihrab* of the 'Uqba Mosque. Examples of these motifs decorate the frame of the *midha* of this same mosque, as well as the facade of the Mosque of the Three Doors, and two tympana of the Great Mosque of Sousse. The striking analogy of these motifs with the stamped terracotta tiles of the Christian era, which can frequently be found across the country, leaves us with no doubts over this local tradition, which was conserved by the Ifriqiyan artists of the 3rd/9th century.

The script employed in the ornamentation of 3rd/9th-century monuments is exclusively the monumental, angular script known as *Kufic,* a very close relative to that of the Egyptian inscriptions on the Nilometer of Rauda and of the friezes of Ibn Tulun. Letters sculpted in the monument's stone form a long horizontal line. The self-restraint and simplicity displayed in the inscriptions affirm the founder's desire to claim merit over his creation without recourse to aesthetic pretension. Examples of Aghlabid inscriptions can equally be seen in Kairouan, in Sousse and in Tunis.

The Sousse School of architecture is mainly represented by monuments like the *ribats* of Monastir, Sousse and Lamta, the cistern called the Sufra, the Great Mosque and the Bu Fatata *masjed,* all situated in Sousse. Massive and austere, the architecture produced by this school is clearly distinct from that of Kairouan, and accurately reflects the defensive role played by its military outposts that consist of the coastal towns of Sahel. In order to prevent the spread of fires, the roofing used is no longer that composed of wood ceilings but is one exclusively composed of barrel vaulting which is reinforced by double semi-circular arches. These supports are no longer antique marble columns but solid pillars, squat and positioned in a cruciform plan, with the exception of the Ribat of Monastir, where the arches stand on large pedestals. Ribbon joints, such as those used by the Romans, persist.

Decoration hardly features other than the rounded merlons which crown the tops of buildings, or the few features conceded to in the construction of the Great Mosque. There is nothing to distinguish the *ribat* of

Qubba bin al-Qhawi, scallop, Sousse.

Al-Bashiya Madrasa, capital with acanthus leaves, Tunis.

Ifriqiya from the castles built in the desert or in the mountains of Syria during the 2nd/8th century by the Umayyad Caliphs. This design is composed of the same general layout: a rectangular enclosure, flanked by towers in each corner, with a single entrance at the centre of each side, with rooms which back onto the external walls,

The Ribat, entrance, Lemta.

and with the placing in the corners of several winding ramps or staircases. Only the oratory and the signal tower express the twin character of the *ribat* and its dual military and religious purpose.

In spite of the political rupture of the period, Fatimid art seemed to be an extension of the art and architecture of the 3rd/9th century. It continued to use the same means of structural support, although its way of roofing broke with tradition. The groin vault replaced the barrel vault as well as the timber ceiling, the abandoning of which can be explained through the shortage of wood used in construction. This type of vault is an Eastern import; the first of its kind covers the entrance porch of the Ribat of Sousse.

A closer examination of the Great Mosque of Mahdia, which was the first of the Fatimid Caliphate's foundations, confirms the plan's analogy to that of the 'Uqba Mosque: a hypostyle prayer room, preceded by a courtyard, mirrors the T-plan of the axial nave and transept. The novelty here, other than the existence of a monumental entrance porch, lies in the choice of decoration, whose principal characteristics are displayed on the porch and on the *mihrab* of this mosque. The decoration is distinct for its more or less general use of recessed niches, of arcatures and concentric archivolts, which furnish large facades. These features are divided up into various levels on the vertical plane, and are apportioned out on both branches of a symmetric axis on the horizontal plane. The elaborate facades surprise the viewer through their sheer variety of niches: some have flat backwalls, whilst others are semi-cylindrical, highlighted by arches whose forms are either simple, polyfoiled or recticurvilinear. They are occasionally outlined by concentric architraves, by arches of various shapes or by simple triangles. The most beautiful examples of this repertoire were produced during the Zirid era. The Oriental facade of the Great Mosque of Sfax, the Sidi Ammar Masjed in Sousse, the *bahu* dome of the Zituna, and the western facade of the al-Qsar Mosque in Tunis – these are but a few of the sites where these examples can be admired.

The first applications of this decorative principle by Ifriqiyan architects appeared in the 3rd/9th century in the decoration of Kairouanese domes, whose resemblance to the niches of the Ukhaydir and Qasr al-'Ashiq Palaces, near Samarra, has been pointed out. However, its use was subsequently generalised under the increased influence of the East during the Fatimid era and then during that of the Zirids. Variations of this school of architecture born in Ifriqiya, appeared, accomplished in the West by the Banu Hammad, first in *Qal'a* and then in Bugie, their successive capitals. Similarly it also influenced architecture in Norman Sicily, where the masters of Palermo produced Christian works which attest to Zirid influence, intimately linked to contributions from al-Andalus.

On the other hand, with the departure of the Caliph al-Mu'izz from Egypt, can one speak of a "transfer from west to east" of forms that existed in Ifriqiya? It seems that this channel of contribution is perceptible within certain foundations such as the al-Azhar Mosque and the al-Hakim Mosque in which the central nave, which leads into the depths of the mosque, is magnified by a border of twinned columns and is endowed with two domes, one at each end. The entrance which protrudes from the facade of the al-Hakim Mosque is reminiscent of the porch of the al-Mahdi Mosque of Mahdia.

Meanwhile Ifriqiya gained far greater enrichment from the East, to the "point of obliterating that which was left over of antique tradition" according to Georges Marçais. The author adds that these imports *"would even go on to multiply after the departure of the Fatimids and with the institution of the Sanhajain Amirs who replaced them and their position ... so much so that one can conclude with the following paradox: while what was local to Ifriqiya still survived under (and thanks to) masters who themselves were from the Orient, the Islamic art of Ifriqiya in fact became purely Oriental under its first native, local dynasty."*

The Ribat, viewed as a whole, Monastir.

Burj al-Ghazi Mustapha, loopholes, Humt Suq.

From the 5th/11th century onwards, the emergence of Berber political forces in the Maghreb, with the appearance first of the Almoravids, followed by the Almohads, brought with it a far clearer distinction between Western and Eastern Islamic art. The native dynasties, heirs to the Almohads, produced buildings whose Berber sobriety was brightened up by the brilliance of Cordoban Umayyad art, sealing the birth of a new and original style called Hispano-Maghrebic, more commonly referred to as Hispano-Moresque or al-Andalus ("Moorish").

Ifriqiya, relieved of Almohad domination, was ruled for three and a-half centuries by the Hafsids, who did not fail to enrich the arts, nourished by both Antique and Oriental traditions and through the importation of influence from al-Andalus. The impact of this trend grew even greater when the Hafsid sovereigns facilitated the settlement of a solid and spirited al-Andalus population fleeing from the Reconquest. Among the refugees were master masons and artists widely experienced in ceramics, and in *naqsh hadida*, in wood. The western syncretism which took place had an Ifriqiyan specificity.

Whilst the use of brick was becoming more common in Spain and in the western Maghreb, Ifriqiya kept its loyalty to stone. The minaret of the Almohad Mosque belonging to the Kasbah of Tunis copied in stone the design of interlacing diamond-shapes which decorated the Almohad towers of the Giralda, the Kasbah of Marrakesh and the Tower of Hassan. Ifriqiya also kept its taste for colourful materials. The juxtaposition of black and white marble placed alternately in the keystones of the arches or incrusted into mural panels, or used to enhance the paving of a courtyard, is what makes the monuments of Tunis, such as the *mihrab* of the Almohad Mosque, the *Midha al-Sultan*, and the Sidi Qacem Zawiya, distinct and original.

While the Hispano-Maghrebic School is unique for its astonishing variety of arches – foiled, scalloped, recticurvilinear or with pelmets – Ifriqiya continued to use the semi-circular horseshoe arch, and only employed different types of arches in the building of decorative arcatures (like the fountain of *Midha al-Sultan*, the courtyard of the Shamma'iya Madrasa, and the intrados of the *mihrab* of the Almohad Mosque). A stalactite dome rises up in front of this latter *mihrab*. Stalactite or *muqarnas* is a decorative process used in vaulting, made up of stacks of honeycombed cells. Persian in origin, it was first seen used in the Maghreb in the 5th/11th century in the *Qal'a* of the Banu Hammads. It was copied in Tinmal and in Marrakesh, quickly taking root in Ayyubid and Mamluk Egypt.

Ifriqiya, in adopting the Hispano-Maghrebic-style capital, created a typical Hafsid one. The former is made of a lower cylinder decorated with large meanders, surmounted by a more lavishly decorated parallelepiped. Beautiful examples of this capital can be seen within the *madrasas* of Fez, in the Court of Lions in the Alhambra, and within the monuments of Tlemcen, as well as in several Hafsid monuments in Tunis like the *Suq al-Qumash*, the *Midha al-Sultan* and the Sidi Qacem al-Zelliji Zawiya. The more common Hafsid capital is in the shape of chalice which flares out from its cylindrical shape into that of a square; it is inspired mostly by the Sanhajian capital of the 5th/11th and 6th/12th centuries.

The *naqsh hadida*, plaster sculpted with iron tools, blossomed to its fullest in the 7th/13th and 8th/14th centuries in Granada, Fez and Tlemcen, and made a comeback in Ifriqiya, where several Aghlabid attempts can be seen in Raqqada. Its decor is rich in planes; it consists of an arabesque of interlacing braids which contain palms and flowerets; it is occasionally embellished with painting. *Zellij* underwent a considerable boom in the western Maghreb, but would not go on to achieve the same kind of success in Ifriqiya, where ceramic tiles were used more willingly. This single tile, small in size, existed in green, white, brown-black, ochre yellow and very occasionally blue. Knowledgeable use of this simple single element brought about the brightening up floors in rooms and courtyards (like al-'Abdelliya Palace). One must also note here the exceptional series of *cuerda seca* tiles in the Zawiya of Sidi Qacem al-Zelliji.

Hispano-Maghrebic art thus greatly influenced the work produced by the Hafsids, without however dethroning ancient traditions. The result is an artform which, though certainly less sumptuous than that of the western Maghreb, does not lack in force nor in elegance.

The settlement of the Turks in Tunisia brought with it both the Hanefite rite and the Malekite sect, as well as the Ottoman governmental elite. In terms of architecture, the model of the Ottoman mosque, with its domes at various levels, never really took off or was replicated, save for

Mosque of the Kasbah, Tunis.

Panoramic view of Tunis.

19th-century watercolours.

the Sidi Mahrez Mosque (1085/1675). On the other hand, the Ottoman model was used in the building of *turbes* (funerary monuments) and *zawiya*s, such as the Turbe al-Bey and the *zawiya*s of Sidi Mahrez, of Sidi Shiha in Tunis, of Sidi Hmam in Menzel Temime, of Sidi Ahmed Ben Hammuda in Kelibi, and the Qadiriya in al-Kef. The Turkish Mosque in Tunis, with its octagonal minaret, is a funerary mosque, and its courtyard does not precede the prayer room but frames it along three of its sides (like the Yussef Dey and Hammuda Pasha Mosques). Places of worship were becoming complexes linking, other than the founder's tomb, one or two *madrasa*s, and a *sabil (sabil Kuttab)* (such as the al-Jedid and Yussef Sahib al-Taba'a Mosques).

Turbe al-Bey, window, Tunis.

Decoration demonstrates the influence of Andalusian art and manifestations of Turkish art. Chiselled plaster, without repudiating the Andalusian arabesque, also takes on another form. Motifs, featuring the oriental cypress, the star, or the bouquet of foliage, reveal themselves on a plain background. Woodwork also presents two styles: Hispano-Maghrebic ceilings are decorated with small interlacing beading and with *muqarnas*, whilst the others are embellished with sculpted rosettes. The paintings feature geometric designs in one instance and floral designs in another; they are enhanced with gold leaf.

However, if there is one area in which local tradition could not resist outside competition, that area is ceramics and marble cutting. Enriched by the decorative repertoire and the colourful palette of tiles imported from Iznik (such as those on the Sidi Mahrez and Jedid Mosques), the school of potters in Tunis produced tiles decorated with elaborate vegetal motifs. But from the $12^{th}/18^{th}$ century onwards, columns and capitals, pilasters and marble lintels were all made by one and the same hand – a European one, whose work was imported directly from Italy. Fluted columns, doric and composite capitals, pilasters, lintels and inlaid panels in polychrome marble all carry the hallmarks of the Renaissance or the Baroque. They became more and more common within noble buildings, both public and private. More discreet low-relief sculptures in stone can be seen on the facades of buildings in Sfax, Gabès, Gafsa and certain villages of the Sahel. They are attributed to Sfaxian artists of the modern era and seem to have been inspired by the woodwork practised by the Berbers since Antiquity. Of particular note is the brick surfacing on the buildings of Tozeur and Nefta, the ornamentation of which presents

Noria, 19th-century watercolour.

the most ingenious combinations that exist. The beginnings of the Italicising style would grow and reinforce itself, particularly after the country's confrontation with Europe in the 13th/19th century, the repercussions of which was felt not only on the political and economic level but also culturally. Architecture and the construction industry were submitted to external market forces. The materials used were no longer manufactured from indigenous resources but were imported. Tool-replacing engines were also imported. The rules of the game became mixed-up and confused, and the craftsman could no longer pass on his thousand-year old know-how. For the first time during the long history of Islamic art in Tunisia, the rupture between age-old tradition and the present-day was brutal and it would be a long while before any syncretism would again take place.

ITINERARY I

The Medina

Jamila Binous

I.1 TUNIS
- I.1.a Sidi Qacem al-Zelliji Zawiya
- I.1.b Bab Jadid (option)
- I.1.c Turbe al-Bey
- I.1.d Dar Ibn 'Abd Allah
- I.1.e Dar 'Uthman
- I.1.f Dar Husayn
- I.1.g Dar al-Haddad
- I.1.h The Kasbah Quarter
- I.1.i Cafe Mnouchi
- I.1.j Al-'Attarin Barracks
- I.1.k Sidi al-Morjani Barracks (option)
- I.1.l The Great Mosque of Zituna
- I.1.m Al-Baschiya Madrasa
- I.1.n Turbe 'Ali Pasha (option)
- I.1.o Slimaniya Madrasa
- I.1.p The Suqs
- I.1.q Dar Lasram
- I.1.r Bab al-Bhar

Tunisian Ceramics

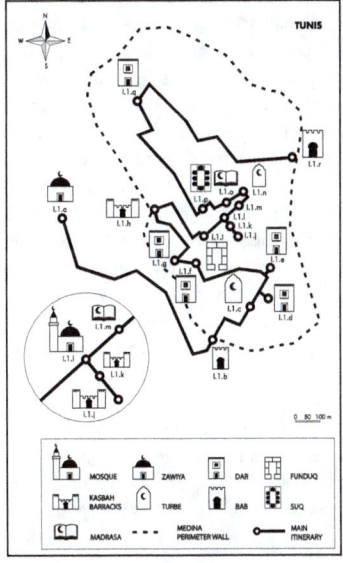

The outside of a herbalist shop, al-Blat Suq, Tunis.

ITINERARY I   *The Medina*

The *medina* maintains and perpetuates a typically Islamic urban plan whose initial formation can be traced back using investigative research undertaken by certain contemporary writers. At first, the expeditionary body sent on the mission of conquest, the *futuhat*, began by building a rampart around an area of land, usually one already occupied by the military camp. A mosque would be built at the centre of this outlined area, and would open out onto a large esplanade used for holding both markets, public meetings and military parades. The main roads, each reaching a gate within the rampart, would radiate out from this esplanade, and would thus divide the town into large neighbourhoods. Troops stationed under tents, grouped by kind, often in terms of ethnicity, occupied small islands within the town which were outlined by internal ringroads. Through being settled thus, the military camp had all the time it needed to establish a city: the island-camps transformed into housing complexes, and shops appeared around the esplanade. The principal characteristics of this core urban prototype allowed it to multiply itself through juxtaposition – which it needed to do as a result of its growing needs and the natural constraints imposed on it through its geographical positioning – without altering the unity and homogeneity of the urban system. The road network could be extended voluntarily or empirically to serve the new neighbourhoods in the same way as it served the initial core. The general permanence of the organisation and forms of the urban fabric guaranteed the unbreakable unicity of the Islamic town, despite obvious evolution in terms of building density.

The Islamic city shows itself to be both a homogenous whole and a juxtaposition of sub-units: each neighbourhood is, in some way, a miniature city, complete with everything a city contains. The great innovation in urban design introduced in the form of the *medina* model also exists within the organisation of the commercial zone, known as the area of *suqs*. It required the codification of each economic activity, and the rationalisation of its pursuit. Each sector of economic activity is thus assigned a work-place, so that each discipline of work is grouped together and given its own area. Concentric zones are established around the Great Mosque, determined by the amount of disruption to the peace each activity risks causing, in particular noise, which could break the silence practised in and around religious buildings. While participating in the life of the city, these *suqs*, which were usually covered with a series of vaults for reasons of security as well as climatic, constitute an exclusively economic quarter, reserved for the production and trade of articles of craftsmanship. The residential quarters are spread around the *suqs*. To satisfy their need to expand, while unable to settle outside the ramparts for reasons of security, the inhabitants used all available

Weaver's workshop, 19th-century watercolour, Tunis.

free space, such as the gardens on the inside of the city walls. In cases of extreme densification, the necropoles next to the ramparts would be dismantled at the expense of urbanisation, and new cemeteries would be built outside the city walls. Nonetheless, it is difficult to determine the exact mechanism of this densification in terms of how the land was divided and how the ground was surveyed due to lack of sources. In the meantime, from observing the texture of the developed site, one can deduce a few certainties. Constructions were subject to common ownership; thus their proliferation often entailed the enclosure of certain plots of land and buildings that were far away from the main roads, which explains the presence of alleyways and impasses opened through being assigned the right of way. This density of residential building, so that houses are built folding over themselves again and again, reinforces the segregation between public and private domains.

This urban concept, outlined above, is very well reflected in the Medina of Tunis. The *medina* locates itself around a central pole which is made up of the Zituna Mosque and its surrounding *suq*s. While the Great Mosque is the main place of learning and of worship, the *suq*s house the central economic nerve of the city. The main roads leading towards the gates of the town lead out from this centre. Facilities pertaining to urban life can be found along the lengths of these roads, and they are open to or can be used by the whole community as well as foreigners admitted into the town. These facilities cover religious needs (such as mosques and *zawiya*s), purification rites (*midha, hammam*), knowledge (*madrasa*) and the shelter of travellers (*wikala, funduq*). Secondary roads, that branch off the main ones, irrigate the residential quarters, and house necessary amenities such as the mas-

A Tunis street, 19th-century watercolour.

jed, the *kuttab*, the mill and the oven. As for the houses, they are grouped into compact islands served by impasses that end in cul-de-sacs. Both impasses and houses are kept apart strictly for family life, governed by the rules of the patriachate. This city, the focus of economic wealth, was carefully protected by its ramparts, isolating it from the countryside in which the nomads lived, who were ready to attack it at the slightest sign of a weakening of central government. The dismantling of Tunis's ramparts, which began at the end of the 19th century and was completed in the aftermath of Independence, did not compromise the homogeneity of the medina. A ring-road replaced the city wall, and despite changes in the town's economic basis and its evolution in relation to the countryside, the age-old circular spatial structure remains perfectly evident within the Medina of Tunis as within the majority of Tunisian *medina*s elsewhere.

Historical Overview

Polybe once said that Tunis "was well protected by nature and by man". Built on raised ground, cut off behind the lake at the back of the Gulf, first called the Gulf of Carthage then the Gulf of Tunis, it holds in its clasp a network of roads which links it as easily to the centre and south of Tunisia as it does to the rich lands of the north. Tunis, "daughter of the road", is also such through its toponymy. Its name, *Tounes* or *Tenes*, comes from the Berber root "*ens*" which means "to be asleep" and, by extension, "to spend the night at …", hence the meaning of the word *tounes*: the place where one spends the night, the roadside inn. This Libyc toponymy is evidence that it existed before Carthage did, but when the Carthaginians had wanted to strengthen their hinterland, they seized Tunis, as its strategic position provided a protective cover over their capital. According to Diodore of Sicily: *"from each of these towns one could see what was happening in the other".*

In fact, for centuries, Tunis provided a base or trench camp for all enemies of Carthage: the Libyc rebels in 396 BC; Agathocles, the tyrant of Syracuse; the Roman general Regulus and finally, during the first of the Punic wars, Scipio the African, who defeated Hannibal. Carthage dragged Tunis down with it when it fell in 146 BC. It was destroyed by the Romans as Carthage was, its natives forced into servitude and its lands incorporated into the public domain; henceforth it became a mere satellite of Carthage, first Roman, then Vandal, then Byzantine.

In 78/698, the Amir Hassan Ibn Nu'man seized Carthage for good, through which he succeeded in the conquest of Africa. The capital of the latter, which became Ifriqiya, was Kairouan, but, although the strategic importance of Carthage did not go unnoticed by its new masters, they preferred Tunis, which was more sheltered from naval attacks. Tunis was not intending to turn its back to the sea, much the opposite in fact, as the first great Islamic project to take place there was the building of a naval dockyard, *Dar al-Sina'a*, between the city and the banks of the lake, where it would remain to be seen until the $10^{th}/16^{th}$ century. A thousand Coptic families were brought from Egypt to help build this project. A canal dug along the coastal line at the level of the Goulette, the port, "brought the sea to Tunis", allowing ships to sail straight to the open sea. Tunis lay claim to the hegemony of the western Mediterranean, after the destruction of the Byzantine fleet.

The town ordered itself around its Great Mosque, the Zituna. From the $2^{nd}/8^{th}$ century onwards, this place of worship asserted itself as an important place of scholarship, and illustrious doctors like 'Ali Ibn Ziyad taught Islamic law there. This scholar went as far as Medina to study the Malikite branch of Islam which became and remained the rite of the Maghrebis. Defended at first by a "circular ditch", the town was, from the $2^{nd}/8^{th}$ century onwards, encircled by ramparts built of clay and brick, and numbered amongst the great towns of Ifriqiya capable of competing with Kairouan. Right through the $3^{rd}/9^{th}$ century, several revolts which began from within Tunis nearly toppled the Aghlabid Dynasty, so much so that the sovereigns were obliged, on two occasions, to come and settle themselves in Tunis in order to bring it under greater control.

The Shi'ite Dynasty of the Fatimids succeeded that of the Aghlabids at the end of the $3^{rd}/9^{th}$ century. Shortly afterwards, Kairouan lost its status as the country's capital to Mahdia (303/916) and was subjected to severe repercussions from this loss, whilst Tunis, which had remained at a distance from all of this, became a place of refuge for Malikite doctors as well as heir to Kairouan's cultural prestige. This period was marked by the existence of Mahrez Ibn

Khalef, otherwise known as Sidi Mahrez, "*Sultan al-Madina*", the undisputed patron of Tunis. His achievements were considerable, undertaken in order to protect the town from the troubles which arose through the arrival of the Shi'ites. Tradition attributes to him the settlement of the Jews into a neighbourhood which was within the city-walls called the *hara*, not far from where he resided himself. Until that time, this active population of Tunis had had to leave the city at nightfall to retreat to their quarter located near Mellassine. When he died in 412/1022, Sidi Mahrez was buried in his house, which became a site of veneration for Muslims and Jews alike, and it remains the most visited of the *zawiya*s.

The arrival of the Hilalians in 441/1050 put an end to peace in the country. The weakening of central government brought with it proclamations of Independence from principalities like that of Banu Khurasan in Tunis. These sovereigns agreed to pay tribute to the nomads in return for them putting a stop to their raids, whilst also establishing commercial relations with the Normans of Sicily. They set up the seat of their government in a neighbourhood south of the Great Mosque, the memory of which is preserved by Sidi Bu Khrissan street. They built a palace on what is now the site of the Chateau (Castle) and of a mosque belonging to the Castle, the *Jama' al-Qsar*.

The geographer al-Bakri, writing under this dynasty, spoke of the *suqs* of Tunis overflowing with merchandise and groceries, and of house doors being "*ornate with white marble*" in his *Description of Northern Africa*. "*In fact*" wrote he "*marble is so abundant in Carthage, in the amphitheatre, the circus, and the thermae, that even if all the inhabitants of Ifriqiya got together to take away the blocks of marble, there still would not be enough people to complete the task.*"

Bab al-Bhar, 19th-century watercolour, Tunis.

In 554/1159, the Maghreb and al-Andalus were for the first time united under the leadership of the Almohads. These caliphs, from the south of Morocco, relegated the government of Ifriqiya to the Hafsids and chose Tunis as their capital. Soon after, the Governor Abu Zakariya al-Hafsi proclaimed his Independence. From being the capital of a province, Tunis became the capital of an Independent State. The Hafsid Dynasty were without doubt the most important dynasty in the history of Ifriqiya and particularly in the history of its capital. Prosperity and peace were reflected in the extension of the town with the building of the *kasbah*, the foundation of mosques, of *madrasa*s, of *zawiya*s, the creation of an important network of *suq*s, and great water conveyance works (see the remains of the aqueduct, at the western exit of Tunis). The city changed its appearance, neighbourhoods spilled out of the enclosures; the extension of suburbs to the north and the south necessitated the erection of a second line of fortification. The example of royal summer palaces, like Ra's Tabaia, Abu Fihr, al-'Abdelliya, was followed by those belonging to notables.

Dar Lasram, sculpted marble lintel, Tunis.

Neighbourhoods such as the Ariana, the Marsa, the Goulette and the Bardo developed.

Tunis' renown attracted a number of foreigners. First came the Almohads from the Moroccan Anti-Atlas, who then formed the military and administrative elite. The Andalusians, chased out of their land by the Spanish and Portuguese Reconquest, then came to settle in Tunis and in its surroundings. The one transformed the face of certain neighbourhoods like the Suqra and the Ariana through the introduction of meticulous gardens; the others made themselves known for their intellectual superiority and their refinement of taste. The poet Ibn al-Abbar and the Cadi Ibn al-Ghammaz were originally from Valencia; Hazem of Carthage was the poet of Sultan al-Mustansir; the Banu Khaldun's of Seville settled in what became rue Turbe al-Bey where 'Abd al-Rahman Ibn Khaldun was born, who affected universal thought through founding the basis of modern sociology. The Jews expelled from Spain came to join their fellow Jews, bringing with them more advanced commercial practices. There were already quite a number of Christians in Tunis, both enslaved and free. The Hafsid Sultans usually recruited 2,000 Christian lancers and Italian and Spanish cavaliers, Aragonians and Catalunians mostly, for their personal bodyguards. They were stationed in the south of the *kasbah,* in *"a street separated off as if it were another neighbourhood",* as Leo the African describes it; it was the suburb of the Nazarenes, *Ribat al-Nasara*, in which they had their own church dedicated to Saint Francis, the sound of whose bells ringing was even tolerated. A certain number of these Christians converted to Islam, like the Majorcan monk Anselme Turmeda, who became known as 'Abd Allah al-Torjman and whose tomb was conserved by Tunis at the entrance of the Sakkajin Suq.

Merchants and shipowners of European origin, from Pisa, Catalunia, Marseilles, Provence, Ragusa, Sicily and Venice, formed a new elite that occupied a quasi-monopoly over maritime transport. They resided in *funduqs* under the protection of their consul, according to the rule which was very much in place. Consuls appeared during the middle of the $7^{th}/13^{th}$ century. The archives of Marseilles mention an authorisation, dated 652/1255, that was accorded to merchants from Marseilles who had settled in Tunis, which gives them leave "to chose from amongst themselves one who will act as a consular agent as a representative of their nation to the authorities."

At the beginning of the $10^{th}/16^{th}$ century, according to Leo the African, *"another suburb appeared on the outside of the Gate called Bab al-Bhar, which is the gate of the navy ... There, Christian merchants of foreign origin reside, like those from Genoa, Venice, Catalunia, all of whose boutiques, shops and hostels are separated from those of the Moors."* Piracy also developed hand-in-hand with regular commerce, giving rise to frequent conflicts which were amiably resolved by the sultan. A letter from Barcelona, dated 8 January 1434, addressed to Sultan Abu 'Uthman, illustrates this well: *"Following the accident of the small galleon commanded by Antoine Gil, which was lost on the shallow depths of a place known as the Bône of our Lordship, we have learnt through letters sent by merchants who were in Tunis that Your Great Highness, in his royal forethought, had prescribed and ordered for your officers and subjects of Bône to help those saved from the aforesaid galleon and restore all the lost robes and goods that had belonged to the merchants ... The Qa'id of Bône and the rest of your subjects did not obey your prescriptions and orders ... therefore, having misled the great renown and friendship which, by divine grace, rules between the very high and very noble Prince King and our Lord and his subjects and vassals and Our Great Highness and your subjects and vassals, we ask for the grace that you show in your royal edicts and prescriptions, and chastise and punish and immediately put a stop to those who show insolence towards the merchants of the aforementioned galleon, and order the compensation and restoration of the cloths and robes which have been taken from them ... In return, the aforementioned merchants and all the other inhabitants of your kingdoms and lands of which the city-dwellers and inhabitants of maritime cities are a part, should rejoice with grace and special favour, as the very great and excellent Prince King and Lord of our nation and our natural subjects will do in this case and situation ...".*

Signs of the decline of the Hafsid Dynasty began to show in $9^{th}/15^{th}$ century: nomad tribe rebellions, dynastic rivalries, and a resurgence of piracy. Following a Spanish "protectorate" (941/1535–981/1574), the Turks entered Tunis and declared the end of the Hafsids. Under the Deys 'Uthman (1002/1594–1018/1610) and Yussef (1018/1610–1046/1637), the influx of Andalusians, including a great number of craftsmen, brought with them a fresh breath of life to several working bodies and guilds including that of the *shawashis*, the silk manufacturers, the ceramicists, the stone sculptors and wood sculptors. Alongside the ruling aristocracy of "natural Turks" lived the "Turks of the nation", renegades of European origin who occupied positions of trust. Usta Moratto Genovese, son of Francesco Rio de Levante from Genoa, began his career as a close adviser to Yussef Dey, and then rose to power under the name of Hammuda Pasha. The Englishman, Ward, who became Issuf Ra'is, introduced sailing ships to the country, thus solving the recruitment problem with respect to warders of galley slaves.

The $11^{th}/17^{th}$ century was undeniably the Golden Age of privateering by pirates from the Barbary Coast. But the loot was only partially used for the internal development of their country. Its dispersal and sale across Europe was undertaken by Leghornese' Jews, descendants of the Spanish and the Portuguese, who had settled in Tunis in the $8^{th}/14^{th}$ century and whose number had increased through new settlers in the $11^{th}/17^{th}$ century. They were distinct from the native Jews, the *twansa*, in terms of their dress, language and culture. They played an important role in external commerce, and occupied high positions in the financial departments of the State.

The enrichment of Tunis manifested itself through creations in areas of both architecture and urban design in which Turkish influence was evident. Several new *suqs* appeared from the beginning of the $11^{th}/17^{th}$ century, when Yussef Dey came to power, onwards. They competed amongst themselves in the production of luxury

ITINERARY I *The Medina*

Tunis

goods in response to the demand posed by a refined urban clientele, of Turkish or Tunisian origin, but victims of Turkish fashion.

From the point of view of religion, the arrival of the Turks introduced a new orthodox sect, the Hanafite. Funerary mosques featuring octagonal minarets proliferated: there was that of Yussef Dey (1025/1616), that of Hammuda Pasha (1065/1655), the domed mosque of Mhammed Bey (1103/1692), that of Husayn Ibn 'Ali (1129/1717) and finally that of the Minister Yussef Sahib al-Taba'a at the start of the 13th/19th century. Sovereigns and dignitaries erected religious and public utility foundations as a mark of their stay: *madrasa*s, funerary *turbe*s, *zawiya*s, watering holes and public fountains characterised the town. Sumptuous palaces were built to house the political and military aristocracy as well as the industrious bourgeoisie of the *suq*s.

The town's remarkable boom came into difficulties, beginning in the 1245/1830s. The hold over the Mediterranean passed into the hands of European powers. Their economic penetration and political interference weakened the Tunisian government which was in fact trying to activate a chain of reforms. The face of the town began to change even prior to the Protectorate: thus a municipality was instituted in 1858. In 1861, Mohamed Sadok Bey promulgated a Constitution which included granting Europeans the right to own property there. Tunis therefore exploded in size, moving beyond the ramparts eastward. In 1881, the regime of the Protectorate entrusted the actual administration of municipal affairs to a vice-president who was an important French Civil Servant. This resulted in the rapid growth of the "European" town, and began the long crisis that was to affect the *medina*. Independent Tunisia was to inherit a capital that was colonial in type – divided, lacking in equilibrium, and characterised by the juxtaposition of a dynamic "modern" quarter and a *medina* in stagnation. Successive building and development plans tried to redress this imbalance. Through tourism, and through hosting international events and conferences of all kinds – political, economic or cultural in nature – Tunis has rediscovered its identity as an open and welcoming city.

1.1 **TUNIS**

I.1.a **Sidi Qacem al-Zelliji Zawiya**

This monument can be reached via the "boulevard du 9 Avril", not far from the new town hall of Tunis. It is advisable, from this point onwards, to continue this part of the itinerary on foot. Cars can be parked around "la place du Leader", the square on which the monument is situated.
Entrance fee. Opening times: 08.00–13.00 from June to September and 08.00–12.00 from October to May. There are toilet facilities.

From the "boulevard du 9 Avril", one can see the Sedjoumi, a sebkha *or salt-water lagoon, on the shores of which developed shantytowns, which today have been rebuilt and improved, such as Mellassine which has a flea market and a secondhand market.*

Abu al-Fadel Qacem, known as Qacem al-Zelliji, must have derived the name he used from the job title referring to the creation of *zellij* (ceramic tiles), for which he had a rare talent. Andalusian in origin, he lived in Tunis during the second half of the 9th/15th century. He was known for his great piety and generosity towards Andalusian immigrants who found comfort and lodging in this *zawiya*. These qualities earned him the respect of the Hafsid princes and the veneration of the population. According to Ibn Abi Dinar, he died in 895/1490 and was buried in his *zawiya*. This remark leads us to assume with accuracy that the *zawiya* preceded the tomb. Decorated by himself, if not by his spiritual and artistic disciples, the *qubba* illustrates a harmonious mix of Ifriqiyan and Hispano-Moresque elements. The general plan is classical in style, even if only through the addition of an oratory in the 12th/18th century, situated on the left of the entrance. The funerary chamber and rooms originally kept aside for pilgrims and the poor are spread around a courtyard of porticoes. The originality of the paving of this courtyard rests in the incrusted braid motifs in black marble which highlight the floor. This decoration is reminiscent of the Mamluk buildings of Cairo. The *qubba* is divided into an ante-chamber followed by the funerary chamber, which are separated by an arch of black-and-white marble keystones supported by columns whose capitals are fashioned in true Hispano-Moresque tradition. The flat niches that pierce the walls of the first room are decorated with slabs of ceramic on their bottom halves with plaster-sculpted arabesques on top. The *zellij*, displaying a star motif, is made using a technique called "*cuerda seca*", which is well-known in Spain.

From the exterior, the silhouette of this *qubba*, with its pyramidal roof covered in green tiles, cannot but evoke Hispano-Moresque monuments, while the blind arcatures and stone bonds are echoes of Ifriqiyan origin. The second room holds the tomb of Sidi Qacem, which has been the object of continuous visits and veneration for five centuries. Following a project of restoration completed in 1981, which took place thanks to aid from the Spanish government, the Zawiya of Sidi Qacem houses a museum of Tunisian ceramics as well as the National Centre of Fine Art Ceramics instituted to educate future ceramicists, all without interrupting the worship which continues to be practised there. In addition to an important selection of fine-art ceramic tiles, the museum offers a collection of items from the site of Raqqada (3rd/9th century); others exhumed from the Kasbah of Tunis (9th/15th century); and some which were made in the workshops of Qallaline (13th/19th century). The pottery modelled and decorated by the women of Sejnane are astonishing in terms of the way in which they were made, a method whose roots go back to the dawn of time.

Sidi Qacem al-Zelliji, peristyle, Tunis.

ITINERARY I   *The Medina*

Tunis

Turbe al-Bey, patio, Tunis.

I.1.b **Bab Jadid** (option)

To get to Bab Jadid, take "rue Abdelwahab", then "rue Morkad" until you reach boulevard Bab Jadid.

From our starting point, one crosses Humet al-Haua or the Neighbourhood of Air, called such due to its being located on the outskirts of the town. This is a neighbourhood full of old bourgeois houses; Isabelle Eberhardt stayed at the Dar Abdelwahab, found in the street of the same name. This very popular neighbourhood contains numerous antiquarian shops as well as a second-hand market.

The only gates to remain amongst the seven that pierced the interior enclosure of the *medina* are Bab al-Bhar (the Gate of France) and Bab Jadid. The latter, which translates as the New Gate, was opened in 674/1276 to link the *medina* to the southern suburb which had experienced a leap of urbanisation due to its proximity to the Hafsid Kasbah. This gate would have been flanked by two segmented towers, similar to those of the Sqifa al-Kahla of Mahdia, in keeping with its proportions. One can still imagine the tearing away of these two bulging towers from each side of the horseshoe bay. The entire floorplan can be deconstructed into two square areas of equal proportions, placed in a zig-zag from one another. The first is open roofed: it allowed the defenders of the gate to attack the assailants by throwing projectiles at them. The second area is a hallway covered by a groined vault. From there, after having to change direction yet one more time, one is led out into the heart of the city. The presence of the Suq of the Blacksmiths reflects the original layout of the economic area of a *medina* that pushed polluting activities out to the outskirts, keeping the centre on reserve for *suqs* that were considered "noble".

I.1.c **Turbe al-Bey**

From Bab Jadid, take "la rue des Forgerons" (the street of the Blacksmiths) and then "la rue des Juges" until you reach "rue Turbe al-Bey" (one of the main crossroads of the medina). Follow the arrows on the orange-coloured ceramic tiles. Entrance fee. Opening times: 09.30–12.00 and 13.00–16.30. Closed Mondays.

Certain facades which can be seen on the "rue des Juges" (the street of the Judges) are particularly remarkable.

Islamic funerary customs, particularly of the Malikite sect, recommends simplicity to its believers, as can be seen by the anonymity of the tombs. The Hanafite Turks had introduced the habit of building elaborate monuments in honour of the dead, which were known as *turbe*s or *turbet*s. The Turbe al-Bey, built during the reign of 'Ali Pasha II (1171/1758–1195/1781), houses the burial place of the Princely Husaynite family. It has a imposing ochre sandstone facade from which pilasters, as well as Italian-styled stone entablatures sculpted in low-relief floral motifs, branch out.

It is interesting to compare this facade to that of Turbe al-Fellari which is situated in the opposite corner. Dating from the 12th/18th century, this monument subscribes to local tradition. Each of its three facades is furnished with a blind arcature, and the median arch is punctured by a saddle-barred window which is surmounted by an epitaph.

Leading on from a straight-lined entrance, Turbe al-Bey is composed of a complex succession of rooms, a result of successive extensions done according to various needs and at the expense of bordering buildings. Next to the tombs of the sovereigns and their families, the monument retains tombs belonging to a certain number of their ministers or of privileged faithful servants.

Within this complex, it is the square room which houses the tombs of the "*beys* of the throne", in other words the tombs of those who actually reigned, that is the most attention-grabbing. It is a miniature replica of Ottoman mosques which themselves derived from Agia Sofia. Four fat pillars support a central dome which is buttressed by semi-domes on each of its four sides. Four smaller domes (cupolas) finish the roof, covering each of the room's four corners. The interior decoration combines the Italian-style, polychrome marble inlaid work with the sculpted plaster perfectly.

The tombs dug out of the earth are covered with marble chests which are abundant with low-relief motif ornamentation, above which rise prismatic columns engraved with epitaphs, which are surmounted by a hat when the deceased is a male. The turban or Fez-form sculpted in stone corresponds to the change of fashion within official costumes. The tombs of women are indicated by two marble plaques, and that which lies on the end where the head is placed is engraved with an epitaph.

Dar Ibn 'Abd Allah, incrusted polychrome marble coping, Tunis.

ITINERARY I   *The Medina*

Tunis

Dar Ibn 'Abd Allah, patio, Tunis.

I.1.d **Dar Ibn 'Abd Allah**

Follow the signs until you reach "rue Sidi Kacem". Entrance fee. Opening times: 09.30–16.30. Closed Mondays. There are toilet facilities.

> *A fruit and vegetable and grocery market occupies the first stretch of the "rue des Teinturiers" (the street of the Dyers), an important axis in the* medina *which links boulevard Bab Jadid to the Great Mosque.*

The Dar Ibn 'Abd Allah, whose history is known to us since 1796, changed hands twice before being bought by Mohamed Tahar Ibn 'Abd Allah, who gave it his name. A wealthy silk weaver, 'Abd Allah lived there from 1291/1875 until 1316/1899, before it was bought by a French painter, Albert Aublet. This aesthete proceeded in undertaking important repair works which were resumed in 1941, when the Office of Public Education and Fine Arts set up the Office of Tunisian Arts there. In the aftermath of Independence, the Dar Ibn 'Abd Allah was transformed into a Regional Museum of Tunis.

Its design and decoration does not differ from those of the *medina*'s other palaces. On the other hand, we are stopped in our tracks by the traditional $13^{th}/19^{th}$ century furniture which it displays. The floorplan of the room is configured in the form of an inverted T-shape. A *qbu*, or central recess, faces the entrance, which is furnished with small horseshoe-shaped benches. The conventional decor of this alcove demonstrates the predilection for mirrors and crystals imported from Venice. Suspended at ceiling height, the mirrors surmount a painted wood shelf on which collections of coloured crystal phials and vases are displayed. The large chandelier highlights the importance of this alcove for holding receptions.

Two *maqsura* or small rooms, the use of which vary according to need, branch off each side of this *qbu*: they could be used as children's rooms or store rooms. At each end of the room, two alcoves house side beds. To accentuate the intimacy of this space, a painted wood canopy reduces the height of the ceiling, whilst heavy curtains isolate the space from the rest of the room. At the foot of the bed, the slightly lower bench allows one to rest, get dressed or eat breakfast. In the *maqsura* of the "bridal chamber", a beautiful collection of chests demonstrates, through its variety, the importance of this item in traditional furnishings. The chests, coated in silver or mother of pearl and lined inside with velvet or quilted satin, were used to store silver and jewels whilst the larger wood painted coffers, which were sculpted or adorned with studs, were used to store linen and clothes.

I.1.e Dar 'Uthman

On "rue Mebazza". Opening times: 08.30–13.00 and 15.00–18.00. Closed on Friday afternoons.

From the time when the Almohads built the *kasbah* to when it was rebuilt by the Hafsids, the citadel united the seat of government to the residential palaces of the sovereigns. 'Uthman Dey (1002/1594–1018/1610) chose to separate the affairs of State from those of his familial life by having a residence built in the Dyers' Quarter which was still relatively non-urban as it was only endowed with a mosque a century later. The security that was established enabled the development of agriculture in the countryside, and the rise of arts and crafts and commerce in the towns. The favourable reception with which this sovereign greeted Andalusian immigrants also contributed to this economic boom. Furthermore, thanks to a well-armed flotilla, he "managed the pirateering and filled his hands with loot".

'Uthman Dey lived in this palace until his death in 1018/1610, after which it was used for various purposes. These included its use as the residence of Bey Husayn Ibn Mahmoud (12th–13th/first half of the 19th century) as well as the military service's supplies office, from which the name *Dar al-'Awla* (provisions house) is still used to refer to the site. Following restoration work carried out by the Antiquities department, it was used as quarters by the Ethnological Museum (1936-1957). Today it is used by the Medina Conservation Department (the National Institute of Heritage).

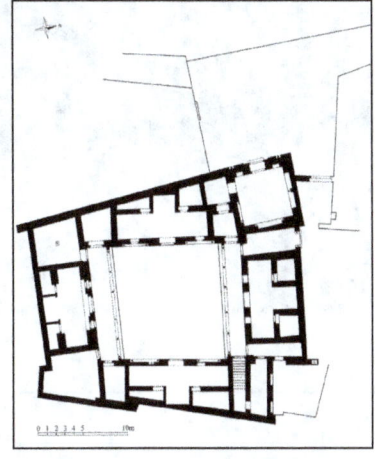

Dar 'Uthman, ground-floor plan, Tunis.

Dar 'Uthman, patio, Tunis.

ITINERARY I The Medina
Tunis

Dar Husayn, first-floor gallery, Tunis.

Dar Husayn, ground-floor plan, Tunis.

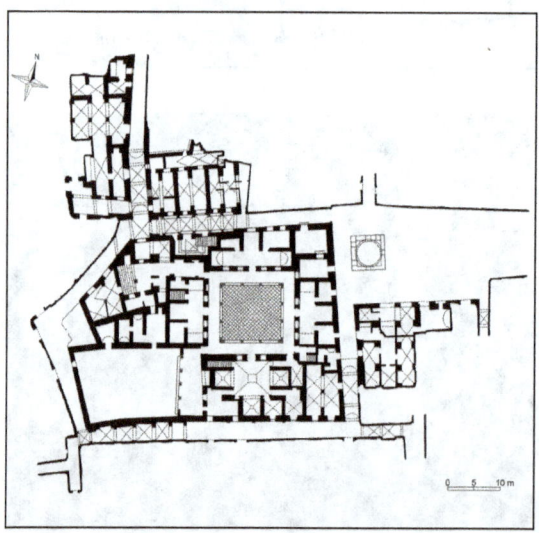

It is distinct for its majestic facade. The right door is surmounted by two (stone) bonded lintels, separated by a Horseshoe arch with bicoloured keystones. Two superposed marble colonnettes symmetrically flank each side of the facade. The overall use of white marble surfaced with incrustations of black marble, and of Hispano-Moresque capitals (*sqifa* and courtyard), cannot but recall Hafsid monuments of the $9^{th}/15^{th}$ century, such as the Midha al-Sultan or the Sidi Qacem al-Zelliji Zawiya. The patio, a later addition, lies between two porticoes, each featuring five Horseshoe arches of unusual elegance. This succession of arches is repeated along the two other sides of the courtyard in the form of two blind arcatures on one side and as an Italic-Turkish-style baroque arch on the other.

ITINERARY I The Medina
Tunis

I.1.f Dar Husayn

From Dar 'Uthman, return via the "rue des Teinturiers" on the right, follow the "rue suq al-Blat" and go back up the "rue Kachachine", then take the "rue du Dey" until you reach the "place du Chateau" (Castle Square).
Opening times: 08.30–13.00 and 15.00–18.00. Closed on Friday afternoons. Toilet facilities available.

> Suq al-Blat today belongs to the merchants who sell medicinal plants at stalls which spill out onto the street. One can also find several cheap fast-food places and popular restaurants on this street.

The framework of the building was built by Isma'il Kahiya, minister and son-in-law of 'Ali Bey (1171/1758–1195/1781). At the beginning of the $13^{th}/19^{th}$ century, Yussef Sahib al-Taba'a, Hammuda Pasha's favourite minister, who had made a fortune in maritime commerce thanks to having his own personal flotilla, undertook the expansion and embellishment of this palace in view of his marriage to Princess Fatma, Hammuda Pasha's sister. His assassination committed by his rivals put an end to this project (1230/1815).
The palace was chosen by the *bey* as the municipal seat which had just been created in Tunis (1274/1858). General Husayn, the first President of the new Municipal Council, was allowed to live in a section of the palace, which henceforth carried his name. In 1882, when General Forgemol, commanding French troops from Tunisia, entered Tunis, he decided to settle in this building with his administrative staff, which symbolised authority over the capital. A square, the actual Castle Square (place du Chateau), encroaching on an old cemetery, was constructed to mark the occasion. The entrance began from the *driba*, designed to serve each different section of the palace. Today, one enters the "great house" directly from the square. The peristyle courtyard displays elaborate cladding. The *mihrab*'s "Qallaline" panels alternate with those made of marble, encrusted with Turkish floral elements. Italian sculptors were without doubt responsible for the creation of the neo-Corinthian styled capitals and for the Baroque decoration of the cistern.
Amongst the various rooms, those facing south are based along the lines of the *bayt diwani*, a reception hall whose model was adopted for the Dar al-Bey and the Bardo Palace. The three alcoves of the classic T-shaped room no longer look upon a long room but upon a room which is nearly square. A vault of cloistered arches, completed above by three cupolas of the same style, constitutes the roofing of this room in which stucco craftsmen have deployed their entire knowledge, repeating various styles which were well-known at the time: festooned, Andalusian vault friezes and four-curled circles embellished with geometric

Dar Husayn, peristyle, Tunis.

ITINERARY I *The Medina*

Tunis

I.1.g Dar al-Haddad

It is located at 9, "impasse de l'Artillerie". From Dar Husayn, take a right towards "rue Ben Mahmoud". The "impasse de l'Artillerie" is the first on the left before "rue Ben Mahmoud".

Built south-west of the *suqs* in the Old Quarter of the Bani Khurasan, the Dar al-Haddad is, without doubt, one of the oldest palaces of the *medina;* its construction dates back to the 10th–11th/end of the 16th century.

At the beginning of the 12th/18th century, the palace belonged to Sa'id al-Haddad al-Andalusi, a wealthy maker of tarbooshes, Fez hats. The Haddad family is one of the largest families of Andalusian origin. Having arrived in Tunisia in the 10th/16th century, this family settled in Tunis after having spent some time in Tebourba.

The tarboosh trade established between Tunis and the countries of the Mediterranean was thus a prosperous one. During the 13th/19th century, following the country's economic crisis, the Haddads' fortune was in jeopardy; thus the palace was abandoned, and was rented to various families. In 1966, it was acquired by the City of Tunis and classed as an historic monument. Its restoration, directed with care by the National Institute of Heritage, has just been completed.

One is made aware of the originality of the design, the scale of its size and the elegance of its architectural solutions, making the palace functional yet pleasingly comfortable. On each side of the *driba* – which in fact is an impasse, and which, in the old days, was closed off by a set of doors – lie the outbuildings of the palace. At the far end of the impasse, a double door leads into the heart of the palace. The courtyard, isolated from the outside by

Dar al-Haddad, chimney, Tunis.

and floral motifs, eight-pointed stars and Turkish cypresses, Italian vases unravelling large amounts of foliage across the four corners of the main vault. Beneath the painted wood shelves, the walls are lined with European *faience*.

The guests' floor, or *dar al-diaf,* which was added on by Yussef Sahib al-Taba'a, and which before had an open roof, has a marble columned peristyle, supporting Italianised round arches. The shells above the lintels of the doors and windows, and the Sicilian *faience* panelling the walls, are signs of the renewed architectural decoration that occurred at the beginning of the 13th/19th century.

ITINERARY I *The Medina*
Tunis

three *sqifa*s, is surrounded by porticoes on three sides.

The *kadhal* columns, topped with Hafsid capitals, are raised using imposts. The fourth side of the courtyard is furnished with three long niches. Two stone benches sit alongside the base of these side niches. Upstairs, a corridor gallery runs along the four sides of the courtyard. Columns, sitting on supports, the corners of which have been cut off, and which are grouped in threes in each corner, are linked together by a turned wooden balustrade. Contrary to the usual layout of palaces, the work area has not been separated from the masters' quarters. The work area is spread out on each side of the reception hall, which faces the entrance. One section was used as a storage room, whilst the other, which housed the well, led out onto a small courtyard, which was surrounded by the kitchen, *hammam* and latrines. One of the six large rooms of the palace, situated upstairs, is laid out and designed in such a unique way that there are no further examples of it to be seen elsewhere. It consists of a room with a central recess, flanked by four smaller side rooms. It is within this section of the palace that the unique Turkish chimney, well-known in the Medina of Tunis, can be found. Its opening consists of a pelmet arch, topped with a conical chimney-hood. Its presence, in a town where, even in winter, one only came across the fire of a brazier, deserves a special mention.

I.1.h The Kasbah Quarter

From Dar al-Haddad, walk back up to the "place du Gouvernment" (Government Square) via the Sakkajine Suq and the boulevard Bab Mnara on the right.

The Kasbah Quarter developed itself around the citadel, on the heights of the western fringe of the *medina*. Ever since the $3^{rd}/9^{th}$ century, it has been a site privileged by the the powers that be. It was there that the governors under the Almohad Caliph of Marrakesh settled in the $7^{th}/13^{th}$ century. One of them, Abu Zakariya al-Hafsi, proclaimed independence from the *caliph*, made Tunis his capital, and proceeded to rebuild the *kasbah*. It is a "royal" mosque whose minaret, which still stands, echoes the ornamentation of the Almohad towers of the mosque in the Kasbah of Marrakesh, of the Hassan Tower in Rabat, and of the Giralda in Seville.

Turbe Laz, the kasbah, Tunis, 19th-century watercolour.

ITINERARY I   *The Medina*
Tunis

The Kasbah of Tunis, defended by powerful walls, housed the palace in which the sultan gathered together his council and gave audiences, as well as being his private residence, and the barracks for his own bodyguards and for the soldiers in charge of defending the palace. Its structure remained thus until the Husaynite period (12th/18th century), after which the sovereigns decided to live outside the *kasbah* walls, in the Dar al-Bey, right at the foot of the citadel. The latter had in the meantime neither lost its military role nor its worth as a symbol of power. Occupied by the French army during the Protectorate, it was demolished as soon as Independence was achieved. The new Town Hall marks the affirmation of authority of the Tunisian State. On each side of the citadel and around the Dar al-Bey, an administrative quarter has been developing since the 13th–14th/19th century, and is distinct for the homogeneity of its Arabian-style architecture. This trend defines itself as an attempt to "bring together the respective elements of one with the stylistic key of the other." From this utterly original adaptation of Islamic art, Tunis – like all great Maghrebi Capitals – jealously guards its finest examples, such as the Ministry of Finance (1892), the Ministry of National Defence (1894), the Sadiki College (1897) and the High Courts of Justice (1902).

I.1.i **Cafe Mnouchi**

This – an old wikala *with beautiful* faiences *which was transformed into a cafe – can be found half-way into the Leffa Suq, in the tail end of the Sakkajine Suq.*

The Mnouchi *wikala*, named after its current proprietor, is an old inn which lodged foreign merchants visiting the town. As opposed to *funduqs*, which are often located near ports and lodge wholesale merchants, *wikala*s are reserved for merchants that trade in precious goods such as gold, silk, perfume and spices. This more "noble" character explains their location near the Great Mosque as well as their more refined architecture, both of which is demonstrated by the *wikala* featured here.
The Mnouchi *wikala* does not distinguish itself over the originality of its design layout: it has a central courtyard framed by porticoes, surrounded by rooms. What

Café Mnouchi, ceramic mural, Tunis.

ITINERARY I   *The Medina*
Tunis

does give it its unique character is the thematic design of the ceramic tile cladding which decorates it. It is the only example of its kind in Tunis, and indeed in Tunisia, of a design in which the depiction of animated beings is the principal feature. These fresh figurative compositions, undertaken using pure (primary) colours, reveal animals (a bird, a peacock, a gazelle, a lioness) as well as people, including a woman. She is seated by a tomb of a wealthy person, and is shown draped in a veil; her face remains uncovered and her arms are bare. It is the imaginative creation of an anonymous artist, complete with a love poem inscribed in the horizontal cartouches which run across, frieze-like, crowning the entire piece.

The *wikala* has today been reincarnated into a lively cafe by young, and not so young, card players.

Al-Dar, which is located at the exit of the Leffa Suq in the Truk Suq, is an old apartment which has no patio as it is housed within more classical buildings. It has been turned into an antiquities shop. The old kitchen gives an idea of the sites' layout.

I.1.j Al-'Attarin Barracks

Go down along the Leffa Suq towards the Great Mosque and turn onto "rue Suq al-'Attarin", on which the barracks, which today house an annex of the National Library, can be found. Photography here is forbidden.

The Bey Hammuda Pasha, the founder of these barracks, paid particular attention to works which were military in nature. Five barracks, all built within the city walls, were erected, including this one, the al-'Attarin Suq. The entrance on the right leads into an oblong courtyard surrounded by galleried corridors which are stacked above one another. Barracks rooms branch off from the shelter of the galleries, some of which still carry, above their doors, the name of the janissaries corps that occupied it. Right from its beginning, the colonial administration of the Protectorat installed the Department of Antiquities and a Library within these barracks. In 1958 the National Institute of Archaeology and the Arts replaced the Department of Antiquities, which was transferred to the Dar Husayn. The library, reorganised and enriched by thousands of Arabic works and manuscripts from the Great Mosque and

Al-'Attarin barracks, patio, Tunis.

ITINERARY I *The Medina*

Tunis

the *medina's madrasa*s, has since become the National Library. It is the best endowed and most important of the Tunisian Libraries.

Al-'Attarin Suq: perfumes, incense and henna (a green powder which produces a reddish dye, used by women in the dyeing of their hair and in the decoration of their hands and feet).

I.1.k Sidi al-Morjani Barracks
(option)

Take "rue des Tamis" which is on the right, followed by "rue Jama' al-Zituna" on the left. This monument, which houses an annex of the National Library, looks out onto "rue Jama' al-Zituna". Photography here is forbidden.

The Great Mosque, nartex, Tunis.

Built by Hammuda Pasha in the middle of the 13th/19th century, it was vacated in 1290/1874 to make room for a new institution, the Sadiki College, before the construction of modern sites on the heights of the *kasbah* (1897). The barracks housed the administration in charge of managing *habus* until these were abolished in 1956. Today it is annexed to the National Library next door.

I.1.l The Great Mosque of Zituna

Walk back up "rue Jama' al-Zituna".
Entrance fee. Opening times: 08.00—12.00 daily except Fridays.

Situated in the heart of the town, the Great Mosque, also called *al-Zituna*, which means the Mosque of the Olive Tree, is the largest and most venerated sanctuary in Tunis. Its foundation is linked with that of the city (78/698). It benefited from the great building works undertaken by Governor 'Abd Allah Ibn al-Habhab in 113/732, a date to which its foundation is often falsely attributed. It is to the Aghlabid Amir Abu Ibrahim Ahmed (241/856–249/864) that we owe the basic structure and essential elements of the actual monument. This prince completely demolished the first, original mosque and rebuilt it.

Like the mosque of Kairouan, Zituna Mosque is a reflection of the basilical plan in which the naves run downwards perpendicular to the back wall. It is a type of plan which appeared quite early on in Syria-Palestine, within the design of the Aqsa Mosque in Jerusalem. As in Kairouan, the hypostyle prayer hall is preceded by a courtyard, *sahn*, the sloping roof, which rests on 184 columns and antique capitals outlining the 15 naves of the 6 bays. The antique elements used in this building derive, for the most part, from the ruins of Carthage. Their use attests to the ingenuity of the architects of the 3rd/9th century who, from various scattered elements, created works of perfect harmony. The median nave as well as the transversal nave of the transept are larger than the others and cross at right angles in front of the *mihrab*. The T-shape created by these two naves can be linked, according to certain art historians, to basilicas like that of the Nativity in Bethlehem. The front of the *mihrab* is highlighted by a dome dated by an inscription as being from 249/864. From the outside it displays a fluted segmental arch which rests on an octagonal drum sitting on top of a square base. An inscription, also from the 3rd/9th century, runs as a frieze across the facade of the prayer hall.

The mosque used to be encircled by a great wall of stone; two corner towers – one of which can still be seen in the north-east corner to the right of the main entrance – attest to the defensive role played by the earliest mosques. Amongst the six gates that lead into the mosque, the Gate of Imam – which faces out onto the wool *suq* – features a Roman frame, decorated with acanthus leaves through which one can see the hammering-out of certain figurative motifs.

The Zituna owes its narthex, and the dome of its *bahu* that emphasises the axis of the facade, to the Fatimids, or rather to the Zirids. The appearance of alternate bicoloured assizes echoes back to Cordoba or to the Umayyad monuments of Syria-Palestine, like the Dome of the Rock; unless what we are witnessing here is the revival of a local tradition, an example of which can be found in a Roman mosaic of the Bardo. The profusion of niches ties the dome to Fatimid art. In the 5th/11th century, the Banu Khurasan greatly opened up the mosque to its surrounding environment by increasing its number of gates from six to twelve. The one looking out onto the *al-'Attarin* Suq is surmounted by an inscription dated 473/1081. The Hafsids involved themselves in the enrichment of the Zituna with Hispano-Moresque decorative elements in geometric interlaces like those created on the woodwork of the doors isolating the prayer hall from the courtyard: this work was done by Abu Yahya Zakariya. The beautiful facade of the Abu 'Amr 'Uthman Library, with its twin windows, forming the south-east corner on the extreme left of the main entrance, dates from this era. This period witnessed an important demographic

The Great Mosque, patio and minaret, Tunis.

ITINERARY I   *The Medina*

Tunis

increase, which necessitated the creation of another side courtyard to the east.

During the Turkish and Husaynite eras, only three architectural styles are noteworthy, as they transformed the look of the building. They involve the covering of the side courtyard, as well as the embellishment of three galleries in the main courtyard and of the minaret. In 1096/1685, the Imam al-Bakri ordered that the side courtyard be covered with a flat roof, supported by a triple colonnade with Hafsid *kadhal* capitals, *kadhal* being a local limestone. Prime Minister Khaznadar endowed the three galleries of the main courtyard with columns featuring composite capitals made of white marble from Italy, imported directly from the Peninsula, as was the case from then on with respect to all the marble used in the Tunisian construction industry.

The final touch to this prestigious monument was the erection of the minaret we see today which replaced a former, more modest one. The tower is 43 m. in height, and its decor is inspired by that of the Almohad minaret of the Mosque of the Kasbah.

I.1.m Al-Baschiya Madrasa

On leaving the Great Mosque, take a right onto the "rue des Libraires"; the monument faces the Kashashin Hammam.

As its name indicates, the "rue des Libraires" (the street of the Booksellers) is an old book suq, *a noble trade thus situated in the surroundings of the Great Mosque. Facing the* madrasa, *the Kashashin Cafe and* Hammam *are places which are typical of the* medina.

The *madrasa* is an institution that appeared in the Orient in the 5th/11th century. A place of lodging and centre of study, it also received foreign students. The first *madrasa* to be set up in the Maghreb was the "*Shamma'iya*", founded in Tunis in 635/1238 by the Hafsid Sultan Abu Zakariya. Ever since, and right across the Hafsid period, sovereigns and princesses, ministers and patrons of the arts did not stop building *madrasas*, confirming Tunis's importance as a University town and cultural centre.

Whilst having been neglected at the start of the Turkish era, education and learning improved with the accession of the Husaynite Dynasty, who needed the support of the religious world as much as they needed the services of good Civil Servants who had mastered the Turkish language. Numerous *madrasas*, teaching along the lines of both the Malikite and Hanafite sects, saw

Al-Bashiya Madrasa, detail of a bench, Tunis.

the light of day. 'Ali Pasha, founder of the Bashiya, went on to build four more *madrasa*s.

Constructed in 1165/1752, the building is based on the classic building plan of a *madrasa*. Individual rooms accommodating students open out along the three sides of the central courtyard whilst the fourth side is taken up by a *masjed*: a prayer hall that also acts as a classroom and library. To the right of the entrance, one can see a *sabil* or public fountain which 'Ali Pasha added to his pious foundation. A stone tank, placed behind the bars of a window, was always full of water. Passers-by could always help themselves to the water through the bars with the help of copper cups which were placed on the window sill.

In order to guarantee the maintenance of this establishment, the founder set up *habus*, a non-transferable endowment of 40 buildings, the rent from which was used exclusively for this purpose. The document regarding this matter, taken from the register of Husaynite *habus*, reveals to us the nature and ruling of the establishment, the main points of which are the following:

The *madrasa* must teach according to Hanefite beliefs. It contains 13 rooms, to be used strictly by individuals only. (Later on, *madrasa*s were over-subscribed and students shared rooms, two or three to a room after having moved out of the mezzanines).

On top of housing, students benefited from funding. They were obliged to follow, with regularity, the three daily lessons, and to reside permanently on site. They could nevertheless take leave of absence, lasting no longer than two months in cases of travel and one year in the case of making a pilgrimage to Mecca.

The teacher must be a follower of the Hanafite sect. He must teach three classes a day, divided into three sessions. Moreover, he holds the title of *Imam* of the *masjed* of the *"madrasa"* and must be responsible for leading the five daily prayers. In return he receives a regular salary.

Today the students live in modern halls of residence, and the old *madrasa*s have been restored and brought back to life for various uses. The Bashiya houses an arts and crafts vocational training school.

Al-Bashiya Madrasa, main entrance, Tunis.

I.1.n **Turbe 'Ali Pasha** (option)

The monument is located at the corner of the "rue des Libraires" and the "rue de la Madrasa Slimaniya", next to the preceding monument.

ITINERARY I *The Medina*
Tunis

Slimaniya Madrasa, prayer hall, Tunis.

In order to adapt it to the papered surfaces, the artist plays around with this composition, which has since become a classic, by creating within it forms that vary greatly: slender, pointed shapes that radiate out from the central keystone of the vault, triangular ones on the pendentives, rectangular ones on the cylinder. Four-cornered columns, grouped in threes, are in place to receive the fall in the vault's arch. The polychrome marble inlay cladding the walls takes after a decorative style introduced a century earlier by Hammuda Pasha al-Muradi. It echoes the Italian technique of inlaid work. This monument today houses the Association of Alumni of the High School of the "rue du Pasha". Both the young and old ex-students meet up there for social occasions and cultural events or use it simply as a place in which to relax.

I.1.o **Slimaniya Madrasa**

Located in the street of the same name, the monument is around the same corner as that of the previous monument.

The construction of this *madrasa* was ordered by 'Ali Pasha in 1167/1754. It was dedicated to the memory of his son, Sulayman, who was killed with poison by his own brother. In order to gain sympathy from the local population, he created this building for students of Malikism, in opposition to the sect of the Bashiya. In terms of architecture, this *madrasa* is distinct for its entrance found under an elegant, monumental porch supported by columns featuring Turkish capitals which are crowned by a cornices made of green tiles.

Situated between the two *madrasa*s he founded, 'Ali Pasha could not have chosen a better site for his burial place. His work, dedicated to education, is the best way of gauging the peace in which his soul rests. This monument is composed of an elbow-shaped entrance that leads into a portico courtyard. The slim marble columns and wall cladding of the courtyard do not differ in the slightest from the decoration of a dwelling place. The domed room, formerly the funerary chamber, is the most beautiful example of the stucco-craftsmen's skilfulness; they have transformed the stucco into true lace. The base motif is nothing other than a vase holding a bouquet whose abundant foliage spreads out.

ITINERARY I *The Medina*
Tunis

I.1.p **The Suqs**

The al-'Attarin Suq

The creation of the *suqs*, at the heart of which lies the Great Mosque, is attributed to the first Hafsids (7th/13th–8th/14th century). Only the "noble" *suqs* – those that neither caused a nuisance in terms of noise or smell – could locate themselves near this venerable sanctuary.

Situated alongside the northern facade of the Zituna, the Suq of the Perfumers, *al-'Attarin*, has retained its original function, which is for the sale of perfume essence and incense, as well as the sale of different ingredients (both mineral and plant) used in the preparation of traditional beauty products which continue to be popular despite the invasion of industrial products.

Candles and wax products can be found here in abundance. Brought together in the form of a five-arm chandelier, they constitute the most privileged offering that can be made to the saints, and burn during the ceremony of henna application on the bride. The baskets lined with pastel-coloured satin are designed to hold the gifts offered by the groom to his future spouse.

The counters and shelves made of sculpted wood (see stall no. 43) attest to the age-old wealth of this corporation. In the 15th century, Anselme Adorne noted that "the perfume stalls sold their long, decorated perfume bottles to a wide clientele, and each day were the last to shut for the night".

The al-Qumash Suq

To the west, the Great Mosque looks out onto the Suq of Fabrics, *al-Qumash*, founded by Sultan Abu 'Amr 'Uthman in the 9th/15th century. Its homogenous architecture appears to be a response to a vision of it as a unified complex. A *suq* is thus not the result of a spontaneous juxtaposition of stalls in a straight line.

Two rows of stone columns divide the space into three alleys. The central alley, intended as a pedestrian walkway and for traffic, is larger than the side alleys onto which the stalls spill out. Covered by longitudinal barrel vaults, the alleys are filled with daylight through lanterns that pierce the central vault. The same system of lanterns also allowed for the stalls to be naturally lit once, before the widespread use of false ceilings, mezzanines and the invasion of neon.

Two gates defend access to the *suq*. That on the *al-'Attarin* Suq side is flanked by two

Suq of the Sheshiyas, a craftsman's boutique, Tunis.

ITINERARY I   *The Medina*

Tunis

Dar Lasram, patio, Tunis.

columns topped with Hispano-Maghrebic capitals, which as Georg Marcais explains: "... looked like they had come from Fez or Granada had certain details in their composition and manufacture not given away the fact that they were made locally".

I.1.q Dar Lasram

Take "rue Sidi Ben Arus", continue down "rue du Pasha" until you reach the "rue of the Hafsia". Turn right, and then take "rue du Tribunal" on the left until you reach the monument. Dar Lasram is about 15 minutes from the Mosque of the Kasbah. There is parking on the "place du Tribunal". Toilet facilities are available.

The "rue du Pasha", which was one of the most aristocratic streets of the medina, features a number of drapery merchants.

The Romdhane Bey Square features several Rococo-style balconies.
On "rue du Tribunal", a hammam stands on the other side of the same corner on which one can find the entrance to the old stables of Dar Lasram, known today as the Tahar Haddad Cultural Club.
As a residential neighbourhood, this part of the medina offers several unique sights, like that of the twisting and very narrow "rue de la Noria".

Hammuda Lasram, a rich landowner and high-ranking military officer, built this palace at the dawn of the $13^{th}/19^{th}$ century, providing a house for generation after generation of his descendants up until 1964. Put up for sale, it was acquired by the council and given over in 1968 to the Association for the Conservation of the Medina, who proceeded to restore and rebuild it.

ITINERARY I   *The Medina*
Tunis

The essential components expected of a palace are spread across three floors. The ground floor was occupied by servants, a raised ground floor encompassed the main dwelling area, and the first floor was reserved for guests. The facade is distinguished by a large, studded door framed within a double band of *kadhal* and sandstone, *harsh*. A barely recognisable Roman sarcophagus forms a large step which allowed horsemen to get off their mounts easily, without setting foot on the ground. A high dormer window, *guenariya*, held up by solid corbels made of freestone, ornaments this facade.

The entrance, through its elbow-shape design, protects the heart of the residence from outside inlookers and all other undesirables. The succession of halls allows one to access the interior space, and they are set out according to a hierarchy determined by their more or less intimate connection to the proprietors. The *driba*, the first hall, furnished with stone benches, was used as a reception room for short visits and for business meetings. One room to the right of the entrance, called the room of the evening, "*bayt al-sahra'* " was exclusively used by the teacher, the *meddeb*, during the day, and at night by the men of the house and their closest friends for their evening chats. To the left of the entrance, a staircase leads to the floor on which the hosts live, the "*dar al-diaf*". This independent floor, planned out around a courtyard, allowed them to receive guests without interrupting their own family life, as guests were not always friends or close to the family. Distinguished visiting foreigners who were passing through town – dignitaries, famous scholars, important merchants – were, in view of their social status, received by the town's notables. Most of the travellers had a network of *funduqs* at their disposition.

The *driba* extends through a second hall used as the "*dar al-harka*", the house of domestic staff. Kitchens and servants' rooms encircled a courtyard, the simplicity of whose materials stands out in great contrast to the opulence of the masters' courtyard. Pink *kadhal* replaces marble; it forms the frames of the doors, the columns and the capitals, as well as the paving on the floor. It is through this courtyard that one can reach the *makhzen*, the grocers, stables and carriage shelter. Arches and brick vaults, falling back onto large stone pillars built with great care, demonstrate the thousand-year old mastery of the art of building. Two very small internal gardens extend this space linked directly to the street outside through a single door. The entire building, redesigned, now serves as a centre for cultural and artistic events: the Tahar Haddad Club.

The main residential area, the "*dar al-kebira*", gathers together the apartments belonging to the different branches of the patriarchal family that occupied the palace. Built raised above the *makhzen*, it is located at the back, kept at a distance from the street by the *driba* and the three halls that lead on from it. The

Dar Lasram, painted ceiling, Tunis.

ITINERARY I   *The Medina*
Tunis

courtyard is adorned with two porticoes facing each other, composing marble columns and neo-Doric capitals. The two side rooms conform to the classic T-shape layout whilst the reception room, situated in front of the entrance, is marked out by its cruciform layout. This particularity is only seen within certain impressive palaces. The courtyard, as well as these three rooms, display a unified style in terms of decoration: *Qallalin* ceramic on the base of the walls, sculpted plaster higher up, and a wooden ceiling decorated in a floral Italian style. The decor of the room occupying the fourth side of the courtyard comes from a different source of inspiration. It is rectangular, and is reached through a door at the far end rather than a central one, which stands under a small, elegant portico composed of four small columns and three arches linked together. A row of low windows and cupboards featuring sculpted wood panels framed in polychrome marble, furnish the three sides of the room. The sculpted wood ceiling is guilded and has painted features of Hispano-Moresque inspired star motifs. This room is modelled on the *"bayt al-ftur"*, the dining room of the Dar al-Bey and of the Bardo Palace. These rooms suit the European furniture adopted by the reigning family from the 13th/19th century onwards, which was then copied by the aristocracy.

I.1.r **Bab al-Bhar**

Located at the end of the street "rue Jama' al-Zituna", at the far end of the "Avenue de France", this monument marks the border between the medina *and the "colonial town". Bab al-Bhar is about 25 minutes from Dar Lasram.*

On one side of "place de la Victoire", the "rue des Glacieres" features several antiquarian shops; on the other side, the "rue de la Commission" abounds with wholesalers and Genoese facades dating from the beginning of the 20th century.

Bab al-Bhar, 19th-century engraring, Tunis.

Up until the 13th/19th century, the waters of the lake of Tunis reached the town's street level: hence the name given to this gate, Bab al-Bhar or Gate of the Sea, known of since the Hafsid era. In 1263/1848, following his voyage to Paris, Ahmed Bey ordered the demolition of the Hafsid gate and the construction of today's gate in its place. The latter was built on a different site to that occupied by the former, in order to be positioned on the axis of "avenue de la Marine", which today is known as "avenue de France". The defensive purpose of the gates seems to feature less in the second construction. Perhaps this was due to changes in the art and technology of war and to the consecration of the era of artillery! Ahmed Bey used this gate to symbolise his capital's entry into the modern age.

When the Protectorat became established, the Bab al-Bhar was rebaptised Gate of France. Today, it has changed back to its old name, but, no longer attached to the city wall that branched off from its right and left sides, it looks like a piece of decoration which, despite everything, has conserved its wooden double door portal which is plated with iron.

TUNISIAN CERAMICS

Jamila Binous

Example of a wall-facing incrusted in marble.

In Tunisia, the production of terracotta crockery dates back to the Neolithic age. The decoration composed of strokes and dots etched into the wet clay was replaced, ever since the protohistorical era, by decorative paintwork. Since then, the rural world has not ceased in producing crockery modelled by women and featuring elaborate, rectilinear decoration created through the use of mastic-tree sap which attaches itself permanently once fired. The Mogods, Sejnane, Kesra and the villages of Douiret are all centres for the creation of this thousand-year old craft, as are the mountainous regions of the whole of North Africa; one can find the practice of this art among the Kabyls of Algeria and the Rifians of Morocco. Egypt and Persia had invented the potter's wheel at the height of the age of Antiquity. It was introduced to Tunisia at least 2000 years ago. The potter's wheel allowed for the development of a style of pottery whose shapes were increasingly elaborate. Elsewhere, the improvement of firing techniques, thanks to the perfecting of the traditional kiln, consecrated this mastery in the art of firing, this skill whose evolution through the entire duration of Islamic history shall be traced.

Various centres of pottery prospered until recently: Tozeur, Kairouan, Beja, Tunis. Others resisted, and continue to resist, the recession affecting this craft, namely Moknine, Jerba and Nabeul. What are the great moments of Tunisian ceramics? What have the various decorative repertoires been throughout the ages?

The Aghlabid era, of the $3^{rd}/9^{th}$ century, is characterised by the sobriety of its palette. A bichrome brown-and-green decoration composed of geometric motifs plays off a yellow background, created through the use of antimony oxide. The same oxides created from antimony, from manganese and from copper, as well as the same geometric decor, remain very popular and fashionable within a form of traditional pottery called *motli*, made in Nabeul and Jerba.

The works dating from the Hafsid era of the $7^{th}/13^{th}$–$9^{th}/15^{th}$ centuries, which were discovered during excavations of the Kasbah of Tunis, reveals the secrets of the potters of this period. Conical dishes – *hallab*s – and cups and goblets, all in which slate-blue or ashen-blue and brown with a light violet tint feature predominantly, do not differ in the slightest from ones of the same period discovered in Spain or in the south of Portugal. The decorative paintwork is geometrically inspired: the designs are either rectilinear, expressed in herringbone, oblique, zig-zag and lattice designs, and dipped in the tradition from its earliest beginnings – or they are curvilinear, expressed as spirals, rosettes, and circles placed concentrically or as listels. One also notes the presence of stylised vegetal forms, zoomorphic motifs and depictions of boats and ships. This period saw the introduction into Tunisia of the Andalusian processes of "*cuerda-seca*" and of "*cuerca*". Both cases involve isolating the enamel through the means of a partition, to prevent it from running and spreading out, as it risks mixing with other colours. In the first process described, that of "*cuerda-seca*", a brown manganese tint is used which is thicker and more solid than the enamel itself; in the second process, a fine relief moulding is used. The decorator then paints within the contours that have been created. The Potters' Quarter in Tunis, located outside the town walls between Bab Swiqa and Bab Carthagene, was destined for greatness. In the $11^{th}/17^{th}$ and $12^{th}/18^{th}$ centuries, the Turks brought with them the know-how and techniques developed in the Anatolian workshops. Greyish-white enamel from the Hafsid period appears against a cream white background, whilst their palette is enriched by a symphony of blues and greens. Meanwhile, note is taken of the fact that the "tomato" red, which gave Iznik its reputation and which is very close to the Chinese and Japanese red known as "beef's blood", is not used in the production of the *Qallalins* of Tunis, despite the importation of beautiful tile specimens which were brought for the needs of monuments such as the Sidi Mahrez Mosque or the Dyers' Mosque (Mosque des Teinturiers). This period, between the $11^{th}/17^{th}$ and $12^{th}/18^{th}$ centuries, marks the height of Tunisian ceramics known as *Qallalin*. The shimmering quality of the colours and the exuberance of the vegetal decoration transformed the creation and production of this artform. The foliage, leaves and flowers mingle together to form an abundant mass which only the inexhaustible imagination can make sense of. One recognises the fine outline of tulips, carnations spread out like a fan, the lavish pomegranate flowers and delicate buttercups.

From the beginning of the $13^{th}/19^{th}$ century, the use of ashen-blue enamel is gradually abandoned, and is replaced more or less exclusively by the traditional yellow, brown and green tones. Zoomorphic forms, in

"Tree of Life", polychrome ceramic, $12^{th}/18^{th}$ century.

TUNISIAN CERAMICS

Calligraphic polychrome ceramic, 12th / 18th century.

The 1900s saw the rise of another ceramic centre that followed in the footsteps of the masters of *Qallalin* production: the workshops of Nabeul.

We cannot conclude without mentioning the cladding tiles that lit up the monuments of Tunisia, and even those across the Mediterranean, with their bright, shimmering colours. Tunisian tiles are characterised by their great variety in size, ranging from 6 to 9, 12, 15 and 20 cm. The old samples are recognised by the thickness of their biscuit, and are often bevelled on the non-enamelled side in order to facilitate their placement and adhesion to vertical surfaces. These tiles are used as floor paving for "noble" areas such as bedrooms. However, they are mostly used for the cladding of walls. Particular care is taken in ornamenting interior walls, the bases of which, reaching up to 3 m. in height, are transformed into frescoes through the use of the harmony and warmth of polychrome tiles.

Tiles used in repetitive motifs, able to cover unspecified surfaces and to create friezes of variable lengths, can be distinguished from those used in panelling, through the way in which the bird and the lion hold pride of place, proliferate. The depiction is rough and sketchy and seems to herald the beginning of the end for the workshops of Tunis, which are destined to disappear despite the pathetic venture instigated by Jacob Chemla. This master ceramicist, a Tunisian Jew, took the decision in 1296/1880 to immerse himself in the rediscovery of ancient enamels. With the help of his three sons, and following 30 years of research that cost him his fortune, in 1910 he succeeded in producing pieces that were of unique quality. His reputation extends beyond the boundaries of Tunisia and his work is in demand in Algeria, Libya, Egypt and in the United States. which they have been assembled and put together. Repetitive motifs are either used within the design of a single tile, or are created through placing four tiles together to form a pattern. The panel known as *Qallalin* measures approximately 1.5 m. in height and 0.75 m. in width. Usually it is composed of 50 tiles, each measuring 15 cm. along its side, placed in 10 rows of 5 tiles. The panel is located about 60 cm. above floor level and is easy to place, even on a wall already wainscoted with repetitive tiles; in this case it is isolated in a frame made of *qdhib*, a black border about 2 cm. to 3 cm. thick, made from cut out and varnished terracotta.

The *Qallalin* panels, otherwise known as the *mihrab* panels, come in two variations. In each case, decoration covers the entire surface without leaving an inch to spare, and the main motif sits within an arch (*mihrab*) held up by two small columns. The whole composition is based along the axis of vertical symmetry. The originality and uniqueness of each one lies in the central design drawn within the *mihrab*. The design involves the reproduction of either an Ottoman-style domed mosque, or a large Turkish bouquet composed of foliage, leaves and flowers, all flowing out of a vase.

ITINERARY II

The Summer Palaces

Jamila Binous

II.1 SIDI-BOU-SAÏD
    II.1.a Nejma al-Zahra'

II.2 THE MARSA
    II.2.a The al-'Abdelliya Palace

II.3 ARIANA
    II.3.a Burj Ben 'Ayed

II.4 THE MANOUBA
    II.4.a The Rose Palace, National Military Museum

II.5 THE BARDO
    II.5.a Bardo Palace (Museum only)

II.6 AL-HNAYA
    II.6.a Hafsid Aqueduct (option)

II.7 THE BELVÉDÈRE
    II.7.a The Qubba of the Belvédère (option)

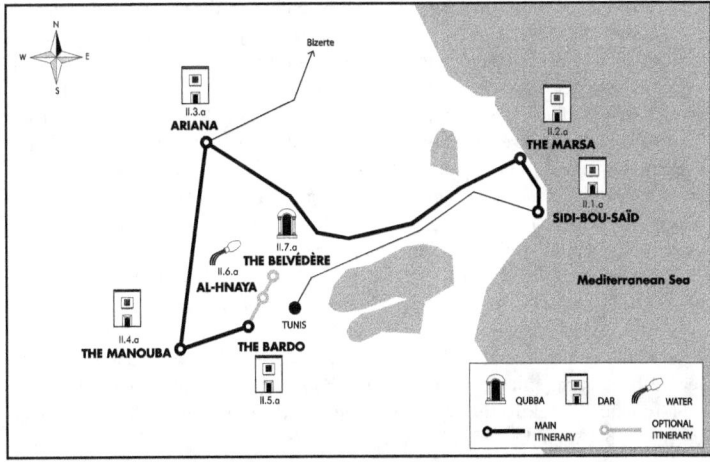

The Rose Palace, Hall, The Manouba.

ITINERARY II   *The Summer Palaces*

Summer residence, Dar Alkamila, the residence in fact of the French Ambassador, 19th-century watercolour, The Marsa.

Anselme Adorne describes the surroundings of Tunis at the end of the 15th century thus: *"Around the town there are in fact close to four thousand gardens, and not a single inhabitant outside the city who does not have their own garden, very pleasantly filled with the perfume of a diverse variety of flowers, and very abundant with all kinds of fruit (...); each garden contains a beautiful building, composed as usual of a large square tower, with (...) an attractive cistern ..."*. To divide one life between town and country was a way of life which was not unknown to the Punics nor to the Romans. There are numerous mosaics in this very countryside which reveal the physiognomy of these villas, erected by the masters of proconsular Africa. These constructions were motivated by the same reason of wanting to be in a semi-urban, semi-rural location, but they were also encouraged by the same desire to enjoy the view onto the gardens or onto the sea, as well as the same forethought of being prepared against eventual attacks during periods of insecurity.

Except for the 'Abdelliya and the Bardo, which were founded by the Hafsids, the Summer Palaces that can still be seen in the region of Tunis date back to the reign of the Husaynites, between the 12th/18th and 13th/19th century. These residences are only known as *qsar* or *seraya* when they house princes or *viziers*; the rest are known either as *burj*, a fort or fortress, perhaps due to their character as a fortified residence, or they are known as *senia*, garden, due to the importance of the plantation that surrounds the *burj* in certain cases.

From the 12th/18th century onwards, foreign consuls were seduced by this way of life. They obtained from the *bey* the privilege of having summer residences. "Since 1187/1774, the bey *had conceded to du Saizieu, the French consul, the free enjoyment of a beylical building as a summer house which was situated at la Marsa, close to the sea"*. In 1274/1858, Mhammed Bey placed *"a burj with its surrounding gardens"* to the disposition of the British Consul, Richard Wood, allowing him to reside there for the summer, in close proximity to the Beylical Palace of the Marsa. Whatever the rank and status of their owners or whatever their dimensions, these Summer Palaces shared a few common characteristics. They displayed architectural elements of city dwellings whilst introducing several new features. They are raised buildings; the ground floor, which is vaulted over, was often occupied by the servants and housed the grocery provisions, spaces for cars and carriages as well as stables for the horses. The design of the apartments situated on the first floor facilitates having large bays and windows, allowing for a substantial amount of ventilation as well as a generous view over all the gardens and parks. These are equipped with one or more wells which provide the water for the plant irrigation reservoirs, for the basins, baths and for the creation of an effect that pleases the eye. These estates were enclosed by high walls or by impenetrable cactus hedges, which guaranteed them both privacy and security.

ITINERARY II The Summer Palaces
Sidi-Bou-Saïd

From Carthage to Gammarth

The region that lies between Carthage and Gammarth was, since the Golden Age of Antiquity, *"planted with gardens and trees ... each plot of land was separated from the next by walls and hedged"*. This description by Appien (in the 2nd century AD) has been confirmed by archeological research that has brought to light a network of cisterns, along the western slope of Carthage's headland. Following the abandonment of Carthage in favour of Tunis from the $2^{nd}/8^{th}$ century onwards, the remains of its Roman civilisation, overgrown with greenery, pricked the sensibilities of the *Sufis*. Through it they saw the blinding proof of God's greatness and a call for humility. Sidi Mahrez, patron of Tunis (end of 4th/end of 10th century) left an eloquent poem to this effect to posterity. Others found these sites to be a peaceful retreat which they could turn to within their ascetic lives, and chose to be buried there: Sidi 'Abd al-'Aziz, Sidi Bu Fares, Sidi Dhrif and the famous Sidi Bu Sa'id. On an economic level, the region regained its agricultural strength in the $5^{th}/11^{th}$ century. Al-Bakri mentioned prosperous villages which provided Tunis with fresh supplies of agricultural produce. Tunis was no less strong under the menace of foreign attack. This included the involvement of the troops of Saint Louis in 668/1270, the nomadic incursions right through the Middle Ages, and above all the sack of the town led by the army of Charles Quint who debarked at la Goulette in 941/1535. Whilst the area of the Marsa had become the place of choice for those in power, the mystical character of the actual headland had been reinforced.

II.1 SIDI-BOU-SAÏD

This area of retreat, which dominates the Gulf of Carthage, previously called the Gulf of Tunis, would have been occupied by a fortress, in the $3^{rd}/9^{th}$ century, which would have stood on the site of the actual fort we see today. Like the *ribat*s, this site was guarded by *murabitun*s. Abu Sa'id al-Baji was in the habit of spending pious periods in retreat on this headland, where he was buried in 628/1231. The area around his tomb was chosen as a burial site on which a necropolis was built, remains of which can still be seen today. At the beginning of the $12^{th}/18^{th}$ century, the Bey Husayn Ibn 'Ali organised the building of a mosque featuring a monumental entrance with a grand staircase. This entrance is today the "café des Nattes", also called *Qahwa al-'Aliya* (the high Café). Mahmoud Bey (1229/1814–1239/1824) built his summer residence there, privileging Sidi-Bou-Saïd as the holiday destination for the notables of Tunis. Here, hardly any *burj*s are sur-

Nejma al-Zahra', cloister, Sidi-Bou-Saïd.

ITINERARY II   *The Summer Palaces*
Sidi-Bou-Saïd

*Nejma al-Zahra',
great salon,
Sidi-Bou-Saïd.*

rounded by vast parks. This is probably due to the accidental character of the relief of the land, or to the desire to be the closest to Saint Sidi Bu Sa'id to benefit best from his "baraka" and from his protection. The houses are built in a continuous line, each one standing shoulder to shoulder with the next, very much in accordance with the urban plan of *medinas*. The village is situated along a steep axis, starting at the point at which the road to Tunis and the road to the Marsa meet, and ending at the point occupied by the mosque. Daily trading, which today has adopted the form of touristic bazaars, took place along this main road which the villagers call "*suq*". A second pole of attraction was created in the 1870s, around the Sidi Cheb'an Zawiya; Sidi Cheb'an was another mystic, musician and fine poet. Extensions and changes to the place came to a head with the opening of a cafe that faces the Gulf of Tunis, against the backdrop of the Jabal Bu Kornin. Since the beginning of the 20th century, numerous artists and foreign aesthetes, seduced by the beauty of the place, set up their home on this hill. The most famous amongst them was the Baron Rodolphe d'Erlanger. It was he who introduced the blue known as "the blue of Sidi-Bou-Saïd", as well as in 1915 inciting Naceur Bey to promulgate a decree protecting the village.

II.1.a **Nejma al-Zahra'**

At the roundabout below the village, take the road on the right that leads to the mosque climbing up towards the village. Leave your car in the pay-and-display car park. The entrance to the palace is directly opposite.

ITINERARY II The Summer Palaces
The Marsa

Entrance fee. Opening times: 08.30–12.30 and 14.00–17.00. Closed Mondays. Toilet facilities available.

Make your way up to the top of the village and admire the view of the sea from the lighthouse. The "café des Nattes" houses various ancient objects, but is also one of the liveliest places in the village. "Café Sidi Cheb'an" offers a beautiful view over the Gulf of Tunis and the port.

"*The construction of Nejma al-Zahra' over a period of ten years (1912-1922) was not initiated on the back of a whim of a rich layabout but was a kind of a step on the way to recreating an Orient that had been dreamt of passionately*", wrote Ali Louati. The Baron Rodolphe d'Erlanger, son of a wealthy family of French bankers of German origin, was 16 years old when he discovered Tunisia. He had come for reasons relating to his health, and left with the decision to swap the banking world for painting, for as long as the light and colours of the land exalted themselves as they did. At 26, he married Elizabeth, known as "Bettina", who had come from a noble Roman family. Right from the start, she shared his love of Tunisia, which they visited regularly. In 1912, they began to create "*Nejma al-Zahra*" (Resplendent Star). Nothing interrupts the harmony of the village whose mass descends from the *zawiya* down to the sea through marrying together with the slope of the hill. In respect to this "velum", the baron built an esplanade leaning back against the hill, on which he erected his palace, facing the sea. From the outside, a porch entrance, which could be closed with a modestly studded door, subscribes to the spirit of introverted buildings. The slightly rigid composition of the main facade, featuring a projecting gallery as well as perfect symmetry, provides a contrast to the finesse and element of fantasy displayed by the interior spaces. This later residence provided the occasion to restore some honour to a body of professions that were having the life squeezed out of them by shareholders. It is the embodiment of all that is most noble and most refined within the arts of building and interior decoration of the times, whilst showing a preference for the Hispano-Moresque style. Acquired by the Tunisian State, today Nejma al-Zahra' is the Centre for Arabic and Mediterranean Music. It has preserved its sumptuous furniture and its rich collection of manuscripts, paintings, rugs and other items, and offers the visitor an insight into the private family life of the Baron d'Erlanger. A museum of Tunisian musical instruments has also been opened here in homage to the baron, who was a great connoisseur of Arabic music.

II.2 THE MARSA

Leo the African described The Marsa, at the beginning of the $10^{th}/16^{th}$ century, as "*an*

Bardo Palace, cavity ceiling, Tunis.

103

ITINERARY II *The Summer Palaces*
The Marsa

ancient, small town, built on the shores of the sea. It is where the Port of Carthage once stood. It was once upon a time ruined, and remained as such for a long time. However, today it is inhabited by fishermen, farmers and laundrymen. Royal palaces and properties in which the present king habitually spends his summers are located close by". This relates to the three palaces known as al-'Abdelliya, which were first occupied by the Hafsids, then the Muradites followed by the Husaynites. At the beginning of the 13th/19th century, Mahmoud Bey (1229/1814–1239/1824) built the Dar al-Taj not far from the 'Abdelliya. It was then enlarged and modernised by the Bey Mohamed in the middle of the 13th/19th century. An urban centre was to grow up around this beylical palace, a development that was described by Charles Lallement at the end of the 19th century. *"After crossing the palace courtyard"*, writes he, *"one reaches a street bordered by the outbuildings. These are then followed by private houses and* funduqs *overrun by Jews. Another street to the right leads to the sea (...). The main street spills out into a square which has nothing remarkable about it save for a strange café, the Café of the Source of the Poplar* (safsaf). *This café provides entertainment through having a well in the middle, the mill of which is turned by a dromedary ..."*.

The example of the sovereigns was followed by ministers and dignitaries, and soon the gardens of the *burj*s were spreading out to the hills of Gammarth. The consuls, namely those from France and Britain, benefited from the privilege of having summer residences in the neighbourhood of the *bey*s. Today, under the effect of urbanisation, only certain residences remain, separated from their orchards (Dar al-Sa'ada, Seniet Ben 'Achur, Seniet Isma'il Bey ...). As for the Dar al-Taj, it was demolished in the 1960s, together with the urban cluster that surrounded it. The only buildings to be spared were the Hafsid Mosque, which was restored at the end of the 19th century, the Safsaf café, and several later buildings. Small squares and car parks link this old centre to the most recent neighbourhood, that which has risen around the station and the al-Hafsi Café.

II.2.a The al-'Abdelliya Palace

From Sidi-Bou-Saïd, two roads lead to the Marsa; one heads off from the lower end of the village, and is adjacent to the small suburban train station (Tunis-Goulette-Marsa); the other heads off from the upper part of the village and runs via Sidi Dhrif. Once in "Marsa Ville", take "rue A. Chtiui" to the left of the bus station, then take the first road on the right.

It is possible to stroll along from Marsa Beach up to the cliffs of Gammarth. The café-restaurant "du Safsaf" serves up good-quality local cuisine within a typical decor. A stroll on the hill of Gammarth is ideal for the enjoyment of a beautiful view over the coastal beaches.

Built at the beginning of the 10th/16th century, by the Hafsid Sultan Abu 'Abd Allah Mohamed, this palace was composed of three main buildings at the centre of a vast garden which stretched as far as a place known as al-Hafsi, not far from the actual station. Only the great 'Abdelliya remains for us to see. The main entrance opens out under a portico into a square-plan *driba*. A staircase leads to the courtyard which is embellished with a water feature and framed by a portico along two sides.

Three large, median-alcoved rooms look out towards both the courtyard and the outside. In the north-eastern corner, opposite the entrance, stands a square tower that looks as if it has descended from ancient Almohad constructions. Other than the panoramic vista, the top of this tower offers a view over the terraces below, revealing the astonishing variety of domes that cover halls and rooms. The succession of high corner vaults, and barrel vaults intercut with groined vaults and hemispheric vaults, attest to the skill of vault roofing, a skill inherited from the Golden Age of Antiquity. On the ground floor, the vaults, reinforced by beams, pillars and partition walls support the apartments above.

These constructions were used for household storage space, as stables, as guards' quarters and as prisons. A projecting part of the building forming an extension covered by groined vaults which largely opens out onto the garden, was used as a place of rest and relaxation, *maq'ad*. If one looks at historical documents (Ibn Abi Diaf), one learns that in the $10^{th}/16^{th}$ and $12^{th}/18^{th}$ centuries, the palace was not used as a summer residence, but was only used as a refuge in cases of emergency. At the beginning of the $13^{th}/19^{th}$ century, the Husaynite court began to use it again before Bey Ahmed (1250/1835–1271/1855) abandoned it. The English Consuls were allowed to come and stay there for the summer. Classed as a historic monument in 1923, al-'Abdelliya was put in the hands of the municipality. Indeed, it was to benefit from restoration works due to it having been given a cultural use.

II.3 ARIANA

Did Ariana already exist in the age of Antiquity? Whilst a text written by Marmol

The al-'Abdelliya, north-east wing, The Marsa.

ITINERARY II   *The Summer Palaces*
Ariana

Burj Ben 'Ayed, patio, Ariana.

describes it as *"built by the Romans"*, and Leo the African attributes it to the Goths, there is not a single piece of archaeological evidence that corresponds to these claims. On the other hand, a text dated from the 4th/10th century, relating to the biography of Sidi Mahrez, mentions Ariana as being the place where this *shaykh* lived before settling in Tunis where he became the Patron Saint of the town. We know from other sources that in the 5th/11th century, this city had its own mosque and a *hammam*, and was considered sufficiently prosperous to justify the sending, by the Zirids, of a governor in charge of raising taxes.

This plain was chosen by the Sultan al-Mustansir, for the salubrity of its climate and its rich resource of water, as the site on which to build his *Abu Fihr* pleasure residence, which became the object of admiration for all visitors (Ibn Khaldun, Dimamini the poet …). Ariana is known equally for its role as an outpost, defending Tunis from incursions made from over the sea, from over the plains of al-'Auina and from Suqra. This period was followed by the Crusades, led by the King of France, Saint Louis. Military contingents, which included among them Sidi 'Ammar al-Ma'rufi, a mystic recruited from Kairouan in response to the call to Holy War, departed from Ariana. He himself died of dysentery a short while after the departure of the Crusaders, and was buried at the entrance to Ariana. Considered as the Saint Protector of the town, his tomb became the object of assiduous veneration for all Arianese.

In the 11th/17th century, Ariana welcomed an important Morisco community which brought with it new customs in terms of culinary skills, dress, ways of speaking and in terms of arboricultural, market-gardening, evidence of which still exists today.

In the 12th/18th century, Ariana witnessed the arrival of the first Jewish families from Algeria, and the foundation of the first synagogue, the Ghriba. This community underwent such growth that in the 1930s it became a majority. In the 13th/19th century, Ariana attracted important dignitaries from Tunis, who built their *burj*s there at the centre of huge gardens in which grew the rose of Ariana (Burj Ben 'Ayed, Burj al-Baccush, Burj al-Zawush, Burj Raffo …). The Tunisians of modest means, whether Muslims or Jewish, rented a room or two in the village, when the resort was in the full bloom of springtime.

Little by little, holiday makers settled in Ariana for good, and the village took the shape of a town, governed since 1908 by a municipality. Following the urban boom, only a main road now divides Ariana from Tunis.

II.3.a **Burj Ben 'Ayed** (this monument is not open to visitors)

Take the road which serves the Tunis-Carthage airport, and then take the boulevard "du 7

ITINERARY II   *The Summer Palaces*
The Manouba

II.4 THE MANOUBA

Novembre" until you reach the first interchange. Turn right towards Ariana and follow the main thoroughfare round until you reach the monument.

This Palace (13th–14th/19th century) built by 'Abd al-Rahman Ben 'Ayed, nephew of the minister Mahmoud Ben 'Ayed, reiterates the layout that is typical of Summer Palaces: servant quarters and stables on the ground floor, apartments and reception rooms on the first floor, entirely surrounded by gardens. The recently rebuilt, small square that can now be seen in front of the entrance had once been planted with cypresses and palm trees, and had been defended by high enclosure walls, as well as an iron-forged portal. The facade is marked by an imposing *mashrabiyya* overhang, *guenariya*, above the semicircular arch of the door. The elbow-shaped entrance contains a *driba* and a *sqifa* both of which are covered over by flattened, pendentive vaults cladded with sculpted plaster. A large, marble principal staircase with a cast-iron ramp leads to the floors above. The first floor is designed around an open-roofed courtyard, whilst the second floor is designed around the covered area of a *raqba*. It resembles the upper floors of the Bardo Palace in terms of its rectangular floorplan and its circular balcony, which is upheld by corbel brackets and bordered by a forged-iron balustrade which runs up to the floor above. The decor of the Ben 'Ayed Palace reflects the ornamental taste prevalent towards the end of the 19th century. The abundance of Italian earthenware from Naples, and the sumptuousness of the marble from Carrara, were both very sought after. The Ben 'Ayed Palace, having once housed a school, is today the seat of the Municipal Council of Ariana.

II.4.a **The Rose Palace, National Military Museum**

Return to the boulevard "du 7 Novembre" heading towards the Manouba. Cross over the railway line, take a left before the roundabout, followed by the first street on the left.
Entrance fee. Opening times: 09.00–16.00. Closed Mondays. Toilet facilities available.

The Rose Palace, patio, The Manouba.

ITINERARY II   *The Summer Palaces*
The Manouba

The Rose Palace, polychrome marble framing of the door, The Manouba.

This residence was built by Hammuda Pasha (12th–13th/18th century) at the centre of a rose garden – hence its name, the Rose Palace, *Qasr al-Ward*. It is also called Grand Burj, *Burj al-Kebir*, given its former importance.

Hammuda Pasha came here to relax, whilst also loving to organise sumptuous receptions there in honour of foreign guests. His successors occupied the palace until the reign of Ahmed Bey. In 1255/1840, Ahmed Bey turned the palace into barracks for the cavalry. Under the Protectorate, it was used as barracks for the artillery corps before becoming the post of command for the administrative staff of the occupying forces. Abandoned in the aftermath of Independence, it was restored by the Ministry of National Defence, who opened the National Military Museum there.

Whatever the disadvantage and loss caused by the disappearance of the gardens and the removal of its kiosk, *Qubbat al-Hawa'*, to the Belvedere Park, this palace has still kept its essential floorplan and decoration. As in the Bardo, a large staircase links the main courtyard to a raised gallery that precedes the patio. From the vast *driba*, one enters the Hall of Justice, divided by a double row of columns into three naves. The throne was placed right at the end, whilst the members of the court stood or sat here or there, depending on the circumstances. The sovereign listened to the complaints of the plaintiffs, and the defence of the accused, all of whom were allowed to plead before him, and the sovereign pronounced judgments which were executed without delay.

The apartments encircle a large peristyle patio, which has a large basin at its centre. The rooms are in the form of a T-plan or of a cruciform plan. The central *qbu* lacks a *maqsura*. It protrudes out of the facade, and on each of its three sides it is pierced by windows, in order to give a greater view to the outside. Note that these windows have been transformed with glass panes in accordance with the Museum's needs.

The reception room faces the entrance, and is of particular interest in terms of its dome, which, following the example of certain Ottoman monuments in Istanbul, forms a roof over a cruciform floorplan. Its sumptuous ornamentation is of a composite style, as it is for the entire palace – a style that was already very fashionable in Tunis since the middle of the 12th/18th century. This style is distinct for its mix of different artistic trends that prevailed at the time. The wall

ITINERARY II   *The Summer Palaces*
The Bardo

Bardo Palace, music room, capital, The Bardo.

cladding alternates panels of Neapolitan earthenware, mainly in yellow and green, with earthenware that is Tunisian in inspiration (mainly in blue and influenced by Turkish floral motifs) as well as with *qallalin* panels depicting vases, and finally with panels displaying polychrome marble inlaid work. The types of capitals are no less varied. Their range extends from the Hispano-Moresque capital that twists and turns, which can be seen in the *driba*, to the Turkish capital, with its double row of leaves, which can be seen in both the gallery and the Hall of Justice. The *naqsh hadida* displays Hispano-Moresque motifs – rosettes and interlacing stars, a succession of pelmeted archways – as well as several Husaynite motifs – the vase overflowing with foliage and the star between two cypresses that hang against a smooth background. This astonishing mix is in fact only a prelude to a period in which the influence of the West, notably from Italy, would come to dominate architectural decoration in the official monuments of Tunis, up until the introduction of the "Arabist" style.

II.5 THE BARDO

II.5.a **Bardo Palace** (Museum only)

Head towards the Bardo Palace along the boulevard "du 7 Novembre". The Museum is at the town's entrance.
Entrance fee. Opening times: 09.30–16.30 from 16 September to 31 March, and from 09.00–17.00 the rest of the year. Closed Mondays. Toilets available.

The Bardo Palace has been widely described by the foreign visitors who were received at court throughout the centuries. From

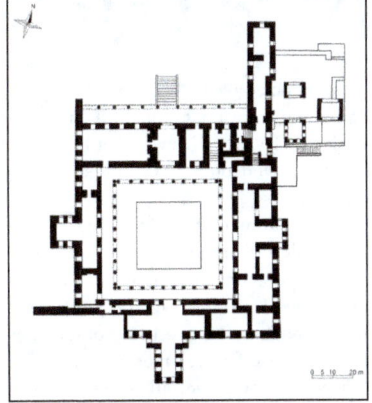

The Bardo Palace, first floor.

ITINERARY II   The Summer Palaces
The Bardo

Bardo Palace, staircase of the lions, 19th-century engraving.

memory one can cite Anselme Adorne who had come from Bruges in 1470, Leo the African, Cavalier d'Arvieux in his Memoires received on 30 May 1724, among many others.

The Bey Husayn Ibn 'Ali decided to turn the Bardo into the official Beylical residence, rather than having it just as a second home. He transformed it into a veritable fortified city, consisting of lodgings for superior officers, a mosque, a *madrasa*, a *hammam* and a *suq*, all of which were located next to the palace. This residence represents a rare insight into the evolution of domestic architecture, thanks to the successive alterations and works that it underwent.

Only one of the five circular towers that defended the Beylical city remains: that of the north-west corner, to the left of the entrance. Not far from here, both the mosque and the old military buildings still stand, with their monumental doors whose pediments are decorated with Beylical emblems.

The official palace, reached via a staircase framed by marble lions, houses the Chamber of the Deputies since the advent of Independence. The Bardo Museum, opened in May 1888, occupies what was once the old seraglio or the old quarters where the women had their apartments.

The vaulted ground floor is linked to the old outbuildings over which rise two floors, each of which subscribed to a different style. The first, built by Husayn Ibn Mahmoud (1239/1824–1250/1835) takes after the look of traditional dwellings, laid out around a central open-top courtyard adorned with a basin.

The two reception rooms open out under the shadow of two porticos that stand side by side. One of the rooms is designed in a cruciform plan. Marble from Carrara and earthenware panels from Tunis unfurl themselves under vaults surfaced entirely with Hispano-Moresque style *naqsh hadida*.

The second part of this palace, built by the Beys Mohamed and Sadok (13th–14th/second half of the 19th century), displays an Italian style that borders on the excessive. The rooms look out onto a covered courtyard, but possess high windows through which they are lit. Two luxurious salons face one another, the "domed salon" – a vast room crowned by a beautiful sculpted wood dome which is painted and gilded in gold – and the hall of women, whose space is designed in a cruciform plan, and is decorated traditionally. The Italian influence is more pronounced in the side rooms, whose coffered ceilings are entirely painted over with excessive polychrome floral Baroque ornamentation.

Islamic art seems to be the poor parent within this internationally renowned Museum. The rooms allocated to Islamic art exhibit a reconstruction of a room, as well as display cases showing clothes worn by women, jewels, and examples of goldsmithing and leather crafts.

II.6 AL-HNAYA

II.6.a **Hafsid Aqueduct** (option)

Up until the $7^{th}/13^{th}$ century, Tunis's water was supplied from wells and cisterns situated in different places. Via a system of pipes, this water was distributed to various drinking troughs and fountains across the town. The demographic increase, which came as a consequence of Tunis becoming the capital city, resulted in greater demand and a need for new sources of water, which the Hafsids, following the example of the Romans, found on Mount Zaghouan.

The Aqueduct, built by Hadrian between AD 120 and 130, was restored by the Sultan al-Mustansir. The works were completed in the year 665/1267. The Hafsid Aqueduct differs from the Roman one in its mode of construction. Instead of being built from blocks of stone, it is built from rubble with a facing of freestone. The superior arches that link the archways are built of brick. The conveyance of water towards Tunis branched off from the water conveyance of Zaghouan, 4 km. north of the capital, which followed a trail via Ra's al-Tabiya, then went through the hill of la Rabta, before reaching the *kasbah* and the Great Mosque. It is the remains of this branch that we can still see in the Quarter known as Hnaya – the Arcades.

II.7 **THE BELVÉDÈRE**

II.7.a **The Qubba of the Belvédère** (option)

This monument is located at the heart of the Belvédère Park.

The pavilion called "Qubba du Belvédère" once adorned the Rose Palace of the Manouba. In 1901, having fallen into ruin, the kiosk was brought to the hills of this public park. The space divides itself into two halves. The first is arranged around a central dome, held up by four columns and surrounded on the outside, on three sides, by open galleries. The second part of the kiosk extends along the fourth remaining side, and is composed of a room featuring median alcoves. Designed as a place for relaxation and for enjoyment of the view over the gardens, the construction includes elements of airiness and transparency. The decor ingeniously brings together the different influences that have affected Tunisian art: white marble columns with Italian-style Doric capitals, recticurvilinear arches, ceramic and sculpted plaster inlaid work of Hispano-Moresque inspiration, and Tunisian earthenware *(faience)* panels.

ITINERARY III

The Andalusians

Ahmed Saadaoui

First day

III.1 GHAR AL-MELH
    III.1.a The Old Port
    III.1.b The Naval Dockyard
    III.1.c The Eastern Fort
    III.1.d The Central Fort
    III.1.e The Western Fort

III.2 BIZERTE
    III.2.a The Old Port
    III.2.b The Kasbah
    III.2.c The Qsiba (option)
    III.2.d The Fort of the Andalusians

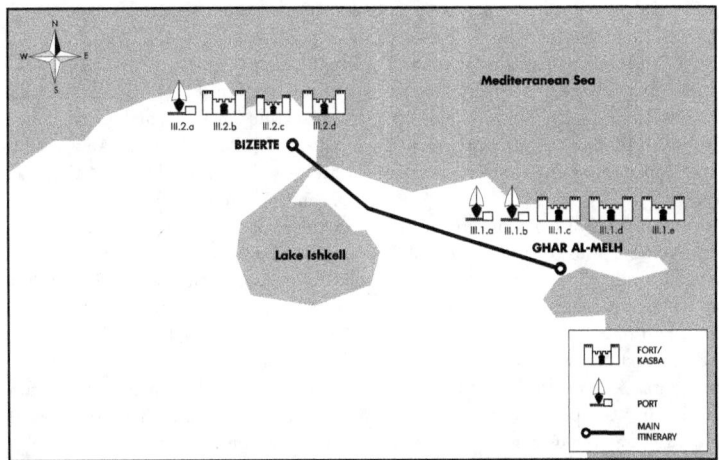

Great Mosque, patio, Testour.

The Andalusians derive their name from that of their country, Vandalusia, the "Land of the Vandals", which the Arabs then transcribed as *al-Andalus*. It would not be long before the Spanish Reconquest, which began at the end of the $5^{th}/11^{th}$ century, would provoke the departure of the Muslim population. It was this that led to the successive waves of migrants received into Hafsid Ifriqiya. The first influx, which dates as far back as the $7^{th}/13^{th}$ century, was marked by the arrival of numerous refugees who settled in and around Tunis. It was the fall of Valencia, of Jaen and of Jativa and finally of Seville that resulted in this first waves of departure. They were attracted by the presence of Abu Zakariya al-Hafsi (633/1236–646/1249) who had formerly been the Governor of Seville. Establishing a community that showed both dynamism and solidarity, the Andalusians were able agriculturalists, artisans and merchants; but, above all, it was their artistic and literary competence which made them stand out. Therefore Ibn Khaldun describes them thus: *"Some are distinguished poets, while others are eloquent writers, illustrious scholars, magnanimous princes, intrepid warriors."* Held in esteem by the Hafsids, they vied easily against the Almohad Shaykhs. Towards the end of the $9^{th}/15^{th}$ century, following the fall of Granada, the second wave of Andalusian immigration towards Tunisia took the route of its predecessors.

The brutal and definitive expulsion of the Moriscos under Philip III in 1017/1609 resulted in one of the most significant waves of Andalusian immigration to Tunisia, and one which was to have the greatest impact on the collective memory of the Tunisians. In fact from that time on, and following the precedent set by the Hafsids, the natives under the reigns of both 'Uthman Dey (998/1590–1018/1610) and Yussef Dey (1018/1610–1046/1637), encouraged Andalusian immigration to the north-east of Tunisia. A good number of these refugees settled in Tunis, in the "rue des Andalous" (the street of the Andalusians), where their compatriots had lived since the $9^{th}/15^{th}$ century; however, the majority settled in a new neighbourhood, between Bab Swiqa, Bab al-Khadra and Bab Carthagene, located around a mosque, the *jama'* Subhan Allah, and affirmed their monopoly in the field of terracotta craftsmanship. In the town of Bizerte, they settled similarly into a relatively spacious suburb north of the *medina*, outside the city walls by the Spanish Fort. They brought with them their skills and know-how, and injected a new lease of life into the commercial and craft industries of Tunisia, opening Fez hat, ceramic and silk weaving workshops in each of the towns they inhabited.

However, the Moriscos' most significant contribution, as was noted by various travellers, took the form of urban building developments. In effect, they constructed, both partially or completely, about 20 different localities spread across four regions of north-east Tunisia. They stretched from the Bizertine Sahel – which included the localities of Qal'at al-Andalus, Aousja, Ghar al-Melh, Raf-Raf, Metline, al-'Alia, Ra's Jabal and Menzel Djemil – to the Valley of the Medjerda, including Jedeida, Tébourba, Grich al-Oued, Medjez al-Bab, Slouguia and Testour; and from the Cap-Bon, including Soliman, Grombalia, Turki, Belli, Nianou and Jédida, to, finally, the straggling villages neighbouring the capital, like the Manouba, Ariana, Hammam-Lif and, further south, Zaghouan, which was built on the site of a Roman town.

In the 11th/17th century, Ibn Abi Dinar, who attributed 14 towns and villages to them, emphasised the nature of their activities: *"They planted vines, olive groves, extended gardens, and built roads"*. Following a long period of recoiling from settling down in these rich, north-eastern plains, the Andalusians had succeeded in reversing this tendency of not staying-put by creating agglomerations which were to profit from the relative security instilled by the Turks. In 1724, Peyssonnel went even further in the appreciation of their role: *"Most of the towns one sees today owe their foundation, or at least their re-establishment, to them"*. The writings of European travellers of the 17th and 18th century expressed a certain admiration for their villages, *"well opened up through roads and clearings and well built like the villages of Europe"* and *"full of enough beautiful houses like those in Christendom"*. In fact, these towns were very prosperous compared to the local nomadic environment; furthermore, the Hispanic origin of the inhabitants seems to have given them a particular cachet and, according to Peyssonnel, *"the inhabitants were from Granada, and they had named the squares and streets of their towns and villages with the same names as those of their former hometowns"*.

In fact, the most important Moriscos cities, like Testour, Soliman, Tébourba, Medjez al-Bab or Ghar al-Melh were built in accordance with a regular urban plan; moreover, certain elements of the building technique and of the concept of the Morisco city were reiterated within small towns and villages, for example paved roads, drains for rainwater and squares that were probably very similar to the *"plaza mayor"*. "Spanish bull festivities", which were very popular, contributed to reviving Andalusian tradition and culture in Tunisia.

The main road in Testour, 19th-century engraving.

Meanwhile, it is within the field of agriculture that the Andalusians contributed most during the 11th/17th century. The centres that had welcomed a substantial community of Moriscos or that were founded by them themselves possessed an architectural quality which reflected now and then an obvious Spanish influence, and at other times an adaptation of local traditions. From the moment they were founded, these centres endowed themselves with a dense network of religious and civil monuments. Even small straggling villages such as Slouguia or Grich al-Oued, in the lower valley of the Medjerda, whose population, in the 11th/17th century, numbered no more than a few hundred inhabitants, made themselves stand out by having beautiful mosques of an architectural quality rarely to be seen in other villages. In fact, the authors of the time underlined the beauty of the aforementioned mosques by mentioning that they were comparable to the "sanctuaries of the larger towns." A study of the buildings that belong to these cities reveals that part of these Andalusian architectural creations combine Spanish techniques with architectural elements of the country. On the

General view of the port and the village, Ghar al-Melh.

other hand, the architecture of the first generation of immigrants, a generation very much impregnated with Spanish influences, did not undergo any diffusion whatsoever. This applied in particular to pediments, pinnacles, obelisks, clocks, keystones and diagonal ribs built in the Andalusian style; these delicate ornamental fantasies based on Christian themes, which one encounters at Testour or at Soliman, were, under the circumstances, unable to sustain a long posterity. The descendants of the founders, who had no knowledge or experience of Spain, conserved and retained only the simplest elements, those that were then passed into the architecture of the day and could be easily transposed into local techniques, such as a mixed device known as Toledan and roofs covered in trough-like (hollow) tiles. The elements imported from Spain quickly became combined with the techniques and architectural forms of local origin.

The Bridge of Bizerte

The Andalusians built roads to facilitate transport and trade of their market produce or crafts; they also constructed four bridges over the Medjerda in the 11th/17th century. The first of these, erected during the reign of 'Uthman Dey (1018/1610) is the one found along the route from Tunis to Bizerte, and is called the Bridge of Bizerte. Taking the shape of a donkey's back, it is made of freestone and has seven arches; six openings through which water was discharged were used when the river flooded.

Qal'at al-Andalus

Situated on the left bank of the Medjerda, not far from the sea, the village of Qal'at al-Andalus welcomed ethnic groups after it was founded by the Moriscos, each of which settled into distinct neighbourhoods. Thus, one can distinguish three neighbourhoods: the Andalusian one, that belonging to the Turks – also called the Hanafite Quarter – and finally that of the Kairouanese.

The village population decreased during the 13th/19th century and its public buildings fell into ruin. This explains why the actual city lacks monuments that date back to its foundation. The Great Mosque of the 11th/17th century was recently completely reconstructed and restored.

ITINERARY III *The Andalusians*
Ghar Al-Melh

III.1 GHAR AL-MELH

From Tunis, take the north exit in the direction of Bizerte. Ghar al-Melh is reachable via the main road to Bizerte (GP 8), turn right at the road sign, or turn right before that towards Utique. Cross the village of Aousja, and then take the road on the right towards Ghar al-Melh.

Before reaching the village, the road runs along a beautiful agricultural plain and lush orchards, which are worked in the "Andalusian way".

Ghar al-Melh is a small coastal town situated half-way between Tunis and Bizerte; its foundation, which dates back to 1047/1638, was decided upon by the Dey Usta Murad for strategic reasons. The city, created around a Portuguese and military compound, was colonised by the Andalusians mostly from Tunis, who were attracted by particularly favourable concessions. Squeezed in-between the mountain and the lake, Ghar al-Melh is located on an exceptional site. Its plan is based on a regular design: two large thoroughfares run across the town from one end to the other. The median thoroughfare crosses the central square, whilst the meridional crosses the small covered *suq*. The two thoroughfares are linked via smaller perpendicular streets.

The Medina of Ghar al-Melh, which has suffered relatively little from the renovations and reconstructions that have recently taken place, contains several buildings of a certain architectural and archaeological value, including a few old houses, two *hammam*s, the maritime complex, the fortifications and several religious buildings (mosques, *madrasa*s and *zawiya*s).

The Madrasa of Ghar al-Melh, which dates back to the 11th/17th century, is actually known under the name of Mosque of the Madrasa. Of medium height, it is composed of an oratory, an open-top (roofless) courtyard, an ablutions hall, a recently rebuilt minaret and eight rooms. When it was founded, this building was intended for the teaching and accommodation of young, rural men who came to learn and attend classes for several years.

Bridge of Bizerte, general view, road to Bizerte.

117

ITINERARY III   *The Andalusians*

Ghar Al-Melh

The old port, view of the port and the arsenal, Ghar al-Melh.

The 11th/17th century Mosque of the *Rahba* is located at the centre of town, bordering the central square, which gave Mosque of the *Rahba* its name. Its small square minaret, rising up in the courtyard of the building that precedes the oratory, dominates the town square and the neighbouring houses.

The Port Complex and its Fortifications

Ghar al-Melh is distinct for the importance accorded to its maritime buildings and fortifications. Its naval dockyard, the artificial port to which it belongs, and its three defensive forts, all of which date back to the 11th/17th century, constitute an architectural complex, one of a few that best represent the military architecture of Ottoman Tunisia. In addition, these works were constructed by Morisco engineers and carry the mark of the Andalusian school.

III.1.a The Old Port

Travel right across the village until you reach the old port and the naval dockyard.

The construction of the port shares the same origins as the building of Ghar al-Melh. Usta Mussa al-Andalusi al-Gharnati, the engineer who oversaw the construction of the port, was an Andalusian from Granada who was ordered to come from Algiers by the Dey of Tunis, Usta Murad (1047/1638–1049/1640), where he had worked on the rebuilding of the port and on the for-

ITINERARY III   *The Andalusians*
Ghar Al-Melh

tifications of the town. The restoration works carried out at a later date have not altered the appearance of Mussa al-Andalusi's work, as can be seen from 11th/17th-and 12th/18th-century engravings. It consists of an artificial port with three jetties that enclose a basin. Entrance is made via a passage 25 m. wide, defended by two bastions between which an iron chain is attached to close off access to the basin. The quays are bordered by a wall, pierced by large windows on the one side that faces the lake, which were formerly used to house canons for shooting just above water level.

III.1.b The Naval Dockyard

The naval dockyard, which was built several years after the construction of the port, stands as an architectural complex which is in partial ruin. It includes a series of storage spaces 7 m. wide and 18 m. deep, covered by barrel vaults on beams. These storage spaces are preceded by a gallery which was used as a shed to shelter the boats which were taken out of the water. Other than the store rooms and the gallery, this naval dockyard included two penal prisons, housing both the warder and Christian slaves, who were employed in the naval constructions; it very probably included a chapel for them to practise their faith.

III.1.c The Eastern Fort

This is situated near the naval dockyard.

The construction of the eastern fort in 1069/1659 was ordered by the Dey Mustapha Laz, as one can see by the Turk-

The arsenal, vaults, Ghar al-Melh.

ITINERARY III *The Andalusians*

Ghar Al-Melh

Eastern fort, corner column, Ghar al-Melh.

ish inscription above the lintel of the building's entrance. The decision to build it was taken after the English attacked the town in 1063/1653. The building, built on a rectangular plan, was surrounded by a ditch and had four bastions, one at each corner. Prior to the partial filling-in of the ditch, one had to cross a drawbridge in order to enter the monument via a single door which opened onto the small western courtyard, preceding a vaulted hall. The rectangular, open-top courtyard is surrounded by the cells and block-houses; the oratory meanwhile stands in the north-eastern corner. The terraces of the block-houses and the walls of the small courtyards form round paths that are very wide, particularly on the south side overlooking the lake. The paths are protected by parapets that jut out to the exterior through the use of round mouldings.

III.1.d The Central Fort

This monument faces the headquarters of the Association for the Safeguarding of the Medina (ASM).
Today it houses the offices for the Ministry of Social Affairs.

The central fort of Ghar al-Melh was also designed by Mussa al-Andalusi, who built the port. Its construction dates back to 1047/1638, as is indicated by the inscription above the entrance. The recent building works have completely modified its interior. It is rectangular in plan, flanked at each corner by four octagonal bastions. Entry into the interior is gained via a straight doorway which opens into the monument's small northern courtyard. A drawbridge once existed over the ditch that surrounded the fortress. The enclosure wall, approximately 10 m. in height, is surfaced with freestone facing and crowned with rounded merlons. The point of departure of the parapets from the walls is indicated by a moulding cut into the stone. The bastions, also made of freestone, are crowned with canon-filled embrasures.

III.1.e The Western Fort

This is the first fort one notices to the right on entering the village.

Built the same year as the preceding fort – that is to say in 1069/1659 as is indicated by the inscription on the tympanum of this

ITINERARY III *The Andalusians*
Ghar Al-Melh

Central fort, corner tower, Ghar al-Melh.

Western fort, view from the sea, Ghar al-Melh.

building's unique entrance – and also on the orders of the Dey Mustapha Laz, the building, rectangular in plan, is flanked to the south by two octagonal bastions, and to the north by a crescent moon. The courtyard, which fits within the form of the building, is surrounded by numerous block-houses and by 13 vaulted shelters. The latter are pierced by loopholes (windows) and support a circular pathway 5 m. wide which is protected by a parapet pierced with canon embrasures, as in the preceding forts. The Western Fort is endowed with a small mosque and a cistern.

ITINERARY III   *The Andalusians*

Bizerte

Suq, 19th-century watercolour, Bizerte.

III.2 **BIZERTE**

From al-'Alia, take the road in direction to Bizerte.

The road runs alongside the Lake of Bizerte on the approach to the town, and from afar one can see the silhouette of Jabal Ichkeul plunging into its surrounding natural park.

Bizerte is a maritime town in northern Tunisia, and it lies along the mouth of a canal that links the sea to the lake. It occupies the ancient site of *Hippo Diarrhytus,* a Roman colony, and was named *Binzart* after the Arab Conquest. The Mediaeval town, with its bazaars, its Great Mosque and its baths, was enclosed by walls. Following a period of lying dormant, it experienced a certain amount of prosperity when it became the seat of a small independent principality governed by the Banu al-Ward (444/1053–599/1203). During the late Middle Ages, the town once again went into decline and became, throughout the 10th/16th century, the site on which terrible confrontations took place between the Spanish and the Turks. During the modern era, and particularly during the 11th/17th and 12th/18th centuries, the town profited from the relative stability secured by the Ottoman *Beys* and *Deys*. As the seat of the Admiralty, Bizerte had one of the highest rates of Barbaresque piracy, which contributed greatly to its prosperity. The arrival of the Andalusians around 1017/1609 in numerous villages across the Bizertine Sahel and into one of the neighbourhoods of the *medina*, which still to this day carries their name, also had a positive effect on the demographic expansion and on the revival of military, commercial and agricultural activities of the town. Up until the end of the 19th century, Bizerte, enclosed behind town walls, was composed of various distinct units: the *medina*, the *kasbah*, the *qsiba* (a small citadel), the Frank Quarter and the Andalusian Quarter.

The Medina

The *medina,* which lies to the west of the *kasbah,* was, until the end of the 19th century, encircled by ramparts that were pierced

ITINERARY III *The Andalusians*
Bizerte

by several gates. Only two sections of these walls, mostly ruins, remain, one of which links the Spanish Fort to the Andalusian Quarter. A study of the sections that remain reveals that each section of these walls were high, about 6 m. long and 3.5 m. thick, and were crowned by a parapet pierced by loopholes.

The Great Mosque which rises up from the *medina* was built on the site of a Mediaeval Mosque in 1060/1650 by the Dey Mohamed Laz. It stands at the centre of the *medina*, on the quays of the old port. The building is constructed on top of a platform, the area beneath which is occupied by five small shops that open out onto the banks of the port.

The minaret, which is distinct in that it has an octagonal shape, is situated on the north side of the courtyard. Supported on a square base, it is crowned by a balcony which is protected through the presence of a canopy. An octagonal lantern rests above the octagonal tower, and is topped by a pyramidal roof. This minaret, though less slender than those of Tunis, is no less original; it too reveals the Ottoman influence on the religious architecture of this town, which once housed one of the principal ports of this period's Regency.

The Zawiya of Sidi al-Mostari, the Patron Saint of the town, is situated not far from the Great Mosque. Built on a platform below which there are shops, it was constructed on the orders of Murad Bey in 1083/1673. It forms an architectural complex that includes all the regular elements of a *zawiya-madrasa*, that is to say an ablutions hall, a domed funerary chamber branching into a long hall that leads out onto a beautiful, paved courtyard, surrounded on all four sides by galleries. Several chambers, a *kuttab* and a prayer room branch off these galleries.

III.2.a The Old Port

Return to the quay of the old port and park your car in the area near the "place du 18 Janvier 1952".

The Old Port, which still welcomes in boats of fishermen from the surrounding

Minaret of the Great Mosque, 19th-century watercolour, Bizerte.

ITINERARY III *The Andalusians*
Bizerte

The Old Port, quay running alongside the kasbah, Bizerte.

area, is a natural port built on the canal which links the lake to the sea. The port defences, which until the $9^{th}/15^{th}$ century consisted of the *kasbah* and the *qsiba*, were later reinforced with the construction of two piers, at the north and south of the entrance, as well as with the building of an enclosure wall which protected it from all sides. A thick iron chain, which was hung between the two bastions of the kasbah and of the *qsiba*, closed off the entrance to the narrows. Both piers and the enclosure no longer exist today. On each of the two quays of the port there is a fountain that provides it with water; the fountain of Yussef Dey on the northern quay was built by an Andalusian in 1029/1620. A beautiful inscription engraved on a marble plaque situated on the tympanum of the bichrome arch of the fountain, indicates both its construction date and the name of the craftsman who made it.

III.2.b The Kasbah

Access to this monument is gained via the Khemais Tarnen Quay.
Entrance fee. Opening times: 09.00–11.30 and 15.00–19.30. Closed Mondays. Toilets available.

From the terrace café at the top of the monument, one can enjoy a wonderful panoramic view over the rooftops of the medina *and the sea.*

The Kasbah, sealed behind its own walls, consists of a small town with its own mosques, public *hammams* and houses. Its enclosure wall, rectangular in shape (approximately 170 m. x 110 m.) is flanked by eight towers that stand in its corners. Built in beautiful freestone, it is pierced by a single gate that links the *kasbah* to the *medina*.

ITINERARY III   *The Andalusians*
Bizerte

III.2.c **The Qsiba** (option)

This neighbourhood is located at the other end of the Old Port, opposite the kasbah. *By car, take "rue Sidi el-Henni"; otherwise on foot, walk via the quay of the Qsiba.*
The Burj Sidi al-Henni houses an Oceanographic Museum.

The *qsiba*, or small citadel, which was declared a fort in the 5th/11th century, rises up on the south bank of the channel, thus facing the *kasbah*. Both monuments controlled entry into the Old Port; a chain, hung between the two, closed off the entrance to the port, whilst a donjon bared down over it. The monument gave its name to a small neighbourhood that was once lived in by fishermen.

III.2.d **The Fort of the Andalusians**

One reaches this monument via the "avenue du 15 Octobre".

This monumental fort occupies an end point in the north-west of the enclosure which allows it to survey and control the town, the port and the harbour of Bizerte. Its construction was begun by the Pasha of Algiers, 'Alj 'Ali, on the basis of a design mapped out by a Sicilian engineer, and, after having been conquered by the Spanish, its construction was then completed by them, hence its name. This fort was built in the shape of a five-point star, but, following a series of modifications, it stands today as a 13-sided polygon, made in part from pounded earth with a freestone fac-

The kasbah, viewed from the quay, Bizerte.

125

ITINERARY III   The Andalusians
Bizerte

Fort of the Andalusians, 19th-century watercolour, Bizerte.

ing. The fort is pierced by a single entrance door, which faces the town and is preceded by a porch, opening out onto a round arch crowned with merlons, and defended by a pole-axe. This gate leads into a polygonal courtyard; a ramp that runs along the side of this courtyard offers access onto the fort's platform, the level of which is indicated on the outside by a large, semi-circular moulding. This latter, which serves as an artillery platform, is protected by a parapet 1.9 m. high pierced with tiny arches.

The Andalusian Quarter

The Andalusian Quarter is a suburb that lies outside the city walls, lying north-east of the *medina*. Begun by the Moriscos around 1018/1610, it grew lengthwise along a stretch 450 m. in length and was 130 m. at its widest point. This Quarter possesses a more or less regular layout: it is arranged around a main thoroughfare which runs across it from north to south, and has its own mosque, the Mosque of the Andalusians.

Rafraf
This small fishing village which leans against the hillside has become an important town, stretching along the length of a very beautiful beach. The road that leads to it from Ghar al-Melh crosses an undulating agricultural landscape, renowned for its muscat grape.
On entering Rafraf, one is blessed with an impressive view over the entire village below as well as over the desert island of Pilau opposite.

ITINERARY III

The Andalusians

Ahmed Saadaoui

Second day

III.3 JÉDEIDA
  III.3.a Jédeida Bridge

III.4 TÉBOURBA
  III.4.a The Bridge-Dam of al-Battan

III.5 MEDJEZ AL-BAB
  III.5.a Medjez al-Bab Bridge

III.6 TESTOUR
  III.6.a The Great Mosque
  III.6.b The Mosque of Rihbat al-Andalus
  III.6.c The Mosque of Sidi 'Abd al-Latif

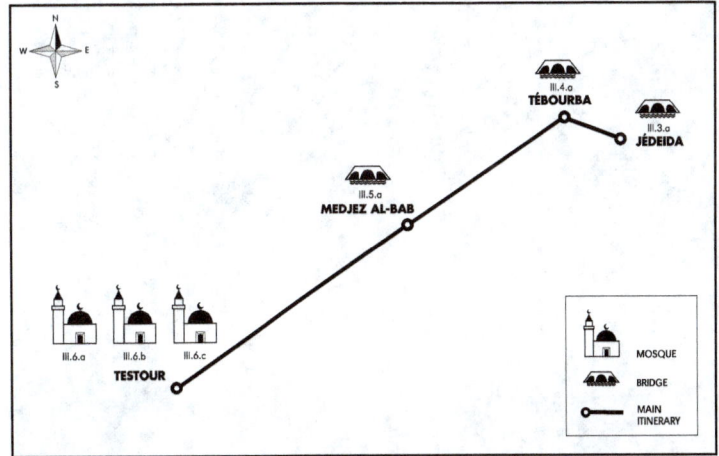

III.3 JÉDEIDA

Amongst the four bridges erected over the Medjerda by the Andalusians, two function also as dams: the Jédeida Bridge and the al-Battan Bridge near Tébourba. The latter's name comes from the Spanish "*batanar*" which means "to press or tread upon", "to give a dressing to a piece of cloth"; this name is due to the mill press that is used for the fabrication of Fez hats (*sheshiya*s). These two bridges provided the water for the *sheshiya* presses and irrigated the plains of the river by raising the height of the river to the required level.

III.3.a Jédeida Bridge

From Tunis, there is a roundabout at the exit of Jédeida; follow the signs towards Bizerte. The bridge is approximately 3 km. from here, on your right-hand side.

The Jédeida Bridge, completed in 406/1016, was built under the order of Yussef Dey. 116 m. in length and 6 m. wide, it numbers seven equally sized arches supported on quite a high floor built along the entire length of the river, in such a way that the water keeps cascading down as it flows along. Following the Second World War, this bridge was partly torn down and carried away by the water; now only three arches remain, whilst the others have been replaced by a metal construction. A certain Shelebi, son of Yussef Dey, ordered for a summer residence to be built next to this bridge, whose charm and beauty was boasted about in the literature of the day.

The Jédeida Bridge.

ITINERARY III   *The Andalusians*
Tébourba

The bridge-dam of al-Battan, Tébourba.

III.4 TÉBOURBA

Tébourba is another Morisco centre and is located near the ancient site of Thuburbo Majus, 35 km. from Tunis, on the left bank of the Medjerda. It is surrounded by gardens, natural beauty and vast olive orchards as well as other plantations. The cultivation of olives on this site went through great developments thanks to the settlement of the Moriscos. The *medina* is based on a regular enough plan: the roads cross each other at right-angles, eight of which converged towards the great rectangular square which constitutes the main element of the urban structure. This layout is evidence of well thought-out urban planning; the town was built by Morisco immigrants around 1018/1610. The central square, surrounded by mosques, *funduq*s and shops, is an element of urban planning that originates from Spain.

The population's attachment to its origins remained strong during the 17th and 18th centuries, as was vouched by Ximenes, the religious Spaniard who visited the town in the 1724; he reveals to us that a section of the population preserved the use of the Spanish language, after more than a century of having settled there: *"Following their arrival from Spain, they established schools in our language"*, he writes.

The *medina* of Tébourba possesses three neighbourhood oratories and a Great Mosque that dates from the 11th/17th century. It also contains various *zawiya*s erected at different times. One of the oldest, that of Sidi Thabet, goes back as far as the middle of the 11th/17th century; it was renovated, according to an inscription, in 1112/1701.

III.4.a The Bridge-Dam of al-Battan

Return to Jédeida and drive towards Tébourba. The monument is situated at the entrance of al-Battan.

ITINERARY III   *The Andalusians*
Medjez al-Bab

The bridge, complete view, Medjez al-Bab.

The bridge, monumental inscription of dating, Medjez al-Bab.

Throwing itself over across the Medjerda, 2 km. downstream from Tébourba, this bridge-dam was built around 1101/1690 by the Bey Mohamed, son of Murad II. It is one of the most commendable works, pierced by 16 arches that stand raised up on an invert that serves as its foundation. Gates closed the arches and raised the water-level to set the press mills in action and to irrigate the river plains. The *bey* ordered for a summer house to be built next to this bridge.

III.5 **MEDJEZ AL-BAB**

A very pretty country road links Tébourba to Medjez al-Bab.

Medjez al-Bab is a small town, renowned for being Andalusian, that is situated on the right bank of the Medjerda, between

ITINERARY III *The Andalusians*
Testour

Tébourba and Testour. In 1271/1855, according to a fiscal register, the town included 38 persons of Andalusian origin out of 100 inhabitants. After 1881, the small town that had become a rural colonial centre was transformed completely.

III.5.a Medjez al-Bab Bridge

Attributed, like the two bridges mentioned above, to the Andalusians, this work of beautiful freestone was completed in 1087/1677. It is a "donkey-back" bridge pierced by eight equal arches, supporting a roadway protected by a parapet. Crossing over the Medjerda, it links the town to its gardens and to nearby Andalusian cities.

III.6 TESTOUR

Testour is a small town situated in the middle valley of the Medjerda. The town was founded at the beginning of the 11th/17th century on the site of a Roman city called *Tichilla*. The Morisco *medina* is composed of three neighbourhoods: the Andalusian Quarter, the Tagarins Quarter, and that of the *Hara*. Three main thoroughfares, delineating lengthening blocks, run parallel to each other, each one being relatively wide and linked together by smaller side streets that run at right-angles to it. The large square constitutes an important element, a key stitch, in this urban weave. It is the centre of town life and can be considered as the public space *par excellence*. Several important buildings look out onto it: the Great Mosque, the *hammam*, the cafés and, at one point in time, the *funduqs*. Moreover, this square constitutes an early example of the European-type square in the Maghreb.

The *suq* occupies the central thoroughfare, which carries its name, crosses the town from one end to the other and extends itself via the shops that border the sides of the central square. Not a single residential

Orchards, Testour.

ITINERARY III   The Andalusians
Testour

The Great Mosque, view of the roofs, Testour.

The Great Mosque, interior courtyard, Testour.

house can be found amongst the stalls and shops, but the *suq* does house several public buildings, notably mosques.

Tradition attributes 14 mosques to the town of Testour, the majority of which are small neighbourhood oratories. Five of these are actually open for worship, whilst the others are either in ruins or have completely disappeared. Most of these buildings, like the town, were built in the 11th/17th century. Testour also houses other religious or civil buildings such as *madrasa*s, a synagogue, an Israelite mausoleum, a *hammam*, *zawiya*s, all of which date from the 11th/17th century.

In terms of the *zawiya*s, that of Sidi Nasr stands at the far western end of the "rue *al-Hara*". It contains all the characteristic elements of a *zawiya-madrasa*, encompassing two domed funerary chambers, an oratory, two courtyards – the larger of which is surrounded by porticoes, and several outbuildings whose rooms are reserved for accommodating students.

III.6.a **The Great Mosque**
(this monument is not open to visitors)

The entrance to the monument borders the central village square.

The Great Mosque represents one of the most elegant examples of Morisco architecture in Tunisia. In fact, it reveals original forms as well as techniques. The master craftsman of this building, while employing some usual features which are visible in the local mosques, used architectural and decorative techniques that are Spanish in origin, creating thus an utterly uncensored work of synthesis. Well ordered, the building is distinct for its imposing tiled roof

ITINERARY III   *The Andalusians*
Testour

which is supported on an armature of attics consisting of a structured system that rests on top of the vaults's extrados with the help of 48 intermediary pillars.

Its minaret consists of a square tower surmounted by two octagonal towers; its very unusual form, as well as certain other details, confirm its relation to Spanish bell-towers, and more particularly to those of Aragon. It is the same in the way that its square tower has small pinnacles on its corners of as well as a decorative clock. The construction of the minaret, in its assembly-line of bricks and rubble-stone filling, and the structure of its spiral staircase, also reveal an affiliation to Spain.

III.6.b **The Mosque of Rihbat al-Andalus** (This monument is not open to visitors)

This monument is situated behind the Great Mosque, on "place al-Andalus".

The Mosque of Rihbat al-Andalus is the first Morisco Great Mosque of Testour, as the building dates from 1018/1610. After the building of a new Great Mosque in around 1024/1615, the former lost its place as the town's first sanctuary; however, it continued to hold a Friday *khutba*. The monument was abandoned towards the middle of the 13th/19th century, a period during which the town went into decline. Since then, the monument became considerably degraded, falling almost entirely to ruin. In fact, the only remains that can be seen today are a half demolished minaret, two corners of the walls of the oratory, and various other remains that are barely apparent. The corners of the walls that still stand, stripped of their facing, reveal the stone bonds that constitute their construction. It consists of a

The Great Mosque, mihrab, Testour.

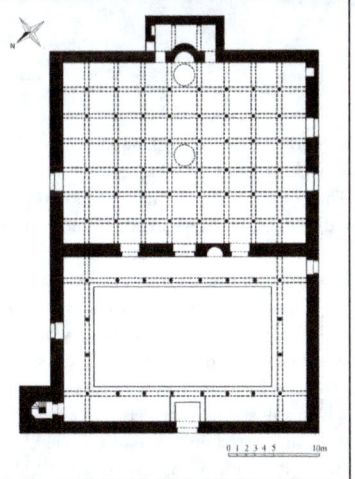

Floor plan of the Great Mosque of Testour.

ITINERARY III *The Andalusians*

Testour

Rihbat al-Andalus Mosque, the rihba and the minaret, Testour.

composite bonding technique composed of a brick frame and concrete filling.

The minaret is actually missing its entire top half; its original appearance is known to us thanks to photographs that were taken at the beginning of the 20th century. It was made up of two superimposed towers, a lower one that was a square-plan tower whilst the other was octagonal. The two towers were crowned by a lantern. The square tower, which still stands today, rises to a height of 9 m; supported on a base of recycled free-stone, it is built using a mixed bond. The bricks in each of the four corners form chains of dog-tooth ornamentation cut across by horizontal levels. This framework of bricks is filled in with rubble bonded with lime mortar.

III.6.c **The Mosque of Sidi 'Abd al-Latif** (This monument is not open to visitors)

This Mosque is found in the "rue du 2 Mars", perpendicular to the avenue Habib Bourguiba.

ITINERARY III   *The Andalusians*
Testour

The avenue Habib Bourguiba, the main thoroughfare of the suqs, *is full of life and has retained its authenticity.*

The mosque of Sidi 'Abd al-Latif is also known as the Hanafite Mosque. It is located in the Tagarins neighbourhood, very close to the main thoroughfare from which it is separated by a series of shops.
The unique facade of the mosque looks out onto the "rue de Seville". Several elements come together to create one of the most beautiful facades of Testour's religious buildings: the bonding, the cornice that crowns it, the doors and windows that pierce through it, and above all the minaret.
The prayer room, which is preceded by a portico that leads into a small courtyard, adopts a square plan. It is divided into three naves, each possessing three bays through a network of 16 columns carrying Hispano-Maghrebic capitals. The vaults belonging to the oratory are doubled over with a roof of concave tiles, sloping on two sides over gabled walls. It stands at the far northern side of the facade, and is divided into four stacked levels which are separated by registers that were originally surfaced with ceramic polychrome tiles. The third level has the most decoration. It shows large panels from which square pieces of brick emerge from the casing, forming diamond-shaped patterns. Here, the use of brick, through placing it in relief, is inspired by Mudejar architecture. The minaret is crowned by a cylindrical lantern.

Sidi 'Abd al-Latif Mosque, facade and minaret, Testour.

135

ITINERARY IV

Sufism

Mohamed Tlili

IV.1 AL-KEF
    IV.1.a   The Kasbah
    IV.1.b   The Rahmaniya Zawiya, Museum of Popular Arts and Traditions
    IV.1.c   The Synagogue of the Ghriba

IV.2 HAFFOUZ
    IV.2.a   Fatimid Bridge-Aqueduct of Chrechira (option)

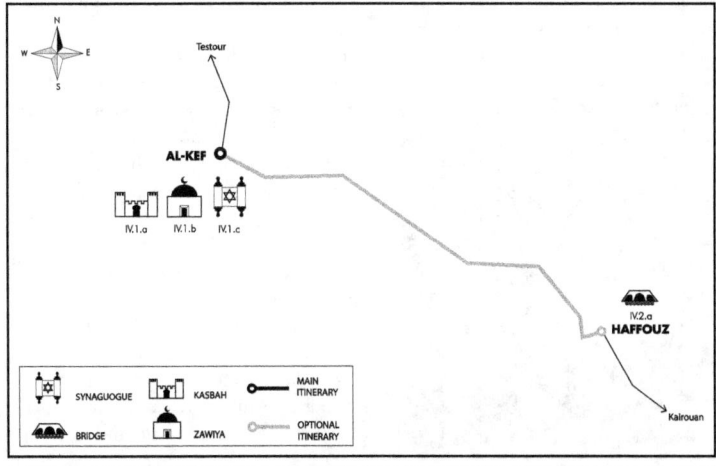

Dome, al-Kef.

ITINERARY IV *Sufism*

Al-Kef

The road from Testour to al-Kef travels through agricultural land, the pine forests of Alep, and undulating landscape.

IV.1 **AL-KEF**

The old Numid city of Sicca had already emerged, under the protection of an exceptional goddess – the Oriental Ishtat, goddess of love and war. The town was christened and known of in Antiquity under the name of Theodore of Sicca Veneria, derived, through its Latin root, from *Shikabeneria*, which the Arabs transformed into *Shaqbanariya*. Popular good sense wanted to attribute it to "*shaq bi-l-nar*", he who travelled across hell.

Its name today, al-Kef, appeared during the course of the 10th/16th century following the completion of transforming the country into an Arabic one, priming it for confusion and bringing it very close to ambiguous acts of sacrilege. Al-Kef, "he who prevents and puts a stop to harm and evil", above all signifies a place of refuge. Its long history as a safe haven situated in the open country, particularly for the inhabitants of Lorbeuss, and as a sophisticated fortress of the Regency of Tunis, confirms its vocation and clearly justifies its name, which can also mean plateau in geographical terms.

Founded on the last areas of headland of the plateau of Jabal Dyr, the town of al-Kef has been profoundly affected by its history as a stronghold and as a religious centre. Here, the particular natural characteristics of the site favour the emergence of the paradox, applicable to all high altitude sites, that describes its foundation: a paradox in which sanctity combines with the gregarious protective instinct to create a place high above sea-level that is both unique and fecund. It is as if the fate of al-Kef is sealed by this binary invocation, in which the paths of two histories – one of war, the other, religious – have often crossed. The urban and architectural landscape illustrates and identifies the historic journey of a town that is both truly and simultaneously a citadel and a temple.

The town is more suggestive of a large *shawi* village of the Aures, or of a Kabyle hamlet, hanging on to its rocky outcrop. Roman and rigid during the Age of Antiquity, Oriental and supple in Paleo-Christian and Arab-Islamic times, it is a place of transition between two superimposed urban landscapes, one vernacular, the other Mediterranean; the archaeological structures, inherited from each and every era, make themselves felt and push their forms into the morphology and dense fabric of the present *medina*.

Built in a series of steps on the side of the original rock, at the foot of the citadel and on the same level as the sanctuaries, the Medina of al-Kef cascades its building blocks out and downwards, dominating the large Ra's al-'Ayn source and its green enclosures. A landscape that reveals as much of the genius of its land as it does of the successive

Courtyard of a Jewish house, al-Kef, 19th-century engraving.

ITINERARY IV *Sufism*
Al-Kef

external contributions; a happy synthesis that creates an exceptional, natural, site and an ancient and rich history. From its past military grandeur, the old town has retained both its *kasbah* and its fortifications. The minarets and uncountable number of domes, which punctuate here and there the ever-changing landscape, are reminders of the brotherhood metropolis and the centre of marabouts that described the town long ago. Probably Libyc in origin, the first urban centre of the town dates back to the 5th century BC. As the site of a bishopric since the 3rd century, its church experienced its hour of glory, thanks to its bishops; it was thus that Arnobe taught rhetoric there, Saint Augustine enlivened its monastic life, and Saint Fulgence attempted in vain to found an Order. Sicca was endowed, from the time of the Byzantines, with solid fortifications and several basilicas; they were intended for the surveillance of great centres of "Moorish" resistance.

After the settlement of the Arabs, *Shaqbanariya* for a while remained a Kharijite stronghold, up until 171/788. It became famous for its fortress, *qal'a*, right through the Middle Ages up to the beginning of the 7th/13th century. Situated on the road of the citadels, *tariq al-qila'*, the town retains its souvenir of 40 "citadel men", *rijal al-qila'*, who are like holy warriors. As the seat of government during the Zirid era, *Shaqbanariya* became a City State in the 5th/11th century, at the time of the Hilalian invasion. Its importance was nevertheless diminished by the neighbouring town of Lorbeuss, despite the presence of the Sidi Ahmed Ibn Harz Allah who was already teaching mysticism there.

As the stronghold of the Banu Shannuf during the dismantling of Hafsid power, *Shaqbanariya*, which became al-Kef during the 10th/16th century, was recaptured by the Turks of Tunis who turned it into a solid centre of support. In 1046/1637, after the neutralisation of the Banu Shannuf, a permanent garrison, *ujak*, was installed in al-Kef, and it was depended upon by the *'arrush senjaq* – tribes that were linked to the central power known as *makhzen*. The growing importance of its strategic role, following the fixing of the borders between Algiers and Tunis, made it into an advanced bastion of the Regency of Tunis, turned to the west, facing the independent tribes of the region. Because of its fortifications, the town was the perpetual desired prize of various armed conflicts that marked the end of the 11th/17th century and the beginning of the 12th/18th century, opposing the Muradite Pretenders supported in Algiers by Brahim Sherif. Taking advantage of these conflicts, Algiers tried, in 1089/1679, to seize the *senjaq* of al-Kef. The final cycle in the history of al-Kef, beginning in the 11th/17th century, was marked by a power-driven *kasbah-zawiya* duality. If the *kasbah* and its *ujak* were aligning themselves more closely with the power of central government, then the brotherhoods, in retaliation,

Panoramic view of al-Kef, 19th-century engraving.

ITINERARY IV *Sufism*

Al-Kef

General view, al-Kef.

had prepared their assimilation to the country via their proselytism. This fusion, whether through the expediency of the *makhzen* or through the affiliation of the brotherhood, brought the town closer to its countryside and facilitated sedentary nomadic relations. The military and religious chiefs had been active agents in the diffusion of multiple cultural and social trends, and in the interweaving of the town and its region to larger areas.

During the whole of the $12^{th}/18^{th}$ century, al-Kef acted as principal stage to the wars between the *Husayniya* and the *Bashiya*, supported by the intervening Turkish armies from Algiers. As the stronghold of the *Bashiya*, al-Kef stood up against Husayn Ibn 'Ali under the leadership of Sidi Ramdan Ibn Shannuf, a town saint. Following the failure of the revolt, the *kasbah* was converted back into a *ribat*, to house marabouts. The final campaign of 1169/1756 saw, once and for all, the ruin of the town and the destruction of its fortifications.

At the beginning of the $13^{th}/19^{th}$ century, Hammuda Pasha, in his desire to free himself from the tight clutches of Algiers, once again raised its ramparts. This allowed him to secure victory over Algiers, to expand the territory of the Regency of Tunis, and to preserve its independence as well as his own. During this period, help from the Saints of al-Kef, *rijal al-Kef* – such as Sidi 'Amor, the bearer of the cemetery, *al-bala*, and Sidi al-Bdiri, who died, as did his companions, defending the town – was often beseeched. From the end of the 12th–beginning of 13th/end of the 18th century, al-Kef existed as a brotherhood metropolis, and the great brotherhoods – like the 'Issawiya, the Rahmaniya, and the Qadriya – were already in place by the end of the 19th century.

The last of these, founded in 1239/1824 by al-Haj Mohamed Ibn 'Ammar al-Mazuni al-Gharbi, who was originally from Mazuna in Persia, underwent an extraordinary growth and expansion in Tunisia and in eastern Algeria. Thanks to the radial area over which it spread, estimated to be greater than 150 km., and the number of its followers in the region, numbering more than 5,911 persons recruited in particular from the Unifa tribes, as well as to its wealth, evaluated to be over 3 million francs at the time, the brotherhood had been able to amass great political weight. Having died in 1294/1878, Sidi al-Mazuni was replaced by his adopted son, Qaddur, as head of the brotherhood, who built ties of friendship with Bernard Roy, a French intelligence agent who became the Secretary-General of the government. Shaykh Qaddur welcomed the occupation of the town of al-Kef by French troops in 1881. This attitude, coupled with the favours accorded to them by the French, did nothing but discredit this brotherhood.

On Qaddur's death in 1916, his grandson Ahmed took over from him until 1941, the year that he himself was succeeded by his own son 'Abd al-Hafid. The latter was wit-

ITINERARY IV *Sufism*
Al-Kef

ness to the struggle for Independence, the dissolution of the *zawiya*, and to the liquidation of its assets as well as to other trials and tribulations. The Qadriya's considerable property inheritance extended beyond the actual road that leads to the *kasbah*. A large section of it was demolished in order to build an official residence. Only the areas that were deemed sacred were saved from this fate. Having housed a library for a number of years, they regained their original religious functions. The mosque still includes some of the elements that once composed a set of brotherhood buildings. The facade was modified in 1919, through the addition of the present minaret which replaced the old one. Maghrebi in design, it consists of a square tower, repeating on each of its four sides the decorative interlacing diamonds, a pattern taken from the Almohad minaret of the Kasbah of Tunis. A poem engraved into a marble panel, recessed into the base of the minaret, attributes merit to Shaykh Ahmed Qaddur.

In 1280/1864, the town found itself at the heart of the insurrection of the regional tribes against the beylical power. During these troubled times, the town's brotherhood chiefs acted as the restraining, moderating force. Following the calamities of 1283/1867, al-Kef went into notorious decline that was aggravated by the French Occupation of 1881, particularly so as certain brotherhood leaders did not act unfavourably towards the colonisers. Dissolved in 1958 for their demobilising role in the course of the national struggle, the brotherhoods, save for their architectural heritage, no longer possessed any political nor economic weight; however, maraboutism has regained its past importance. In fact, the town of al-Kef is the administrative and political headquarters of the government administration, and has undergone important urban, socio-economic and cultural transformations.

The Magnificence of the Town

As a centre, established on the great invasion routes, for the integration of nomadism, transhumance, trade and pilgrimage, the town had always been the centre of Mediterranean, Eastern, Maghrebi and Saharan confluences. If, from the point of view of the power established in the east, it was the furthest sentinel to the west, then for the nomads of the south, those from Jerid and those from Aures, it was the gateway of the mythical and promising *"Friguah"*. A jetty between two seas, it is the final push towards the shy setting sun, rebelling against the soothing nature and salvation offered by the Mediterranean and the Orient. The fate of the improbable meeting between the Mediterranean and the Sahara depended on their confrontation, on their dialogue.

A European traveller would have been surprised to find in al-Kef locals who spoke

The kasbah, wall of the enclosure, al-Kef.

Al-Kef

their *"lingua franca"*; Father Ziminez's informer was a Christian slave who lived in al-Kef; the confidante of the Kahiya Salah was a Neapolitan gentleman; the miners were from Malta and from Greece; most of the *kasbah*'s master masons were Europeans. There is no shortage of examples to describe the bizarre cosmopolitan mix that existed in this inland, and moreover mountain, town.

It suffices to describe below examples of significant synthesis. A first attempt at an alliance between the regional tribes and the central power of Tunis, in this instance between the Hananshas and the Muradites of Corsican descent, was sealed through marriages and resulted in important repercussions. One of these marriages, that of Prince 'Ali, became the object of a remarkable romantic novel within Western literature of the 17th century. This first attempt failed, giving rise to a monster, the bloodthirsty Murad III, as well as to a tremendous increase of Hanansha power during the course of the interminable wars of Muradite succession (11th–12th/end of 17th century). The second attempt, which ended more happily, was that of 'Ali Turki; a Greek from Crete who converted to Islam, he settled in al-Kef as its commander and as commander of the *makhzen* tribes of the region, where he took two wives of whom one gave birth to Husayn Ibn 'Ali, founder of the Husaynite Dynasty which governed over Tunisia for over two and-a-half centuries.

Benefiting from important migratory trends, drawing as many Moroccan *shorfa*s as Andalusians, Orientals, people from south Tunisia – *Jridi*s, *Suafa*s, Jerbans – as well as Algerians, *Bahussah* Jews, Bedouins, Leghornese', Blacks, Kabyls and the Maltese, the town has, since the $11^{th}/17^{th}$ century, become a veritable cultural melting pot. The different founders of the brotherhood orders, most of whom were Maghrebi in origin – such as the *shrishi*s (Andalusians) Sidi Salah Bu Hambil (Saguiet al-Hamra'), Sidi Bu Makhluf (Morocco), Mustapha Trabelsi (Tripoli), Ahmed Bu Hajjer (Persia), Mohamed al-Mazuni (Persia), Budali (Constantine, a city in northeastern Algeria), Dhia (Black, from Tunis) – reflect the extraordinary wealth of different tributaries which the town must have benefited from since. An example of this involves Sidi 'Abd Allah Bu Makhluf who, in 1099/1688, came to Morocco with his two brothers, Bu Baker and 'Allala, to settle in al-Kef as leather craftsmen. On his brothers's death, 'Abd Allah erected a dome, on the outskirts of the *suq*s, on the exact same spot to where he retreated in order to meditate. Around this initial centre grew the *zawiya* of the 'Issawiya Brotherhood. Its facade has become more noteworthy since the ascent up has been levelled, forming a small square. It stands on the one side between a *funduq* and a Byzantine basilica which was, for a number of centuries, the town's Great Mosque, whilst on the other there is a Moorish café. It has a slightly unusual appearance; the ribbed Kairouanese dome stands shoulder to shoulder with the octagonal Turkish minaret.

On the inside, a rich decor highlights the ceremonial aspect of the particularly bewitching liturgical and musical sessions of the *Tariqa 'Issawiya*.

The al-Kef branch of the 'Issawiya, created in 1232/1817, was only recognised by its parent-*zawiya* of Tunis in 1249/1834. It experienced moments of glory towards the middle of the $13^{th}/19^{th}$ century, obtaining from the *bey* the privilege to have its own *senjaq*, set of standards. After the dissolution of the 'Issawiya as a brotherhood, in the

ITINERARY IV *Sufism*
Al-Kef

aftermath of Independence, the *zawiya* preserved the ritual of hosting musical performances until the death of the last Shaykh, *al-'amal* Bashir Dhib Shannufi.

The music of al-Kef was a further example of its cultural diversity: nomadic as well as marabout music, Andalusian Maluf music as well as African and Eastern music, all settled comfortably against its native mountain background. Certain pieces of music from the 'Issawiya, other than possessing Berber origins from the High Atlas mountains of Morocco, relay ancient polyphonic Gregorian chants via Turkish Bektashi music. The Bu Makhluf Zawiya was a veritable musical conservatoire. Other indications of the multiple and wealthy contributions to the life of al-Kef, facilitated through an intense circulation of goods, men and ideas which irrigated and revived the thirsty, open and tolerant town, were its architecture, its traditional (and especially female) dress, its gastronomy, certain socio-cultural habits and attitudes – in particular the use of terracotta or clay pipes (*sibsi*), made in the workshops of Smyrna (Izmir) in Anatolia – the conservation of snow, and the fabrication of norias.

IV.1.a The Kasbah

Walk up to the entrance of the village, take the road on the right which climbs up to the Museum square and walk down the lane on the left which leads directly to the monument. Parking and toilets available.

> There is a beautiful panoramic view from the top of the kasbah. On a clear day, one can see the craggy mountain of Jugurtha's Table.

Sitting alongside the prominent rock with which it merges to form a single body, the Kasbah of al-Kef is built of large limestone blocks, mostly taken from the amphitheatre and the theatre. It is composed of two forts joined together via a string of buildings which seem more recent. The main gate leads to an outside courtyard that borders, to the left, some cisterns, and to the front, a small fort. The entrance to the small fort, built in 1008/1600, is surmounted by a watchtower. Antique elements – like two Corinthian capitals, and a section of pilaster – are curiously affixed to the facade in the guise of a pediment. Trapezoidal in layout, the fort is flanked by four square towers. A hallway gives access to the central courtyard whose south side has regrettably been transformed. The ancient chambers lie in a L-

The kasbah, facade looking onto the courtyard, al-Kef.

143

ITINERARY IV *Sufism*

Al-Kef

The kasbah, Cannons, al-Kef.

shape formation around the north and west corners. The corner room offered a secret exit for surreptitious escapes. A balcony led to the terraces and the towers. A series of block-house embrasures, surmounted by a circular wall-path, assured the protection of the ancient western town gate, Bab al-Hwareth.

An exceptional panoramic view allows one to see the large field that contains the road crossings, the flow of the *wadi*, the natural pits and forest plains, reaching the frontier of Algeria.

At the exit of the small fort there is a copper mortar cast in Algeria at the end of the 12th–beginning of the 13th/end of the 18th century, a war trophy taken off the Algerian armies. It was offered by Hammuda Pasha to the town as a sign of recognition. Up until quite recently, its salvo announced the breaking of the fast during the month of Ramadan.

The ancient gaol of the colonial era, which is situated between the two forts, is a preserved example of military prison architecture. The town of al-Kef was thus a very well-known disciplinary camp (*biribi*). The Great Fort built in the $11^{th}/17^{th}$ century is imposing in size; it introduces itself with a beautiful iron-bordered, wooden gate, which is ensconced into a traditionally Maghrebi, large-stone frame. It is preceded by a draw-bridge, one of the few existing examples left. The entrance is composed of two elbow-shape hallways, separated by a door placed within a curved arch, sculpted into a rounded hump, with piedroit at key cornerstones. This style of framing curiously harks back to European Baroque art. Could it be the work of several Mediterranean master stone-cutters, often mentioned in the construction-site registers of the *kasbah*?

The vast courtyard of the Great Fort, a veritable courtyard of weaponry, is surrounded – with the exception of its south side – by chambers, *'uda*. In the northwest corner stands the only example of a concave interior corner tower. It is covered by four groined vaults held up on a central pillar, capable of supporting the terrace and its batteries of artillery. This room was in fact used to house pieces of artillery. Powder rooms were built beneath the eastern chambers, whilst cisterns were placed under the enormous courtyard.

The south wing is occupied by the ancient Turkish Mosque: a hypostyle room, composed of naves and three bays, covered in groined vaults, resting on reused columns featuring Antique capitals. The wall of the *qibla* is pierced by three windows, one at the back of the *mihrab* and the other two on each side. These unusual openings seem to have been added later to reinforce control over the southern side of the site.

The *seraya* was built above the old northwest tower, where the main entrance to the fort is now situated. It was used as the residence of the military commander of al-Kef, the *agha*. It is made distinct by a large room endowed with a *guenariya*, a protruding balcony, closed off with panels of fretted woodwork screens, *mashrabiyya*. It looks over the town and constitutes a preferred observatory from where the entrance to the fortress, as well as its various wings and all the different town neighbourhoods, can be supervised. In this respect, one must highlight the ingenuity of this military site. From the circular path that contours the fort, one can, thanks to a judicious system of embrasures (doorways), look over an exceptional sequence of panoramic views of the town

The kasbah, crenellations, al-Kef.

ITINERARY IV *Sufism*

Al-Kef

and the vast countryside that surrounds it. On a clear day, one can make out the horizon at a distance of about 50 km., over a view at a 210-degree angle. These openings are embrasures whose corners are blocked in, but are open-topped elsewhere; sometimes they reduce themselves to simple loopholes. The south side looks over the *medina*, its various neighbourhoods and monuments, and the vast surrounding landscape. The northwest corner, from the small fort, offers the same quality of view in the direction of Algeria. From the terraces of the northeast bastion one can see the ravine of the *wadi* Ben Smida, the heights of the Darduria – an ancient disciplinary camp, Kudiat al-Bumba and a section of the Dir plateau. From these terraces,

one surveyed the city-wall, which one can still see today unrolling itself into the distance, as well as the gates Bab Sharfein and Bab al-Ghadr that serviced the Burj Ruah. The fortified complex constituted by the *kasbah* and the town was conceived rationally and scientifically, in order to assure protection and make the place impenetrable. One can discern, among other things, the direct relationship between the various defensive sections of the *kasbah* and their ability to offer mutual protection, as well as the solidarity between the artillery batteries of the forts and the outworks, like the town gates and the bastions. Certain bastions and their guns cover the blind spots and survey the heights from which one could justifiably fear an attack, as was the case between Kudiat al-Bumba and Burj Ruah. This military compound possesses practically every constituent piece of a coherent and integrated defence system, as well as constituting an important example of defence architecture.

IV.1.b The Rahmaniya Zawiya, Museum of Popular Arts and Traditions

Climb back up the main avenue until you reach the Museum square.
Entrance fee. Opening times: 09.30–16.30 from 16th September to the 31th March; 09.00–13.00 and 16.00–19.00 the rest of the year. Closed Mondays. Parking in the small square permitted. Toilets available.

A section of the buildings that once belonged to the Rahmaniya Brotherhood, and which were then absorbed into the public domain following the liquidation of the *habus*, now houses the Museum of Popular Arts and Traditions of al-Kef. Two white

Rahmaniya Zawiya, door, al-Kef.

Sufism

Al-Kef

domes stand as reminders of the past religious function of the building. Two gates come away from the lime whitewashed walls. The main gate sits within a curved archway with black-and-white coloured keystones; the stone frame and the two columns which flank the piedroit link this entrance's style to that of classic Tunisian gates. An elbow-shaped hallway leads into a small courtyard that serves the *turbe* and the old oratory. The *turbe*, where the *shaykh*s who were the successive heads of the brotherhood now rest, leaves one guessing, through the richness of its decoration, as to the prosperity attained by the Rahmaniya during the time of Sidi Yussef Bu Hajjar, 1213/1799–1247/1832, allied to the sovereign, Hammuda Pasha, and to the powerful minister, Yussef Sahib al-Taba'a. The door to the *turbe* is, like the two windows which flank it, framed with white marble imported from Italy. The design features architectural elements that became henceforth classic within the Turkish funerary chambers of Tunisia. The square room is covered by a dome that rests on top of a circular drum and is pierced with small fretted windows fitted with coloured glass panes. Blind angle corners replace the squinches. Corner-columns in white marble, surmounted by Italian-styled, neo-Corinthian capitals, support this roof.

The wall decoration follows the classic design of superimposing registers of enamelled ceramic tiles along the lower half of the wall, and *naqsh hadida* on the upper half. Between the two, a double frieze lists, in the form of calligraphy, the 99 attributes of God. This stucco is both "Moorish" and Turkish in inspiration. It harmoniously brings together geometric motifs and bouquets of foliage. The chiselled plaster is highlighted with paint, featuring once again the colours brown-red, green and blue. No

Rahmaniya Zawiya, music room, al-Kef.

longer used as a funerary chamber, the *turbe* now houses a rich collection of female official dress, traditional jewels in solid silver, and beautifying objects and products traditionally used by the women of al-Kef.

The old oratory is a hypostyle room which includes three naves and three bays, covered by groin vaults. A recently added central dome has modified the roofing style without changing the rest of the layout. It seems that the work done in the 1970s has sacrificed the essence of this oratory's decoration. Only a few chiselled stucco motifs remain, that decorate the *mihrab* and the top sections of the walls. The room is a re-creation of a nomad tent, with its natural grandeur, furnished with all the items pertaining to a Bedouin habitat, as well as displaying diverse aspects and techniques of the agricultural and transhumant life of the region: shearing of sheep, weaving and feeding practices.

Through a second doorway, probably the only entrance into the prayer room, one reaches a courtyard surrounded by galleries, supported on huge sturdy pillars. This

ITINERARY IV *Sufism*
Al-Kef

Synagogue of the Ghriba, catafalque of Sidi 'Abd al-Kader, al-Kef.

courtyard serves a second domed room and a vaulted corridor which lead to the stables. The room, an incomplete *turbe*, is designed along the same plan as the first which lacks only in its decorative dressing. It was used as a *madrasa* run by the brotherhood, and today holds an exhibition on the art of horse-riding, as well as some of its accessories: saddles, guns, official clothes and head-dresses, some of which are specific to certain tribes, like the feather head-dress worn by the warriors in Neolithic rock paintings.

The vaulted passage is used for the exhibition of local village pottery that displays a variety of techniques and materials. Out of all this utilitarian pottery, one mostly notices the curious shapes of the utensils used to close the beehives. A series of newly built rooms present various forms of urban employment: the hairdresser, the traditional coffee shop, the blacksmith, the miller, the weaver and the tailor-embroiderer, as well as other aspects of traditional life – primary education taught at the *kuttab*, popular medicine and food.

IV.1.c The Synagogue of the Ghriba

The old Jewish Quarter is located below the museum. One reaches the monument via "rue Maraket al-Karma".

At the heart of the *hara*, the Jewish Quarter, stands the Synagogue of al-Kef, called al-Ghriba, "the foreigner". This name has not ceased to intrigue; legend attributes its origin to three Jewish sisters who separated, one settling in al-Kef, one in Annaba, and the third at Jerba. In each of these three towns there is indeed a synagogue called *al-Ghriba*. But what about the fourth *al-Ghriba* Synagogue, located in Ariana?! The Ghriba of al-Kef is doubly sacred: alongside the Hebraic faith, Muslims worship a cult dedicated to Sidi 'Abd al-Qader al-Jilani. Without either one assuming priority over the other, both communities venerate this site with equal fervour and tolerance.

Little is known about the Jewish community of al-Kef. Meanwhile, it is said that, among the Bedouins, there have always been tribes with Israelite beliefs, notably amongst the Hanansha and the Arabs of Drid and of Sers, who were known as the Bahussah. This long history is attested to by the Jewish Cemetery of al-Kef, where one can see Roman funerary steles reused as tombstones. They still feature Latin characters over which epitaphs in Hebrew have been superimposed.

The entrance to the Ghriba leads directly into an oblong courtyard featuring a groin-vaulted portico along its left side. Two arches held up by an Antique column are proof that the side portico belongs to the ancient form of the building. The large room, which has been entirely rebuilt, probably in the aftermath of the Second World War, houses the catafalque of Sidi 'Abd al-Qader alongside a rich collection of objects that were used in the synagogue: an important collection of chandeliers, textiles, manuscripts, and in particular a parchment *Torah*, carefully kept rolled up in its wooden box.

IV.2 HAFFOUZ

IV.2.a Fatimid Bridge-Aqueduct of Chrechira (option)

One of Tunisia's most important hydraulic works, without doubt, is the Bir al-Udhin system of harnessing underground water, situated 36 km. west of Kairouan. In his concern to provide its capital and its palaces with water, in 348/960, al-Mu'izz built an aqueduct that crossed hills and ravines, bringing water to Sabra and as far as the agalacties basins. This project, which without doubt made use of pre-existing Roman constructions and agalacties, consisted of a system of harnessing, conveying, collecting, stocking and distributing water that is still apparent today. The most majestic part of this work is the aqueduct of the *wadi* al-Muta, which stretches over 70 m. in length. Consisting of a continuous wall, it transforms, on the level of the river bed, into a bridge made up of four arches surmounted by semicircular arches. It is 38 m. long, and reaches 10 m. in height. The conveyance system is composed of two superimposed canals, one dating back to the Fatimid era; the date of other is indeterminate, perhaps from the Aghlabid period. The construction of this aqueduct does not conform to Roman architectural norms; its Islamic origin is indisputable. Having become a specific model of the aqueduct in North Africa, it found further applications, mainly in Morocco.

ITINERARY V

Architecture and Spirituality

Mourad Rammah

V.1 KAIROUAN
 V.1.a Sidi 'Abid al-Ghariani Zawiya
 V.1.b Bir Barruta
 V.1.c The Suqs
 V.1.d Husaynite Madrasa (option)
 V.1.e Ibn Khayrun Mosque, or Mosque of the Three Gates
 V.1.f The Great Mosque
 V.1.g The Aghlabid Reservoirs
 V.1.h Abu Zama'a al-Balaui Mausoleum
 V.1.i Sidi Amor 'Abada Zawiya and Museum
 V.1.j The Ramparts

The Rugs of Kairouan

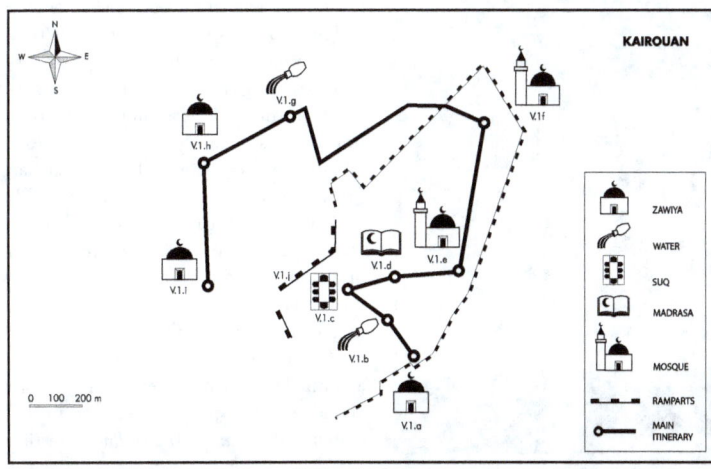

Abu Zama'a al-Balaui Mausoleum, interior passageway, Kairouan.

ITINERARY V   *Architecture and Spirituality*
Kairouan

V.I KAIROUAN

Once inside the medina, *follow the signs leading to the monuments.*

Following several fruitful expeditions, General 'Uqba founded the town of Kairouan in the year 49/670, with the thought of being able to assure Muslims of an everlasting presence in the Maghreb. Strategically, the choice of its site was judicious. In fact, Kairouan is a day's walk from the sea, which was still under the domination of the Byzantine fleets, as well as being a day's walk from the mountains, in which Berber tribes, hostile towards Islam, were entrenched. The new town formed a bridgehead along the demarcation line following the withdrawal of the Byzantine army after the defeat of Sufetula in 27/648. 'Uqba devised the town plan of Kairouan by placing the Great Mosque at its centre, next to which he built the Government Palace and established the basics of the main thoroughfare, later called "Grand Simat", before he proceeded to distribute portions of land to his soldiers. Kairouan became a town and people arrived in droves from all around. Neither the Revolt of Kusseila (64/684) nor the Rebellion of the Kahina against Hassan Ibn al-Nu'man (78/698–82/701) succeeded in swallowing up the new-born town, which came into existence in an extremely hostile environment. Indeed, after the country's pacification, the town was the target of Kharijite Berber plots who organised revolts in the name of racial equality. They sacked the town and massacred its population at various intervals during the years 124/742–139/757. Consequently, protection over the town was imposed: this was the work of Mohamed Ibn al-'Ach, the first Abbassid chief who settled in Kairouan and busied himself with protecting it against invaders through the building of a rampart in 144/762. The Abbassid Caliph al-Mansur wrote to al-Aghlab Ibn Salam Tamimi, his Governor in Ifriqiya, about this matter, advising him *"to be just towards his subjects, to fortify the town of Kairouan and its defences and to arrange for its protection"*. It is true that these measures did not prevent further assaults against the town from occurring, but nevertheless they did help to improve its security and create more favourable conditions for its urban growth. Under the reign of the Banu al-Muhallabs, Kairouan went through a relatively peaceful period. Yazid Ibn Hatim undertook building and extension works on the Great Mosque, which became a reason for Kairouan's rise and demographic growth. He organised the *suqs*, and filled them with different professional bodies. Earlier, various *suqs* had proliferated in the heart of the *medina*, attesting

The Great Mosque, view of the domes, Kairouan.

ITINERARY V   *Architecture and Spirituality*
Kairouan

to intense commercial and economic activity. Since the Ist/2nd half of the 7th century, Kairouan began its preparation to become a significant, and heavily populated, Arab-Muslim centre, without, however, aspiring to become a great luxurious and opulent capital; its houses remained modest. Merit is due to the Aghlabids for propelling it to the rank of great Mediterranean capitals. Yet, the new era had begun ominously. The founder of the dynasty, Ibrahim I, distanced himself from the Kairouanese by founding, in 185/801, a new capital, al-'Abbassiya, 5 km. to the south. His son, Ziyadat Allah, punished the inhabitants of Kairouan for supporting the Arab rebel leader Mansur al-Tanbudhi, and destroyed its ramparts. However, after the consolidation of power among the Aghlabid princes, Kairouan stood out for its loyalty to the dynasty, which then endowed the town with its most beautiful monuments. It was thus that Ziyadat Allah I undertook, beginning in 220/835, the reconstruction of the Great Mosque, so as to render it worthy of the spiritual role which had not ceased to befall the town of Kairouan. Abu Ibrahim placed his freed slave Khalef (246/860) in charge of building a cistern which came to be considered as one of the most important hydraulic works of the Muslim world.

Historical sources attest that Kairouan attained its level of growth with the Aghlabids and did not cease to develop. Its intellectual life was no less abundant, and Kairouan became one of the most brilliant centres of Islamic culture, from where Malekism would spread out across the whole of the Muslim West due in particular to the work of the great scholar Sahnun Ibn Sa'id (159/776–239/854).

When the Fatimids settled in Ifriqiya (296/909), they did not bestow any kind of particular importance on Kairouan, which was fighting back stubborn Shi'ite resistance, forcing them to seek refuge on the coast and to found the town of Mahdia. The Kairouanese even rallied themselves around the Kharijites during the revolt of the "man on the donkey" in 329/941. However, aggravated by the demands of the Berbers, they ended up supporting the Fatimid Caliph al-Mansur, who after his victory, pardoned the Kairouanese and founded his new Capital, Sabra al-Mansuriya in 337/949, on the doorstep of their town. Later on, al-Mu'izz built an aqueduct that supplied the town's cisterns with drinking water after first providing for his own Capital, Sabra. Kairouan seemed at the height of expansion:

Abu Zama'a al-Balaui Mausoleum, patio, Kairouan.

153

ITINERARY V *Architecture and Spirituality*
Kairouan

it numbered around 15 thoroughfares, each emanating from the Great Mosque, creating a circulatory urban configuration, which leads to the assumption that the town-plan was based on that of Baghdad, the round city. Fifteen cisterns, situated outside the town walls, supplied the town with water and one could count the presence of over 48 *hammam*s. The town constituted a commercial centre, linking the two extremes of the Muslim world and the economic one which received caravans from al-Andalus and from the auriferous deposits of the southern Sahara. Kairouan was surrounded by well-populated villages like the Sardaigne, Jalula, Husr and Sadaf, that provided it with foodstuffs and agricultural produce. Furthermore, the town of Kairouan became one of the largest centres of textile, ceramic and pottery fabrication. It could thus fulfil the necessary criteria required in becoming one of the biggest towns of the era. It is probable that it was, alongside Cordoba and Fustat, one of the greatest metropolises of the Mediterranean.

After the departure of the Fatimid Caliph al-Mu'izz to Egypt (361/972) in the wake of Cairo's foundation, Ifriqiya became a Zirid province. Closer ties began to form between the Zirids and the Kairouanese following Prince al-Mansur's move to Sabra in 375/986. These were reinforced in 406/1016, in the aftermath of the Shi'ite persecutions in Kairouan, and came to a head in 438/1047, when al-Mu'izz repudiated his Fatimid allegiance and Sunnism was proclaimed. The Fatimids' reaction bore tragic consequences for the town.

Indeed, in 442/1051, the Fatimid Caliph al-Mustansir sent the Hilalians to Ifriqiya: tribes from lower Egypt swarmed over North Africa and sacked its capital, Kairouan, which was deserted by the majority of its population. From then on, the town lost its political-economic role and retreated back within its city walls, cutting itself off from a hostile countryside and retaining an essentially spiritual role, whilst transforming itself into a market-town dedicated to commercial activities and craft-making. Meanwhile, the town went through a relative renaissance under the Hafsids. In fact, from the end of the $7^{th}/13^{th}$ century, Kairouan began to rebuild its ramparts along new lines, and the success of maraboutism provoked the proliferation of mausoleums and *zawiya*s that marked the urban development of the town. It transformed itself into a centre for tanning, fur-trading, and weaving, and its *suq*s were again reorganised. Following the decline of Hafsid power, Kairouan was conquered in 944/1538 by the Chiefs of the Shabbiya Brotherhood who turned it into their capital for 40 years and into the bastion of national opposition to the Spanish Christians who had come to rescue the Hafsid Sultan Hassan. In the $11^{th}/17^{th}$ century Kairouan benefited from the care and concern of the Muradites, in particular that of Hammuda Mohamed; he transferred his capital there following the rebellion lead by his uncle and his brother 'Ali. But in 1112/1701, Murad III turned against the Kairouanese, burning down their homes, taking advantage of the allegiance of the Husaynites, after which Husayn Ibn 'Ali paid particular attention to Kairouan through reconstructing its ramparts and building the Husaynite Madrasa. His successors followed his example as a sign of gratitude for the position taken by the town during the rebellion of 'Ali Pasha. The French traveller Desfontaines, who visited the town in 1784, noted that it was *"the largest of the kingdoms after Tunis. It is even better built and*

ITINERARY V Architecture and Spirituality
Kairouan

less dirty than the latter ...". The traveller Guerin estimated that its population, in 1861, was 12,000 inhabitants. In fact, Kairouan was the seat of the government administration with a population of 130,000 inhabitants. It was an essentially agricultural region, focusing on cereal cultivation and arboriculture. The town was reputed for its crafts, mainly for its rugs and brassware.

V.1.a Sidi 'Abid al-Ghariani Zawiya

One reaches the monument via the street of the same name. Take the second road to the right via Bab al-Shuhada' (Gate of the Martyrs).
Opening times: 08.30–13.00 and 15.00–18.00. Closed Friday afternoons and Sunday.
Parking spaces outside the medina, around Bab al-Shuhada'. Toilets available.

This monument was built in the 8th/14th century by a Kairouanese scholar called al-Jadidi. Having died on a pilgrimage to Mecca in 786/1384, he was succeeded by his disciple Abu Samir 'Abid, who was from the Jabal Gharian in Libya. He taught at the *zawiya* for 20 years and was buried there on his death in 804/1402. The *madrasa* was then named after him. The monument appears to have undergone several changes and enlargements across the centuries, but it is difficult to trace its evolution clearly due to a lack of documentation. It was completely restored in the 1970s in order to house the offices of the Association for the Safeguarding of the Medina of Kairouan. One enters the *zawiya* via an elbow-shaped entrance typical of Kairouanese houses; the hallway, covered by a pretty, Hispano-Moresque painted ceiling, leads into a courtyard paved in marble, decorated in geometric interlac-

ing patterns and black in colour. This type of paving essentially existed in Tunisia from the Ottoman era onwards, and in this particular case it can be dated from the 11th–12th/second half of the 17th century. The courtyard is surrounded by four porticoes whose walls are faced with stucco panels and *faience* tiles which were added during the last set of restoration works. Each of these porticoes is composed of three semi-circular arches in fitting with pure Kairouanese tradition. Running along above these porticoes are galleries covered with a wooden canopy which delineates the horizontal lines of green tiles on top, level with the terraces. The entire design displays a rare harmony that respects the proportions between the curves and the

Sidi 'Abid al-Ghariani Zawiya, passageway, Kairouan.

155

ITINERARY V *Architecture and Spirituality*
Kairouan

Bir Barruta, bucket elevator, Kairouan.

various lines. It all seems to point to being the handiwork of an experienced and meticulous architect. At the far end of the south-east portico lies a prayer room consisting of three naves and three bays, in line with the classic plan of Muslim oratories. Note that the studded doors of the prayer room and of the entrance porch reflect the wood sculpturing techniques that were practised by the Kairouanese in the 12th/18th and 13th/19th centuries. The funerary chamber, on the north-eastern side, houses the tomb of the Hafsid sovereign Mulay Hassan, who died in 957/1550, next to the tomb of Sidi 'Abid. It has a beautiful, painted wood ceiling in the form of a staircase. The decor consists of geometric and floral motifs and recticurvilinear arcs conforming to the Hispano-Moresque repertoire. This ceiling is surmounted on the outside by a pyramidal dome covered in green tiles. This type of dome displays certain analogies with the dome of the Sidi al-Uhayishi Madrasa in Kairouan, dating from the middle of the 11th/17th century. The other outbuildings of this part of the monument consist of student accommodation and classrooms. In the south-east corner one can enter into a second courtyard surrounded by porticoes whose Byzantine and Zirid capitals, and columns adorned with ring ornamentation and *kufic* inscriptions, no doubt originate from Sabra. This courtyard ends in an ablutions chamber and yet another, smaller courtyard which leads to the exit.

V.1.b Bir Barruta

Return onto avenue Habib Bourguiba, take a right and continue until you reach the "rue des Cuirs" (Street of Leather). Toilets available.

Sources attribute the digging of Bir Barruta to the Governor Harthama Ibn A'yan, in 180/796. However it seems that the Bey Mohamed, son of Murad, carried out a renovation of the whole construction in 1101/1690, to which he added a marble fountain. Although it is not amongst the first wells to be dug out at the centre of the town, it is an object of special veneration for part of the population. According to legend, the wells are linked to those of Zemzem in Mecca. Another legend states that whoever drinks water from Barruta is sure to return to Kairouan. The room that houses the wells, reached via a staircase, is covered by a dome on squinches based on the Kairouanese dome type. It stands out for its profound bareness, and rests on four arches that lean against the walls. It is doubtless a contemporary of the dome covering the dome room in the Mausoleum of Abu Zama'a al-Balaui, built at the time of Mohamed Bey. Both are the works of the master mason Mohamed al-Zakraui whose name features on a panel

ITINERARY V   Architecture and Spirituality
Kairouan

of fretted stucco. The room is occupied by a noria that is worked by a camel. This system of drawing water, which dates back to the Middle Ages, exists here as one of the last that work at the centre of Tunisian city life. Outside the building, standing up against the north wall, there is a fountain with a drinking trough and marble taps.

V.1.c **The Suqs**

It seems that the neural centre of the town has moved since the Hafsid era, from the area surrounding the Great Mosque to the site that the *suqs* occupy today, within the area that links Bab Tunis to the Jalladin Gate. Kairouan included the most important commercial zone in the Regency of Tunis, after the capital. Like everywhere else, the *suqs* were divided and grouped by trade. The leather industry and wool-weaving were probably the most significant crafts inside the town centre. This was on par with the development of cattle breeding in the Kairouanese countryside. One can identify the *al-Blaghgia Suq* (makers of babouches) built by 'Ali Pasha II in 1181/1768, as well as the *suq* of the cisterns (near the Husaynite Madrasa) reserved for the clog-makers. The *suq* of the saddle-makers used to be situated near the Gate of Tunis. The *al-Sakkajin Suq* (near the Bey's Mosque) was restored in 1884. The *suq* of the Jerbians (near the Mosque of the Three Gates) is reputed for its work in the weaving of Kairouanese wool blankets alongside black wash cloths. All of these *suqs* have in fact lost their original vocations and now specialise in arts and crafts related to tourism. Only the rug *suq*, still flourishing as ever, has escape this act of deformation.

V.1.d **Husaynite Madrasa** (option)

This is an annex to the Kairouanese municipal offices.
Opening times: 08.30–13.00 and 15.00–18.00. Closed Friday afternoons and Sundays.

Founded in 1122/1710 by the first Husaynite Prince, Husayn Ibn 'Ali, it is one of the oldest Kairouanese *madrasa*s that has been past down on to us; as such, it holds a special place within the history of Kairouanese architecture. The rectangular doorway, framed by *kadhal* piedroits, leads to a hall whose ceilings are painted with geometric and floral motifs based on the Hispano-Moresque model. The elbow-shaped entrance ends in a courtyard surrounded by four galleries featuring horseshoe arches resting on Ottoman-type capitals. The acroter is made of green tiles, definitely Hispano-Moresque in influence. There are 11 rooms surrounding the courtyard; they are covered by barrel vaults. On the south-east side stands the mosque: it is composed of two bays and of three barrel-

A main suq street, Kairouan.

ITINERARY V   *Architecture and Spirituality*
Kairouan

Ibn Khayrun Mosque, facade, Kairouan.

vaulted bays, supported on circular pillars. In earlier days, a stucco decor adorned part of the walls; nothing but a few fragments of it remain. The niche of the *mihrab* is surmounted by a semi-circular horseshoe arch. The plan of this *madrasa* is based on that of the *ribat*s, composed uniquely of a ground floor. This monument was restored during the 1980s by the Association for the Safeguarding of the Medina. It is now used as the old town's local Town Hall.

V.1.e Ibn Khayrun Mosque, or Mosque of the Three Gates
(this monument is not open to visitors)

Head towards the "rue de la mosquée des Trois Portes" which extends on from the "rue des Cuirs".

Although not open to visitors, a visit to this monument is recommended as its main feature of interest lies in its facade. In fact, the Ibn Khayrun Mosque, otherwise called the Mosque of the Three Gates, possesses the oldest sculpted and decorated facade in Islamic art to survive, and is a veritable inventory of the Kairouanese decorative repertoire of the Aghlabid period. The use of soft sculpted stone has conferred a majestic aura to the entire appearance. The facade is composed along the lines of axial symmetry, possessing three gates, the largest of which stands in the middle. Framed by panels of floral and geometric motifs, composed of five or three-lobed leaves, open or folded, it is surmounted by *kufic* writing attributing its foundation to Mohamed Ibn Khayrun (252/866). The mosque has a modest look. It consists of three naves parallel to the wall of the *qibla*. Each of the two columns that support the ceiling is surmounted by semi-circular arches. In the north-east corner stands a minaret that was added during the Hafsid era as stated in the last line of the *kufic* inscription which bares witness to the renovation of the entire oratory in 843/1440. Like all Kairouanese minarets, it has a rectangular base, and is adorned with twin bays framed in *faience* tiles, indicating a clear Andalusian influence.

V.1.f The Great Mosque

Follow the ramparts heading north until the "rue Ibrahim Ibn al-Aghlab", then continue up this street until you reach the monument.
Entrance fee. Opening times: all year from 08.00–12.30. Afternoon opening times: 16.30–17.30 from June to September. 14.45–16.30 pm from October to May. Closed Fridays. Parking available close by.

ITINERARY V *Architecture and Spirituality*
Kairouan

The Great Mosque of Kairouan is considered to be the oldest and most prestigious sanctuary in the Muslim West. Its architectural model served as an example for the majority of Ifriqiyan mosques until the arrival of the Ottomans. Through the diversity of its forms and the richness of its ornamental repertoire, it incarnates the essential elements fundamental to the school of Kairouanese architecture. The first oratory was built in 50/670 by ʻUqba Ibn Nafi. Constructed using crumbly materials, it was completely rebuilt by Hassan Ibn Nuʻman in 84/703. The mosque underwent extension works on its north side during the reign of the Umayyad Governor Bishr Ibn Safwan (103/722–109/728) before being renovated by Yazid Ibn Hatim in 155/772. But the mosque, in the form and dimensions it takes today, is the work of the Aghlabid Prince Ziyadat Allah I who, in 221/836, demolished the entire building and built it up again in its entirety. In 247/862, Abu Ibrahim Ahmad added a narthex gallery built against the prayer room and surmounted by a dome. The enclosure of the Great Mosque of Kairouan is rectangular, measuring 125 m. in length and nearly 75 m. in width. From outside, the mosque looks like a fortress, prickling with towers and bastions and pierced by eight gates. In fact, this is due to the porches and buttresses that were added later on, essentially between the $7^{th}/13^{th}$ and $12^{th}/18^{th}$ century, in view of embellishing the mosque or of sustaining its Aghlabid walls which were definitely showing signs of decrepitude. This explains why a gate through the western facade (Bab al-Maʼ or Gate of the Water) as well as one

Ibn Khayrun Mosque, detail of the facade, Kairouan.

ITINERARY V *Architecture and Spirituality*
Kairouan

The Great Mosque, nartex, Kairouan.

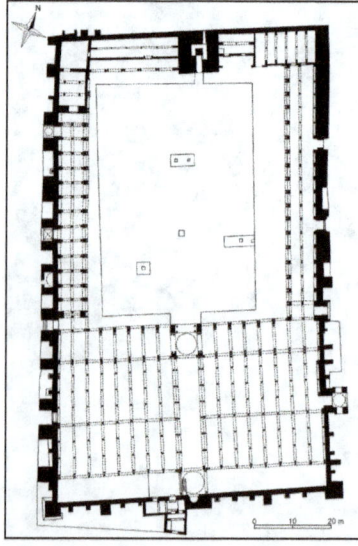

Plan of the Great Mosque of Kairouan.

belonging the eastern facade (Bab Lalla Rayhana) date from the reign of the Hafsid Caliph al-Mustansir, from 692/1293. The porch of the latter, surmounted by a superb fluted dome with stucco ornamentations, was erected by the *imam* of the Great Mosque in 716/1316. The other gates date either from the Muradite or the Husaynite periods.

The central courtyard is surrounded by galleries displaying a rhythmic symphony of semi-circular horseshoe arches supported on columns and capitals taken from ancient sites. Thus, paradoxically, this mosque is the largest museum of Roman and Byzantine capitals ever to be formed under the roof of a single Muslim monument. The galleries that no doubt date from the time of Ziyadat Allah were certainly restored during the Hafsid era and then again in the

ITINERARY V *Architecture and Spirituality*
Kairouan

Muradite era, as is attested to by a stone panel sculpted with floral motifs which can be seen in the south-west corner. An *impluvium*, whose labyrinth-like design consists of horseshoe arches, furnishes the centre of the courtyard. It no doubt dates from the era of Mohamed Bey (11th–12th/end of the 17th century). In the middle of the *qibla* gallery stands a dome on squinches called the dome of the *bahu*, which was completely renovated at the beginning of the 13th/19th century. In front, at the centre of the north side, rises the minaret built by Zidayat Allah. With a square-base foundation, it is composed of three levels reaching a height of 32 m. Its robust yet sober allure is a reminder of Roman lighthouses and of Syrian bell towers; it would become a model for future Ifriqiyan mosques up until the arrival of the Ottomans. The prayer room, formed in a hypostyle design in the Umayyad tradition, is composed of 17 naves and 8 bays, following the example of the Mosque of the Prophet in Medina. The crossing between the axial nave and the bay of the *qibla* forms a square on which a dome on squinches was erected, made of sculpted stone, whose forms and motifs (shells and polyfoiled rosettes) are of Umayyad inspiration. Most of the gates in the prayer hall, and essentially the central gate adorned with Maghrebi floral motifs, were re-built in 1244/1829. The prayer hall roof is made of wood. It was the object of several repairs throughout the ages. The oldest part dates from the 3rd/9th century; it has a pretty decor of flowers and foliage. The work undertaken by the Zirids during the 4th–5th/first half of the 9th century is marked by *kufic* inscriptions, the shafts of whose letters end in small, two-foiled flowers. The ceilings were restored under the Hafsids towards the end of the 7th/13th century. The last repairs date from the time of Murad I, in 1027/1618. The *mihrab* dates from the time of Abu Ibrahim Ahmad (247/862). It is adorned with a half-dome made of painted wood, and furnished with 28 fretted *champlevé* marble panels decorated with a variety of floral and geometric motifs, amongst which one can distinguish the vine leaf, in all its varied, stylised forms, as well as a shell design, inscribed within an arched bandwidth imitating the form of a *mihrab*. The decor, of Byzantine influence conveyed through Umayyad art from Syria, is as such imbued with Islamic creed. The frame of the *mihrab* niche is decorated with a unique collection of 139 tiles that have a metallic sheen, dating from the middle of the 3rd/9th century. Doubtless Iraqi in origin, this niche possesses a

The Great Mosque, mihrab, Kairouan.

ITINERARY V   Architecture and Spirituality
Kairouan

The Great Mosque, view of the minaret from the cemetery, Kairouan.

stylised floral ornamentation that can be viewed as a precursor to modern abstract art. The *minbar*, a jewel of Ifriqiyan art, dates from the middle of the 3rd/9th century, and is the oldest Muslim preaching pulpit to have survived. It consists of more than 300 Indian Teak wood panels. Its elaborate ornamentation, in which Byzantine and Mesopotamian influences are combined, denotes the maturity of Kairouanese art. The *maqsura*, situated to the right of the *minbar*, was built by the Zirid al-Mu'izz in the 4th–5th/beginning of the 11th century. It enabled princes and governors to pray separately from the rest of the worshippers. Made of cedarwood, it is distinguished by its beautiful epigraphic frieze, written in flowery *kufic* script. The panels above this frieze were completely restored in the Ottoman era (1075/1665).

V.1.g The Aghlabid Reservoirs

It is advisable to use your car when visiting the following monuments.

The reservoirs are located outside the ramparts, north of the town, on the "avenue de la Republique".
Opening times: 08.30–18.00 from September 16th to March 31st, and from 07.30–18.00 during the rest of the year. Parking and toilets available.

The Aghlabid reservoirs are considered to be amongst the most important and most famous hydraulic works of the Islamic world. They represent some of about 15 reservoirs located outside the city-walls that supplied the town with water. Arab chroniclers and geographers were continuously amazed by the impressive majesty of these installations, which necessarily led to Kairouan being called the "town of the cisterns" during the Middle Ages. They were filled by draining rainwater as well as water from the tributaries of the *wadi* Merguelil that flow in the surrounding low lands. Its waters were harnessed by small dams and a conveyance canal equipped with a breakwater that transported it to the small pool. But in 350/961, the Fatimid Caliph al-Mu'izz built an aqueduct that brought water from the sources of the Shreshira, located 40 km. to the west of Kairouan, to the town's cisterns after having already supplied his Capital, Sabra, along the way. The Kairouanese generally had wells and cisterns at home; and it appears that water collected in these reservoirs was used in times of drought and by the most impoverished members of the population, as well as to supply caravans and supply water to the herds. These famous reservoirs were built between 246/860 and 248/862 by the Aghlabid Prince Abu Ibrahim Ahmed. They are built of rubble surfaced with a waterproof coating and are rounded at the top. They are composed of three main sections:

ITINERARY V   *Architecture and Spirituality*
Kairouan

– The small reservoir, 17 m. in diameter, is enclosed within a polygonal wall made of 17 internal buttresses and 26 external ones that alternate against each other, thus consolidating the construction to enable it to withstand pressure. These buttresses are semi-cylindral in shape and topped with semi-spheres. This reservoir, which has a holding capacity of 4,000 cubic metres, serves to filter the water from the debris and alluvial deposits that it carries. The purified water then runs into the large reservoir through a semi-circular opening called the outlet.

– The large reservoir, also polygonal, is flanked by 64 internal buttresses and 118 external ones. Measuring 128 m. in diameter and 4.8 m. deep, its holding capacity exceeds 57,000 cubic metres. A fat poly-foiled pillar rises up from its centre and was once surmounted by a dome, serving as a leisure pavilion. This large reservoir is used to stock the water necessary for the needs of daily life. In the meantime, this process allows for a further filtration of the water, the purest parts of which would become drinking water and would as such be poured into dispensing water tanks.

– The water-tanks consist of two parallel basins standing perpendicularly to the reservoirs. They are covered with barrel vaults held up by arch-beams that rest on pillars. Six openings, at the top of the vaults, allow water to be drawn. The holding capacity of each reservoir exceeds 1,000 cubic metres.

These reservoirs of gigantic dimensions stand as a reminder of the town's past glory and of its past struggle against thirst and water shortages. They seduce the viewer with their simplicity and their impressive majestic quality, and enchant through the elegance of their style and through the harmony of their forms.

V.1.h Abu Zama'a al-Balaui Mausoleum

This monument is situated on the same avenue as the preceding monument.
Entrance fee. Opening times: 08.30–18.00 from September 16th to March 31th and from 07.30–18.00 during the rest of the year. Parking and toilets available.

This cultural complex was built in memory of one of the Prophet's companions, Abu Zama'a U'bayd Ibn Arqam al-Balaui, who died, in the year 33/654, during a military expedition in Ifriqiya following a battle waged by the Muslim troops against the Byzantine army near Jalula, 30 km. west of Kairouan. His body was buried on the site of this town before its foundation. This venerable character carried about on his person, hair that had belonged to the Prophet, which explains why Europeans call his Mosque "du Barbier". The mausoleum consisted in the 9th/15th century of a simple, octagonal-based dome, surrounded by a wall. Hammuda Pasha (1040/1631–1075/

The Aghlabid reservoirs, detail of the buttress, Kairouan.

ITINERARY V *Architecture and Spirituality*
Kairouan

Abu Zama'a al-Balaui Mausoleum, Kairouan.

1665) initiated building works which no doubt involved repairing the mausoleum dome and its enclosure. But the essence of the building is the work of Mohamed Bey, constructed between 1092/1681 and 1096/1685. This architectural complex consists of the following:
– A warehouse situated to the left of the entrance which is used to stock the produce bought using the saint's *habus* and donations.
– The apartments of the Pasha which are known as *'alwi* and which are located above the warehouse. They were formerly used to receive the chief of the detachment in charge of overseeing the regional taxes and, at a later date, were used by distinguished guests of the mausoleum.
– The *madrasa* situated next to the warehouse. It is the prototype of the Tunisian *madrasa* and it is made distinct through its elongated prayer hall, composed of only two naves. The *mihrab* is surmounted by a dome on fluting squinches. The *madrasa* is made up of two small courtyards and of porticoes that surround the rooms of the students. An elegant minaret, Hispano-Moresque in type, rises up in the north-east corner. It is decorated with a ceramic facing which surfaces the area above twin horseshoe arches. In contrast to other Kairouanese minarets, whose crenels are rounded, those of this *madrasa* are serrated. They recall the minarets of the Great Mosque of Tlemcen and of the Kasbah of Tunis. Everything is imbued with Andalusian art; the two master masons who supervised these works were the two brothers Ahmad and Mustafa al-Andalusi.
– The mausoleum whose entrance faces the main gate has a doorway consisting white and red marble frames, Italian in style. The hallway possesses an angled, elbow-shape entrance leading to a large patio that looks Andalusian. It is bordered by two porticoes whose horseshoe arches, typically Kairouanese, are supported on neo-Corinthian capitals that reveal crests which have been sculpted so as to depict, in relief, the Ottoman emblem. This patio spills out into a room surmounted by an attractive dome on squinches. Its ornamentation consists of stucco panels which display the full range of Hispano-Moresque, as well as, Turkish decoration (the bouquet of flowers and the pine tree). Then comes the mausoleum and its courtyard which are reserved for worship. The walls, clad with polychrome enamelled tiles, are surmount-

ITINERARY V *Architecture and Spirituality*
Kairouan

ed by stucco panels which have been sculpted with rare finesse. The wooden ceilings which have been painted and sculpted are of a Hispano-Moresque style. The tomb of the Prophet's companion is crowned by a dome on squinches whose recent decoration dates from the 13th–14th/end of the 19th century. Although recently built, the architecture of this compound distinguishes itself through its visual harmony and decorative beauty. It reflects new influences on Tunisian architecture: first Turkish with a certain Byzantine imprint, then Andalusian following the arrival of craftsmen expelled from Spain, and Italian through its relationship with the European Renaissance – all of which are combined with local traditions perpetuated by the Kairouanese school of architecture. This intermixing of different civilisations that swept through Tunisia during the Modern era reflects the ability for assimilation that has always characterised the Tunisian personality throughout the ages. Abu Zama'a, renamed Sidi Sahbi, considered to be the town's Patron Saint, enjoys a special sort of veneration. His mausoleum is the most visited by the Tunisians, who come in droves particularly during the official celebration of *Mulud*, commemorating the birth of the Prophet. Ceremonies celebrating the contract of marriage, as well as those celebrating circumcision, are also held here. Young Kairouanese girls offer their first rug to this saint, famed for his prophylactic talents.

V.1.i Sidi Amor 'Abada Zawiya and Museum

Continue along the "avenue Zama'a al-Balaui". The museum is reached via "rue al-Gadraou". Entrance fee. Open every day from 08.00–18.00. Toilets available.

Abu Zama'a al-Balaui Mausoleum, funerary chamber, Kairouan.

Renamed the mosque of the Sabres, this *zawiya* is the work of a marabout who lived during the first half of the 13th/19th century: Amor Ibn Salam al-'Ayari, known as 'Abada, who originally came from the region of Makhtar. He was a master blacksmith and enjoyed favours from the Beys Mustapha (1250/1835–1252/1837) and Ahmad (1252/1837–1270/1854). He was an extraordinary character, a megalomaniac endowed with a remarkable presence of spirit. Scholars were suspicious of him whilst local people feared him and sought his blessing, believing that he possessed supernatural powers. Oral tradition has woven various tales and myths around this character, which have been held in the collective memory up to this day. At his death in 1271/1855, he was buried in his *zawiya*, the architecture of which reflects the personality of its master craftsman. In fact, situated in a modest suburb, it is distinct for the spread of its floor area, which exceeds 1,500 sq. m., and for the majesty of its six ribbed domes which are of a Kairouanese type, characterised by the presence of a

165

ITINERARY V *Architecture and Spirituality*
Kairouan

Sidi 'Amor 'Abada Zawiya and museum, catafalque, Kairouan.

square base and an octagonal drum. The internal layout of the monument is incomprehensible: galleries covered in groined vaults end in spaces which surmount domes. The thickness of the walls exceeds 2 m., indeed exceeds 4 and 5 m. The few columns and capitals are Ottoman in type, and their abaci reveal small flowers and Turkish crests. It is probable that these were dedicated by the *bey* to the saint, but each and every architectural form belonging to the monument complies with pure Kairouanese tradition. A large room in the *zawiya* that houses the saint's tomb was transformed into a museum, displaying objects that either belonged to Sidi Amor 'Abada or were made by him. These objects, disproportionately enormous in size, are effectively of little functional use, and reflect the megalomania of this character: very heavy iron-forged sabres sheathed in solid wood scabbards, shelves, a colossal pipe, giant anchors, storage trunks … recuperated from the Ghar al-Melh naval base and offered by the Bey Ahmad. Each object dates from the first half of the $13^{th}/19^{th}$ century and some of them carry inscriptions in Maghrebi script in the form of intaglio engravings. These texts contain Qur'anic verses, some prophesies, some aspects of Sidi Amor 'Abada's life and his position in respect to certain problems and events of the period. Nevertheless, these objects constitute a range of iron and wood production techniques, employed in Kairouan in the $13^{th}/19^{th}$ century.

V.1.j The Ramparts

The ramparts are pierced by four gates: Bab Tunis, Bab al-Khukha (Gate of the Hatch/Counter), Bab al-Jalladin (Gate of the Leather Workers), and Bab al-Shuhada' (Gate of the Martyrs).

The first ramparts of the town of Kairouan were built by the Abbasid Governor, Harthama Ibn A'yun, in 144/762. Equipped with six gates at the time, these were then destroyed by the Aghlabid Prince Ziyadat Allah I. Rebuilt by al-Mu'izz in 443/1052, along the lines of a perimeter that exceeded 9 km., they were completely neglected following the Hilalian invasions and the ruin of the town. The contour of the new enclosure, 54 hectares in surface area, hardly covered a tenth of the town's sprawl when it was at its height; it took a while for it to be redrawn. It seems that the first designs were done as early as the restructuring of the town, at the end of the into weaving this sort of rug. At the heart of the decoration that ornates the Kairouanese rug one finds motifs already seen in the *minbar* of the Great Mosque of Kairouan, the imprint of the lion that one finds in Andalusian ceramics. This demonstrates the extent to which the Kairouanese rug is a symbiosis of different influences that have come from an already well-established tradition, one that was no doubt established before Kamla's arrival, but whose contribution to the evolution of the Kairouanese rug remains relatively unclear. The texture of the authentic Kairouanese rug was made up of 40,000 knots per sq. m.; its colours, which possessed a sumptuous array of tones, were polychrome. At the start of the 20th century, the craft industry decided, in response to clients' needs, to move away from traditional colours, which are now only used for dowry rugs, towards more natural tones like white, black, beige, grey and brown; this type of rug was named "Agnelle", *Allucha*. The vogue for Kairouanese rugs incited certain other regions of Tunisia to weave imitations, which, through changes in the decorative motifs or perhaps through the desire to innovate, have given birth to a new form of mixed rug, that possesses enough originality, such as the rugs of Bizerte or, created within our times, the rugs of Ksiba al-Mediuni. In fact, rugs of different textures are woven that consist of 90,000, 160,000, indeed 250,000 knots per sq. m. Alongside the "urban rug", there is the *gtif*, a nomad rug par excellence. It constituted the furnishing for tents of the Drid, Hmamma, Zlass and Mhedhba tribes. It was made by men, *raggams*, travelling craftsmen who offered their services to the wealthiest nomads. The *gtif*'s colour spectrum is nearly always the same: it has a red background, and its motifs, usually outlined in white cotton, are polychrome. Goat and camel hair is relatively long, able to grow over 4 cm. in length. The number of stitches per square decimetre is limited to no more than 40–45. The *gtif* is divided into rectangular or square outlines, usually four but sometimes five. They are decorated with motifs which are, more often than not, geometric – diamond-shapes, crosses, eight-point stars – are, more rarely, figurative – people and camels, a palm drawn within the shape of a diamond. It should be noted that the techniques and the decorative repertoire employed by the Tunisian *gtif* are close to those of Algerian and Moroccan nomadic tribes. Independently from the type of rug they happen to be, rugs are sold as three different qualities, attested by an official stamp, dependent on the regularity of its motifs, the symmetry of its designs and the tightness of its knots. They are distinguished as "superior quality", "first choice" and "second choice", and there exists a fourth category for rugs that have not been stamped, or have been refused an official stamp.

Polychrome rug, featuring traditional tints, used as a form of dowry.

ITINERARY VI

The Towns of the Princes

Mourad Rammah

VI.1 RAQQADA
    VI.1.a Museum of Raqqada

VI.2 MAHDIA
    VI.2.a The Sqifa al-Kahla
    VI.2.b The Great Mosque
    VI.2.c Burj al-Kebir
    VI.2.d The Inland Port

Tunisian Manuscripts

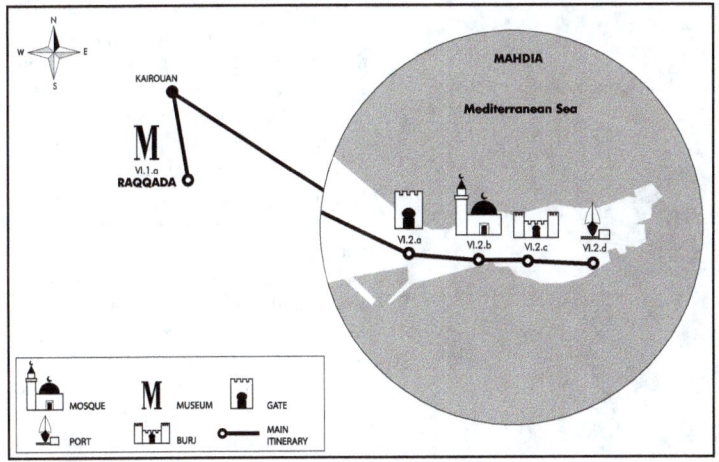

Window and wall fountain, Mahdia.

Raqqada and Mahdia constitute, alongside Sabra and al-'Abbassiya, the only Capitals in Tunisia to have been founded by princes between the arrival of Islam up to the present day. Their destinies differed, even though one was heir to the other, confirming the definite influence exerted by the geopolitical context on the evolution of Ifriqiyan princely towns in the Middle Ages. Raqqada was built in 262/876 by the Aghlabid Prince Ibrahim II in the Kairouanese suburbs, and was transformed into a holiday retreat equipped with grandiose hydraulic installations and luxurious palaces, remains of which still exist today. It reflects the relative symbiosis that existed between the Aghlabid Dynasty and the Kairouanese population. The town even lacked town walls at its inception, and was built within Ifriqiyan territory, thus betraying the continental, indeed Maghrebi, vision of the Aghlabids', who had just restored peace to the country. Furthermore, Raqqada constituted, on an architectural level, a continuation from the Kairouanese School, mainly in terms of architectural models and building materials – the use of fired brick and wooden beams – as well as in terms of decoration, through the creation of floral and geometric motifs carved in stucco. The foundation of Mahdia, in 308/921, proved fatal to Raqqada and spurred its decline. It was born as the fruit of the new political-spiritual context within which Ifriqiya evolved during the 3rd–4th/beginning of the 10th century. More precisely, surrounded by an atmosphere of Sunnite hostility, the Fatimid Caliph, belonging to the Shi'ite faith, sought refuge on a nearby rocky island off the eastern coast of Tunisia, where he erected the fortress of Mahdia, intended to fend off all dangers. In contrast to Raqqada, the founding of Mahdia marked a rupture between the reigning dynasty and the Ifriqiyans, but, simultaneously, it revealed the Fatimids' ambitious gaze eastward, and, after the Fatimid fleet imposed itself as the most powerful of the Mediterranean, it denoted the start of Tunisia's maritime age. It followed that Mahdia became the Maghreb's most important stronghold. It was supplied with terrestrial and maritime ramparts, a port, and two naval dockyards, that would later gain reputations of "pirate niches" and would bring about the wrath, aimed against the town, of the Spanish Armada during the middle of the 10th/16th century. Mahdia's military architecture is similar to that of the neighbouring *ribat* towns, but the town's urban morphology

Medina, facade, Mahdia.

ITINERARY VI   *The Towns of the Princes*

View of the Great Mosque from the coast, Mahdia.

also reflects the Shi'ite beliefs of its founders.

Raqqada, the Aghlabid Capital and heir to al-'Abbassiya, was founded in 262/876, 9 km. south-east of Kairouan. Worried by the presence of an agitated and violent population, and wanting to surround himself with a hefty army, Ibrahim II built his new town in a green plain, reputed for its clean, healthy air, as he suffered from depression. In the same year that he moved, he built a sumptuous palace called the Palace of Victory, *Qasr al-Fath*. From then on, the town did not stop growing, and sources confirm the presence of several other palaces including the Palace of the Courtyard, *Qasr al-Sahn*, the Palace of the Sea or of the Lake, *Qasr al-Bhar*, and the Palace of Baghdad, *Qasr Baghdad*. There, one comes across a mosque, *hammam*s, *caravanserais* and *suq*s, all essential elements of a veritable city. Ziyadat Allah III built a protective enclosure around it, the perimeter of which al-Bakri claims as being over 10 km. Several cisterns were constructed to supply the town with drinking water as well as with water for the numerous gardens and orchards surrounding its castles.

Following Ziyadat Allah III's departure in 296/909, the town was pillaged by the Kairouanese over several days and the Aghlabid Palaces were stripped bare, but the arrival of al-Mahdi breathed life into it for a second time, and for a further 12 years Raqqada remained the Capital of a Fatimid Caliphate that spread from Cyrenaica, a province of Libya, to the Atlantic before relinquishing its position to Mahdia in 308/921. The departure of al-Mahdi had dire consequences on the town, which fell into a state of apathy. Disbelieving what certain authors have written on the hateful destruction of Raqqada led by the Caliph al-Mu'izz, it appears that the town trans-

173

ITINERARY VI The Towns of the Princes
Raqqada

*The Museum,
view of the entrance,
Raqqada.*

formed itself into a residential suburb and thus lost all economic and political significance, even though the Zirid Prince al-Mansur sojourned there in 374/985 before moving into his new palace at Sabra. The final straw came in the form of the Hilalian invasions, which took place during the middle of the $5^{th}/11^{th}$ century: the conquerors completely devastated and pillaged the town. The rising levels of the rivers and the damage done by surreptitious searchers ended in the carrying off and destroying what was left of its remains.

VI.1 **RAQQADA**

VI.1.a **Museum of Raqqada**

Raqqada is about 7km. away from Kairouan on the way to Sfax.

Drive along the enclosure of the ancient palace, which has been converted into a museum, until you reach the vehicle entrance. Entrance fee. Opening times: 09.30–16.30. Closed Mondays. Parking and toilet facilities are available.

Whilst the second section of the museum is awaiting completion, several rooms have already been opened to the public.
The ceramics' room is distinct for the variety of its collection, which brings together objects that have come mainly from archaeological digs on the sites of Raqqada – the Aghlabid Capital during the $3^{rd}/9^{th}$ century – and Sabra al-Mansuriya, the Fatimid and Zirid Capital during the $4^{th}/10^{th}$–$5^{th}/11^{th}$ century. Several beautiful specimens of Egyptian, Syrian and Iranian (Persian) ceramics add to, and embellish, the exhibition. The Kairouanese potter, certainly inspired by Berber decorations, demonstrates his rich and creative imagi-

ITINERARY VI *The Towns of the Princes*
Raqqada

nation through the creation of clever compositions in which stereotyped flora and timeless fauna are mixed together, interwoven or placed next to geometric patterns.

The medals' room presents an exhaustive display of Islamic money in Tunisia. This display allows one to follow its evolution and its typology during a period of over 1000 years. Generally genuine in worth, the Ifriqiyan *dinar* has seen its weight vary from 4.25g. – in accordance with official metrology of the Aghlabid, Fatimid and Zirid periods – to 4.76g. during the Hafsid period. A map showing the main centres of coin stamping is also displayed within this window.

The money collection is exhibited in chronological order, divided into dynasties:
— Aghlabid coinage, which was minted and stamped along the lines of eastern models, is characterised by the presence of the sovereign emblem, the *ghalaba*. It also carries the name of the prince and, in certain cases, the name of the servant, *mawla*.
— Fatimid coinage reflects the Shi'ite religious beliefs of the new masters of Ifriqiya, and changed in appearance when al-Mu'izz came to power (341/953): the number of circles that figure is brought to three, on the right and on the reverse, and its features become more obviously Shi'ite. Fatimid money was greatly sought after during the Middle Ages, denoting a flourishing economy.
— Zirid coinage: the Zirid princes did not implement any changes to Fatimid coinage, they just added their names to it. But in 440/1049, al-Mu'izz Ibn Badis repudiated his allegiance to the Fatimids and proceeded to change the coinage through incorporating Qur'anic verses extolling his return to Sunnism.

— Almohad and Hafsid money differs from the rest in terms of shape, a square inscribed within a circle, its diameter, ranging from 26–31mm., and weight, ranging from 4.61 to 4.76g. Its form reflects the Almohad and Sunnite creed, which states that the Mahdi is the Caliph of God.

Finally, the dome room houses the crowns of light that once served to illuminate the Great Mosque of Kairouan. Dating from the $4^{th}/10^{th}$ to the beginning of the $5^{th}/11^{th}$ century, this extremely rare collection presents a sort of analogy to earlier Coptic chandeliers, but the crosses here take a floral and heart-shaped form, marking a change within the faith.

Lastly, a variety of other collections are exhibited in the museum.

Most of the glass objects originate from two fortuitous discoveries made on the site of Sabra al-Mansuriya in 1922 and 1983.

The weights and measuring tools presented next to a modest panel of general informa-

Pottery with decorative calligraphy, Museum of Raqqada.

ITINERARY VI *The Towns of the Princes*
Mahdia

tion date from the $2^{nd}/8^{th}$ to the $4^{th}/10^{th}$ century and were used to set the monetary standard and to weigh pharmaceutical products. An interesting collection of lead weights, discovered on the site of Raqqada, dating from the end of the Aghlabid period and from the beginning of al-Mahdi's reign (end of $3^{rd}/9^{th}$–beginning of $4^{th}/10^{th}$ century), constitutes evidence of the highest scientific importance on Ifriqiyan metrology of the Middle Ages. The weights are engraved with a *kufic* inscription carrying the name of the reigning prince or his *qadi*, and calling for equity and generosity.

The Qur'an room holds a display of parchments from Kairouan. It consists of one of the most important and most famous collections of parchments of the Muslim world. This collection was put together through the use of endowments, *habus*, donated to the Great Mosque of Kairouan. The specimens on display cover a period that extends from the end of the $2^{nd}/8^{th}$ century to the middle of the $5^{th}/11^{th}$ century. It allows one to trace the development of calligraphy and gilding, illumination, binding and writing techniques employed in Ifriqiya for over three centuries. Writing, which was generally done in *kufic* script, evolved to give birth to a Maghrebi *kufic* script (window display 2), *rayhani* (windows 3 and 4), represented most eloquently by the Qur'an of Fatima, the wet-nurse, *al-hadina*, of the Zirid prince Badis. This Qur'an was written using diacritical signs, and was then gilded and bound by 'Ali, son of Ahmad al-Warraq the librarian, in 412/1022. The diacritical signs are generally highlighted, according to an elaborate system conceived by Abu al-'Aswad in the $1^{st}/7^{th}$ century, by using red dots, in line with the Iraqi method (windows 5 and 2), or by using multicoloured dots in line with the Andalusian method.

VI.2 MAHDIA

Leave from Kairouan on the al-Djem, then head towards Ksur Essaf and Mahdia.

The growing hostility of the Sunnite Kairouanese in opposition to the Shi'ite Doctrine, coupled with the various different rebellions that kept rising up all over the Maghreb, resulted in al-Mahdi's decision, in 301/914, to seek a suitable site for the foundation of a town-refuge. Furthermore, the *caliph*'s designs on the East – focused on the conquering of Baghdad, the capital of the Abbasid "usurpers", in view of dominating the Muslim world by right – were not inconsistent with the final choice of a site on the eastern shores of Ifriqiya. The site of Mahdia presented ideal guarantees for the security of a dynasty that was heir to an important naval fleet and that dominated a central area of the Mediterranean. Built on a spur rising 1,400 m. above sea level, the town was impenetrable if approached by land. Only 25 years after its foundation in 303/916, it was put to a hard test. Indeed, after having devastated the whole of the Ifriqiya, Abu Yazid, the "man on the donkey", took siege of Mahdia in 329/941. The Fatimid Caliphate was at a hair's breadth from losing its position of power, and found its saving grace in Mahdia's defences. Having crushed the revolt, al-Mansur built a new capital at Sabra. Nevertheless, Mahdia continued to be the fleet's naval base, and the central pivot of Maghrebi maritime commerce. Its port constituted a point of departure for Kairouan in the exportation of oil and textile goods towards the East and Sicily. Mahdia rediscovered its role as Capital of a tiny principality following the

ITINERARY VI *The Towns of the Princes*
Mahdia

Hilalian invasions that had forced al-Mu'izz Ibn Badis to seek refuge there in 448/1057, face-to-face against the assaults perpetrated by Christian fleets. In 479/1087, the Pisans and Genoans became the masters of Mahdia, burning and pillaging the suburb of Zawila. The fratricide struggle between the Zirids and the Hammadites, who took siege of Mahdia in 528/1134, weakened the town's resistance against the Normans, who succeeded in enslaving it in 542/1148. The town was liberated by 'Abd al-Mu'min Ibn 'Ali in 555/1160, during his campaign to reconquer Ifriqiya. The end of the 6th/12th century proved to be a turbulent one for the population of Mahdia, following the Revolt led by the Town Governor against the central Almohad Authority in 595/1199. In the 7th/13th century, Mahdia returned to a state of relative prosperity thanks to the development of its trade with Italian towns, and to pirateering, which provoked the exasperated Christians to mount a Crusade against the town in 792/1390. Despite the failure of the expedition, Mahdia had to pay a ransom and a tribute for a further 15 years. In the 10th/16th century, Mahdia was stage to various conflicts between the Turks and the Spanishs over Western Mediterranean supremacy. The Ra'is Dragut succeeded in seizing Mahdia in 951/1545, and turned it into a Port of Registry for his fleet which spread terror along the Christian coastlines. These misdemeanours provoked a strong reaction from Charles Quint, whose Admiral, André Doria, prevailed in penetrating the town following a memorable siege. In 961/1554, the Spanish abandoned the town, having attacked its maritime ramparts with canon-gun powder. From then on, the town played but a secondary role in the country's history.

Sqifa al-Kahla, Mahdia.

VI.2.a **The Sqifa al-Kahla**

Take the "rue des Martyrs", the gate faces the Town Council building.

From the solid terrestrial and maritime fortifications that al-Mahdi provided his Capital with, only the Sqifa al-Kahla and several large pieces of rubble remain, scattered along the banks of this peninsula, reminders of a past splendour. In terms of terrestrial fortifications, the hefty wall, which blocked off and steered the isthmus was 175 m. in length and over 10 m. in width; it was flanked by six towers. Textual sources tell us that the entrance to Mahdia consisted of two gigantic gates that featured statues of lions. The present Sqifa al-Kahla seems to be the last small fort in this defence system; it was certainly revised after the destruction of the

ITINERARY VI   *The Towns of the Princes*
Mahdia

The Great Mosque, detail of the mihrab, Mahdia.

town's ramparts by the Spanish in 961/ 1554. These revisions no doubt date from the 12th/18th century. The facade, whose height exceeds 11 m., features two projecting polygonals to allow for pieces of artillery, placed at the top of the fort, to undertake side shots and cross-fires. The relatively squat entrance is surmounted by an arch the tympanum of which features rosettes and a crest, the emblem of the Turks. It dates from the 12th/18th century. The gate leads into a single hall covered in barrel vaults. The median section is covered by a groin vault; this corridor is elongated over a length exceeding 44 m. Access to the floors above can be found on the eastern side. On the first floor, there are gun posts directed towards the *medina*, and a central shooting gallery flanked by two guard rooms, one of which is bricked up. Little remains of the maritime rampart. A section of Fatimid wall and the ruins of a rectangular tower can be found remaining on the southern side.

Towards the tip of the African headland stands a tower that cannot date from before the 5th/11th century. The groove cut out of the rock in which to lay the foundations of the maritime ramparts gives an approximate idea of its width, which varied from 2.5 m. along the isthmus to the port, to only 1.5 m. in other places. The height of these walls did dot exceed 3 m. Everything points to the belief that the Fatimids feared an attack overland rather than one launched from the sea. They appeared to have confidence in their naval fleet.

VI.2.b **The Great Mosque**

From the Sqifa al-Kahla, follow the "rue 'Ubad Allah al-Mahdi" until you reach "place Kadi Noamene".

The Great Mosque of Mahdia was built by the Caliph al-Mahdi. Both it and the Audit

ITINERARY VI   *The Towns of the Princes*
Mahdia

Department were built on embankments, encroaching on the sea to the south of the peninsula. This mosque was subject to various modifications. It was completely rebuilt between 1961 and 1965 by the French architect, A. Lezine, who re-established the basic plan of the mosque as it had been in the 4th/10th century. Even though the accuracy of this plan is based on scientific evidence, it nevertheless remains the case that only the porch and north gallery are authentic: everything else has been completely renewed. The Great Mosque is nearly perfectly rectangular; it is 75 m. long by 55 m. wide, following a 3:2 ratio. It is flanked by two round towers that were once used to retrieve water from the terraces. It is probable that at a certain time in history these towers were supplied with water from the aqueduct, which carried the water from the underground sources of Miyyanish, situated 6 km. from Mahdia, to as far as the al-Mahdi Palace. The mosque does not seem to have ever had a minaret: the call to prayer was no doubt carried out from the top of one of these towers. The main entrance, which is fronted by a projecting porch, is the first of its kind to be seen in Maghrebi religious architecture. The porch, harmoniously proportioned, is surmounted by a semi-circular horseshoe arch flanked at the level of the upper register by niches in the shape of *mihrab*s. Below, the different wall-faces feature flat niches. These decorative elements already existed in the Aghlabid architectural repertoire, as shown in the minaret and *mihrab* dome of the Great Mosque of Kairouan, but it was the first time that they were used in the ornamentation of the facades belonging to an Ifriqiyan mosque. This decor, which served as a model for future Fatimid monuments, pre-empted the decor of the Zirid period, essentially affirmed by the Qubba bin al-Qhawui and by the lateral facade of the Great Mosque of Sfax. This porch recalls, and owes its allure to Roman Triumphal arches. Galleries surround the courtyard on all four sides. The presence of a portico preceding the prayer room is in itself an innovation with respect to earlier Ifriqiyan mosques. The north portico, whose pillars support curbed arches covered in groin vaults, dates from the 5th/11th century. The prayer room is composed of nine lateral naves and three bays; its plan has been visibly influenced by that of the Great Mosque of Kairouan; only the dome rests on polygonal pillars, used for the first time in Ifriqiya.

The Great Mosque of Mahdia has inspired certain Egyptian Fatimid mosques, in particular the Mosque of al-Hakim and the Mosque of al-Aqmar in Cairo. This monument owes its beauty to the simplicity of its forms, the candour of its openly visible materials, the absence of all superfluous decoration, and the harmonious unity of all its parts.

Columns belonging to the Great Mosque, Mahdia.

ITINERARY VI   *The Towns of the Princes*
Mahdia

VI.2.c **Burj al-Kebir**

On leaving the mosque, take the path on the right, which runs alongside the sea until you reach the monument. Opening times: 09.30–16.30 from 16th September–31st March, and from 09.00–12.00 and 14.00–18.00 the rest of the year. Parking and toilets are available.

This *burj* seems to have been built on the ruins of the palace belonging to the Fatimid Caliph al-Mahdi. The fortress as it stands is the result of several repair and rebuilding works. At the end of the 10th/16th century, it was still a rectangular building. The great bastions flanking the corners are no younger than 12th/18th century, no doubt dating from the period of Ibrahim Sharif Pasha who, according to the historian al-Wazir al-Sarraj, proceeded to carry out works on Mahdia's citadel in 1115/1704. One enters the fort via the south-western bastion; a slightly angled passageway leads to the entrance gate whose lintel and *piedroits* are decorated with stone-sculpted rosettes. A commemorative plaque engraved in beautiful *naskhi* writing mentions the construction date of the primitive, small fort: 1004/1596. This gate opens out onto a vast, barrel-vaulted hallway, modelled on the Sqifa al-Kahla. The hallway is broken up by a series of niches the function of which is not clear, unless they were used for illuminating lamps. At the end of the passage is a large reception room that was completely renovated during the colonial era. An elbow-shaped passage leads into the courtyard that is furnished with a small, very simple oratory. A staircase runs up to the first floor, which has many outbuildings, including a T-shaped room that must have belonged to the Commander of the place.

Burj al-Kebir, corner bastion, Mahdia.

ITINERARY VI   *The Towns of the Princes*
                    Mahdia

Quay of the inland port, Mahdia.

The corner bastions incorporate platforms on which to hold large pieces of artillery. These bastions offer a superb panoramic view over the peninsula and the neighbouring cemetery. A bas-relief can be found on the south-western bastion, adorned with a lion surmounted by an *arbalistraria*, or arrow loop. This decoration appears to be very old, and to have been re-used. It looks as if it is a Fatimid design. Indeed, the texts mention that the town of Mahdia was founded under the zodiac sign of the lion, which featured as a symbol on the gates of its terrestrial ramparts.

VI.2.d The Inland Port

The port is below the Burj.

Even though Fatimid sources attribute the inland port of Mahdia to the Caliph al-Mahdi, it seems that this port, tailored and cut into the rockface, was successor to an ancient Punic port that was completely covered over in sand. Al-Mahdi would have gone ahead with its enlargement and its rebuilding. The channel, 15 m. long, which gave access to the port, was defended by two towers linked together by a thick chain. The base of these towers, their lower structures reinforced with column shafts, still exists today. An opening bored out of the side parallel to the entrance allowed sea water to flow in and out. The basin, practically rectangular in form (126 m. x 657 m.) could, according to al-Bakri, contain up to 30 vessels. The port had its own ramparts from the time of al-Mahdi onwards, of which only a few remains still exist in the south, consisting of a redan wall that deserves to be pulled down. The inland port of Mahdia belongs to the same family of protected (*Marsa Ma'mun*) Maghrebi basins: those of Sousse (3rd/9th century), of Bougie (6th/12th century), of Salé (7th/13th century) and of Honaïn in Algeria (8th/14th century).

TUNISIAN MANUSCRIPTS

Mourad Rammah

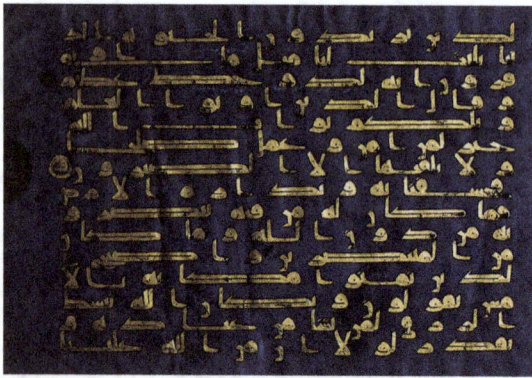

The blue Qur'an, blue parchment, kufic script.

Ifriqiya, one of the great centres of Arab-Muslim culture, contributed to the propagation of the Qur'an, and of all the manuscript techniques, thanks to the involvement of its scholars, calligraphers and bookbinders. A love for scholarship and learning soon implanted itself in Ifriqiya. The *Bayt al-Hikma*, built in Raqqada during the Aghlabid era, and then in Sabra at the time of the Fatimids, contributed, along with the mosques and *ribats*, to the perpetuation of knowledge and bookish techniques. Documents from the ancient Synagogue of Genizah in Cairo confirm irrefutably that Ifriqiya, during the $4^{th}/10^{th}$ and $5^{th}/11^{th}$ centuries, was an important centre of book production, exporting its manuscripts to Egypt, Syria and Spain. *'Umdat al-Kuttab wa 'Uddat Dhawi al-'Albab*, written by a Kairouanese in the 4th–5th/beginning of 11th century in honour of the Zirid Prince al-Mu'izz Ibn Badis, constitutes a first-class reference to the techniques of calligraphy, on the components of inks and colours, as well as on gilding.

The Hilalian invasions proved to be a fatal blow to this spirited enterprise. However, the arrival of Andalusian refugees brought new life to literary and artistic creativity, which favoured unity between Maghrebi cultural elements and the renaissance of book production under the Hafsids: schools, such as the *suq* Madrasa of *al-Shamma'in*, proliferated and brought craftsmen back together again. The Hafsid Princes encouraged this spiritual trend and built themselves libraries, like al-Mustansir bi-Allah. But the Spanish, settling in Tunis at the start of the $10^{th}/16^{th}$ century, ransacked and burnt down its manuscript treasures. Later on, the Husaynite *beys*, no doubt influenced by the spirit of the European Renaissance, created new libraries, like those of the 'Abdelliya and of the Sadiqiya in the Zituna, to which they added the Ahmadiya at the beginning of the 20th century. The latter contains manuscripts from the Pasha Mosque in the Bardo, as well as books belonging to Hassan Mamluk, to Shaykh Ibrahim al-Riyani, to the *vizier* Mustapha Khaznadar, and to the historian Ahmad Ibn Abi Diaf. Since the Byzantine era, writing on parchment was the most widespread in Ifriqiya. This lasted until the $8^{th}/14^{th}$ century, at least for the writing of the Qur'an, and until modern times for marriage and property certificates. The use of paper was rare, and only became more popular during the Hafsid era, when it was used mostly for works of science. The production of parchment went through various stages, consisting of *ebourrage*, polishing and hide tanning. The finishing itself obeys certain rules: for the Qur'anic text, the hides that have been sanded down best are chosen, in particular for the centre part of the parchments which in general were without fault. The rest, especially the hides ruined by the tanner's knife or through *ebourrage* imperfections, were used instead for the writing of legal texts and legislative acts. Cotton fibre was the main component used for the production of paper, although the Ifriqiyans do not seem to have excelled in this field. The ornamentation of Ifriqiyan manuscripts is demonstrated most eloquently through the collection of parchments belonging to the library of the Great Mosque of Kairouan, and through the paper manuscripts of the National Library of Tunis. The genius of the calligraphers and gilders continued to be seen up to the Hafsid period, essentially through the production of the Qur'an; it is only later that interest grew in the ornamentation of *hadith* books, and it is only since the modern age that books on other branches of knowledge, such as the martial arts, astronomy and cartography have attracted similar interest. The most ancient dated Qur'an, from the Kairouan collection, goes back to the year 294/907. The form these particular editions of the Qur'an take is usually oblong; their ornamentation originally distinguished the title of the *sura* through the use of a different colour from the ordinary black writing. Since the end of the $3^{rd}/9^{th}$ century, this title, which came to be written in gold, has been underlined by a platform ending in a palmette that runs into the margin. During the $4^{th}/10^{th}$ century and $5^{th}/11^{th}$ century, frontispieces and illuminations decorated with geometric and floral forms begin to appear, occupying a whole page of the Qur'an. Another means of ornamentation, more elegant and costly, consists in tracing the outlines of letters using a fine-nibbed feather pen. Following that, the calligrapher goes over each letter with gold ink. Since the Hafsid era, Ifriqiyan ornamentation, while in keeping within the same genres, was influenced by the Hispano-Moresque repertoire, formed essentially of pure geometric shapes, hexagons and stars. Up until the Hafsid period, the dominant script in Ifriqiya was *kufic*. However, from the end of the $4^{th}/10^{th}$ century, the form of this script was transgressed through the rounding of letters in order to lessen and smooth down their angular and rigid appearance. This technique gave birth to a Kairouanese style that was a prelude to Maghrebi cursive script. Ibn Khaldun notes that it was this calligraphy that was used most commonly in Ifriqiya until the $6^{th}/12^{th}$ century. Following the capture of Seville, Ifriqiyan calligraphy was abandoned in favour of an Andalusian style, introduced by the Andalusian calligraphers who sought refuge in Tunisia. This script was used in various different Ifriqiyan manuscripts until the modern age. Despite the evolution of calligraphic writing, the Qur'an continued to be written, up until the 4th–5th/beginning of the 11th century, according to the ancient method developed by Abu al-Aswad al-Duali (68/688) and these editions were characterised by the use of diacritic dots to indicate vowels. The system devised by Abu al-Khalil Ahmad, used today, only appeared for first time in Ifriqiya in 409/1019, in the *Qur'an* of the Hadida belonging to the Zirid Prince Badis.

Qur'anic manuscript, vellum, Kairouanese kufic script called "rayhani".

ITINERARY VII

The *Ribat* Towns

Mourad Rammah

VII.1 MONASTIR
VII.1.a The Ribat
VII.1.b Sidi al-Ghedamsi Ribat (option)

VII.2 LEMTA
VII.2.a The Ribat (option)

VII.3 SOUSSE
VII.3.a The Ribat
VII.3.b The Great Mosque
VII.3.c Al-Zaqqaq Madrasa
VII.3.d Qubba bin al-Qhawi
VII.3.e Sidi 'Ali 'Ammar Mosque
VII.3.f Buftata Mosque
VII.3.g The Kasbah and the Ramparts

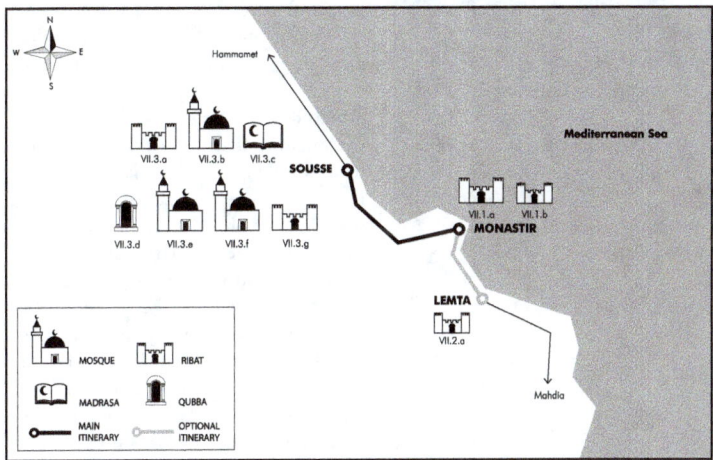

The Ribat, Monastir.

ITINERARY VII   *The* Ribat *Towns*

Monastir

The assaults of the Byzantine fleet along the coast following the Muslim Conquest forced the Ifriqiyans to build a continuous line of defence consisting of fortresses called *ribat*s. They rose along the coastline from Tangier to Alexandria and communicated via the use of fires lit up at the top of the towers. The *ribat*s served as a refuge for the inhabitants of the surrounding countryside and were lived in by warrior monks. The prolonged stays and visits of the most illustrious Ifriqiyan scholars, jurisconsults and ascetics reinforced the spiritual prestige of these buildings, transforming them into veritable monastery-fortresses and centres of learning that transmitted Arab-Muslim culture along the north coast of North Africa. The proximity of Sousse and Monastir to Kairouan, as well as their strategic positions as frontline watch towers defending the capital, meant that they possessed a military role of the first order. Their *ribat*s gained an utterly unique renown and became the core for future urban developments. Their dual military and religious purpose were reflected in their robust and austere architecture, characterised by the use of stone and vaults made of rubble and the banishment of wood coverings and light structures. This type of architecture spread across the whole of the Tunisian Sahel, and Sousse and Monastir became the two *ribat*-towns *par excellence*.

Whilst all making reference to the same school of architecture, they nevertheless each underwent a slightly different evolution. Sousse became in the 3rd/9th century the headquarters of the Aghlabid fleet and the most important naval military base, which was involved in the Conquest of Sicily in 211/827, as well as being the crucible of Mediterranean commerce, all without losing its appeal to Islamic scholars, some of whom preferred it to all other bastions of Islam.

Monastir's evolution took a more spiritual turn, and became, during the Middle Ages, a place of pilgrimage during religious festivals, and there are still many Sahelians, especially the Mahdians, who wish to bury their dead in its blessed earth. In fact, the evolution of Sousse and Monastir complemented each other perfectly, incarnating the whole dialectic of the spirit of the *ribat*.

Situated at the far end of the headland, the antique Ruspina derives its name from the Punic "Rus Penna", which into Latin translates as *Caput Anguli*, a name justified by the very marked corner that forms the coastline on this site. This headland was an ideal place from which to defend the coastline, thus explaining the Abbasid Governor Harthama Ibn A'yun's choice, in 178/795, of it as a site on which to build his model *ribat*, a type imported from the East. The passion Ifriqiyan

The Ribat, interior courtyard, Lemta.

ITINERARY VII The Ribat Towns
Monastir

scholars and ascetics felt for such institutions facilitated the population of this new *qsar* and, during the 2nd–3rd/first half of the 9th century, several *ribat*s were built in Monastir, such as the Ibn al-Ja'ad Ribat, and the Dhuayib Ribat in 239/854. Overtaken first by Sousse, which became the Aghlabid naval base, and then by Mahdia which became the Fatimid Capital, Monastir had to content itself, throughout the Middle Ages, with its essentially spiritual role, becoming a place of pilgrimage, a *ribat*, and one of the bastions of orthodoxy to face the Shi'ite challenge. Nevertheless, the town continued to grow, and was described by al-Bakri, writing in the middle of the 5th/11th century, as follows: " ... *it is a vast fortress, extremely high, enclosing a considerably large suburb. At the heart of this suburb, one sees a second, very large fortress, full of lodgings, mosques and castles with several floor levels. In this secure and powerful place one discovers a great number of baths. Not long ago, the inhabitants of Kairouan donated large amounts of money and charity to it. Close to al-Monastir is a huge salt marsh that provides ships with cargoes of salt intended for export to other countries. Al-Monastir has, within its area, five* mahri*s, built very solidly, which are inhabited by pious people".* Monastir does not seem to have suffered from the Hilalian invasions in the same way that Kairouan did, and al-Idrissi reports that, during the middle of the 6th/12th century, *"Mahdia had neither gardens nor orchards. Neither did it have palm trees. Fruits are brought in from Monastir ... Monastir"*, he continues, *"consists of three fortresses grouped together, full of devout inhabitants. The Arabs (Hilalians) do not cause damage to their orchards, nor to their plan-*

Ruins of the Ribat of Sidi al-Ghedamsi, Monastir.

tations. The inhabitants of Mahdia use small boats to transport their dead to Monastir where they are buried". The exodus of Muslims from Sicily following the Norman Conquest, followed by the exodus of the Kairouanese, contributed to the growing urbanisation of the town. It seems that even when Mahdia was seized by the Normans in 542/1148, Monastir managed to escape this fate and served as a refuge for the Mahdians. Without doubt, it is from this time onwards that one can date Monastir's extension and the birth of one of its suburbs. The decline of Kairouan followed by that of Mahdia, during the Hafsid era, led to the decadence of Monastir, which folded back onto itself and continued to grow stagnant. Leo the African, who visited Monastir at the start of the 10th/16th century, describes it thus: *"It is surrounded by forts and high walls. The houses within it have also been built with an equal amount of care. One thing is for certain and that is that the inhabitants are*

ITINERARY VII   The Ribat *Towns*
Monastir

The Ribat, facade looking over the courtyard, Monastir.

poor ... Within Monastir, a great number of properties are planted with fruit trees such as apricot trees, fig trees, apple trees, pomegranate trees and an infinite number of olive trees. But the sovereign cripples the town with taxes". In fact, Monastir would end up by revolting against the Hafsid Sultan Mulay Hassan, who became an ally of the Spanish. Between 945/1539 and 955/1549, the town was sacked several times by the naval fleets of Charles Quint, lead by André Doria. In the 10th–11th/end of 16th century, it was conquered by the Turks. In the Muradite era, during struggles between the two Murad brothers, Monastir sided with Mohamed, who took refuge there in 1091/1680. Throughout the modern era, Monastir regained its strength, becoming a centre for the transmission of Sufism and asceticism.

VII.1 MONASTIR

Take the coastal route towards Sousse.

VII.1.a The Ribat

This monument is situated on the coast road. Entrance fee. Opening times: 08.3–17.30 from 16th September–31st March, and from 08.00–19.00 the rest of the year. Closed Mondays. On-site parking. Toilets available.

The *ribat* was built in 178/795–179/796 by the Abbasid General Harthama Ibn A'yun, and underwent various enlargements throughout the ages. Originally, in its first stage of construction, the *ribat* was composed of a rectangular enclosure with towers in each corner. In the south-east corner rose a high cylindrical minaret that made reference to Mesopotamian influences. Inside, the courtyard was surrounded by porticoes onto the which the rooms looked out. The prayer hall, on the first floor, was composed of two bays and seven naves, the axial nave being larger than the others. This architectural layout, applied for the first time to a prayer room, would become the norm for all Ifriqiyan mosques.

The architectural plan of Harthama's *ribat* would serve as the model for the main Ifriqiyan *ribat*s built along the coast in the 3rd/9th century. The north wing of this *ribat*, which must have had an area of 1,300 sq. m., was completely modified, and the monument underwent several enlargements of which four major stages can be marked out.

In the first stage, a pavilion, composed of a porch flanked by two columns supporting a semi-circular horseshoe arch, was added to the primitive entrance, separated by a small courtyard. This porch, recalling the one belonging to the Great Mosque of Mahdia (with hindsight), leads onto rooms covered in barrel vaults. On the first floor one found the prayer room composed of seven naves rhythmically divided by two bays and covered, with the exception of the central nave, by barrel vaults; the southern half of the median nave was covered by a surbased segmented sphere without squinches. Everything points to there once being a prayer room here whose *mihrab* was sealed up. Its architectural design evokes that of the early *ribat* which is situated along from it. This pavilion dates, according to a inscription in the Louvre, from the middle of the 4th/10th century; this succinct inscription refers to works carried out by Abu al-Qassim al-Tammar in 355/966, which seems to apply to this wing of the *ribat*. This pavilion, which would later serve as a *ribat* for women, is mentioned by al-Bakri in the middle of the 5th/11th century. This function explains why it was necessary to provide the *ribat* with a new gate, to separate the passage used by women from that of men. The present angled entrance of the *ribat* seems to date from this time. The decoration featured above its archway consists of five flat niches, surmounted by horseshoe arches topped by a floral frieze, an ornamental design characteristic of the Fatimid-Zirid style; one also finds it on the facade of the porch of the Great Mosque of Mahdia, on the east-facing facade of the Mosque of Sfax, and on the facade of the Sidi 'Ali 'Ammar Mosque.

The second phase of construction consisted of extending the north and east sides that dated from the Aghlabid era, an era that saw the consolidation of the monument via the building of square towers. Works undertaken in 827/1424, as indicated by a Hafsid commemorative plaque in *naskhi* script above the door of the angled entrance,

The Ribat, an upstairs room, Monastir.

increased the area of the fortress to 4,200 sq. m.

The third stage of the construction dates unquestionably from the era of Ibrahim Sharif Pasha in 1115/1704. It encompasses modifications undertaken on specific areas, such as the rebuilding of the east wing; turning the ground floor of the women's *ribat* into a prayer hall; adding polygonal towers to the north-west and south-east corners, as well as the circular tower of the north-east corner, all of which related to an armaments initiative.

The fourth stage, initiated by Hammuda Pasha (1195/1781–1228/1813) incorporated the building of a fortress and the decision of transferring students to the Zawiya of Sidi Dhuib. Similarly, Husayn Bey II restored and consolidated the *ribat* in 1250/1835. The bastions built at the north-east and south-east corners must date from this time. The lack of homogeneity in the appearance of the external walls of the fortress is due to the multiple consolidations staggered across the $11^{th}/17^{th}$ century and $13^{th}/19^{th}$ century.

Elsewhere, the prayer hall of the early *ribat* has housed a small museum of Islamic arts since 1959, whose exhibits include:

— a collection of funerary steles from Monastir that date from the $5^{th}/11^{th}$ century to the $9^{th}/15^{th}$ century, and whose inscriptions range from flowery *kufic* to *naskhi*.

— A collection of pieces of Egyptian textile, mainly Abbassid and Fatimid.

— Several Kairouanese works of bookbinding dating from the $4^{th}/10^{th}$ and $5^{th}/11^{th}$ centuries.

— Pages from Kairouanese and Egyptian copies of the Qur'an and manuscripts dating from the $4^{th}/10^{th}$ to the $12^{th}/18^{th}$ centuries.

Standing next to these latter exhibits are bronze objects, originating mostly from the Zirid and Fatimid eras, amongst which one can pick out a rare bronze chandelier from the Hafsid era, and Aghlabid and Fatimid ceramic plates.

VII.1.b Sidi al-Ghedamsi Ribat
(option)

One reaches the monument via the route of the marina. During 2001 the site was in the process of excavation.

Situated on an island which is now reattached to *terra ferma*, the *ribat* underwent various excavations that revealed the essence of the site, bringing to light its initial plan as well as the different phases of its extension. This island is named after a saint, originally from Ghdamas, who lived during the $4^{th}/10^{th}$ century, and who was buried on this site. The *ribat*, in fact, was erected in 257/871, by a wealthy Kairouanese, Ibn al-Ja'ad. Its construction reflects strategic considerations and demonstrates the necessity of securing more effective communications between the *ribat*s of the Monastir headland, through building a watchtower on the island situated at the tip of the headland. The monument was built on the remains of Roman villas and mosaics. It is a square-plan construction, each side measuring 22.5 m. in length. Flanked by four circular towers at each corner, the centres of the two north and south walls are consolidated by two square towers used as cisterns, recuperating water from the terraces. One can clearly see the hallway and ground-floor rooms through the entrance on the eastern side. It seems that this *ribat* consisted of only one floor level, like the *ribat* of Lamta.

The Bourguiba Mausoleum is an example of contemporary, elaborately decorated, Islamic art.

VII.2 LEMTA

The town is situated half-way between Ksar Hellal and Monastir.

Originally a Libyc-Punic agglomeration, *Leptimus* is mentioned for the first time in the 4th century BC Allied to Rome. During the third Punic War, in 146 BC, it benefited from the status of a "liberated town" following the defeat of Carthage. Elevated to colonial status by Trajan, it became the principal town of the regional area of *Leptiminensis*. After the Byzantine Conquest, it became the home base of the Byzantium military command. Its renaissance dates from the Aghlabid period: from a simple *ribat* that served as a refuge to fishermen, Lemta became one of the most important ports of Ifriqiya. Nevertheless, it was supplanted by Mahdia in the 3rd–4th/beginning of 10th century. Around Lemta there is a salt marsh that, according to al-Bakri, produced fine-quality salt.

VII.2.a **The Ribat** (option)

Entrance fee. In order to visit the ribat, you must first go to the municipal offices.
Opening times: weekdays from 08.30–13.00 and 14.00–17.45, Fridays and Saturdays from 08.30–13.00. Parking available in the small square.

It was built by the Aghlabid Prince Abu Ibrahim Ahmad, in 245/860, and is the prototype *ribat* for *ribats* with only one floor level. As opposed to Sousse and Monastir, which were important towns whose populations needed spacious fortresses in which to take refuge in case of an enemy attack, Lemta it seems was, during the 2nd–3rd/beginning of 9th century, a sparsely populated hamlet, which explains the difference between it and the *ribats* of Sousse and Monastir, the latter two being more sophisticated and endowed with more crucial defence systems. Indeed, the *ribat* of Lemta did not possess a watchtower but was flanked at each of its four corners by a tower. Its prayer hall is on the ground floor, on the south side. Its very simple entrance is made up of a squat semi-circular arch which constitutes direct access.

VII.3 SOUSSE

Take the coastal route again. until you reach Sousse.

Founded in the 2nd century BC by the Phoenicians to serve as a base for their trading ships in the western Mediterranean, Sousse experienced a remarkable boom during the Roman era, distinguishing itself as one of Africa's main cities. Nothing significant occurred during the Vandal period or the Byzantine period, and this also applied to the first Muslim period. Facing the supremacy of the Byzantine navy in the western Mediterranean as well as the anarchy that dominated Ifriqiya throughout the 2nd/8th century, the Muslims decided to retreat inland into the country, while Sousse, which was composed of numerous hamlets, lived under the protection of its *ribat*, a sort of fortress

Sousse

that served as a watchtower and refuge for its inhabitants. During the middle of the 2nd–3rd/beginning of 9th century, the Aghlabids succeeded in pacifying the country and becoming the new masters of the sea. They chose Sousse as their naval base and Ziyadat Allah I endowed it with a *kasbah* in 205/821 that encompassed the *ribat* and the naval dockyard where a military garrison were stationed; the whole compound was enclosed by a rampart. It was thus that Sousse was used as the departure point for the Conquest of Sicily in 211/827, reviving the conflict between the Aghlabids and the Byzantines, resulting in a series of clashes that have been well documented in historical sources. The threat of danger incited the Aghlabid princes to reinforce the defensive infrastructure of their base at which the most vicious assaults were aimed.

A new *kasbah* was built by Abu 'Abbas in 229/844; then, 15 years later, Abu Ibrahim Ahmed encircled the town with a freestone enclosure. Sousse then benefited from a time of relative peace, which favoured its growth and development. From being purely a military base, it rose to being one of the largest towns in Ifriqiya, serving Kairouan as the main maritime outlet.

Crafts were developed, particularly the weaving of fine materials, which was greatly admired abroad. The problem of supplying the town with drinking water was resolved through the rebuilding of the *sofra*, an ancient Roman cistern that had been turned into a prison during the Aghlabid period. A canal brings the water from the surrounding area to inside the town walls. The foundation of Mahdia in 304/917 by the Fatimid Caliph al-Mahdi, relegated Sousse to second place; Sousse suffered greatly under the siege imposed by the Kharijite Abu Yazid in 333/945.

Nevertheless, it was able to pick itself up again due to its ideal location in terms of the economic geography of Ifriqiya. Throughout its history, and depending on political fluctuations, Sousse sometimes developed in direct relation to inland areas, whilst at other times it developed completely separately from it, but it always counterbalanced itself with maritime activities.

The end of the 4th/10th century and the beginning of the 5th/11th were notably periods of great urban growth. However, this prosperity was abruptly halted by the arrival of the Hilalians who ransacked the country. Sousse's fate slipped through the hands of Jebara Ibn Kamel, an Arab Chief allied to the Zirids. Cut-off from the rest of the country, it retreated back into itself, surviving only thanks to its maritime commercial trading links with the other ports of the Mediterranean. Like many coastal towns, it was annexed by the Normans of Sicily and dwelled under their domination for 15 years, until the arrival of the Almohads in 555/1160.

During 7th/13th century, the town benefited from the great attention paid to it by the Hafsids, who endowed the town with several monuments. But when, in the 10th/16th century, the Sultan Mulay Hassan called on the Spanish to help him reclaim his throne, Sousse rose up against the invaders and endured severe damage following two punitive expeditions.

The Turks, in restoring peace to the country, reclaimed the town. The 11th/17th century was marked by two events. From within, Sousse was deeply shaken by internal struggles that afflicted first the brothers Mohamed and 'Ali Bey from 1085/1675 to 1097/1686, then Murad III and his cousin Ramdan who had taken refuge in Sousse only to be persecuted and decapitated there

ITINERARY VII   The Ribat *Towns*

Sousse

in 1110/1699. In the outside world, Sousse took part, as did most coastal towns, in privateering activities, rampant throughout the Mediterranean, and because of this was often the object of reprisals by European States, most notably France and Venice. In the 12th/18th century, during the rebellion of 'Ali Pasha in 1140/1728, Sousse sided with Husayn Ibn 'Ali's camp and was stage to various battles, until the final victory was won by the Husaynites in 1170/1757. In recognition of this, the Bey Mohamed accorded Sousse various rights and privileges. On the other hand, in the Revolt lead by 'Ali Ibn Ghdhahum during 13th/19th century, Sousse sided with the rebels. After this insurrection failed, General Ahmed Zarruk, sent by the *bey,* exercised a pitiful regime of repression over Sousse, whose importance suffered a continuous decline until the debarkation of the French troops in September 1881. By that time, it had been reduced to a town of merely 8,000 inhabitants.

The Ribat, corner tower, Sousse.

VII.3.a The Ribat

Leave your vehicle at the foot of the ramparts, on avenue Mhamed Ali, and walk about 100 m., via the "place des Martyrs".
Entrance fee. Opening times: 08.30–17.30 from 16th September until 31th March, and 08.00–19.00 the rest of the year. Parking available in the square.

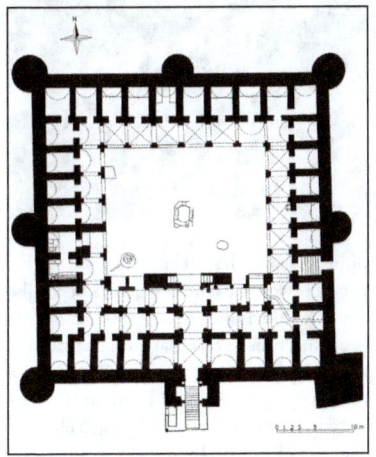

Plan of the Ribat of Sousse.

The *ribat* faces the Great Mosque. This monastery-fortress was no doubt founded towards the end of the 1st/beginning of the 8th century, but was completely rebuilt by Ziyadat Allah I at the heart of the Great Fortress, *al-Qasr al-Kabir*, which he had erected in 205/821. A garrison composed of about 50 warrior monks, who had avowed themselves to the *jihad*, lived there permanently. This in particular, gave the army base a dual character, one that was both military and religious, that was manifested through the austerity of the building, the crampedness of the rooms and the choice of layout. The *ribat*, square in shape measuring 36 m. on each side,

ITINERARY VII   The Ribat *Towns*
Sousse

The Great Mosque, kufic inscription mentioning the name of Mudam, Sousse.

entrances of the Abbasid palaces of Ukhaydir and Atshan, palaces that also heavily influenced the exterior architecture of Sousse's *ribat*. In all other respects, the *ribat* is a reproduction of the original plan of the Monastir Ribat founded by Harthama, the author of several similar military construction works found on the eastern front.

The *ribat*'s porch is surmounted by a defence feature consisting of a group of machicolations made of parallel stone openings or slits. Its pole-axes are surmounted by a domed kiosk on squinches, made of freestone, constituting the oldest specimen of its kind known to us. This allows for the study of the evolution of this prototype dome, which originated in the East, was adopted in Ifriqiya in the $2^{nd}/8^{th}$ century, and reached its maturity as the dome of the *mihrab* of the Great Mosque of Kairouan ($3^{rd}/9^{th}$ century). The dome of the Ribat of Sousse constitutes an intermediary stage in its evolution, as it demonstrates by the direct transformation from octagon to circular skullcap. From the porch, one enters a square hallway covered by a well-bonded groin vault, appearing to confirm the survival of certain Byzantine and Roman traditions. The central courtyard is surrounded by four galleries, covered by a series of barrel vaults, whose arcades rest on freestone pillars. The north and east wings, rebuilt in 1134/1722, are covered by groin vaults. The ground floor is composed of 33 cramped rooms, covered by barrel vaults made of rubble. One reaches the first floor via a staircase that leads onto a passage used by rooms on three of the sides; the fourth side houses the prayer hall. The latter consists of 11 naves and two bays. The wall of the *qibla*, the same wall as that of the rampart enclo-

built in stone, has been fitted out with a round tower in each corner except for the south-eastern one, where, instead, there is a square-base circular minaret of outstanding beauty. It was inspired by the prototype of Abbassid minarets that became popular across the Maghreb from the end of the $2^{nd}/8^{th}$ century. Semi-circular towers stand half-way across the walls except on the south side where there is a rectangular porch that precedes the sole entrance to the fort. This direct-access entrance, a form that preceded the elbow-shaped entrance which became common in defence buildings, appeared in Ifriqiya from the $3^{rd}/9^{th}$ century. The building's entrance seems to take after the sure, is pierced with arches: the worshippers could thus transform themselves at any moment to soldiers of war in order to defend the *ribat*.

There is not a single element that expresses more eloquently the mixed nature of the *ribat* than this: it is an institution that is both simultaneously religious and military. After the confrontation between the two Mediterranean shores had come to an end, and the techniques involved in warfare had evolved, the military role of the *ribat* ceased, and the essential purpose retained therein was that of the spiritual. Several *ribat*s were transformed into schools in which the religious sciences were taught; in fact, the architectural plan of *ribat*s directly inspired that of Tunisian *madrasa*s.

VII.3.b The Great Mosque

This is 100 m. south of the preceding monument. Entrance fee. Opening times: 08.00–13.00.

The Great Mosque of Sousse was built by the Aghlabid Prince Abu al-'Abbas Mohamed in 236/851. It is quadrilateral in form (59 m. x 51 m.) and is composed of a prayer hall which is preceded by a courtyard. The latter, greater in width than in depth (41 m. x 26 m.) bordered by porticoes along three sides, also dates from the Aghlabid period. The fourth portico, situated on the outside of the prayer hall, is a later addition which probably dates back to the $5^{th}/11^{th}$ century, but which was completely restored in 1085/1675.

Along the top of the portico's facade runs a *kufic* inscription mentioning the name of Mudam, the freed slave put in charge by the prince to supervise the work. This inscription is the oldest epigraphic frieze decorating the courtyard of a mosque to survive. Unlike the majority of Tunisian mosque-cathedrals, Sousse does not possess a minaret; this absence can be explained by the proximity of the *ribat*'s vigil tower. Nevertheless, the call to prayer was proclaimed from the top of the north-eastern tower, which is surmounted by a domed kiosk dating from the Zirid period ($5^{th}/11^{th}$ century).

The hypostyle room features 13 naves and six bays. It echoes the T-plan of the 'Uqba Mosque in terms of its median nave, which is larger than its lateral ones, and in terms of the dome in front of its *mihrab*, but differs from the 'Uqba Mosque in terms of its architecture. The naves are covered by rubble vaults rather than ceilings, which are reinforced by semi-circular beam arches, supported on robust pillars laid out in the plan of a cross. This prayer hall seems to have developed through three stages. It is probable that Abu al-'Abbas Mohamed proceeded to extend the oratory of Ziyadat Allah's kas-

The Great Mosque, prayer hall, Sousse.

ITINERARY VII   The Ribat Towns
Sousse

Al-Zaqqaq, courtyard, Sousse.

bah in order to obtain a room to accommodate 13 naves and three bays, covered by barrel vaults. The three bays at the back, covered by groin vaults, were added by Ibrahim II in 247/862. The *mihrab*, however, is from the Zirid era, as is attested to by the decoration of the semi-spherical dome, which consists of a series of niches with semi-circular backs and bands covered in flowery *kufic* inscription circling the columns that flank the *mihrab*. These architectural and decorative motifs are taken from the Zirid repertoire. The prayer hall is surmounted by two domes on the same line as the median nave. The Zirid dome, in front of the actual *mihrab*, is simple and austere; it is surmounted by a hemispherical skullcap dome placed directly on top of a square drum. The dome's interior reveals the use of squinches, devoid of all decoration, encircled by archivolts that are linked together by arcatures. The second dome, which preceded the *mihrab* of Abu al-'Abbas, and is situated on the same level as the fourth bay, as counted from the actual *mihrab*, echoes the construction principles of the Aghlabid domes of the Kairouanese school of architecture. The circular smooth skullcap sits on top of a an octagonal drum-base on scalloped squinches which fits within two arches resting on small protruding pillars, themselves supported by small corbels. Horseshoe drafted arches, the backs of which are pierced with openings, link the squinches together. An epigraphic band of *kufic* writing unravels itself above it. The entire piece is supported on sculpted tympanum featuring floral decorations inspired by the Kairouanese decorative repertoire.

ITINERARY VII   The Ribat *Towns*
Sousse

VII.3.c Al-Zaqqaq Madrasa

On exiting the mosque, turn left towards "rue Tazerka".

This monument consists of a cultural centre made up of a *madrasa*, a mosque and a funerary chamber. It derives its name from a pious man who lived during the $4^{th}/10^{th}$ century and who was buried in his own house which was later rebuilt as a *madrasa*. An entrance covered by a groin vault leads to a portico courtyard surrounded by students' rooms on three sides; the southern section was completely destroyed during the bombings of 1943. The mausoleum's dome, erected in the north-east corner, dates no doubt from the Husaynite era ($12^{th}/18^{th}$ century–$13^{th}/19^{th}$ century). Inside, the square drum features scalloped squinches at each corner, engraved within polyfoiled arches. The skullcap, made of pottery segments, is a form frequently seen in, and very common to, the Sahel region of Tunisia. An octagonal minaret, Ottoman in type ($12^{th}/18^{th}$ century), rises up in the north-west corner; it is composed of three registers of flat niches, graced with polyfoil arches which are clad in *faience* tiles. It dates from the $12^{th}/18^{th}$ century.

VII.3.d Qubba bin al-Qhawi

Go down "rue Sidi Bouraoui" until you reach the covered passageway of "rue Mustapha Rezam" which ends on reaching the monument. The Bin al-Qhawi Qubba houses the museum of Popular Arts and Traditions of Sousse and its surroundings.
Entrance fee. Opening times: 09.000–13.00 and 15.00–17.30. Sundays open from 10.00–14.00. Closed Fridays. Toilet facilities available.

This very unusual and bizarre building dates from the $5^{th}/11^{th}$ century. It was most probably a funerary monument that contained the tomb of a religious or political personality of the town. The entrance porch consists of a drafted rectangular gate, surmounted by a sculpted, scalloped cut-out of a polyfoiled arch, opening out into three horseshoe archivolts framed by a serrated cornice. Flat or semi-cylindrical niches furnish the corner stones. On the right, eight niches in the shape of a *mihrab* embellish the facade of the external wall, above which rises the dome. This decor cannot but recall the lateral facade of the Great Mosque of Sfax of the Zirid period (end of $4^{th}/10^{th}$ century).
The inside of the building is composed of a square room covered by a vault with fluting

Qubba bin al-Qhawi, dome with zig-zagging furrows, Sousse.

197

ITINERARY VII *The* Ribat *Towns*
Sousse

Sidi 'Ali 'Ammar Mosque, facade, Sousse.

that radiates outwards. Archivolt squinches in the form of a scallop shell establish the transition between the dome and its square base. Triple archivolt recesses link the squinches to each other. One will note the evident analogy between this dome and the funerary monument called Qubba of the Banu Khurassan (5th/end of 11th century). On the outside, the skullcap dome is decorated with furrows rising up from its base to its summit. This decor evokes that of certain Almoravid domes, notably that of the Qarawiyin of Fez, that of Marrakesh, as well as the dome of the Mosque of Sidi Marwan in Annaba built in 424/1033. Everything points to the conclusion that it is a monument of the 5th/11th century, but the origin of certain decorative elements, especially the Z-shaped furrows, remains obscure. A

caravanserai was added to the building relatively recently, probably in the 11th/17th or 12th/18th century; it was completely renovated during the 1980s and actually houses the municipal Museum of Popular Arts and Traditions.

VII.3.e **Sidi 'Ali 'Ammar Mosque** (this monument is not open to visitors)

From "rue Mustapha Rezam", enter the Rba'a Suq, then walk towards "rue de Paris", in the direction of "rue el-Mar", where the monument is located.

The *masjad* of Sidi 'Ali 'Ammar is distinct for its sculpted facade which breaks with the sobriety of the architecture of Sousse from the Aghlabid era. It is composed of two registers:

— The lower register consists of three horseshoe arches, the last keystones of which do not fall beyond the abacuses of the pillars, which is the first indication that the monument dates from the end of the 4th/10th century. The central arch, which is more elaborate than the others, with a protruding keystone, concurs with the entrance gate.

— The upper register consists of seven flat or semi-cylindrical niches; they are surmounted either by polyfoiled or simple arches or by triangles. Medallions featuring floral motifs and six-point stars calls to mind certain motifs on the porch of the Great Mosque of Mahdia. The whole is topped by a jagged moulding, like the one already seen in the dome of the Aghlabid *mihrab* of the Great Mosque of Sousse. The decor on the facade of the Sidi 'Ali 'Ammar Mosque is very characteristic of the Fatimid-Zirid repertoire, as attested to already by the eastern facade of the Great

Mosque of Sfax and the Zirid dome of the Great Mosque of Tunis. Everything seems to confirm that this mosque was built between the middle of the $4^{th}/10^{th}$ century and the beginning of the $5^{th}/11^{th}$ century.

VII.3.f **Buftata Mosque** (this monument is not open to visitors)

Further south, head towards the end of "rue el-Mar" which ends in a sabat, *or covered passageway. The Buftata Mosque faces this passageway, in "rue al-Ma'aser" in the Bab Qibli neighbourhood.*

A beautiful *kufic* inscription sculpted in relief on the facade of the oratory attributes the construction to the Aghlabid Prince Abu Iqal al-Aghlab, who reigned from 223/838 to 226/841. The oratory is preceded by a barrel-vaulted gallery whose facade is recessed with three horseshoe arches. This design is almost unique within the Golden Age of Ifriqiyan architecture.

Sidi 'Ali 'Ammar Mosque, detail of one of the flat niches, Sousse.

Buftata Mosque, kufic inscription on the facade of the oratory, Sousse.

ITINERARY VII   The Ribat *Towns*
Sousse

Kasbah, general overview, Sousse.

The prayer hall, which is nearly square (7.85 m. x 7.70 m.), is divided into three naves and three bays; covered with barrel vaults which support beam-arches that cross at right-angles, resting on cruciform pillars.

The principle of three-nave oratories was adopted everywhere across the Muslim World, from the Atlantic right across to Afghanistan, without enabling its evolutionary history to be traced. The Buftata Mosque is one of the oldest examples of this kind of oratory to have survived. Although a princely foundation, this oratory lacks any element of decoration to distract the eye. The choice of such austere architecture thus seems to reflect an official line taken with respect to the urbanisation of Sousse, distinct for its defensive appearance. The architect of this mosque seems to have elaborated formulas that would later be applied, more forcefully and passionately, by the architect of the Great Mosque, built about 10 years later.

VII.3.g The Kasbah and the Ramparts

Return towards "rue suq al-Qa'id" and go back as far as Bab al-Gharbi. Turn left onto "boulevard Maréchal Tito", until you reach the monument. It houses the Sousse Archaeological Museum.

ITINERARY VII   The Ribat *Towns*
Sousse

Entrance fee. Opening times: 09.00–12.00 and 14.00–18.00 from 16th September until 31st March. 08.00–12.00 and 15.00–19.00 the rest of the year. Closed Mondays. Parking available at the entrance. Toilet facilities.

Sousse's enclosure, which covers an area of 32 hectares, with a perimeter measuring over 2.3 km., was built in 244/859 by the Aghlabid Prince Abu Ibrahim Ahmed. Built of rubble-stone and occasionally of freestone, it is crowned with crenelations whose rounded form perpetuates the Byzantine tradition. The tracery of the ramparts seems to take after the Byzantine wall, some sections of which still exist. The enclosure was pierced by three gates: *Bab al-Bhar* (Gate of the Sea), *Bab al-Qibli* (Gate of the *Qibla*) and *Bab al-Gharbi* (West Gate). Three further gates were later built: *Bab Jadid* (The New Gate, in 1280/1864), *Bab al-Finga* (Gate of the Guillotine), and *Bab al-Jebli* (North Gate) between 1892 and 1895. During the modern age, certain sections of the ramparts were mended and rebuilt in order to accommodate pieces of artillery. The *kasbah* stands in the south-west corner, and was built in 235/850 by the Aghlabid Prince Abu al-'Abbas Mohamed; this fortress housed the military garrison and seat of the governor. The citadel was rebuilt many times, from the $3^{rd}/9^{th}$ century up until the present day, but its oldest part is without doubt the *manar* of Khalaf, named after the freed slave of the Aghlabid prince who supervised the foundation works: in fact it is as old as the foundation date of the *kasbah* itself. This signal tower, 30 m. in height, presents certain analogies shared with the Great Mosque of Kairouan by which it has clearly been inspired, and is an example of the diffusion of the Kairouanese School of architecture in the Sahel region. Composed of two levels accessible via a staircase built into the depth of the wall, the central cluster is served by four superimposed rooms covered in vaults of different shapes. This layout, previously unseen in Islamic art, would appear in Almohad minarets. Note that the construction of the Tower of Khalaf allowed for better control over the maritime coastline than did the Tower of Ribat; indeed, whilst the latter stands 27 m. above sea-level, the Tower of Khalaf stands 77 m. above sea-level, improving the view by over 13 km.

Ramparts, Sousse.

ITINERARY VIII

The Gate of the Levant

Ali Zouari

VIII.1 SFAX

VIII.1.a The Kasbah Museum
VIII.1.b Café al-Diwan (option)
VIII.1.c Sidi 'Amar Kammun Minaret
VIII.1.d Burj al-Nar
VIII.1.e Dar Jalluli, Museum of Popular Arts and Traditions
VIII.1.f The Great Mosque
VIII.1.g The Suqs
VIII.1.h Funduq of the Blacksmiths
VIII.1.i Sidi Bushwaisha Mosque
VIII.1.j Sidi bel-Hassen Zawiya
VIII.1.k The Ramparts

The burj

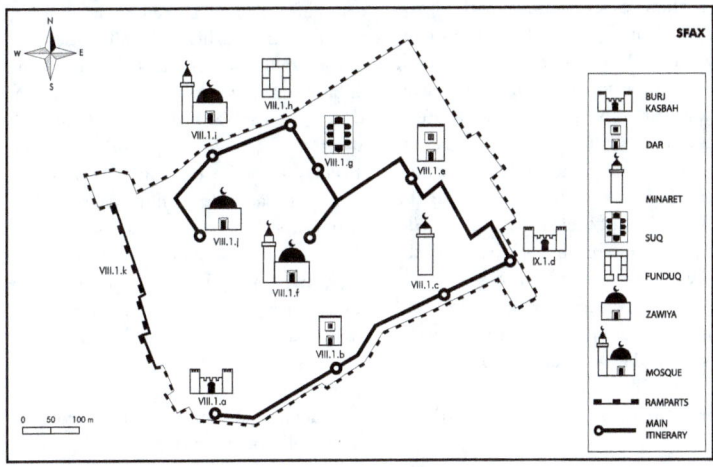

Dar Jalluli, patio, Sfax.

ITINERARY VIII   *The Gate of the Levant*

Southern ramparts, general overview, Sfax.

Sfax is situated where the Sahel and South Tunisia meet, on the shores of a calm harbour facing the Eastern Mediterranean. Its location grants it an enormous advantage in terms of ready maritime and continental influence, whilst its orientation is turned more markedly towards the countries of Africa and the Levant than towards those of the East. With an advantageous cabability of contact with the East via both sea and land, coupled with a spirit of pure dynamism, Sfax was able to become Tunisia's Gate of the Levant, political-economic circumstances permitting, such as in Thyna during the Roman era. Responding to the aims and needs of their town, the *Sharfis*, prestigious inhabitants of Sfax, established a collection of harbour charts in the 10th/16th century for the sailors and the merchants who desired to venture out as far as the Black Sea. Two examples from this collection can be found, one in Oxford, the other in the Paris National Library.

The commercial activity between Sfax and the Levant, upheld by intense caravan traffic, developed throughout the 12th/18th century. Its commercial pulse led to the creation of *funduqs* and *suqs* which are spread along the edge of the town's main thoroughfare. This thoroughfare links the southern gate, Bab al-Jebli, to the northern gate, Bab al-Diwan. The former, which Charles Lallemand called the Gate of the Fields, was composed of a hallway of fair depth, which led into the square in which the caravans were stationed. Bab al-Diwan, elbow-shaped in form, led directly into the mooring. Although it became isolated through the development of the suburb of namely Christians during the 12th–13th/second half of the 18th century, it remained a lively place where money-changers, merchants, porters, fishermen and beasts of burden travelling towards the port collided and mixed with intense movement.

The accumulation of capital provided favourable conditions for the development of agriculture and crafts as well as for urban growth. Outside the ramparts, the zone of gardens encircles the city. The number of *burj*s, summer residences, increases. Within the town, public and private monuments are: rebuilt – the *funduq* of the Blacksmiths; enlarged – the Great Mosque, the Mosque of Sidi Boushwaisha; restored and embellished – the Dar Jalluli and the Sidi bel-Hassen Mausoleum. The ramparts themselves are the object of particular attention.

Sfax, whilst continuing to use the same construction materials and its own architectural traditions, enriched its monuments, without exaggeration, using sculpted *kadhal*, painted wood and *faience* tiles produced in al-Andalus and Turkey. The architecture of Sfax, sober and well-balanced, reflects the taste which characterises the life of this town.

Viewed from an aeroplane, Sfax looks like an immense agglomeration, flat and squeezed in within the fabric of a spider's web. The fortified town, or *medina*, rectangular in form, stands out at the centre. Sfax limited itself for over 10 centuries to the boundaries of this historical centre, which was cushioned by a surrounding area of green gardens, the *jnans*.

In Arabic, the name "Sfax", *Safaqus*, derives according to popular belief from *Safa* – the name of the equerry of the Aghlabid Prince, founder of Sfax, and from *qus* – to cut. *"Cut the hide of the beef in fine strips"* the master would order. The strips were used to outline the edges of the town, like Carthage with Elyssa before. In reality, *Safaqus* is a Berber word which means gulf, belt, just like its name "Taphrura" or "Taparura" during the Roman era, a centre of commerce which was supplanted by Sfax. Through the attribution of one of these two names, Sfax and "Taphrura", it became a protected town.

Kasbah Museum, restoration of a gallery passageway, Sfax.

In the 2nd–3rd/ beginning of the 9th century, Sfax remained a small agglomeration of merchants and fishermen farmers, huddled around a *ribat*. It made its entry into the history books with the construction of its ramparts and its Great Mosque towards the middle of the 3rd/9th century, under the reign of Ahmed Ibn al-Aghlab. The property developer was 'Ali Ibn Aslam al-Jibiniani, a client of the Aghlabid Princes, masters of Ifriqiya. A small village 30 km. from Sfax was named after his grandson, Sidi Abu Ishaq, a great *sufi*. His mausoleum, visible from the main road, is distinguished by its numerous domes.

From the 3rd/9th to the 7th/13th century, Sfax was a great market selling its oils to Italy, the Maghreb, Egypt and Syria. Its olive groves were described by Arab chroniclers as "unique" and "delicious". During this time, Sfax was also famed for its weaving, including a certain "princely moiré, made from the byssus of sea oysters". Meanwhile, it was not at all an era of calm and peace. During the 5th/11th and 6th/12th centuries, Sfax underwent again and again the challenge posed by the Hilalian invasion, and the trials of an ephemeral independence (455/1063–492/1099) under Hammu Ibn Malil, and the torment of a Norman Occupation (543/1149–555/1160). The resistance put up against this occupation, lead by Abu al-Hassan al-Feriani and his son 'Umar, left its mark in the collective memory. One of their descendants, Sidi Abu Bakr al-Feriani, remains at rest in a small mausoleum in the northern part of town, several meters from the ramparts, at the foot of the Sidi al-Lakhmi Mosque.

The Norman Occupation marked a turning point in Sfax's history. Its Jewish population – who played an active role in its Eastern commerce – sensing that the balance in the Mediterranean was about to tip over in favour of the Normans, left the town to move to Sicily.

Following the long dynastic wars that shook Ifriqiya, as well as epidemics and the resulting economic and demographic recessions, Sfax was in a state of collapse. In the middle of the 8th/14th century, its population was down to 400 households. The Sfaxians were, according to Leo the African, weavers, fishermen and sea merchants.

Although small in number, they remained active, voyaging as far as the Black Sea.

During the 11th/17th century, Sfax experienced the beginnings of a general recovery. Becoming more active within the Mediterranean, it got involved in wars of disagreement and contest with Malta. The Shaykh 'Ali al-Nuri (1052/1643–1117/1706), a knowledgeable educator who was also in the trading business as a silent partner, led and organised the struggle against the cavaliers of Malta. He is still to this day considered to be the man responsible for the Sfaxian renaissance.

In the 12th/18th century, Sfax went through a boom. Its commerce with the Levant reinforced its role as a distribution market. Between 1198/1784 and 1201/1787, it was bombarded by Venice on several occasions. At the heart of these events, occurring all along the Tunisian coastline following the defensive intervention by the *Bey* of Tunis Hammuda Pasha, was the breaking of a "nolis" contract by the captain of a Venetian boat which the Sfaxians had engaged for a Sfax–Alexandria journey. From the 12th/18th century onwards, Sfax moved progressively from its status as a small town to becoming the second most important town in the country. It relied on its own dynamism in order to further and structure its economy, thanks to constant,

ITINERARY VIII   *The Gate of the Levant*
Sfax

Kasbah Museum, guard tower, Sfax.

sustained work, thrift and the investment of its people. This enabled it to become a regional capital, the Port of the Steppe and of the South, renowned throughout the Mediterranean to be very active. In 1239/1824 Christians and Jews began to settle in Sfax. The town's commerce thus turned increasingly towards the West. In 1881, in spite of savage resistance against the French Occupation, it capitulated and was submitted to a heavy war indemnity. The sacrifices endured by the town momentarily suffocated its economic vitality. Under the Protectorate, it expanded on the outside of the ramparts. Its olive groves underwent a renewed boom. Its development did not stop once Independence was gained. Today, Sfax is sacrificing its gardens and its agglomeration is growing at their expense. However, a historic area remains: the *medina*. This historic centre is the beating heart of the greater Sfax. A clear projection of 11 centuries of life and of civilisation, Sfax both preserves its past and steps beyond it.

VIII.1 **SFAX**

VIII.1.a **The Kasbah Museum**

Enter the medina *through Bab al-Kasbah, on "avenue Ali Belahouane". The Museum is on the left, in the small square.*
Entrance fee. Opening times: 09.30–16.30. Closed Mondays. Toilet facilities available.

The Kasbah of Sfax is a monumental citadel occupying the south-west corner of the ramparts. The administrative documents of the Ottoman period also describe

ITINERARY VIII   *The Gate of the Levant*

Sfax

Kasbah Museum, ancient mosque, Sfax.

it as a *qal'a* or as a fortress, *qsar*, whilst European texts describe it as a castle-fort. Built on a raised area, it controlled the town stretched out below, as well as the sea which beat against its sides when the tide came in. On its site there once stood a *ribat*, and a section of the *ribat*'s mosque can still be seen today. This *ribat* already existed as far back as the 2nd–3rd/beginning of the 9th century. What remains denotes an austere architecture, similar to that which prevailed in Ifriqiya during the Aghlabid era.

The origins of the *kasbah* remain unknown. Its evolution was moulded by the administrative, political and military requirements of the town. The seat of the Sfaxian government during certain periods, followed by being the seat of the military commander, the *kasbah* underwent important transformations, the dates of which are vague if one wants to ascertain when they were marked out architecturally. The two inscriptions on the facade, dated 1092/1681 and 1150/1738, only mark the times when restoration works were carried out. Aghlabid, Zirid and Ottoman ruins cross over or superimpose one another. This is clearly manifested in its Great Room composed of a juxtaposition of cells, in its two guard towers and the *ribat*'s mosque. The architecture of the *kasbah*, massive and austere, features a slightly curbed arch as its principal feature. Stripped of its later additions, and returned to its original structure and restored since 1987, the *kasbah* now houses a permanent exhibition on traditional Sfaxian architecture. It is a didactic exhibition which, through using examples of tools, materials, reconstructed architectural elements, plans and photographs, offers a precise idea on the techniques, constituent parts, the structures and the typology of the local architecture.

VIII.1.b **Café al-Diwan** (option)

Take the street in front of the entrance to the museum, on the other side of the square. The café is on the right, 100 m. further along. Opening times: daily from 07.00–23.00.

The Café al-Diwan is located in one tower of the ramparts, which is oblong in shape. Dominating the sea below whose waves lapped its foundations, its loopholes were replaced by embrasures with canons to adapt its defences to modern military techniques. It is without doubt thanks to its constantly sustained defensive role and its

ITINERARY VIII *The Gate of the Levant*
Sfax

adaptation to firearms that it is known as the Tower of Lead, Burj al-Rsas.

VIII.1.c Sidi 'Amar Kammun Minaret

From the same street, the monument is located 100 m. from Bab Diwan, in "rue Burj al-Nar", on the right.

This minaret, exceptional in terms of its form and decoration, was part of a mausoleum built in two stages between 1045/1636 and 1076/1666 by Sidi 'Amar Kammun. The construction of a minaret within a mausoleum, previously unheard of in Sfax, can only be explained by the defensive purpose it could have served. This mausoleum, placed back-to-back with the southern rampart, effectively controlled, like a *ribat*, the coastline during a time when Christian privateering targeted Sfax.
Abandoned, then destroyed, it finally relinquished its place to give way to a new mosque. The historic minaret, which has remained intact, stands in the courtyard of the new building, to the right of the entrance door. Square in section and 9.3 m. high, this minaret, which belongs to the type of Maghrebi minaret introduced by the Hafsids, ends in a platform crowned with merlons. A flattened lantern sits above. The minaret's decor is respectful of the symmetry and superposition of bare and ornate areas. Its base is made up of mouldings, indentations and architectonic elements: arcatures, blind niches, starred medallions, twinned windows and calligraphy. Through its rich and varied decor and its freestone masonry, which together create an harmonious aesthetic effect, the minaret of Sidi 'Amar Kammun distinguishes itself from all the other local minarets. Although built in the $11^{th}/17^{th}$ century, it is a remarkable

illustration of the architectural trends in Sfax at the end of the Middle Ages, characterised by the collusion between ancient Aghlabid and Zirid traditions and new influences introduced during the Hafsid era from al-Andalus and Morocco.

VIII.1.d Burj al-Nar

Still on "rue Burj al-Nar", one can find this monument through an entrance on the right. Opening times: 08.30–13.00 and 15.00–18.00. Closed on Friday afternoons.

The Burj al-Nar, literally the Fortress of Fire, derives its name from the luminous signals it once transmitted. Situated in the

Sidi 'Amar Kammun, Sfax.

209

ITINERARY VIII   *The Gate of the Levant*

Sfax

south-eastern corner of the ramparts, it dominates the eastern side of town. This fortress, which constitutes an integral part of the ramparts, was a link in the chain of forts and *ribats* that guarded the Ifriqiyan coast and were responsible for communicating, when required, information which they had received or wanted to communicate through the use of fire or smoke. The Burj al-Nar had without doubt played an important defensive, informative and guiding role for the town. Rebuilt and restored, it has housed the Association for the Safekeeping of the Medina of Sfax for about 15 years. It is actually composed of a vast area, dominated by two donjons in the form of pyramidal trunks, one occupying the south-east corner, the other occupying the south-west. The Mediaeval Burj al-Nar was certainly different. Partial surveys have uncovered, at lower ground-level, stairs as well as corners of walls and a cavern, total-

ly intact, under the south-eastern donjon. Are these the remains of the former Burj al-Nar or of a lower level that was abandoned following a functional change? Only a systematic archaeological dig would be able to give a determinate answer. The present Burj al-Nar seems to be a later construction. Its massive and austere architecture reflects the military function which it has always fulfilled. The archives of the Tunisian Government, as well as accounts of European travellers, indicate that it was equipped with canons during the $12^{th}/18^{th}$ and $13^{th}/19^{th}$ centuries.

VIII.1.e **Dar Jalluli, Museum of Popular Arts and Traditions**

Go along "rue Dar Essabai", then along "rue Driba" until you reach "rue Sidi Ali Nouri"; the museum is at number 5.

Burj al-Nar, corner tower, Sfax.

ITINERARY VIII *The Gate of the Levant*
Sfax

Dar Jalluli, qbu of the T-shaped room decorated with ceramics, Sfax.

Entrance fee. Opening times: 09.30–16.30. Closed Mondays. Toilet facilities available.

The Museum of Popular Arts and Traditions is situated in a neighbourhood that was known as *humat al-Rigga*. This neighbourhood owes its name to the immigrants who settled there in the 6th/12th century, after having abandoned their town, *al-Rigga* – ancient Barbarus – situated next to al-Jem, following the Hilalian invasion.

The museum is housed in an elegant house of the 11th/17th century. It carries the name of its former owners, the Jallulis, who were Governors of Sfax, great property owners and silent partners. The plan of the house is classical: an elbow-shaped entrance, a courtyard with a portico and rooms arranged around it, and an upper floor served by a balustrade turned-wood gallery.

Gathered up together yet well-balanced, and modest in comparison to the bourgeois houses of Tunis, this house is, for Sfax standards, the greatest and most sumptuous. It is distinct for its rich decor of sculpted *kadhal*, of painted wood, of *faience* tiles and of openwork stucco. The *kadhal*, the *faience* tiles, and the openwork stucco windows, *shamsa*, in the courtyard are all so skilfully produced that they add particular impressiveness to the place.

The principle on which the museum is based rests on the simple idea of giving the house its domestic soul back, through furnishing it suitably with traditional furniture. It is often called a living museum.

Buckets full from the wells and the cistern, the doors of the large rooms open, revealing neatly arranged furniture, give the impression of tranquil family occupation.

ITINERARY VIII *The Gate of the Levant*

Sfax

The Great Mosque, minaret, Sfax.

The rooms and their alcoves, the kitchen, and the storage room are so tidy and so clean that they lead you to believe that the lady of the house has just passed through them. The museum also reveals, in the smaller rooms, murals on cupboards which have been transformed into windows, and, in the rooms on the first floor, collections of various objects: head-dresses, crafted wood, male and female dress, paintings under glass, and so on. The visitor also finds recreations and depictions of marriage scenes, particularly the honeymoon, *layl al-dukhla*, and the "jump over the fish", *al-tanguiz 'ala al-hut*. This exhibition, varied and rich, gives us an idea of the other aspects of Sfaxian life, on the creative spir-

it of the Sfaxian, and alludes to the relationships between the home and the *suqs*, between domestic life and economic life. The Sfaxian house was not merely a home, it was a workshop and a goods depot. The women carded, spun and wove the wool; the men, merchants, craftsmen or farmers, tempted into becoming specialised, sold their goods in shops. Did not the military communication of Sire Raynaud of 1036/1627 recommend the canon loaders to take aim at the houses in order to match the Sfaxians in terms of their wealth? He was referring to the oils that filled great jars in the caverns. The museum's caverns, although full of these pottery containers, are closed to the public for security reasons.

VIII.1.f **The Great Mosque** (this monument is not open to visitors)

Take "rue Sidi Khlil", followed by "rue du Bey", the Suq al-Jum'a and then the street of the Great Mosque on which this monument is located.

The Great Mosque of Sfax, *al-Jama' al-Kabir*, occupies the centre of the *medina*, right at the intersection of two main thoroughfares, one that links Bab al-Jibli to Bab al-Diwan, the other being the median east-west thoroughfare. Built in 244/859, it served as the central urban and religious element to the structuring of the town. Surrounded by *suqs*, the Great Mosque was, until the middle of the 13th/19th century, the only sanctuary to practise the Communal Friday Prayer. Its religious privilege, its age, its remarkable location, its spatial and architectural importance and its socio-educational function has guaranteed it the veneration of all Sfaxians.

ITINERARY VIII   *The Gate of the Levant*
Sfax

The architecture of the original mosque of the Aghlabid era has become hypothetical since it was narrowed down during the Zirid era and extended during the Ottoman era. Only a few scattered elements of the original mosque remain, which one can see either in the prayer hall or in the minaret.

During the Zirid era, from the 4th/10th to the 6th/12th century, the mosque was subject to a new layout, particularly in terms of its eastern facade and its minaret. A new *mihrab* replaced the old one in the prayer hall. Made in the same mould as those of Mahdia and Monastir, it must have been enriched with elaborate epigraphic and self-propagating vegetal decoration judging by the little decoration that remains. Abandoned and then walled in in the 12th/18th century because it had become outlying, it was recently uncovered and studied as an archaeological feature.

In the 12th/18th century, the Great Mosque grew into its present form. The prayer hall was enlarged, first in 1171/1758 and then in 1187/1774, through the addition of a wing that runs along the west side of the joint backs of the prayer hall and the courtyard. A new central *mihrab*, decorated with fluting, *kufic* writing and surmounted by commemorative verses by the poet 'Ali al-Ghurab, replaced the Zirid *mihrab*. The plan of the mosque thus developed along original lines: a prayer hall at right angles enclosing a small courtyard surrounded by porticoes.

Having been submitted to these various influences, constraints and judicious interventions, the mosque ended up having original, quirky elements that elicit astonishment, curiosity and admiration. Its eastern facade, completely unique *"has an astonishing layout"* says Ms. Sourdel. It is considered by L. Golvin to be *"the most curious and most elaborate mosque of the Zirid period"*. A succession of tympanum deploys itself across the entire facade, surmounting doors and windows. This design of the layout is achieved through repeating the same motif of a door or window with its lintel, its tympanum circumscribed by three archivolts and a relief arch, and two niches in the shape of a *mihrab* on each side. Some inscriptions dated 377/988 and 477/1085 and written in beautiful *kufic* script state when restoration works took place.

The minaret is of great historical and archaeological value. Sharing the same silhouette as the minaret of Kairouan, it is composed of two superimposed towers

The Great Mosque, door to the prayer hall, Sfax.

213

ITINERARY VIII   *The Gate of the Levant*

Sfax

A suq, Sfax.

and a lantern. The parapets of the two towers are embellished with a varied decor combining epigraphy, geometry and vegetal motifs: palmettes, serrations, mouldings, ovums and deep-set rosettes. According to G. Marçais, the majority of these decorative elements, as well as the merlons cut out into five-foiled flowerets, link *"this work, which is so original, to the style of the Fatimids"*.

The 10 great tympanum doors in the form of *bahu* arches – pronounced *bhu* by the Sfaxians – that link the prayer hall to the courtyard, have been made finely and skilfully by the master carpenter-joiner, Ahmed Sha'abuni. Its doors with two or four shutters are made of sculpted medallions, each with its own decoration, either geometric or floral. There are only vague traces of the polychrome paint that once covered them. The Great Mosque of

Sfax is also distinct from other Ifriqiyan mosques through a resurrected figurative decor. This decor can be seen in the prayer hall on two capitals that face the *mihrab*. Each capital is composed of acanthus leaves and four vultures. On the eastern facade, a Byzantine votive panel features two peacocks faced on each side by a basket from which leafy foliage, bunches of grapes and birds spill out. Was the planishing of the peacocks and one vulture intentional? Everything points to the suggestion that these were tolerated by Islam and that there was a need to profit from antique remains of aesthetic value.

The Great Mosque of Sfax has become a source of inspiration, thanks to its rich architectural and artistic repertoire and its religious prestige. A single example of this is that a copy of this mosque's minaret forms the minaret of Sidi Bush-waisha.

VIII.1.g The Suqs

Cross under the covered passageway of the Suq des Etoffes (the fabric and textile suq), followed by the suq Rba'a.

"*Sfax has very lively suqs*", *aswaq nafiqa*, wrote the Arab travellers and geographers of the Middle Ages. The *suqs* were only beginning to be called and known by their names or activities far later, certainly no earlier than the 12th/18th century onwards. The 30 *suqs* that have been counted, using archival documents and the texts of European travellers, formed the heart of the town's economic life which also included *funduqs*, *wikalas*, and *qaysariyas*. This economic area formed a pocket squeezed in between, to the south by the Great Mosque, to the north by the Bab al-Jibli, and to the east and west by residential neighbourhoods. This pocket is no longer a neat delineation – economic activities have overflown into the residential areas since the beginning of the 20th century.

The *suq* is often defined as a double row of stalls occupied by the same trade or craft. The Sfaxians apply the term *suq* to different specialised economic centres that are physically different. Firstly it is a street or a section of street, uncovered, composed of two rows of shops, sometimes superimposed, a cellar, *dahliz*, a boutique on the ground floor, *hanut*, and a floor above with a staircase and an overhanging balcony, *ghorfa*. These *ghorfas*, which are typical, used to correspond to weaving workshops. Sfaxians wove wool, linen, cotton and silk. There was a regular exchange of basic materials and finished goods between it and the Levant. These perched workshops, which contributed to the charm of the *suqs*, are today occupied by cobblers. These *suqs* are often linked through little alleyways, to areas bordered by boutiques or small shops, known as *qaysariyas*. The *suq* can be covered by barrel vaults upheld by beam arches. This is the case with Suq al-Kamur, Suq al-Truk, Suq al-Raba'a; the latter, the town's most important *suq*, is the only one that is closed by two gates. It is composed of a main north-south thoroughfare, crossed by a mid east-west road. It specialises in the sale of *sheshiyas* and woven woollen goods. During the 12th/18th and 13th/19th centuries, it held a continuous relationship with the Levant. It has increasingly turned

A suq, Sfax.

towards selling clothes that are traditional in character.

The *suq* also corresponds to an enclosure bordered by boutiques surmounted by *ghorfa*s, possessing only a single entrance that leads onto the street where the *suq* is located. *Suq*s like this include the *Suq* of the Cotton Yarn, *Suq al-Tu'ma*. It can also take the form of a more open and spacious area, but with the same layout, as is illustrated by the Friday market, *Suq al-Jum'a*, which some documents refer to as the market of old objects, *Suq al-Qash*. This *suq*, close to the Great Mosque, was originally a weekly market, but is now a daily market.

As in the rest of the Arab-Muslim world, the layout and placement of *suq*s within urban space obeys certain criteria. The *suq*s whose activities are noisy and polluting, like that of the blacksmiths, the carpenters and the butchers, which are in fact linked to the rural world, are relegated to a position next to the Bab al-Jibli. The *suq*s have retained their names, but have been converted; even those which have held on to their traditional activities have been infiltrated with other parasitical activities. The Medina of Sfax is more alive than ever before. What is modern stands shoulder-to-shoulder with what is traditional, and associates itself to it in a move of natural adaptation.

VIII.1.h Funduq of the Blacksmiths

The funduq *is situated in "rue des Forgerons" (Street of the Blacksmiths), on the right after Suq Rba'a.*

The term *funduq*, which signifies an establishment whose character is mainly economic, was at first shared by both the Muslim East and the Muslim West, but in the Muslim East it was eclipsed in the

Funduq of the Blacksmiths, interior courtyard, Sfax.

ITINERARY VIII The Gate of the Levant
Sfax

Funduq of the Blacksmiths, interior courtyard, Sfax.

4th/10th century by the terms *khan* and *wikala*.

Funduq, khan, wikala – although they possess certain architectural differences, their plans are those of a *caravanserai* composed essentially of a huge courtyard surrounded by buildings and with an inn. Caravans would stop there. *Funduqs* appeared in Sfax early on. Ibn Hawqal, in the 4th/10th century, is the first to have notified us of their existence in this town.

Situated inside the *medina*, near Bab al-Jibli and the caravan station, the Funduq of the Blacksmiths derives its name from the *suq* in which it is located. Its name has become more significant since the municipality moved blacksmiths and coppersmiths (boilermakers) there.

Dilapidated during the Hafsid era, and rebuilt and restored in the 12th/18th century, it stands as the only remaining reminder of the neighbourhood of the *funduqs*, Humat al-Fanadiq, which was made up of similar establishments and was very active during the 12th/18th century.

The form taken by the Funduq of the Blacksmiths is a classic one. A narrow hallway-corridor, *sqifa*, leads to a vast courtyard surrounded by porticoes, under which sit shops. Staircases, situated in this same hallway, lead to a first floor of 25 rooms or *ghorfa*s. The ground floor was reserved for the travellers' animals and their goods, whilst the upper floor served as an inn.

The *funduq* is built along the lines of traditional masonry based on time-honoured techniques, using local materials. The conchitic sandstone imported from the Mahdia region is used in bulk for the construction of door frames, arches and pillars. Having calculated the available materials, the width of the spaces required to be covered, and the best means of maximising

ITINERARY VIII *The Gate of the Levant*
Sfax

Sidi Bushwaisha Mosque, entrance, Sfax.

and to *qaysariya*s than to other monuments.

VIII.1.i **Sidi Bushwaisha Mosque** (this monument is not open to visitors)

The monument is situated in "rue des Forgerons" (Blacksmiths' Street) which one can reach via "rue Abdelkader".

The mosque, which has been attributed to Sidi Bushwaisha, the "man with the toupet", is situated in the northern part of town, in front of Bab al-Jibli, the gate that leads to *suqs* seething with life. As his surname, Guardian of the Gate, *Shawush al-Bab*, suggests, Sidi Buchwaicha was probably the guardian of this strategic gate that would have been closed at nightfall. One is tempted to also consider him as the protector and defender of the gate, especially if one thinks of his mosque as a sort of *ribat*.

This mosque limited itself to being a small prayer room flanked by a courtyard. It was enlarged in the 11th–12th/end of 17th century at the expense of its courtyard and of a partition oratory, endowing itself with a minaret and a beautiful facade. The prayer room is thus actually made-up of two linked but neatly distinct parts. The part built in the $11^{th}/17^{th}$ century, whilst imitating the older room in its use of columns and recycled capitals, is more elaborate; its *mihrab* is more imposing, and makes use of *faience* tiles as well as sculpted *kadhal*.

The minaret offers a beautiful view of the Blacksmiths' *suq* from above. Old engravings and postcards have enabled us to follow its evolution. Restoration work undertaken in 1964–1965 have returned it to its original form of two superimposed towers sur-

thermal regulation, the roof coverings are made in the form of groined vaults for the *sqifa*, in thuja-wood joists for the staircases and in a light timber framework for the porticoes. As such, the *funduq* represents every kind of roofing material used previously in Sfax.

In the Funduq of the Blacksmiths, as in other historic Sfaxian monuments, the freestone, the arches, the diagonally ribbed ceilings and the visible joists are all structural elements; they are also, within this type of monument, the only decorative elements capable of attracting attention. Compared to the *khans* of the East, the Funduq of the Blacksmiths appears modest, lacking in all ornamentation, and is located closer to *suqs*

mounted by a smooth skullcap-shaped lantern. Although constructed later, it falls in line with the pure architectural tradition of Ifriqiya. It is without doubt based and modelled on the minaret of the Great Mosque.

The northern facade has been carefully elaborated. Adorned with wrought-iron windows with spiral features, *zlabiya*s, the facade is particularly distinct for the *kadhal* framing of its door and neighbouring windows. The small chain mouldings, the dentils, the three petal rosettes, the solar discs with rays that repeat and revert, all harmoniously combined, constitute a good mix of local architectural elements and Muradite novelty.

Two niched inscriptions, within two sets of twin arches, surmount the entrance on either side. They reveal the date of the mosque's extension in 1094/1683, and mention the five *murabitun*s who supported it as well as the master mason who executed the building work. He was Mohamed, son of the Master Mason Mohamed al-Kotti al-Ansari. This mention clearly demonstrates that the job of a mason, like many other professions, passed from father to son and from one generation to another. This conclusively explains the long-lasting nature of architectural traditions in Sfax.

Restoration works uncovered in the southeast corner of the facade, the fountain (*sabil*), called by one, sucker (*sic.*), *massassa*. It is composed of a large vessel into which a leather tube is submerged; only the outer end of the tube is visible, and is placed at a man's height. Those who were thirsty drank the water they required through sucking on the tube. Great religious and social importance was attached to these *sabil*s, whose purpose was to obtain divine mercy through quenching the thirsty.

Sidi bel-Hassen Zawiya, interior courtyard, Sfax.

Sfax

VIII.1.j Sidi bel-Hassan Zawiya (this monument is not open to visitors)

Continue along "rue Abdelkader" towards Bab Jabli and take "rue Sidi bel-Hassen" on the right which leads to the monument.

The Zawiya Sidi bel-Hassan (a derivation of Abu al-Hassan) looks out onto Barberusse Square, which is squeezed into a lively economic centre. It carries the name of its founder, Shaykh Sidi Abu al-Hassan al-Karray, descendant of Sidi Ali el-Karray, Patron Saint of Sfax and founder of the *Wafa'iya* Brotherhood which his father had brought over from Alexandria. Sidi Abu al-Hassan, scholar and teacher of the 11th/17th century, succeeded in transforming his *zawiya* into an important centre of education and worship. Here, *muwashahat* psalms were chanted which were composed by El-Hassan himself, a kind of *maluf*-adapted liturgical chant. The Sfaxians, who once venerated Sidi Abu al-Hassan, today venerate his *zawiya*.

It was originally a private house. It is composed of a hallway that leads through to a double portico, opening onto the Mausoleum of Sidi Abu al-Hassan, and a courtyard flanked by two further porticoes, and a small prayer hall endowed with an attractive *mihrab* which is framed in sculpted *kadhal* and *faience* tiles. The inscriptions in the hallway, on the facade of the prayer hall, and on the exterior facade, date respectively from 1081/1671, 1113/1702 and 1174/1761, each marking the year of restoration. In architectural terms, this period was a turning-point for Sfax, marking its loyalty to ancient traditions whilst embracing novel creative forms brought over from the East by the Ottomans. This *zawiya* is a good example of this phenomenon. Whilst employing recycled materials, columns and capitals, its builders and restoration workers also made use of sculpted *kadhal*, which in 12th/18th-century Sfax was a sign of great wealth that was linked to economic prosperity. The facade of the prayer hall and the exterior facade of the *zawiya*, the majority of which is surfaced with *kadhal*, makes this entire monument, in decorative terms, the most interesting building in Sfax. To the epigraphic decoration added onto the frames and cogwheel cornices are added Turkish-style motifs that are both remarkably well executed and that are used extensively: rosettes, medallions with rounded rays, starred polygons, small chains, braided cords, and so on. The solar disc, *shamsa*, which has rounded rays – a very popular motif in Sfax – represents *"a decor that does not exist in Tunis"* according to Fawzi Mahfudh, but which, he adds, *"one comes across in the civil architecture of Cairo"*.

VIII.1.k The Ramparts

It is acknowledged that the Ramparts of Sfax were built in 244/859 under the reign of Ahmed Ibn al-Aghlab, Amir of Kairouan. 'Ali Ibn Aslam al-Bakri, Cadi of Sfax and a feudal liege of the Aghlabids, built the ramparts as well as the Great Mosque from his own means, but no doubt with the support of his masters. These two monuments set up the framework for the town's urban plan. The ramparts outline the town in a slightly skewed quadrilateral, measuring 600 m. from east to west and 400–450 m. from south to north, totalling a perimeter of 2,000 m.

This rampart, made up of fruit embellished curtain-walls is flanked by 69 diverse towers: semicircular, oblong, cut-off corners, octagonal or hexagonal. These towers, which the Sfaxians called *burjs* or *ribats*,

ITINERARY VIII *The Gate of the Levant*
Sfax

were fortresses, but above all they were centres of control and defence. The southern side is the most fortified side, with 22 towers in all. Dominating the seafront, it faced the most dangerous of horizons. Indeed it was across the sea that the "Infidels" came in order to attack: Byzantine, Norman, the Cavaliers of Malta, the Spanish ... all of whom were, at this time, the most feared of enemies. Towers and walls end in crenellated parapets and lightly curbed merlon arches.

The Ramparts of Sfax, as a construction for defence purposes, obey the principles of military fortification. One of the basic elements of these principles is to reinforce the fortresses which stand at the corners. In Sfax these corner towers are: the *kasbah* in the south-west, the Burj al-Nar in the south-east, the Burj Mas'uda in the north-east and finally the Burj al-Qsar in the north-west. The Sfaxians were conscious of the importance of their town's enclosure, which sheltered them from all natural disasters as well as from assaults or tentative military incursions. They expressed this feeling of importance through their proverbial sayings as well as through the attention and material support they accorded it. It was good that they bequeathed it endowment gifts, *waqfs*, which allowed its keeper to look after it, restore it and improve it as a means of defence. The canon embrasures that neighboured the arches demonstrate the adaptation of the enclosure walls to the evolution of weapons.

Built initially of rough brick, made from a mix of plaster, quicklime, ash and sand, the construction of the ramparts was carried out during the course of time using more consistent materials. This involved limestone boulders extracted from under the Sfaxian earth and bound together with lime mortar. For the tie rods, the masons used

The ramparts, gate, Sfax.

round logs from olive trees, from vines or from thuja trees to bury into the walls, and used freestone made of conchitic sandstone, imported from Mahdia, for the corner tie rods, the hooks and the protruding pedestals of several towers. This mode of construction was always employed in the modifications and restorations necessitated by the need to defend the town in moments of military activity.

The Ramparts of Sfax express the age-old perpetuity of architectural traditions, of modes of construction and of decorative elements like cornices and denticulations. Their well-preserved state has allowed specialists in Islamic architecture to better understand the system of fortification in Ifriqiya during the height of the Middle Ages.

THE BURJ

Ali Zouari

Sfax possessed beautiful orchards, known as *jnan*s, planted with all sorts of fruit trees and odiferous plants in line with a geometric plan that took space, syntax, soil, species and the proximity of houses into account. These gardens, surrounded by hedgerows of cacti, formed a green countryside, the *ghaba*, which encircled the town. According to al-Bakri, a geographer from the 5th/11th century, this countryside, consisting mainly of olive trees, was strewn with *qsar*s. This word has many nuanced meanings, but it is taken to signify a fortified residence. This countryside receded between the 8th/14th and 10th/16th century, due to military incursions, epidemics, and economic and demographic depressions. It regenerated itself from the start of the 11th/17th century, once political stability was restored. By the 12th/18th century, it had regained its previous form and then continued to grow. European travellers were enchanted by it. The descriptions they have left us speak of an ocean of greenery, punctuated with white dots. These were nothing other than secondary residences that were small in size, which they referred to as *burj*s, as do the Sfaxians, which literally means a tower or fortress. This use stands in contrast to the term employed by Mahmoud Magdish, a Sfaxian chronicler of the 12th/18th century, who preferred to use the word *qsar* like his predecessor al-Bakri. The most ancient *burj*s to have survived to the present day date from the 11th/17th century. They represent the less evolved type of Sfaxian *burj*. Solid but small in surface area (a base floor area of 20–30 sq. m.), they take the form of a pyramidal tower consisting two floors, each about 6 m. in height. With their parapet, their arches and their gatehouses that surmount the entrance door or reinforce a corner parapet, they were designed to resist the incursions of anarchic tribes living in the surrounding area that occurred at a time when the government was unable to guarantee security in the land. They served as places of refuge, from where people were better able to resist foreign invaders. The *burj*s lacked toilet facilities and kitchens. Their occupants satisfied the call of nature, and undertook their culinary preparations, outside, in cabins made of olive branches, known as *kib*. These residences, which belonged to townsfolk, were only occupied during the hot months. The Sfaxians went there in search of fresh air, *jnan*, fruits, the sweet smell of jasmine and marjoram and basil ... and revelled in them all. For families, it was also the time and place to stock up on dried fruit provisions – almonds, pistachios, figs and raisins – as well as stocking up on more staple foodstuffs like barley and durum wheat which were turned into all kinds of flour, couscous and milled wheat. They would return to the town at the start of the autumn, before the heavy rains poured down.

The *burj* progressively evolved from the 13th/19th century onwards following a period of greater security, demographic boom and social and economic development. From being a secondary residence, it became, for a number of both well-to-do and less well-to-do families, a permanent home. An open courtyard, *hush* – which was linked to the outside through a hallway, the *sqifa* – a stable, *rwa*, a kitchen and any new rooms were built alongside the house. One of these new rooms, *bayt al-sahra*, is kept independent from all domestic activities. Opening out onto the terrace, facing the gentle winds blowing in from the southeast, it was set aside for evening gatherings, as indicated by its name, particularly ones held by the master and his guests. Occasionally, this room was used to store wine when the crop was a good year. The *burj*,

Burj on the outskirts of Sfax.

conceived and enlarged thus, played an important role in the conquest of new lands and in the extension of the *ghaba*, as well as in the creation of olive groves in the far depths of the Steppe. Stacks of hay and olive branches, guard dogs, draught animals tied to and stabled under trees, and carts at rest, are all part of the familiar landscape surrounding the *burj*. Inside the *burjs*, rendered sheds, *heri*, and underground rooms, *matmura*, further highlight its rural function, as well as the Sfaxian concern for being prepared to deal with food shortages, created during the years of drought. The *burjs* of bourgeois families, made wealthy through commerce or land exploitation, were the most elaborate ones, possessing interiors decorated in elements and styles which copy those in the urban home. Porticoes in the courtyard, painted ceilings and cupboards, bed posts made of carved woodwork that are jolly but modest and inspire rest, all denote a fondness for well-balanced refinement.

It was thus that the *burj*, which began as a small residence, ended up becoming an architectural feat dominated by crests of majestic palm trees which inspired wonder in the eyes of travellers. This prototype *burj* still exists. It either formed the core of the more evolved *burj* or stood as a separate house in itself, occupied by less wealthy families.

The evolution undergone by the *burj*, which began in the $13^{th}/19^{th}$ century, did not damage or break the umbilical link which attached the countryside to the town. *"Nearly seven thousand gardens surround Sfax"*, wrote Charles Lallemand in 1890. He added: *"Every evening, having finished his work, the content bourgeois Sfaxian, trotting along on his horse, mule, or donkey, returns to his beautiful garden at the centre of which lives his family"*.

Today the Sfaxian countryside has been broken up and dispersed: the *burjs*, with a few exceptions, have been abandoned. The Sfaxians live in villas or in modern apartments.

ITINERARY IX

The Caravan Staging Posts

Kadri Bouteraa, Ali Zouari

First day

IX.1 GAFSA
        IX.1.a The Kasbah
        IX.1.b Dar al-Longu
        IX.1.c Dar al-Sharif (option)

IX.2 CHÉBIKA
        IX.2.a The Room of the Clepsydra

IX.3 TAMERZA
        IX.3.a Sidi Tuati Mosque

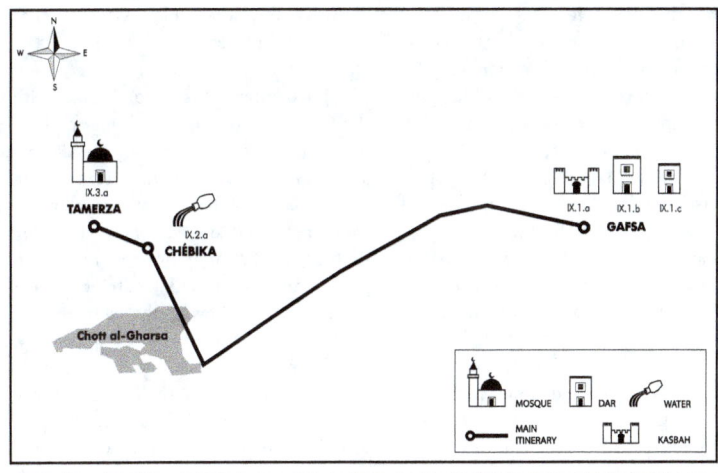

Plain brick architecture, Tozeur.

Ancient village of Tamerza.

The Jérid, an abbreviation of Land of the Palm, *Blad al-Jerid*, was known during the Middle Ages under the name of *Qastiliya*. Grouping together oases cultivated on the tiered plains formed by Tozeur, Nefta, Dégache, al-Hamma and mountains like Chébika, Midès, and Tamerza, they, along with the Gafsa region, composed the northernmost oases of Tunisia, a zone linking the milder Tunisia of the dorsal and the Tell, and the Tunisian desert.

In terms of the Maghreb, this zone is part of a vast corridor of nature, that stretches from the far south of Morocco to the Siwa Oasis in southern Egypt. Ibn Khaldun calls it the zone of the palm trees, *iqlim al-nakhl*. Situated thus, these oases played the role of the Saharan entrance into black Africa – hence the meaning Gate of the Sahara attributed to Gafsa – and of the entrance to the Near East via Gabès. The origin of these centres of water and greenery remains unclear. Arab voyagers considered them to have been eternal and attributed their foundation to heroes or divinities from Arab-Muslim or Libyan mythology. Imaginary stories presented them as initially being hide-outs used by thirsty animal hunters. More acceptable is Gautier's theory which places their origins in the Neolithic Age (3000 BC).

The Jérid entered the history books with the Roman construction of a *limes* which was meant to contain *"the roving nomadic populations to the margins of the Mediterranean world"*. The fall of the Empire opened up the frontiers and led to waves of camel-driving Berbers, the first Arabic groups of the occupation, and later to Hilalian tribes. Made more effective following the submission of the Maghreb to Islam in the $1^{st}/7^{th}$ century, the liberation of the frontiers allowed caravans to perform their duties more effectively, and enabled oases to prosper. Kairouan, engaged in both African and

Maghrebi commerce, made the Jérid an appendage. The sub-Egyptian corridor worked marvelously well. The caravans of pilgrims and merchants, made larger by those who came from al-Andalus and Algeria, stopped over in the Jérid, and joined up with the Tunisian caravans at Gabès. The caravans of merchants took the same corridor but back the other way, in order to trade with Southern Algeria and the borders of Morocco, via Tébessa.

Caravan commerce, which was very lucrative, enabled the managers of the oases to transport their agricultural produce: dates of an amber translucency, *deglet al-nur*, dried fruits, spices ... and crafts goods, especially wool and silk weavings as well as glass and pottery. According to al-Bakri, these products went as far as al-Andalus and Egypt. The economic prosperity allowed for the emergence of strong and animated local powers with autonomist leanings. They succeeded, during moments of weakness on behalf of the central government, in setting up politically and economically powerful principalities, notably those of the Banu Yamlul in Tozeur and the Banu Khalaf in Nefta. Caravan commerce began to slow down from the middle of the $13^{th}/19^{th}$ century onwards, but only disappeared completely much later. Ray, an English voyager who arrived in Sfax in 1294/1877, had to give way with the crowd to two caravans, one charged with dates coming from Tozeur and the other charged with English textiles heading for Tébessa, via Tozeur and Nefta. These latter, he notes, *"were meant to return charged with dates"*.

Nonetheless, the slowing down of the great caravan commerce, the depreciation of agricultural prices and the decline of textile crafts led to the degeneration of the Jérid following a long period of prosperity.

The Jeridis, steeped in ethnic intermixing, and nurtured through the passing of caravans, have also been moulded from a natural landscape that was harsh in its torrid heat

Mountain oasis, Chébika.

ITINERARY IX The Caravan Staging Posts

Gafsa

and mild in its murmuring waters and shaded greenery. Eloquent and poetic but also resisting and judicious, they created an architecture which reflected their own temperament.

In using clay, palm tree wood and brick, all obtained from their surrounding environment, they were able to build monuments, made attractive through their rich decor, which they placed in such a way as to create areas of shade in their battle against the heat. In fact, in endowing his house with a patio surrounded by high-walls, with raised parapets and with small windows which looked like loopholes, the Jeridi could thus limit the amount of hot air, suspend his cluster of dates, provide shaded areas and protect the intimacy of his domestic life.

The material used in the construction of these buildings which is most apparent and most used is blond brick, made in primitive ovens heated with palm-tree wood and placed in a reticulated apparatus; it enables the masons to coat the facades in rich decoration inspired by the environment, by calligraphy and by weavings. This is how Jérid architecture gains its utter originality. Religious architecture adds its own particularities. The minarets, with their lanterns, *jamur*, which are endowed with four domes, are unique within the Arab-Muslim world.

IX.1 GAFSA

Gafsa, descendant of the Roman *Capsa*, gave its name to a civilisation that flowered in this region during Neolithic times. Situated at a crossroads of natural passageways, it was able to transport men between the Tell and the Sahara, as well as commanding the Maghrebi caravans, which had come through the Tébessa and Jérid, and that were en route to Egypt via Gabès. Great and powerful during the 2nd century, and well protected by its ramparts, Gafsa was promoted to town status, and then to that of a colony.

The Byzantines endowed it with strong fortifications and made it a capital of Byzantium. Conquered for good by the Arabs in 78/698, it retained its appearance of an antique town, as well as traces of its Latinisation and Christianisation, for over two centuries.

The Arab chroniclers at the height of the Middle Ages were unanimous in their proclamation that its ramparts, built of stone, were solid and well-preserved, and that its alleyways were paved. Al-Bakri, in the $5^{th}/11^{th}$ century, tells us more precisely that Gafsa *"was built on marble porticoes whose arcades had been blocked up with strong barriers made of rubble"*. The *Kitab al-Istibsar*, the author of which is unknown, adds that Gafsa portrays the name *haniyya*, doubtless because of the arcades, *hanaya*, which it possessed.

Gafsa remained, up until around the $6^{th}/12^{th}$ century, a dynamic and prosperous town. This was because of its agricultural and crafts production, as well as its caravan activity. Its oasis, its fields and its cultivated lands, *mazru'at* – which were irrigated by the currents of water, the *wadi*s, which were fed by two sources, *al-'Ayn al-Kabira* and *al-Tarmid*, which sprung up from inside the town, and by the *wadi* Bayyash – produced, according to chroniclers, dates as large as pigeon eggs, olives, figs, apples, grapes, pistachios and other fruits. The pistachios *"as big as almonds, and better than those of* Bled al-Sham", Syria, were sold in every region of Ifriqiya and were exported to al-Andalus, Sijilmassa and Egypt. Even more eulogistic, the *Kitab al-Istibsar* describes with precision

ITINERARY IX The Caravan Staging Posts
Gafsa

its sources of water and its oasis *"across which are dotted 18 manzils known as* qura's*: hamlets"*. This oasis was surrounded by a rampart known as *Sur al-Ghaba*, which was pierced by four gates, *Abwab al-Durub*, which were surmounted by inhabited towers. *"In Gafsa"*, it adds, *"blankets, shawls, wool turbans, finely pottered utensils that sparkled in their whiteness, works of glass and exceptional utensils and other gilded goods"*. *"Its inhabitants"*, it concludes, *"are well-off"*. Nevertheless Gafsa, which according to all these witness accounts was wealthy, was certainly less so than Tozeur. The tax paid by Gafsa, which according to al-Bakri amounted to 50,000 *dinars*, was only one quarter of that paid by Tozeur.

Gafsa was to be put harshly to the test by episodic events of brutality that related to its political choices. Feeling itself to be sheltered by the distances that separated it from the central power, whilst feeling attached to its old traditions of loyalty to Kairouan and of obedience to the Abbasids, Gafsa opened its doors to dissidents or declared itself independent, under the impulses of powerful families, every time the central government displayed a sign of weakness. It suffered severe reprisals as a result of this attitude.

Following the collapse of Zirid power, Gafsa declared itself independent under the banner of the Banu Rand in 566/1171, which lasted until the Almohad Caliph Abu Ya'qub flushed them out in 575/1180. In 580/1185, Gafsa opened it doors to the Mallorcan Banu Ghaniya in their fight against the Almohads. Al-Mansur punished the town in 582/1187 by razing its ramparts to the ground and by reducing its landowners to share-cropper settlers on their own land. In 795/1393, whilst retaliating against a new Revolt, Abu al-'Abbas utterly destroyed its palm groves. During moments of respite from the fighting, Gafsa's walls were rebuilt, but were once again destroyed at the beginning of the 9th/15th century. It was then given a new

The kasbah, circular pathway, Gafsa.

ITINERARY IX   *The Caravan Staging Posts*
Gafsa

kasbah, only one section of which, however, remains.

Having been challenged severely, Gafsa had, by the 7th/13th century, already lost its energy and drive. Al-Hamawi, writing in the 7th/13th century, whilst reiterating his predecessors in terms of its agricultural production, remarked that it was a small town. Leo the African, in the 10th/16th century, whilst recalling that the town had been repopulated, nevertheless noted the poverty of its buildings, its inhabitants and the unhealthiness of its environment.

Caught up in the events that were inherent to the instabilities of the Ottoman era, and a victim of fiscal exactions, Gafsa fell even further into decline. The town and its monuments were affected even more during the colonial era by additions and transformations. Compact in size, the town has retained from its ancient Roman and Mediaeval splendours only the basins into which water was collected, incorrectly called Roman swimming pools, as well as columns and capitals scattered around in houses and places of worship, and several mosques.

The Great Mosque of Gafsa is outlying, contrary to the normal town-planning of *medinas* which accords the Great Mosque a central position. It is situated in the southern part of town, next to ramparts that no longer exist. The decision to place the Great Mosque next to the ramparts, on an elevated area, accorded it the control and defensive role of a fortress, like a *ribat*. In the Jérid, this was also the case with the Mosque Sidi Mezhud in Nefta and the Mosque of al-'Ayyasha.

The original mosque, probably Aghlabid in origin, underwent several building extensions, the most important of which took place in the 9th/15th century. It encompassed the passageway that separated the ramparts from the constructions on the interior. This move allowed for a corner of the ramparts to be conserved; it was incorporated into the mosque and actually forms its southern side. This extension is perceptible, because its bays do not share the same direction as those of the ancient part.

A small mausoleum, attached to the east-facing facade, is obscurely attributed to Sidi Sahib al-Waqt, known as the Master of the Hours. Was he the person who, employing the sundial, was responsible for determining the hours at which one was called to prayer?

The minaret, which is a clumsy imitation of Hafsid minarets, is of no historic interest. It is a replacement of the original ancient minaret following the First World War, which seemed, according to one surviving photograph, to have been octagonal in section and to have probably dated from the Muradite era.

Meanwhile, the Ottoman era bequeathed several beautiful houses to us: Dar al-Smawi, Dar al-Longu, Dar al-Qarwi … Similar to those in Tunis, in Sfax and in Kairouan, they are all endowed with a *driba*, a patio, and painted ceilings. These houses prove that Gafsa, as an intermediary town, was influenced by immigrant families.

IX.1.a **The Kasbah**

Found in "Avenue Habib Bourguiba". The monument is situated between the local government offices and the courts of justice.

The Kasbah, which is referred to today as a fort, *burj*, stands in the south-west corner of the *medina*. It was once integrated, at its

ITINERARY IX *The Caravan Staging Posts*
Gafsa

The kasbah, Gafsa.

north-east and south-west corners, into the ramparts which today no longer exist. Due to a lack of textual evidence and systematic archaeological digs, it is impossible to give the date of its foundation. Nevertheless it is known that the patrician Salomon built, next to the thermal spas, an important fortress which no doubt was the predecessor of the actual *kasbah*; this is supported by the fact that the remains of the thermal are adjoined to the *kasbah* and can be found on a lower level. These thermal baths actually support the small Mosque of Sidi Salah. It seems that this mosque held greater importance in the 7th/13th century and was called the Mosque of the Apostles, *jama' al-Hawariyin*.

The Byzantine fortress, rebuilt since the Arab occupation and adapted to the defensive needs of Gafsa and its region, transformed itself into a *kasbah*. As a materialisation of the force of order and of supreme authority, this citadel was equally used by dissidents, often strangers to the town, as a base from which to stand up to the central government and from which to gain a good grip over the town. As for the *kasbah*, it underwent counterattacks of indiscipline from the town against the central government: to deprive Gafsa of its citadel was to force it into submission and become its master. In 582/1187, the Almohad Abu Ya'qub Yussef razed its ramparts in order to punish it for having supported Ibn Ghaniya. The Hafsids rebuilt them and restored the *kasbah*; then they destroyed everything at the beginning of the 9th/15th century, again for reasons of indiscipline. During one of his campaigns, Abu 'Abd Allah Ibn Abi Hafs went as far as Gafsa and rebuilt the *kasbah* beyond its former boundaries.

Well maintained during the Ottoman era, this fortress was considered, up until the end of the 19th century, as *"one of the most beautiful in Tunisia"*.

During the colonial period, it was victim to transformations and amputations. The soldiers quarters, the training hall and the Hafsid Mosque disappeared. In fact, only two

ITINERARY IX   *The Caravan Staging Posts*
Gafsa

Dar al-Longu, painted wood ceiling, Gafsa.

walls flanked by oblong and semi-circular towers remain, pierced with canon embrasures and featuring arched merlons of the Aghlabid type. The crenellations and merlons act as a parapet for the circular path, which can still be seen clearly. These walls also offer an idea of the techniques of construction used. Their pedestals are made of freestone, in contrast to the upper parts which are built of rubble.

The little that remains of the *kasbah* badly reflects the role this monument once played and the place it once occupied, both in Tunisian life and in Tunisian military architecture, that lasted for over 1000 years.

There is a beautiful view here of the oasis, which suffers due to its proximity to the far more reputable oases of Tozeur and Nefta.

IX.1.b **Dar al-Longu**

This is inside the medina, *behind the National Museum of Gafsa.*

Opening times: 08.30–12.00 and 15.00–18.00. Closed Mondays.

The traditional Gafsian house, like everywhere else in Tunisia, has a central courtyard. It is accessed via a simple or elbow-shaped hallway. The kitchen, the cellar-vaults which in Gafsa are called *makhzen*, and the bedrooms all open out onto the courtyard, which has no porticoes. The bedrooms are long and narrow, as they are adapted to the length of palm-tree wood and to cross vaults. Each room is furnished at both ends with two masoned rostrums which serve as beds; one surmounts a storeroom full of provisions, the other, which is higher, surmounts a smaller chamber.

It was essentially under the Husaynites, i.e. in the 12th/18th century, with its administrative and military elite, and often with the help of Sfaxian Master-Masons like Mohamed Kammun, that the Gafsian house adopted the look of a bourgeois residence, imitating those of Tunis and of the large coastal towns. T-shaped rooms, courtyards with porticoes, painted ceilings and *kadhal* frames are all embraced.

Houses such as Dar al-Smawi and Dar al-Qarwi are exact copies of Sfaxian houses, right down to the last detail.

Dar al-Longu is an intermediary house. The government, having bought it from its previous owners, the Bakirs, gave it to its Gafsa representative, the Chief Ahmed Ibn Hassan Ibn 'Abd al-Rahman al-Longu. His family, who were of Turkish origin, had set up and secured the town's military and government functions. The first owners of Dar al-Longu had sufficient means to allow themselves to have a relatively sumptuous house, which they chose to place right at the centre of town, close to the Roman pools. A portico endowed with benches, onto which a large room opens, which perhaps once served as stables, leads to a elbow-shaped hallway. The kitchen and outhouses, as well as a reception room and three *qbu* rooms flanked by smaller ones, *maqsura*, all covered in intersecting vaults, are positioned all around the courtyard. Each room surmounts a cellar, which has its own entrance situated inside the courtyard, and acts as a storeroom, *makhzen*. Stairs placed in the hallway lead to the first floor. In terms of typical Gafsian architecture, Dar al-Longu has retained the courtyard without a portico, the intersecting vaults, and the cellars. From Tunis and the coastal towns, it has borrowed the rooms with *qbus* and the painted ceilings. The latter were to be found on the first floor and imitate the Italian-style painted ceilings of Tunis, and thus the house distinguishes itself from Dar al-Smawi whose ceilings, imitating those of Sfax, are of Andalusian production. Mohamed Kammun, who, according to the inscription fixed onto the vault of one of the rooms, oversaw the building works in 1233/1818, had to abandon some architectural dispositions from his hometown in order to satisfy the landowners' attachment to certain forms of traditional Gafsian architecture, and also had to accommodate their weakness for the architecture of Tunis, the thought of which titillated their bourgeois pride. The oratory, *masjed*, integrated into the main part of the house whilst opening out onto the street, was perhaps conceived with this thought in mind.

It seems that Ahmad al-Longu's contribution is limited to purely decorative aspects.

IX.1.c **Dar al-Sharif** (option)

In "rue Mohamed Khadouma".
Opening times: October to May from 08.00–12.00 and 15.00–17.00. June to September from 08.00–13.00. Parking available opposite the entrance. Toilet facilities.

The Dar al-Sharif, situated in the north-east of the *medina*, belonged to the Jewish Moshe before becoming the property of Haj 'Uthman al-Sharif, a great landowner. The passage of Jews through this house has left its trace. On the intersecting vault of the room that occupies the southern side of the court-

Dar al-Longu, hall, Gafsa.

ITINERARY IX   *The Caravan Staging Posts*
Chébika

Dar al-Longu, detail of the door, Gafsa.

yard, an inscription in Hebraic is still visible, but remains to be translated. Furthermore, on the entrance piedroits of the three bedrooms, the following *zwiga* Hebrew invocation, also written in Hebraic script, is chiselled into the plaster: *"May God protect he who occupies this room from all evil"*.

The Dar al-Sharif was built in 1130/1718 by the Master Mason Mohamed Kammun, as is demonstrated by his signature, which accompanies this beautiful saying: *"Oh! you that has entered and departed, know that relief will follow embarrassment and that wealth will wear itself out and that youth will fade"*. Mohamed Kammun also built Dar al-Mufti in 1130/1718 and Dar al-Longu one year later. When carrying out their more often than not expensive commissions, whether regional or domestic, the Sfaxian Master Masons, including Mohamed Kammun and Mahmud Mrad,

shaped the architecture of Gafsa in the mould of that of Sfax. The Dar al-Sharif, the Dar al-Smawi, the Dar al-Mufti … are all replicas of bourgeois Sfaxian homes.

As in Sfax, a hallway, *sqifa*, leads to the courtyard around which are positioned the outbuildings and the three living rooms. Two of these are oblong and narrow, whilst the third, the principal one, follows a T-plan. Its deep *qbu*, embellished with *faience* tiles, is flanked by two tiny chambers, *maqsura*. The architecture, the masonry, and the decor are each a mix of Turkish and Andalusian influences on a Sfaxian background. Gafsian style is only evident on a few scattered elements.

The Dar al-Sharif, like practically all Sfaxian houses, possesses a first floor, accessed via stairs in the hallway. In order to avoid ventilation coming in from the street, the windows on the first floor, like those on the ground floor, face and open onto the courtyard.

IX.2 **CHÉBIKA**

Take the road to Tozeur. At al-Hamma, without entering the village, veer right and get onto a 53 km. track which is suitable for motor vehicles, heading in the direction of the mountain oases. Enquire at the National Guard beforehand as to the condition of the roads, as, if it is windy, the track can be very difficult to drive on.

As soon as one reaches Chébika, the landscape becomes impressive and is imbued with ever-changing colours, depending on the time of day and season.

Chébika clings to the mountain about halfway up, sitting on a platform which allows it to dominate the oasis and the gorge of its *wadi*. The village was once ancient *ad-Speculum*, a Roman defence outpost on the Tacape–Theveste, Gabès–Tébessa track. Built in stone and earth-coloured clay, it blends into its environment. Chébika has actually been abandoned in favour of banal constructions built on the slope. The fabric of the historic village, like a chessboard, evokes that of Tamerza. The axial road, onto which are grafted the secondary roads, leads up to the market square.

IX.2.a **The Room of the Clepsydra**

The monument is situated above the village's unique refreshment room. In order to visit it, ask for the keys to the refreshment room. There are toilet facilities there.

Inside the palm grove, follow the wadi *up to its cascade, then walk up to the summit of the neighbouring hills in order to admire the landscape and the view over the abandoned village.*

Next to the Great Mosque stands a construction with a vault roof. It is the re-conversion of the ancient elbow entrance in Chébika, that takes the form of a deep hallway, and is closed off by two opposing doors. As the interior door was blocked up, the hallway became an oblong room where both the clepsydra and the attendant in charge of it were installed. This water-clock allowed for the equitable distribution of irrigation water to the village's land in the oasis. This room is equipped with a bench that runs lengthwise along its west wall. Facing the bench on the opposite side is an arched recess, sunk into the wall. Its platform was used as a seat by the attendant in charge. Facing him, two Clepsydras in the form of jars were suspended above a vast masoned hole, the purpose of which was to hold the water poured in by these vessels which, once they had emptied themselves, were again filled by the attendant. According to al-Bakri, the clepsydra emptied itself every four hours. Once an amount which corresponds to a certain number of filling and emptying has been consumed, the attendant or his assistant blows a horn to alert a second assistant who is situated in the oasis itself. This latter assistant then closes an irrigation canal called a *seguia* and opens another, thus putting an end to one cycle of water and starting another.

IX.3 TAMERZA

In heading towards Tamerza, the track changes into a tarmac road.

Clepsydra, Chébika.

235

ITINERARY IX   *The Caravan Staging Posts*
Tamerza

> *Impressive landscapes appear successively along the entire length of the road: canyons, disappearing into the chott in the distance, views of oases. Make a stop 2 km. from Tamerza, to visit the Great Cascade located below, 100 m. further on. Directions are clearly indicated.*

Tamerza clings to the sides of a gigantic canyon through which flow abundant streams of water vital to this mountain oasis. Its agriculture, and of late its tourism, depend on them.

Sidi Tuati Mosque, Tamerza.

The site of Tamerza, so well protected by nature, is that of old *ad-Turres*, a site of defence built by the Romans, which became an episcopal seat in the Byzantine era. The history of Tamerza during the Muslim period is unattainable. Nevertheless, the restrained dimensions of this village-oasis, its structure and its monuments allow us to say that it lived for its defensive role. The main street, axial in form, bends further towards the east and ends as a covered passageway, a dark *sabat*, onto which are grafted a maze of pathways that end through dispersing themselves into the mountain. This design was aimed at luring the enemy into surprise to ambush him. Abandoned in favour of a new village, Tamerza increasingly fell into ruin. The Sidi Tuati Mausoleum demonstrates that Tamerza possessed its own architectural objects of interest, such as the Great Mosque, also known as the Mosque of Sidi al-'Abid, which is situated at the far eastern end of the village's axial street.

IX.3.a **Sidi Tuati Mosque** (this monument is not open to visitors)

The monument stands in the old abandoned village of Tamerza which lies on the shores of a dried-out riverbed, wadi. *Cross through the new village in the direction of Mides. Leave your car at the foot of the slope that leads to the Tamerza Palace Hotel. The monument is on the corner of the first two streets as one enters the village.*
There are toilet facilities available in Café République.

Situated at the entrance to Tamerza, at the start of the axial street, the Sidi Tuati Mosque is composed of a prayer hall, a mausoleum where the saint rests, and of rooms reserved for visitors. The prayer hall

ITINERARY IX *The Caravan Staging Posts*
Tamerza

Sidi Tuati Mosque, Tamerza.

is distinct for the orientation of its *mihrab* towards the east, contrary to Muslim norms. One can explain this anomaly if one compares this mosque to churches. Was it originally a church, or did it copy one? These are valid questions if one refers to the writings of al-Tijani, a traveller of the 8th/14th century. According to him, for a long time the Arabs tolerated the churches that were present in the Jérid, they even authorised the construction of a mosque next to each one.

The prayer-hall roof, made of palm-tree wood, is supported by arches resting on indented brick capitals and palm-tree trunk columns, cut octagonally. A piece of apricot-tree wood, functioning as a cushion support, separates each capital from its column, both made of different materials. The use of palm-tree wood to support structures was most widespread in the Jérid. This use slowly decreased in favour of brick and stone. Therefore, the wooden columns made of palm tree in the Sidi Tuati Mosque represent a rare example of its kind in the region. Their octagonal form is even rarer. Could it be a result of foreign influence?

Octagonal pillars transport us to the 12th/18th century, which saw the Italian introduction of this kind of pillar, but in marble. Their use, as much in religious architecture as in the domestic architecture of Tunis, took off a little later throughout the rest of the country. The mausoleum, architecturally different from the prayer hall, is, no doubt, of more recent origin. Its interest lies in its ovoidal dome. This shape recalls that of Sidi al-Kharassani in al-Mahassin and that of Sidi bel-'Abbes in Nefta. This type of dome, which is non-existant if not rare outside the Jérid, is, according to art historians, descended from Oriental art. One can find examples of it particularly in Persia, Yemen and Egypt.

The walk to Mides is worth the detour. The oasis and the old village are extremely picturesque.

237

ITINERARY IX

The Caravan Staging Posts

Kadri Bouteraa, Ali Zouari

Second day

IX.4 TOZEUR
    IX.4.a   Dar Ben 'Azzuz
    IX.4.b   Bled al-Hadar Mosque
    IX.4.c   Sidi al-Lakhmi Zawiya

IX.5 DÉGUÈCHE
    IX.5.a   Ouled Majid Mosque
    IX.5.b   Sidi al-Kharassani Zawiya

IX.6 KÉBILI

Weaving
The mountain Oases of the Jérid

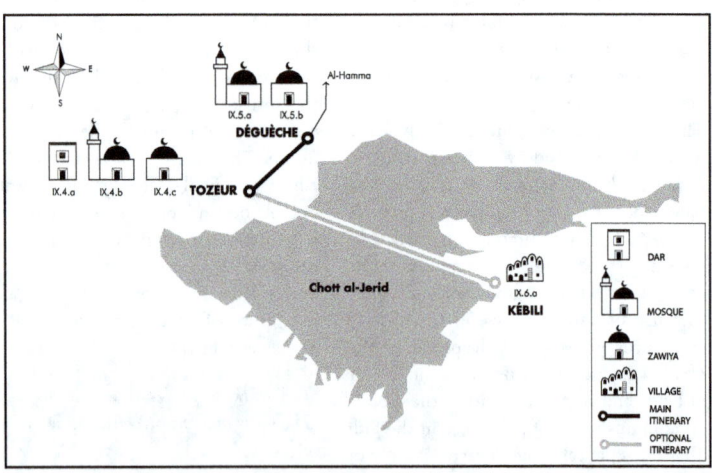

ITINERARY IX   The Caravan Staging Posts
Tozeur

Brick cornice, Tozeur.

IX.4 TOZEUR

Retake the Chébika road, in the direction of Tozeur, passing by al-Hamma.

The name Tozeur comes from the Latin *Thusorus*, a name the Romans gave it when it was nothing but a citadel on the *limes* which was meant to contain Nomadic Berber populations. The Arabs, led by Hassan Ibn Nu'man, in occupying it in 73/693, found it to be a Latinised, Christianised and influential town. Its rapid surrender spared it from reprisals. According to al-Tijani, the conquerors respected the churches and built a mosque next to each and every one of them. The ruins of the churches were still standing when he visited the region.
From the Occupation onwards, the new masters gave Tozeur a second name, equally of Latin origin: *Qastiliya*, from Castella, citadel. The headquarters of the whole of the Jérid, Tozeur, shared its new name with it up until the 13th/19th century. From then on, official documents and travel accounts only refer to it as *Bled al-Jerid*, the Land of the Palm Trees.
Tozeur's population, composed of Arab groups from the Occupation and of Berber offshoots, grafted onto the same Roman backbone, lost its stability and calm in the 6th/12th century with the Hilalian invasion, which was followed by troubles that were often bloody.
The Arab chroniclers at the height of the Middle Ages present Tozeur as the Jérid's main town, as opulent and buzzing with activity. They speak with admiration of its brick and stone ramparts, of its numerous *suqs*, its well-built mosque, its large suburbs and of its luxurious oasis, producing the best and most abundant dates in Ifriqiya. Al-Bakri, in the 5th/11th century, says *"Every day they unload 1000 camels that carry dates"*. Tozeur's wealth was derived from the

ITINERARY IX   *The Caravan Staging Posts*

Tozeur

Dar Ben Azzur, patio, Tozeur.

exportation of dates and crafts, mainly those consisting of woven wool and woven silk.

Opulent and distant, Tozeur, like the rest of the Jérid, was coveted by dissidents who were rebelling against the central government, or who were fired up by vague impulses of Independence, under the pressure of powerful families. The Mallorcan Banu Ghaniya, fighting the Almohads for power, made Tozeur and Gafsa bases from which to mount attack from 582/1187 to 583/1188. Between 732/1332 and 792/1390, the Banu Yamlul were able to become the leaders of this town, despite embargoes enforced upon it by the central government, recognising in name rather than in nature their allegiance to the Hafsid sovereigns.

In spite of these occasionally bloody twists and turns and of the fiscal exactations that ensued, Tozeur continued to shine until the 13th/19th century. Al-Tijani paints a fascinating picture of the place. According to him, the inhabitants of Tozeur lived mainly in the oasis where the houses were bigger and more beautiful than those in town. Stunned by the spectacle he saw through an observatory situated at the point where the waters meet, he described it thus: *"The fullers assemble together and spread out their coloured fabrics and all kinds of decorated objects, so as to cover the entire area. The spectator is under the impression of having found himself in a paradise of blooming flowers and free-flowing streams"*. The "free-flowing" streams were nothing other than currents of water escaping from the *wadi*, and were nourished by the sources as well as by the irrigation canals, *seguia*, of the oasis. The judicious irrigation system allowed for everyone to have their fair share of water, thus enabling the government to collect their fiscal due. *Qadus* were used to determine the dividing up of water, based on chronometric calculations: rudimentary pottery clepsydras that emptied themselves eight times a day.

ITINERARY IX *The Caravan Staging Posts*
Tozeur

Today Tozeur is composed of modern quarters and of old quarters, particularly those of Zebda and the Ouled al-Hadef. The streets of the latter, tortuous and covered in sections by thick vaults, lead to small squares. The facades of the houses, the *zawiyas* and the mosques are adorned with beautiful reticulated brick cladding.

R. Brunschvig, through interpreting the witness accounts of geographers of the Middle Ages as well as those written by Leo the African in the $10^{th}/16^{th}$ century, is inclined to believe that Mediaeval Tozeur was located at Bled al-Hadar, slightly south of present Tozeur: *"It is there, inside a small mosque"*, says he, *"that one can admire a stunning mihrab, dating from 590/1194, built under the Almohads, by Yahya Ibn Ghaniya"*.

IX.4.a **Dar Ben 'Azzuz**

In "rue de Kairouan", go past the sabat *Lalla Ajila which ends up at Dar Ben 'Azzuz.*

Situated in the south-east of the ancient Quarter of al-Hawadif, Dar Ben 'Azzuz bears the name of its former owners: the Ben 'Azzuz's. A family of notables from Tozeur, several of its members became *cadi*s of the town. In spite of changes affecting it, which in fact have only been slight, and have mainly been done with regard to the entrance, this house remains, along with Dar Ben Rhuma in the Zebda Quarter, one of the best examples of traditional houses in the Jérid. Every distinctive element of the oases architecture of this region is represented: palm-tree wood for roofing, reticulated brickwork on the facades of the houses and of the rooms, garret windows to limit the amount of hot air, a high ceiling to facilitate air flow and to suspend bunches of dates, and narrow rooms built to accommodate the length of palm-tree wood. The hallway, *sqifa*, leads to a courtyard with high walls, surrounded by three rooms. The height of the walls creates, here and there, long shadows according to

Dar Ben 'Azzuz, guttering pipe, Tozeur.

241

ITINERARY IX   The Caravan Staging Posts

Tozeur

Bled al-Hadar Mosque, detail of the mihrab, Tozeur.

the position of the sun, areas of shade which are indispensable in this region, given that it undergoes nearly six months of intense heatwaves. Stairs in the hall lead to an upper floor consisting of a room and a privy. Almost separate, it is designed for guests to whom one wants to offer a little freedom and privacy, as well as enabling one to keep one's family life out of their way. Another set of staircases placed in the courtyard leads to the terraces. These terraces, featuring raised parapets, hold an important role in Jeridian daily life. They are used as a place from which to taste the fresh night air of the Saharan climate.

IX.4.b **Bled al-Hadar Mosque** (this monument is not open to visitors)

Take "avenue Abu Kacem al-Chebbi", followed by the first street to the left before the Continental Hotel. The monument can be found on the right after the bridge leading to the oasis, facing the school of the same name.

The Bled al-Hadar Mosque, in the central quarter of Tozeur's old town, stands on the site of an ancient Byzantine church, the remains of which can be seen on the eastern side of the prayer hall. Authorised by the Great Mosque of Tozeur up until the 6th/12th century, it was for this reason, and until this date, remarkably well kept. Because it is similar, in more ways than one, to the Great Mosque of Kairouan, it became, in its moment of glory, a model adopted throughout the Jérid. For instance, the minaret of the Ouled Majid Mosque is a masterful copy of its minaret.

The spread of economic activity from this quarter to the suburbs, coinciding with a population displacement, weakened the interest held in this mosque. Severely damaged, it was rebuilt for the first time, retaining only its principal elements, that

ITINERARY IX   *The Caravan Staging Posts*
Tozeur

is to say, the trunk of the minaret, a section of the *qibla* wall, the *mihrab*, the courtyard floor and the cistern. The thus antagonised architecture lead numerous historians into making errors, such as concluding that the base of the minaret, built of freestone, is from the Byzantine era, and that the actual prayer hall is from Mediaeval times. Nevertheless, the texts by Ibn Shabat as well as archaeological surveys completed in 1970 have discarded these points of view and have allowed us to conclude that the Mediaeval mosque, which was in excellent condition during the $6^{th}/12^{th}$ century, echoes the plan of the Great Mosque of Kairouan, and that the minaret, built in freestone up to the lantern, was added in the $7^{th}/13^{th}$ century. Ibn Shabat states that it was in excellent condition during his time, referring to the $9^{th}/15^{th}$ century. The minaret was truncated much later. A new brick body was built onto its base during the $13^{th}/19^{th}$ century.

An inscription in Maghrebi characters dates its foundation (595/1199), and mentions the name of its founder, 'Ali Ibn Ghaniya al-Mayorqui (the Mallorcan).

One can undertake an agreeable walk through the Ouled al-Hadef Quarter, with its characteristic architecture.

IX.4.c **Sidi al-Lakhmi Zawiya** (this monument is not open to visitors)

Situated 400 m. from the preceding monument, on the right-hand side.

The Sidi al-Lakhmi Zawiya is named after the Shaykh Abu al-Hassan al-Ribi'i al-Lakhmi al-Qayrawani. This Kairouanese scholar had chosen to go and live in Sfax where he was then buried.
An appreciated and celebrated teacher across and beyond the whole of Ifriqiya, students used to flock in droves to his lessons.

Sidi al-Lakhmi Zawiya, ovoidal dome, Tozeur.

243

ITINERARY IX   *The Caravan Staging Posts*
Déguèche

One of them, Abu al-Fadl al-Nahwi, won fame in his hometown of Tozeur for being an eminent scholar of grammar, hence his surname: al-Nahwi, the grammarian. He chose to place his tomb next to the *zawiya* dedicated to Sidi al-Lakhmi, in loyalty and honour to his illustrious master.

The *zawiya* consists of a mosque and a funerary chamber which is in fact only a staged one, simulating that of Shaykh al-Lakhmi's in Sfax. The mosque is of a primitive design, in the mould of Islam's first mosque, i.e. that of the Prophet Muhammad in Medina. It includes a courtyard, endowed with an open arcade, that acts as a prayer hall. The *mihrab*, a simple recess into the wall, is turned – no doubt through misjudgment – eastward like the rest of the mosque, rather than to the south-east which is the exact orientation towards the *qibla*.

The funerary chamber is reached from the courtyard through a small door. This square-plan room is covered by an ovoidal dome built from pieces of pottery and supported on triangular squinches which line the base in such a way as to make it octagonal.

The entire *zawiya*, abandoned, fell into ruin. Affiliated to the ancient religious architecture of the Jérid both in its design and its building materials, this monument is embellished in a rich decor of brick, which is still clearly evident. The decor on the window frames, which are long and horizontal, is particularly elegant and refined.

IX.5 DÉGUÈCHE

It is located 10 km. east from Tozeur.

Déguèche is a derivation of the term *Taqyus*, which was applied to four townships or *qsurs*, fortified by ramparts. These are: Déguèche, Ouled Majid, Kriz and Sdeda. *"These* qsurs *are so close to one another"*, states the *Kitab al-Istibsar*, *"that their inhabitants can all talk to one another from their own home"*.

Sidi al-Lakhmi Zawiya, entrance to the funerary chamber, Tozeur.

ITINERARY IX *The Caravan Staging Posts*
Déguèche

Al-Idrissi cites Taqyus as a town situated between al-Hamma and Gafsa, *"a beautiful town"*, he says, *"well populated. It produces henna, cumin, caraway seeds, and various vegetables. Its palm trees bear excellent fruits"*. Its excellent-quality dates are today still the most popular in Tunisia, and the most wanted for export. Old Déguèche is, together with al-Hamma, one of the rare oases where stone instead of brick is used in construction. The stone is extracted from neighbouring quarries.

IX.5.a **Ouled Majid Mosque** (this monument is not open to visitors)

In what is called Ouled Majid, in the oasis.

Ouled Majid is one of the townships or *qsurs* of the Taqyus agglomeration that al-Idrissi, a chronicler living in the $6^{th}/12^{th}$ century, spoke of. It has actually been abandoned in favour of a new town built alongside the tarmac road. The historic township is located north of the oasis. It still has houses that have nearly kept their entirety, with their palm tree-trunk roofs, their gates and doors, and even with their water supply which has never ceased to run indoors.

The mosque, situated to the north-east of this agglomeration, is in architectural terms one of the most important in the state of Tozeur, although it is not structurally different from the other mosques in the Jérid, which have all been inspired by the Bled al-Hadar Mosque. It differs from the other mosques in terms of the shallowness of its courtyard and the portico, which limits itself to one side only. The tendency for shortening the courtyard between the minaret and the prayer hall would be adopted by a number of later mosques, which means that the Ouled Majid Mosque became a prototype, just like Bled al-Hadar before it.

The Ouled Majid Mosque consists of a prayer hall and a courtyard, endowed on its northern side with a double portico. A minaret stands in the middle of this side.

The minaret, situated at the centre of this northern side, is the oldest of all the minarets in the Jérid. It is worthy for having preserved the form of the minaret of the Bled al-Hadar Mosque, which disappeared but which we know of thanks to the detailed

Ouled Majid Mosque, dome and minaret, Ouled Majid.

ITINERARY IX   The Caravan Staging Posts
Déguèche

Sidi al-Kharassani Zawiya, Déguèche.

description left to us by Ibn Shabat. This square-based minaret has a trunk over 2 m. high, built of freestone. The body of the construction is of brick. Its lantern, *jamur*, which on each side features a twin-arch, is topped by four fluted domes. The flutes are regular in two of these domes, and streaked (striated) on the other two. The four-domed lantern, a design specific to the Jérid, is unique in the Muslim world.

IX.5.b **Sidi al-Kharassani Zawiya** (this monument is not open to visitors)

Situated on the Tozeur–Kebili road, 1km. from Ouled Majid, the Sidi al-Kharassani Zawiya is found at the exit to the village of al-Mahasin, an oases agglomeration grouping together several villages including Sdada and Kriz.

The Sidi al-Kharassani Mausoleum is the most important historical monument in this agglomeration. The man after whom this mausoleum is named remains a mystery to us due to a lack of epigraphic and hagiographic documents on him. If one believes a vague piece of information offered by al-Tijani, he would be a man from the Hafsid era. Nonetheless, oral tradition remembers him as a saint, *wali*, who had the gift of opening up the path of marriage to old maids who came to visit him.

Situated to the east of the road, this mausoleum clutches onto the side of a hill at the foot of which ran the sources that fed the *wadi* of the seven wells, now dried up. This monument is composed of two rooms: that of the tomb, covered by an ovoidal dome, and a communal room covered by a palm-wood roof which is of little interest and kept for visitors. The mausoleum's originality resides in the cippuses, shaped in the form of sugar loaves which surmount the four corners of its terrace and the four corners of the enclosed space outside, out onto which it looks. These cippuses are copies of funerary cippuses which are the original features of cemeteries of the Algerian Mzab. In this way, the Sidi al-Kharassani Mausoleum, through its rare, shaped dome and its chunky stone, represents a masterful example of similar monuments dotted here and there across the Jérid. It bears witness to the influence of the funerary architecture of the Mzab and no doubt to the passage of the Ibadite Kharijites throughout the region. We may even suppose that the man at rest in the mausoleum is himself an Ibadite Kharijite, which leads us to the following admission: that Ibadite Kharijism spread across the Jérid during the Middle Ages, that it firmly influenced social life and behaviour, and that the mausoleum, thought of as a tomb, is an exact copy of the tombs of the Mzab, an Ibadite Kharijite region, and is as such through its placement of four pear-shaped chunky stones at each corner of its terrace.

IX.6 KÉBILI

The al-Jerid Chott
The al-Jerid Chott, like other chotts bordering on the Maghrebi Sahara, is a depression deepened by wind-erosion, whose ground level is below sea level. Formerly the site of a lake that dried out thousands of years ago, to the traveller it looks like an immense expanse of greyish, hilly land which is covered in patches of dried vegetation. This is only a mirage. The al-Jerid Chott was until recently a trap into which all those venturing without a guide fell. For this reason, chotts have remained of interest and have inspired fear. A small temple, situated north of the al-Jerid Chott, offered protection to those who were planning to cross it. The traveller who returned safe and well felt obliged to offer a sacrifice to the gods of the temple.
The Arab chroniclers and voyagers did not omit writing about chotts, insisting on the dangers they entailed. According to these accounts, the swampy and unstable chotts swallowed up individuals, caravans and entire armies. Abu al-Hajjaj thought of them as one of the world's strangest curiosities. A tarmac road built by the Tunisian army around 1970 has since shortened the journey between the Jérid and Kébili.

WEAVING

Naceur Baklouti

Weaving and tapestry have been practised in Tunisia since time immemorial. As early as the time of Pericles, Greek sources spoke highly of the rugs from Carthage. Those which were most likely to have been woven in Kairouan travelled as far as Baghdad, acting as a tribute paid by the Aghlabid Amirs to their Abbassid sovereigns. We know that during the 5th/11th century, mulberry trees were cultivated in Gabés in order to produce silkworms; the town certainly possessed a centre for silk weaving. At the same time, the Hilalian nomads favoured raising sheep and begun weaving with wool, which they executed so well that soon regional and ethnic particularities emerged. There is not a single town, nor village, nor rural area that does not possess its own specific produce.

Thus, there are covers made in Testour, a village in the north founded by Andalusians, that are remarkable in their marriage of geometric and floral decoration and through their use of coloured silk threads in the weft of the fabric.

Kairouan, Bizerte, and the Ksiba in the Sahel, all produced knot-stitched rugs of high-quality wool, woven on a vertical loom that was very smooth. The most famous rug is from Kairouan; Anatolian in inspiration, it features a central hexagonal image, bordered by parallel bands of stylised floral motifs. This image is the projection of the mosque *mihrab* onto the rug through a convergence of religious architecture and the art of tapestry. Today, this kind of tapestry work is fabricated right across the country; the Kairouanese type of rug perfects and improves itself for the purpose of widespread commercialisation and is exported under a quality-control stamp.

Another high-quality wool rug with a less tightly knitted texture was woven by the craftsman, the *reggam*, a travelling craftsman who offered his services to villages and douaniers. The *gtif*, composed of warm colours and geometric decorations that are partitioned like those of the Hammamas and the Mhedhbas, upholstered the tent furniture of the nomads and those of certain bourgeois homes, notably in Sfax.

Further south, in Udref, Matmata and Toujane, the women wove close-cropped rugs, *mergum*, decorated in diamond-shaped, polychrome motifs. The coverings made in Gafsa, which have no wrong or right sides, are distinct for their use of two-colours, red and blue, and for their stylised zoomorphic and anthropomorphic decorations.

On a rudimentary loom, made up of four posts stuck into the ground, the Bedouin woman weaves tent strips, decorated cushions, bags for carrying loads and other rug-coverings, *heml*.

Young woman weaving.

THE MOUNTAIN OASES OF THE JÉRID

Ali Zouari

The oasis of Gafsa, 19th-century engraving.

The mountain oases of the Jérid were for a long time referred to as a *qsur*, as was the case for villages of the region of Gafsa, alluded to under this term by Arab chroniclers. The chroniclers, with the exception of the *Kitab al-Istibsar* (6th/12th century), ignored these oases-villages, perhaps because they were of little interest.

Small, and perching on mountainsides, they were self-sufficient, keeping their equilibrium between production and population. This equilibrium was disrupted by the exploitation of the phosphate mines of the Gafsa region. The inhabitants of these oases thus left their mountainsides in order to work in the mines. The emigration was later amplified for other reasons. Depopulated, and often referred to as "abandoned villages", a fresh lease of life was experienced by the oases, albeit in new villages, thanks to the tourist industry.

The historic villages, which stand mostly in ruin, offer the visitor the opportunity to admire characteristic religious and domestic architecture. The Great Mosque here is called such, not because it is the oldest or the most important or that it is positioned centrally to define urban planning like in the *medinas*, but because it needs to be distinguished from the other places of worship as it is the only one that provides the laudatory prayer on Fridays in line with Orthodox Sunnism.

ITINERARY X

Towards the Land of the *Qsur*

Naceur Baklouti

First day

X.1 GABÈS
      X.1.a Sidi Bulbaba Madrasa
      X.1.b Hush Khrayef
      X.1.c The Jara Suq

X.2 MATMATA

X.3 TAMEZRET

X.4 TAOUJOUT

X.5 TOUJANE

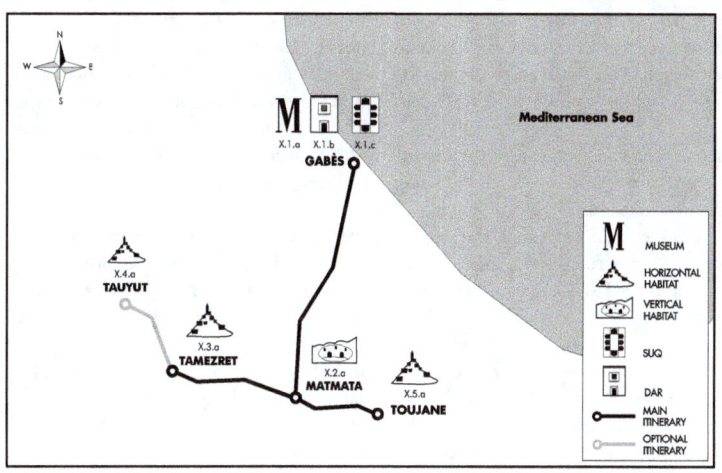

Ouled Soltan Ksar.

Berber handwriting and Arabic inscription, Douiret.

The last of the historic cities before entering the land of the *qsurs*, Gabès is situated in a region of oases which has been graced with a continuous human presence since Prehistoric times. This permanence is due in great part to the existence of sources of water which irrigate the oases that favour an agriculture laid out in tiers, so eloquently described by Pliny the Elder in the 1st century.

Having proven its effectiveness, this cultural system was nevertheless lost, being unable to withstand the gradual draining of its hydraulic resources and the consequences of industrial development, which has effected the town for several decades now.

Gabès is a sprawling town which underwent urban expansion at lightning speed. Since the end of the 19th century, and particularly since 1956 when Tunisia gained its Independence, new neighbourhoods, characterised by their dense and homogeneous urban fabric, spontaneously or voluntarily agglomerated themselves to the historic heart of the town. It is evidently in the historic centres such as Jara and Menzel, or at their outskirts, that one finds the most notable Islamic monuments, such as the Mausoleum of the Prophet's companion Abu Lubaba al-Ansari and the Hush Khrayef. These buildings carry the mark of Muradite architecture of the 11th/17th century, which is distinguished by its nobleness and austerity.

Far from being confined in and around its palm grove, Gabès has always been a town open to the mountains nearby, receiving its overflowing demography and in return benefiting from it as a refuge for its inhabitants in times of trouble. The Jabal, land of the *qsurs* and of troglodytic villages, begins less than 30 km. away from Gabès towards the south-west, continuing in the form of a crescent towards Libya. This region is different in terms of its residual communities that have lived there for a long time, conserving their ancient traditions in terms of housing and agriculture.

Whilst travelling along the sharp bends and paths of the mountains, one is astounded by the tree groves that have been cultivated in the upper valleys. Rainwater streams down the slopes, forming natural *impluviums* which are retained by small dams made of stones or of earth. These dams, known as *jesser*, regularise the flow of the water, enabling the cultivation of palm trees, some olive trees and fig trees, and during a rainy year one can even sow. The mountain habitat, entirely or partially troglodytic, is distinguished by the diversity of its forms, which vary according to the nature of the landscape. In the north, the Matmata range looks like a massif undulating away until it disappears from view. Some villages occupy the basins, such as Matmata, Hadège, Techine ... where houses have been dug out of the sandy, clay formations of the massif. To the west, on the hillocks of the Dahar, a relatively fertile plateau whose western slope, at a gentle angle, joins the oases of Nefzaoua and the basin of the Great Erg, three villages huddle together: Tamezret, Taoujout and Zeraoua, which today are abandoned. Their houses are permanent, consisting of one or more rooms which have been excavated into the flank of the mountain. Further south, the landscape becomes uneven, and the eastern flank of the mountain, that which faces the sea, is steeper. There, like the eagles' nest, the villages are perched on the crests and rocky outcrops, spreading their rows of homes over several plateaus. In Douiret, Chénini, Guermessa, the homes are semi-troglodytic,

each consisting of a section built to last permanently that precedes another hole dug into the tender surface of the mountain, built according to an interconnecting plan. This device is crowned above by the citadel, *qal'a*, or the collective storehouse, *qsar*, which hangs over the village as it hangs over the valleys that surround it. The storage sheds, *ghorfa*s, are built on several levels, mingling together the crests of the *qsurs* with the meanderings of the steep slopes; both in the mountains and in the plains, they are arranged around a central courtyard. In this South Tunisian region, with its arid climate, the tradition of hoarding food reserves for those years when cows were emaciated was an imperious necessity. Whether they were breeders occupying the plains or mountain arboriculturists, the inhabitants' way of life imposed on them the need to preserve their harvest and their precious goods

Oued Gabes, 19th-century watercolour.

ITINERARY X *Towards the Land of the* Qsur
Gabès

from all kinds of damage: a *qsar*, a collective fortified shed, watched over by a permanent guard, was founded in response to this necessity. The *qsar* was also the meeting place for members of different tribes, reunited after their incessant pilgrimages. On such occasions, ties were strengthened, exchanges intensified: social life was at its height. The *qsar* remains to this day the symbol of group cohesion and the affirmation of its identity.

X.1 GABÈS

It was most likely to have been the Phoenicians who founded the town of Tacape, in the Small Syrte, a town known today as Gabès, a veritable gateway to the Tunisian south-east, on a site which without doubt was occupied by the Libycs, as the ancient inhabitants of the land were called. Very quickly, this city trading-post grew in commercial and military importance, gained through its advantageous position of being on the axis of heavy maritime and Saharan traffic. Up until the $13^{th}/19^{th}$ century, the caravan routes from Timbuctoo and Agadès to Niger went through Ghadamès, which is in present-day Libya, in order to reach Gabès.

In the middle of the 7th century, Tapaces, a town first integrated into Roman Africa and then into the Byzantine Empire, became Qabis, an Arab-Muslim city supported by the central power established in Kairouan. Under the Aghlabids in the $3^{rd}/9^{th}$ century, and the Fatimids in the $4^{th}/10^{th}$ century, it lived through a period of political stability which generated a brilliant civilisation, marked in particular by the number and splendour of its monuments. The texts regarding this subject are inexhaustible. The geographer Ibn Hawqal speaks in the $4^{th}/10^{th}$ century of a city belted in by ramparts surrounded by a ditch, possessing several *suqs*. In the $8^{th}/14^{th}$ century, the traveller al-Tijani added that Gabès was surrounded by a rampart made of large bonded stones, built by the ancients, and counted a great number of suburbs, where most of the *suqs* were situated. The texts also speak, in a laudatory manner, of the monuments that were erected, such as the Great Mosque, the citadel, the *kasbah*, the *caravanserai*s and the famous beacon which informed caravans coming in from the East of their arrival into the town.

However, a long period of trouble settled over the town, beginning in the $5^{th}/11^{th}$ century following the weakening of Zirid power and the concurrent arrival of Bedouins from Upper Egypt, affecting both its urban organisation and social life. It would only lift itself up and out of these troubles under the Muradites several centuries later, a dynasty of Turkish origin from the $11^{th}/17^{th}$ century.

In terms of its past, Gabès, this very prosperous town, which Ibn Khaldun had described as a maritime metropolis, has faded into the obscurity of history because, mysteriously, nothing remains of the monuments that were so greatly praised by Arab chroniclers and travellers. Legend therefore takes over from where history left off. Collective memory reports that in those days, when order and security ruled, beasts of burden were trusted to carry vegetables and fruits to the town's market without needing to be accompanied, after which they returned to the palm grove carrying the revenue of their sales in their saddle bags. One day, however, the money they were carrying was stolen, and, made to suffer under God's wrath, the town was completely destroyed from its foundations up,

ITINERARY X   *Towards the Land of the* Qsur
Gabès

and its ruins were used to build the new neighbourhoods of Gabès. Where history regains its position from myth, it tells us that in the 10th/16th century the inhabitants abandoned their homes to go and live on the edges of the palm grove, thus creating a new urban centre from the fabric borrowed from Arab-Muslim urban planning: Jara, Menzel and Chénini.

The timid redress of the situation during the 11th/17th century, resulting from relative stability, is marked by the renovation or construction of several monuments, in a style that is both noble and sober. The Muradite architecture of Gabès is distinguished by an austerity born out of a return to the use of large boulders of freestone which adorn the facades, and by the discreet arrangement of architectural elements composed of vaults, domes and curbed and horseshoe arches, often supported by second-hand columns and capitals, in a scansion that alternates curved and straight lines.

The Oasis of Gabès
The Oasis of Gabès envelopes itself around the town like a cup, covered by the majestic panache of its dark and brightly coloured palm trees. On this burnt soil, the city owes its existence to the oasis. As it is situated on the coast, it produces dates of medium quality but is distinct for the diversity of its produce and above all for its age-old agricultural and irrigation techniques which have been in use for several centuries. Dividing into two branches, the Wadi *Gabès, fed by a number of sources, stretches across the palm grove which is both fresh and fecund thanks to a network of* seguias *that distribute an amount of water allocated to each patch of land according to its area.*
These patches are surrounded by palm trees, fruit trees such as pomegranates and vines; they are divided into strips kept aside for market-gardening and fodder crops, and in particular for henna, which yields three harvests a year. From the first fruits of spring onwards, the vine stocks entwine their branches to form inextractible garlands between the palm trees and the pomegranate trees, endowing the tiered agriculture of the oasis with an eye-catching look of exuberance. Today, the decrease in the wadi's flow, the consequences of chemical industry established nearby, as well as the pernicious urban system, risk eroding away this magnificent palm grove despite the efforts undertaken by the authorities.

X.1.a Sidi Bulbaba Madrasa

The monument stands at the exit of Gabès, in the direction of Matmata. Go down avenue Béchir Dziri, on which the Arts and Crafts Office and the PTT *(Post) are located, then turn right after the bridge and continue upwards towards the Mosque of Sidi Bulbaba: the Museum of Popular Arts and Traditions and the mausoleum face the mosque.*
Entrance fee. Opening times: 09.30–16.30 from 15th September to 31st May, and 08.00–13.00 and 15.00–18.00 from June to September. Closed Mondays. Parking and Toilets available.

Built on a raised mound, which hangs over the cemetery and the residential neighbourhoods that are adjacent to it, the Sidi Bulbaba Madrasa looks like an imposing mass thanks to the sobriety of its bulky dimensions. Bordering a vast, esplanade construction, the monument stands next to the mausoleum of the companion to the Prophet Abu Lubaba al-Ansari and faces a large mosque built about 20 years ago which is remarkable in terms of its tall minaret clad in freestone and its column and arcade porch. The *madrasa* housed

255

ITINERARY X   Towards the Land of the Qsur
Gabès

Sidi Bulbaba Madrasa, patio, Gabès.

students as well as giving them an education.

The Sidi Bulbaba Madrasa, which owes its name to the mausoleum nearby, was founded in 1103\1692 during the regime of the Muradite sovereign Mohamed Pasha.

After two flights of steps, one enters the monument via a door worthy for its stone frame cut into the limestone, the only ornamental feature of this quasi-blind facade.

This door is enhanced by a horseshoe arch, the coving of which falls back onto stone piedroits. Following the example of traditional houses, the entrance to the *madrasa* is in the form of an elbow angle. On the back wall of the first hallway, a panel of *faience* tiles hangs over a bench made of stone. A poem, glorifying Abu Lubaba and

stating the date of his death, is inscribed on this panel. The second hallway leads onto a central open-roofed courtyard, surrounded by gallery arcades and limestone colonnades. The keystone arches are lightly curbed, and the soaring columns are raised on pedestals, and made taller by Hafsid-type capitals, abacuses and imposts. The cornerstones feature six-point (enamel) plated stars; this figure, in terms of Islamic iconography, represents the seal of Salomon. The dimensions and proportions of the *madrasa*'s central courtyard inspire a deep sense of quietude.

The oblong, barrel-vaulted rooms in which the students reside open out onto three sides of the courtyard via low self-closing doors, whilst the remaining side facing the entrance is occupied by the prayer hall. One can enter this room through a narrow door framed with freestone, with a window on each side, placed symmetrically, which are also framed and covered with a woodwork-crafted grill. The door is also covered by a series of cross-vaults surrounding a central dome which is supported by four columns and as many stone arches. In one corner, an opening leads to the minaret.

Built in the same way and at the same time, the minaret is not that high. It consists of two sections: the lower part is built of quarry stone, whilst the higher part, which is more elaborate, is built of freestone and possesses on each of its four sides twin windows, separated by small columns. The whole structure is surmounted by a lightly pointed calotte (flattened dome). To the *madrasa* was added, most probably at a later date, a space kept aside for ablutions in the form of a small courtyard with a portico and latrines; the portico links to a small house which adjoins the *madrasa* and opens directly onto the outside. This house, with its two small narrow rooms, was for years the home of the school master – it is known as the Dar al-Meddeb.

Restored numerous times, notably in the 1960s and then at the start of the 1980s, the Muradite Madrasa of Sidi Bulbaba was actually transformed into a Museum of Popular Arts and Crafts, which was opened to the public in 1984. From that time on, this monument has been part of a cultural body that includes the mausoleum and the mosque which face it.

X.1.b Hush Khrayef

Situated in the "Vieux Menzel" neighbourhood ("Old Menzel"), in "rue Ferjani Mnaja".
It is a lively cultural centre, which was undergoing restoration work at the time of writing. Toilets available.

The *hush* literally means the courtyard of the house, but vernacular language, using a current metonymy, uses it to refer to the whole house, saving the word *dar*, a commonly used term, to refer solely to the room. Situated in one of the historic centres of the town of Gabès, the old *manzel*, al-Menzel al-Qadim, which is characterised by its dense and tightly-knit urban layout, the Hush Khrayef was most probably built at the beginning of the 19th century. Although it resembles local houses in the traditional style that possess a semi-rural, oasian character, particularly in terms of its base made of large second-hand bonded stone, it is distinct for its elegance, its more elaborate architecture, and its relatively expensive construction materials. It also belongs to an Arabic-Mediterranean tradition: large residences with a central courtyard, designed to house extended patriarchal families.

The entrance of Hush Khrayef was once certainly defended by a covered passageway, a *sabat*; witness the arches that flank the doorway, which are still visible. The doorway is enhanced by a freestone frame, of local *kadhal* stone, and features a unique door with its own gate. The hallway leads to a vast central courtyard, surrounded by a circular gallery featuring lightly curbed

Sidi Bulbaba Madrasa, Berber-inspired geometric decoration in stone kadhal, Gabès.

Sidi Bulbaba Madrasa, Hafsid capital, Gabès.

ITINERARY X *Towards the Land of the* Qsur
Gabès

Sidi Bulbaba Madrasa, peristyle with limestone columns, Gabès.

and horseshoe arches supported on columns cut from limestone, and Hafsid-type capitals. The amplitude of this patio, the size of which was quite common for this oasis region despite the tightness of the urban web, leads one to suppose that such a space must have served for activities following on from agricultural productivity, such as the drying of henna or of palm foliage used for making woven baskets, hats and fans.

The central courtyard is as much a well of light acting as a light source as it is a thermic regulator. It also acts as a distributive link between the other spaces in the house. The bedrooms and living rooms open out, through double doors framed by freestone, on each of the three south, north and east sides. The main room possesses, just like those of the grand houses of the *medina*s of Tunis and of Sfax, a central recess, a privileged area, flanked by two side rooms.

We know, thanks to two sale contracts spread over several dates, that the system of shared ownership shook and transformed the original architecture of this grand home, through dividing up the living space in order to create a sort of *wikala*, where rooms are let individually. Restoration work undertaken by the State allowed it to return to its original form, whilst at the same time building up new spaces to fit in with the new use for the *hush* as a centre for cultural activities.

The service rooms on the west side formerly consisted of a kitchen, a store room or larder, latrines and shops; two shops opened out directly onto the street. Today, this whole section, which had completely crumbled, has been rebuilt as a vast exhibition hall.

The roofing of the Hush Khrayef buildings takes the form of a terrace with ceilings made of palm or ordinary wood, combining local construction techniques with techniques known elsewhere in Tunisia. The Gabesian method consists first of attaching a number of joists made of palm stems which are cleaved onto the tie-rods of the walls, then a plank of plaited reeds or palm shafts (on top would go a bed of sand) and the whole lot would be covered by lime mortar. Renovation work has lead to the replacement of the palm wood with imported wood; nevertheless, several examples of this technique are still visible in some places where preservation was possible.

Through its configuration, and the materials and techniques of construction used, the Hush Khrayef is a study of traditional architecture in which common Tunisian elements are mixed with elements from other countries that belong to the same cultural mentality.

X.1.c The Jara Suq

This is situated in "avenue Habib Bourguiba", near the Great Mosque.

Jara is one of the historic centres of Gabès. It is the nerve-centre of the city: the city's essential economic activities, mainly commercial ones, are concentrated here. Like most traditional markets of rural towns which appeared during the colonial era, the Jara Suq is composed of a rectangular enclosure, surrounded on all its four sides by a gallery of solid curved arches held up by stone pillars; small shops open out under this circular gallery. Old postcards from the beginning of the 20th century show the bustling crowd that frequented the marketplace where men, animals and various products convened. Today, the Jara Suq, with its two large arched gates which lead out onto the main road, has become more specialised, focusing on the sale of henna, rare spices, legumes, traditionally woven goods and other basketwork made of palm foliage, the whole lot offered up to the curious gaze of onlookers on multi-coloured stalls of picturesque charm.

The Jabal

Land of mountains, land of the Jabal Demer, the land of *qsurs*, this Saharan plateau, whose abrupt contours hang over the coastal plain of the Djeffara, has forever exerted on the man of the Tunisian south a seductive power from which he could only escape with difficulty. Did he want to find refuge within the mountains, leaving the plains conquered by the Bedouin camel and sheep herder, or did he just want to devote himself to an inconceivable arboriculture elsewhere? As always, history teaches us that the mountains have been inhabited ever since the earliest times; we know of grottoes and under-rock shelters like Insefri and Taguet H'med, discovered on the banks of the rivers of the Ghomrassen region. This prehistoric habitat is enhanced by rock paintings that recount the epic of man's struggle to survive.

Certainly the Carthaginians, inveterate sailors like their Phoenician ancestors, had little interest in the interior of their country; but the Punic civilisation nevertheless left indelible marks, in for instance the

Hush Khrayef, facade, Gabès.

ITINERARY X   *Towards the Land of the* Qsur
Gabès

tombs discovered at the beginning of the 20th century. Let us also not forget that Carthage kept up commercial relations with the Sudan via Ghadames and the Sahara. During this era of antiquity, it is the Romans who left the greatest mark on the region, notably by the military, urban and hydraulic installations they erected. The *limes*, lines of defence staked out with fortifications like Qsar Tarcin and Qsar Ghilan, also acted as an administrative installation which enabled them to push the Zenet Berbers, great camel men, back towards the desert, and to regulate their displacement towards the north, whilst also encouraging the emergence of urban satellites. In the plains of al-Farsh, along the route that links Tataouine to Ghomrassen, the Tlalet fort was the centre of an important agglomeration. The Roman penetration did not succeed without difficulty: historical sources speak liberally of revolts by Berber tribes who were jealous of their autonomy and their freedom of movement. A resistance that was possibly even more savage was originally aimed against their Arab conquerors but, as versatile as they were decisive, the Berbers in general were ready to accept and take on the Islamic faith and culture. From then on, they belonged to the Arab-Muslim cultural era. Having no doubt participated in the shock attacks and revolts that occurred under the various dynasties that governed the country, the Berbers from Southern Tunisia were boldly confronted by the Benu Hilal and the Soleym Bedouins, who came in large numbers from Arabia having spent some time in Upper Egypt during the $5^{th}/11^{th}$ century. Thus rural life invaded the plains, driving the natives further into their mountains and into their arboricultural life, whilst in several residual, isolated areas the language of the

Jara Suq, basket and henna boutique, Gabès.

ITINERARY X   Towards the Land of the Qsur
Matmata

Berbers resisted being overrun by Arabic. In the 19th century, the French army attempted to profit from the ethnic split in order to fulfil their occupation of the South, but this political manoeuvre, which lead to several results elsewhere, was of little success. In fact, for centuries, the Arabs and the Berbers had sown such strong links of patronage and kinship, that belonging to an ethnicity, which in itself was hardly discernible, fell into insignificance; this is demonstrated by the little-known history of the *qsar*. This simultaneously economic, social and military accessory, common to all Maghrebi countries from Libya to Morocco, is very old. The Qsar Zenata or Qsar al-Qadim, probably the oldest visible *qsar* of the region, dates from the 5th/11th century, and is a descendant of Aghlabid military architecture. The *qsurs* owe their existence to the adoption of a lifestyle somewhere between semi-nomadism and seasonal agriculture. At first both a citadel and collective fortified storehouse hanging over the villages of the mountain ridges, the *qsar* made its way progressively towards the plain, where it was also adopted by the Bedouin shepherds.

The last two centuries saw a proliferation in the number of *qsurs*, which was certainly due to the way of life becoming more uniform. It was only from the second half of the 20th century onwards that this institution, due to the decline of the rural economy and the effort exerted by the State to stop the population from moving, was seen to be undermined, so much so that today only a few *ghorfa*s are still in use, whilst a number of *qsurs* are totally deserted. Aware of the archaeological importance of these monuments, the State has for a number of years now undertaken to repair and restore some of them, in the hope of seeing them again in use, either for tourism or as cultural centres.

Vertical cave dwelling, door made of palm-tree wood, Matmata.

X.2 MATMATA

Follow the road signs in the direction of Matmata, via Nouvelle "Matmata".
Toilet facilities in Café Abdou.

The inhabitation of the mountains concerned itself above all else with economics and human geography, so much so that it only responded to purely defensive preoccupations of order. Inhabitation involved, in a region where the climate was dry, finding a means of subsistence, and the ability of implanting oneself into the land and of holding onto a territory: the mountains enabled all of these. The Matmatians

ITINERARY X *Towards the Land of the* Qsur

Matmata

Vertical cave dwelling, bedroom, Matmata.

founded their village, about two centuries ago, on a slate-alluvial massif, after having settled on the mountain summit. All of a sudden, they moved closer to agricultural zones, formed by a multitude of enclosed valleys, and adapted their habitat to the nature and form of the terrain, exploiting the possibilities it offered. The mountain habitat is the result of the convergence of man's work with that of nature. Here, the form of the habitat is determined as much by natural factors as it is by cultural factors, where history, with its trends and its marking of time, has had little effect. Dare one say it, it is an architecture characterised by spontaneity, which has the advantage of being able to integrate itself into its location and to respect the environment. It is also remarkable in terms of its stability: the model in which it is built has changed little, even in terms of its interior.

In Matmata, houses look like a well dug to a depth reaching occasionally as far as 10 m. One enters a house via a subterranean corridor, which has a slight slope, and curbs lightly in order to avoid indiscreet and nosy onlookers. A widening of this tunnel allows for the stabling of a camel or other animal. From there, one is led out onto a central, circular courtyard about 8 m. in width, sometimes more or sometimes less, at the centre of which is a tank built to collect used water; an amount of salt is regularly thrown in for obvious hygienic reasons. The kitchen, bedrooms and living rooms also open out onto this courtyard, dug laterally on the first level. These rooms have streamlined ceilings which prevent the eventuality of mud slides; the walls are whitewashed with lime, while the ground is covered in a gypsum plaster coating, making the rooms sufficiently bright, as they have no other open-

ITINERARY X   Towards the Land of the Qsur
Tamezret

ings other than their palm-wood doors. Built on the second level, one or two sheds have at their summits an opening through which grain, olives and other legumes can be poured without having to carry them from the courtyard. In some houses, the rooms are enhanced with very original, fixed furnishings: there, the shelves attached to the walls are made from a kind of trellis made of olive branches and palm stems coated with slate and gypsum. This see-through lattice ensemble allows for discreet tidiness as well as adding an undeniable decorative and aesthetic value.

Reputed as being isothermal, that is to say warm in winter and cool in summer, these Matmatian homes nevertheless fall victim to mud slides during years of heavy rainfall; that is why in some of them, the walls put at risk by the central wells are upheld by small stone walls. Today, the proliferation of solid, permanent constructions is changing the physiognomy of the village. Only a building plan that regulates the architectural and urban activities of the village can save it from being destroyed; but will cave-dwellings be able to resist the evolution of time?

X.3 TAMEZRET

Take the only road to Tamezret. The road is in a bad state, particularly between Tamezret and Taoujout. Toilets available in the three village cafés.
There is a beautiful view to be had from the terrace of the Cafe Berber, above the village.

A stunning lunar-like and undulating landscape, completely wild, that comes to an end at the village of Taoujout.

View of the village of Tamezret.

ITINERARY X *Towards the Land of the Qsur*

Tamezret

Construction using stone, Tamezret.

Together with Taoujout in the north and Zerawa, now abandoned, in the west, Tamezret constitutes the third component of a group of villages whose urban and architectural arrangement are practically identical. These agglomerations are based on top of hillocks, west of the Matmata massif, where the relief of the land softens out, and where the valleys become less closed in, and where the Dahar begins to unfurl its interminable stretches. It is there that the inhabitants of Tamezret set their meagre herds of sheep and caprines to graze, and where they sow during rainier years, exploiting the cultivable part of the plateau.

At first confined to the area that forms the historical centre of the village, Tamezret descended to a lower level, towards the narrow elevations that jut out over the low neighbouring valleys. The village centre, with its urban and social attributes, found itself all of a sudden displaced. Although up until not long ago it occupied the summit, as can be seen by the placement of the mosque and by the more recent cafe building, the village centre is now located at the foot of the hillock.

The homes in Tamezret are divided up and ordered along ethnic lines: five neighbourhoods, more or less marked out and separated by ascending lanes, are each occupied by a group of peoples from the same family line that was once both impermeable and homogeneous. Within these divisions, all the houses back onto the declining slope of the land at different levels, with no intermediate stages. The various elements, living rooms, kitchen, shed or storeroom ... are arranged around a courtyard accessed through a hall that is preceded by a large gate surmounted by an archway, large enough to let a beast of burden through, very different from the narrow and low doors of the interior. Some houses possess, according to the angle of the slope, a second floor, served by some steep steps that rise up from the courtyard; these houses also feature as often as possible one or more rooms excavated out of the rockface. The walls are built with stone, bonded with a plaster mortar; in the inside they are covered with a coating of the same material; on the outside, they are left bare, giving the village its distinguishing rustic look. The ceilings are built as terraces and are rarely vaulted; palm wood is mostly used here, although cement flagstone is today a preferred material. On some of the houses, large grain silos, woven from esparto-grass, sit on top of these terraces.

Tamezret represents a particular type of mountain village, different from the agglomerations perched on the ridges of the Jabal Demer which are characterised by the organisation of their houses on levels, such as Chénini and Douiret, and also distinct from the straggling villages which occupy the basins of the Matmata massif, whose houses are entirely underground such as in Matmata and Techin. Here, the constructions gather around a hillock, forming a compact and tight-knit group; this demonstrates the diversity of mountain habitats in the south of Tunisia and the ingenuity with which man has been able to adapt himself to the possibilities offered to him by Nature. It also unveils the wealth of this so-called Berber culture which is often spoken about but about which little is known.

X.4 TAOUJOUT

The layout of the houses, the form of housing as well as the architectural techniques adopted in Taoujout are similar to those in Tamezret. The village is perched on a hillock, the highest point of which has been reserved for the mosque, whose minaret can be seen from afar, and includes the remains of an ancient *qsar*, meaning here a fortified site, dominating the valleys and the plateau. However in Taoujout, there are no ethnically divided neighbourhoods: small streets climb up to the summit and serve houses which back onto the sides of the mountain. These houses are built of stone bonded with plaster, comprising outbuildings and living spaces laid out around an open-roofed courtyard. Often, one or more rooms have been excavated, linking this type of house to the group of houses which

The Mosque, Taoujout.

ITINERARY X   *Towards the Land of the* Qsur
Toujane

X.5 **TOUJANE**

One takes either a Toujane mountain road (we recommend you have a 4-wheel drive vehicle), or the road towards the towns of Nouvelle Matmata and Beni Zolten. A café can be found at the far end of the village.

Toujane's name is today a generic term used to describe three urban communities that represent the historical stages of the occupation of the area in this mountain range composed of the south-eastern edge of the Matmata massif, facing the Djeffara plain and the coast. At first the ancient village, which is still spoken of as if it were a distant memory, perched on a mountain peak of the Jabal Toujane not far from the Jabal Zembayet, was known for the crucial source of water that flows down its slopes. Only a few indefinable wall remains are left to be seen on this impregnable site, but we know that a citadel was once perched on this ridge; the locals call this installation "*mrah al-qsar*", the forecourt of the *qsar*. Toujane as it is today, a more recent village, starts further down but without breaking away, and backs onto the mountain sides which, at this level, form a sort of creek pierced by the river; from there, the valley widens out, and one already gets a glimpse of the Djeffara. A new hamlet appeared right on the plain just over 20 years ago, in the Oued Troumane Valley: Dkhilet Toujane. As we cannot date the displacement of Matmata from its perch earlier than two centuries ago, thus similarly, the desertion of the perched site of Toujane must have occurred around the same time. Even taking into account an inscription that are partly or fully cave-like in this part of south Tunisia.

appears to date the foundation of its mosque, we are led to assume that present-day Toujane's existence dates back to about four centuries ago.

The 1,100 or so inhabitants of this village, which today is half deserted, continue to live a traditional way of life that is based economically on mountain arboriculture, in particular on olive groves, on some ploughed land in the shallower regions, and on some amount of breeding; they also exploit fields of esparto-grass which is used for weaving, most notably for the creation of large grain-containers known as *kambut* or *runiya*.

Housing in Toujane is organised in levels on the slopes of the creek. A road traverses the agglomeration, linking it to Banu Zelten and to Mareth. The houses are built of bare stone which is bonded with plaster mortar. Each one is covered by a terrace, and their roofs are made of olive-tree or thuja-tree wood which has the advantage of not being susceptible to rot, except for the sheds whose vaulted roofs have openings through which grain can be poured in. Experience showed that this type of roofing prevented the proliferation of insects that threatened the conservation of cereals. Some houses have one or two rooms that have been created by excavating the mountainside, but every room is laid out on one or two levels around a modest courtyard, given the limited cramped space available. It can also be the case, due to the process of inheritance, that a house is divided into two or three more or less independent houses, whilst still sharing a single principal entrance.

The mosque, gleaming with immaculate whiteness, highlights its contours against the fawn background of the mountain. This oratory is without doubt one of the oldest built in the Jabal: the relief inscription, on the wall that faces the entrance, features a date,

ITINERARY X   *Towards the Land of the* Qsur
Toujane

Tiered village, Toujane.

probably the date of foundation, the year 1004/1596. It features three narrow bays parallel to the *qibla* wall, designed to follow the direction of prayer, and three further perpendicular bays, covered in vaults supported by masonry pillars and semi-circular arches. Enhanced by two small columns and framed with sculpted stone defined by serrated outlines, the *mihrab* is distinct for its accentuated bulge. The *minbar* is reached via two steps which stand against the base of a large window.

Toujane represents a particular type of mountain habitat. It is a village, no longer on its perch, which occupies the two slopes of a creek that is pierced on both sides by the foreshore of the *wadi*. Its houses are built according to an original formula, following a plan consisting of a central courtyard with rooms excavated around it. It is also the prime example of a habitat that exploits the possibilities offered by nature, a habitat which responds adequately to the needs of this way of life.

ITINERARY X

Towards the Land of the *Qsur*

Naceur Baklouti

Second day

X.6 CHÉNINI (of Tataouine)

X.7 DOUIRET

X.8 QSAR AOUADIDE

X.9 QSAR ZÉNATA

X.10 QSAR OULED SOLTANE

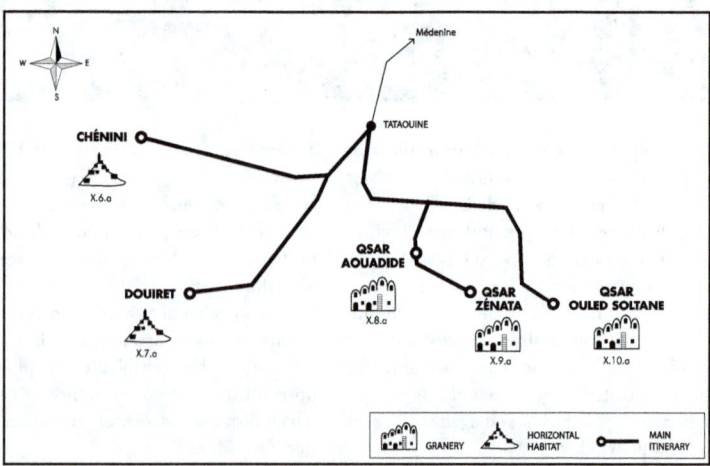

ITINERARY X Towards the Land of the Qsur
Chénini

X.6 CHÉNINI (of Tataouine)

Return down towards Médenine, then take the route towards Tataouine. Turn right 2 km. south of Tataouine. The road is covered in tarmac for a stretch of 18 km. until the new village of Tataouine to the foot of the rocky outcrop, this is where the village of Chénini is located.
Parking and toilet facilities available.

South-west of Tataouine, the region's principal town, a Zenet troglodytic village (the Zenatas were a large Berber tribe in the glory days of the past), Chénini, occupies with its *qsar*-citadel the summit of a rugged and harsh mountain, turning its back on the plain. Constrained in the east by the Farch plain and to the west by the Dahar plateau, the Jabal Demer is slightly narrower in this part, its morphology becoming irregular.

Having completed their settlement in ancient Chénini, situated on one of the foothills of the Jabal facing the Farch and not far from the mosque in sight known as the "Mosque of the Seven Sleepers", the Zenets would have built the *qsar*-citadel towards the end of the $6^{th}/12^{th}$ century, which corresponds to the time, a little over a century, after the arrival of the first wave of Hilalians from Upper Egypt. It is most probably from this time onwards that the present village began to appear lower down, facing the Dahar, the plateau which possesses a stretch which can be cultivated as well as a few pastures.

As in the other villages of this rocky outcrop which marks out the Jabal Demer, the *qsar* of Chénini hangs over rows of houses: it is perched on the crest and consists of several storerooms, *ghorfas*, which are stacked one on top of the other and are reached by narrow alleyways

Cave dwelling, Chénini.

whose paths embrace the form of the land. Now deserted, this fortress, which doubled up as a collective loft, fell into ruin. Further down, the village grew on several levels, occupying the two slopes of the creek formed by the mountain; at the centre of the upper level, a relatively recent mosque is embedded into its white mass. The houses of Chénini are troglodytic and lateral in type, set out in rows. Each house contains one or more rooms which have been excavated out of the soft alluvial layer of the mountain face. The rooms are entered through doors made of palm wood and look onto a paved, open-roofed courtyard, which includes the kitchen, the latrines, the sta-

ITINERARY X   Towards the Land of the Qsur

Douiret

Excavated dwelling entrance, Douiret.

The panoramic view of the neighbouring desert-like, barren hills is extraordinary.

Douiret is a mountain village situated on one of the hillocks of the Jabal Demer, at an altitude nearing 400 m; it is over 20 km. south-west of the town of Tataouine. In this part of the mountains, the relief of the land is uneven and intercut by relatively large valleys.

Oral tradition relating to the origins of the village recalls a legend similar to that which describes the foundation of Carthage. About five or six hundred years ago, a male saint called Dhuieb Ibn Kenana, who had come from Morocco and who preached the good word or simply followed the orders of the central power of Tunis to put down several revolts, allied himself to a tribe of the region. He took many wives and, wanting to settle there, demanded that he be granted a piece of land measuring an area which could be covered by the skin of a goat. This was granted to him, and, like Princess Elyssa, the founder of Carthage, he cut up this hide into very fine strings in such a way as to outline and surround all the land from the mountain to the *wadi*. This marabout, nicknamed the Conqueror, *Ghazi*, thus made his home in this region and was to become the ancestor of the Douiris.

In any case, in this part of Tunisia, where history confuses itself with tradition, we know very little on the dates and the origins of the villages that mark out the mountain range. However, we are on the other hand sure that Douiret experienced relative prosperity towards the end of the 19th century, due its position as a stop-over on the caravan route between Gabès and Ghadamès, and the interest brought to it by the colonial authorities. Shortly after the occupation of the south, Douiret became the seat of the

ble ... the whole built to last. Some houses possess a loft, covered by a terrace or a vault, above their entrance, as a replacement of the *ghorfa*s of the *qsar* which fell into disrepair.

X.7 DOUIRET

Return to Tataouine and head in the direction of Remada until you reach Qsar Ouled Debbab. Take the tarmac-covered road on the right until you reach the modern village of Douiret and carry on for 1km. on the track until you reach the old village. There are refreshment stalls here.

ITINERARY X   *Towards the Land of the* Qsur

Douiret

Bureau of Indigenous Affairs (B.A.I.), that is to say the information bureau; in 1912, the village became the headquarters of the Jebalia Caliphate, in other words an administrative district which grouped together the inhabitants of the Jabal. But, with the creation of the town of Tataouine several years later, the progressive marginalisation of Douiret began. The new centre of administration took over the B.A.I. as well as the weekly market of the regional tribes, more so as the caravan commerce began to wane. The final blow was dealt to this prestigious village towards the end of the 1960s: the Douiris, well-known for their emigration particularly towards the capital, decided to descend for good and settle themselves in a new city built in the valley. Thus, abandoned progressively, the ancient village ended up falling into ruin.

The site of Douiret is crowned by its *qsar*-citadel which hangs over rows of spaced-out houses that follow round the contour line. Acting as a place of safe refuge during periods of instability, the walls of the ancient fortress, which was also a collective grain loft, dominate the landscape, whilst the houses are built on different levels.

The typical Douiret house is a lateral cave-dwelling planned out in a line, comprising of a constructed part which fronts an excavated part. Adopting the form of a corridor, the hallway leads to a courtyard paved with rough stone, onto which opens the kitchen and the latrines which are built of dry stone, just like the walls of the enclosure, as well as the stable and the toolshed which are built to be permanent. This hallway is surmounted by a shed composed of several vaulted rooms. The existence of a space reserved for the ensilage of the harvests, which formed part of the body of the house, marks a stage in the history of the village: it marks the abandonment of the *qsar*-citadel,

the collective tribal loft that was difficult to reach, in favour of a new concept, that of the family grain loft. The living areas have been excavated out of the crumbly parts of the cliff, which alternate with the harder layers; this is certainly what determined the linear organisation of the village. Palm wood doors protect these vast rooms which are whitewashed with lime. At the back, there is a provisions storeroom.

Arriving in Douiret from Tataouine, one is intrigued by the white mass of a mosque whitewashed with lime, which stands out from the ochre background of the mountain: it is the Mosque of the Palm Tree, Jama' al-Nakhla. This sanctuary in fact consists of two parts. The oldest part is exca-

Prayer room of the Palm Tree Mosque, Douiret.

ITINERARY X *Towards the Land of the Qsur*

Qsar Aouadide

Collective grain store-houses, interior courtyard, Qsar Aouadide.

vated from the cliff face; pillars help to support the low ceiling composed of large, flat slabs of stone, whilst two recesses in the *qibla* wall form the *mihrab* and the *minbar*. The second part which is attached to the first is more recent; it is a permanent structure built with modern materials and features a minaret and a vaulted prayer hall.

Walking around the area on which Jama' al-Nakhla is situated, one is surprised to see, huddled at the back of a creek, another mosque partly hidden by an immense fig tree. The sanctuary is named after the tree: Jama' al-Karma. Entirely dug into the mountain, this mosque is remarkable for its simple but also ingenious system of collecting rainwater that streams down the furrowed slope of the cliff.

Douiret, this strange Berber city, with its enigmatic past, today presents its architecture, which, though certainly dilapidated, bares the indelible mark of a misunderstood but very mysterious history which time and again has witnessed the meeting and assimilation of various groups of human beings, each with their own very different origins and traditions. It is trials and tribulations like these which have contributed to the elaboration of a unique architectural art that exploits the possibilities offered up by nature without attacking it.

X.8 QSAR AOUADIDE

From Tataouine, take the road towards Masturia until you reach a sign indicating a track on the right. This leads first to Qsar Aouadid, then to Qsar Zenata or Qadim.

ITINERARY X   *Towards the Land of the* Qsur

Qsar Aouadide

The Qsar Aouadide is classed as a mountain *qsur*, that is to say those founded by factions of semi-nomadic tribes who lived in the valleys whilst exercising their pastoral transhumance, and who adopted the tradition of sedentary mountain people of ensiling their harvests in fortified collective barn lofts.

The Aouadides were a part of the large Oudernas tribe, great nomads who travelled up and down the Djeffara plain, across the Jabal Abiedh, and who frequented the first of its peaks and ridges.

Their *qsar* hangs over the Oued Mazturiya Valley which traverses the Jabal. Here, a hamlet, born just over 20 years ago around a modest and sparse palm grove, continues to develop and grow, welcoming in populations who once either lived up on the perch or lived a semi-nomadic lifestyle: this hamlet is called Mazturiya, situated about 10 km. from Tataouine, on the road to Dhehiba.

The Qsar Aouadide is built of large rough stones at its foundation and of rubble in terms of the rest of its walls, according to the plan of a mountain *qsur*. It is a quadrilateral formation made up of about 160 storage cells, stacked the one on top of the other across two or three floors around a central courtyard.

The entrance projects out slightly, creating a sort of porch upheld by two buttresses which frame the archway of the door; the arch's intrados feature a relief inscription in which appears a date: 1913, but does this date the foundation or purely a renovation? The entrance corridor, forming a hallway, is ceilinged with wood from olive trees; it is furnished with two stone benches sur-

Collective grain store-houses, porch with two buttresses, Qsar Aouadide.

273

mounted by relieving arches. The narrow staircase leading to the terrace also stands in this hall. What used to be the blacksmiths' and carpenters' workshops open out onto the courtyard from either side of the entrance. Corridors leading to the cells have been built in each of the four corners. The cells are vaulted, long and oblong. Some of them feature a raised area supported by arches and with its own vault. Sometimes the space in-between, here occupied by the vaults of two *ghorfa*s which stand side by side, forms a hiding place, *khammala*, where one can leave precious objects, and which one can enter through a narrow opening built inside the cell. During the last few years, the Qsar Aouadide was subject to a great restoration project. Its well-preserved state and its appearance has given it a new lease of life with a view to using it culturally or for the purposes of tourism.

X.9 QSAR ZÉNATA

The Zenatas constitute one of the largest Berber tribes to have populated the Maghreb since time immemorial, together with the Hentatas, the Masmudas and the Sanhajas, and represent the native section of the present population of this region. Historians affirm that the Libyans, cited in Greek and Latin sources, are their ancestors. On the eve of the Arab Conquest, the Zenatas occupied a northern part of Libya, Eastern Algeria and Southern Tunisia. They were either farmers or semi-nomadic camel herders.

The *qsar* which carries their name is probably the oldest of the fortified lofts of the region: it is also known as the old *qsar*, *al-Qsar al-Qadim*. Despite its advanced state of dilapidation, it is solidly anchored to a limestone platform, *rosfa*, on a peak of the Jabal, at an altitude which slightly exceeds 500 m. From its quasi-inaccessible site, it hangs over a row of grotto dwellings which today lie abandoned, and dominates, through its imposing mass which totals an area of 2,500 sq. m., the *wadi* valley and the small palm grove of Mazturiya. Not far from here stand the Qsar Aouadide and the Qsar Dghaghra, one lower down and the other more or less at the same level of altitude.

An inscription at the entrance and another inside one of the cells places the existence of this *qsar* at the end of the $5^{th}/11^{th}$ century, which corresponds to the time about 40 years after the arrival from Arabia of the Hilalian Bedouins following their stopover in Egypt. Is there a correlation between the foundation of the *qsar* and this human influx that precipitated the Arabisation of the country? The Hilalian action, a masterpiece of oral literature, informs us of the turbulent events of this painful and at the same time impassioned contact, bringing famous heroes like the mysterious Jazya, Dhiab and Bouzid on the Hilalian side, and Khalifa and Sa'ada and many others on the Zenata side, face to face. The stakes of this combat was this good land of Ifriqiya, which ended up opening its arms to these brave warriors from afar, who have since impregnated the country with their culture, but have also succeeded to co-exist with their Berber hosts and melt into the whole of the population.

The Qsar Zenata is distinct for its monumental entrance, in the form of a vaulted porch, which was once probably surmounted by a watchtower. The rooms, which number over 100, are placed on two levels around a vast central courtyard. Nevertheless, surveys have enabled us to discover the ruins of other rooms inside the

ITINERARY X   Towards the Land of the Qsur

Qsar Zénata

Store-house citadel, vaulted porch entrance, Qsar Zenata.

courtyard. The *ghorfa*s of Qsar al-Qadim are larger than those known of in other lofts. On the first floor they can measure up to 4 m. in depth, 3 m. in width and 3 m. in height, which allows them to be compartmentalised. Some of them are furnished with a raised alcove supported by arches and a vault. This kind of feature suggests that these rooms were also used as a place in which to stay overnight. The vaults of the *qsar*'s small alveoli feature a plaster decor executed in relief and composed of apparently incongruous signs from which one can make out the motif of a hand, the solar wheel, stylised palm trees, five- or six-point stars, geometric motifs and even small boats!

The Qsar Zenata poses an enigma which is difficult to decipher. It is surely the oldest of the known citadel-lofts. It is thought that it was not originally used solely for economic purposes (the ensilage of grain) but, given the form of its architecture – notably the thickness of the main facade wall which measures up to over a metre – plus the probable existence of a watchtower and the slightly zigzagging outline of its enclosure, it certainly fulfilled an important function in terms of defence. Did it play these two roles simultaneously or did one follow the other? We can only guess. The Qsar al-Qadim is without doubt the result of an evident cultural syncretism, that is to say of a coherent combination of elements taken from various eras whose building and use responded to the necessities of the moment.

ITINERARY X   *Towards the Land of the Qsur*
Qsar Ouled Soltane

Interior courtyard, view onto the ghorfas, Qsar Ouled Soltane.

X.10 **QSAR OULED SOLTANE**

Return along the route of la Masturia, 5 km. from Tamelset, take the road which ascends on the left. Refreshments available.

The Ouled Soltane are a faction of a sedentary Bedouin tribe. In imitation of the Jebaliya mountain dwellers who occupied the crests and isolated mountain-peaks, they ended up building their own collective grain loft. It is situated at a height about 20 km. south-east of Tataouine in the southern part of the Jabal Abiedh. From there one can make out from afar the remains of three pedestrian-only villages – Tazeghdanet, Banu Oussine and Techout – which all had citadel-lofts that have now fallen into ruin. As it was more accessible, the Qsar Ouled Soltane had come to replace them.

The *qsar* is composed of a group of storage rooms, *ghorfas*, which are vaulted, over 300 in number, and piled one over the other across three or four levels around two central courtyards linked via a covered passageway. The first courtyard is over four centuries old whereas the second, clearly of a more recent date, was built on the eve of the Protectorate in 1881.

The small ensilage cavities are deep and compartmentalised, allowing for the conservation of various kinds of foodstuffs like olives and grains. They are protected by low doors made of palm wood which are locked and bolted shut with wooden pegs; in order to open them, the key, also made of wood, must break the pegs. This ingenious device is commonly used in this region. Very steep cantilevered stairs lean procariously against

Qsar Ouled Soltane

the wall offering access to the *ghorfa*s on the floors above. To reach those not served by a staircase, one had to make do with several slabs of stone, cut so as to project outwards like steps, or simply planks of wood fixed onto the wall. Other planks fixed above the doors allow, through the pulling of a cord, for the containers, baskets or sacks of grain to be lifted up to the higher *ghorfas*, to be conserved there. Hiding-places built into the vaults of adjoining rooms are accessible through small doors that open from outside, in the courtyard.

Although partially deserted, the Qsar Ouled Soltane continues to attract the region's inhabitants, whether they be mountain folk or men from the plain, so much so in fact that today it constitutes the centre of an embryonic village, which has progressively been building up around its double enclosure; a recently built mosque consecrates this birth. This *qsar*, which is periodically afforded restoration work, has been converted into a cultural centre which holds the annual festival of the *qsurs*, whatever its manifestation.

ITINERARY XI

Ibadite Architecture

Aziza Ben Tanfous

XI.1 HUMT SUQ
XI.1.a Sidi Zituni Zawiya – The Museum of Popular Arts and Traditions of Jerba
XI.1.b Burj al-Ghazi Mustapha
XI.1.c Funduq al-Zawiya
XI.1.d Sidi Jomni Madrasa
XI.1.e Tajedit Madrasa

XI.2 MIDOUNE
XI.2.a The Oil-Press of Midoune

The Pottery of Jerba

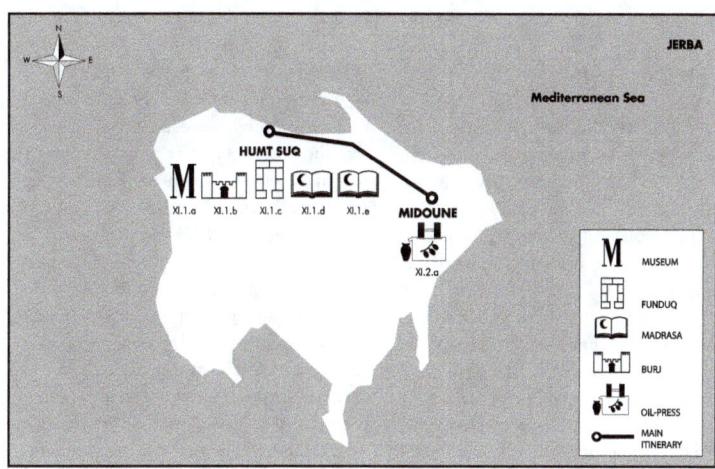

Buttress of a mosque, Jerba.

ITINERARY XI *Ibadite Architecture*

Situated on the same level as the semi-desert zone of the African continent, the Island of Jerba would have been only a piece of the sandy Sahara emerging out of the large gulf of Gabès, but its meeting with man was to give it an altogether different appearance. The island of Homer's Lotophagus, or the "island of great depths", became Girba during the Roman era, hence its present name; it is a large and beautiful island which holds an important strategic position in the Mediterranean. Situated approximately at mid-distance between Ceuta (*Sebta*) in Morocco and Alexandria in Egypt, Jerba possessed a flourishing arboriculture as well as vineyards; it produced all kinds of fruit; and its pottery workshops manufactured large jars used for the exportation of olive oil. Its inhabitants produced olive oil, wool fabrics and a popular cotton cloth. During the Age of Antiquity, its coastal installations worked treating murex, a variety of mollusc that secreted a purple-red colour (*purpura*), a dye much sought-after by the sovereigns of the time as it was used to colour their regal garments. The coastal fisheries provided a variety of fish. Important trading agencies marked out the coastline: Meninx to the south, Tipaza on the site of Ajim, Haribus near Guellala and Ghizen on the northern coast.

Local tradition recalls, during this time, the arrival of a Jewish community who towards the middle of the 6th century BC had left Jerusalem as refugees and who found Jerba a favourable place in which to propagate their faith. Passing into the hands of the Romans after they had taken Carthage, Jerba underwent an even greater boom as can be seen by the size of the city of Meninx, which became the island's capital, and by the construction of a reef linking the island to the continent. The island even gave birth to two emperors, Vibius Galus and his son, Volusianus. With no traces left of the Vandal episode, the island continued to welcome all religions, as illustrated by the fact that, at the end of the reign of Justinian, it housed a solid Christian diocese in the city of Girba, which seemed to have replaced Meninx as the island's capital.

Conquered by the Arabs in 273/887, the island appears to have be unaffected by the events that were acted out on the continent. It was only with the arrival of Ibadism, which slowly gained interest in the Muslim West during the 3rd/9th century, that Jerba was taken note of. One has to briefly remind oneself that during the Great Discord (see the Historical Overview), the first partisans of 'Ali were Kharijites. Hence the latter gave themselves the right to select a leader, whether he be or not descended from Quraysh, the Prophet's tribe, whether he be even a black slave. But Kharijism did not remain unified; ever since its beginnings, it splintered into various sects spreading across the Muslim world; Ibadism, a moderate faction of this movement, implanted itself in the Maghreb. It derives its name from its founder, 'Abd Allah Ibn Ibad al-Murri, who lived in Basra in Iraq towards the end of the 1st/7th century. When and how was this island penetrated by this movement? It is difficult to reply to this question with precision, but it seems that the proximity of Tripolitania played a role in the origins of contact made between Jerba and the first Ibadite State, founded in the Maghreb in 140/758 by five missionaries sent from Basra to preach their doctrine. It was to be an ephemeral state, but it represented the first application of Ibadite political theory of Collegiate power. At the same time, Kairouan was occupied by the Ibadites and was also governed by one of them, 'Abd al-Rahman Ibn Rustum. Tripoli, Ifriqiya and east Algeria seemed for a while to have been converted to the new doctrine. Ibn Rustum, chased out of Kairouan in 143/761, sought refuge with the Berbers and founded Tahert in 161/778, near present-day Tiaret in southern Algeria. Some time after his settlement, he instituted an *imam* diocese (*Imamat*) which would remain within his family until 296/909 to which Jerba was attached. It was a theocracy founded on the Qur'an and on the Tradition in which the *imam* must be a pious theologian supervised by clerks; it was an austere, puritanical and egalitarian regime. His son, 'Abd al-Wahab (171/788–208/824) was elected by a council, but was very soon contested by an Ibadite faction which separated itself from the Rustemids, giving rise to two schismatic movements.

It seems that during this period of Ibadite penetration, Jerba was more of a refuge for these dissident groups created in opposition to the dynastic power of the Rustemids, notably the *Nukkariya* and the *Khalafiya*. The "renouncers", *nukkar*, who constituted one of the main branches of Ibadism, gained their name from the fact that they refused to recognise the second *imam* of Tahert; they also owed their celebrity to their leader, the famous Abu Yazid, "the man on the donkey" who never compromised the existence of the Fatimid Caliphate. As for the *khalafiya*, they derived their name from Khalaf Ibn al-Samh; his father was at first the *vizier* of the *imam* 'Abd al-Wahab, and then Governor of Tripoli (195/811–207/823). On his death, the Tripolitan Ibadite notables elected his son, Khalaf, but he was not recognised by the *imam* of Tahert, which then brought about a schism. Whosoever advocated ideas against the heredity of power and ideas for meritocratic election would have benefited from a good audience if preaching to the population of Jerba. In 296/909, the Fatimids were to put an end not only to the Aghlabid Emirate but also to the *imam* diocese of Tahert, creating a great and powerful kingdom.

Small Ibadite factions gradually regrouped in southern Ifriqiya and Tripoli. No longer able to recreate an *imam* diocese, they adopted the laws of secrecy when it came to matters of faith in order to avoid repression. At the end of the Rustemid reign, Jerba had a *Nukkariya* majority, and the *shaykh* Abu Messwer had a lot of difficulty in creating the first *Wahabiya* school in Jerba (remember that this name was given to the followers of the second Rustemid *imam*, 'Abd al-Wahab, who was mentioned above). He was the founder of Humt Suq, also referred to in sources as Suq al-Khamis. It was only from the beginning of the $4^{th}/10^{th}$ century that *Wahabism*, anchored onto solid foundations, had begun to supplant *Nukkarism* and a harsh, bitter combat was fought between the two parties.

In the middle of the $5^{th}/11^{th}$ century, a new form of government appeared amidst the

Burj al-Ghazi, Mustapha, Jerba, 19th-century engraving.

Banu Yahrassen tribes, which was composed of a council of hermits presided over by a *shaykh*, under which the whole life of the community was submitted. This council was made up of 12 people, each of whom had their own function. They had founded their power on the basis of Ibadite teachings and thought.

During the $6^{th}/12^{th}$ century, the island had to uphold a lengthy resistance against the Normans; on several occasions the latter had the upper hand, as they played on internal dissensions within the island and Jerba was taken in 529/1135. Around 544/1150, Mahdia, Sousse and Sfax, the coastal towns, were also in the hands of the Normans and had to pay tribute to the conquerors. The people Revolted and they were liberated a short while after by the Almohads. The island was taken for a second time in 682/1284 by Admiral Roger de Lauria; it was pillaged and sacked. The admiral organised the building of a fortress and the population was forced to pay heavy tributes. He systematically raided and plundered the Ifriqiyan coasts. Christian domination lasted more or less until 735/1335; the people, overcome and exhausted by the demands of "greedy money grubbing governors", rose up against them, putting an end to their rule. In 835/1432, Alphonso of Aragon took over the island, but his domination lasted but a short while. In 924/1518, Hassan al-Wazzan, returning from a voyage to the East, was captured by a Sicilian pirate during a stop-over in Jerba and was taken to Italy. Offered as a gift to Pope Leo X, John of Medici, he was converted to Christianity and was given the name John Leo the African. He wrote prolifically, but posterity honours him above all for being the author of the *Descriptions of Africa*. In the $10^{th}/16^{th}$ century, the island, having become the den of the famous corsair Dragut, Darguth Rais, was attacked by the admiral to Philip II, André Doria. It turned out to be a disaster for the Spanish and the apogee of Turkish power in the Mediterranean. Despite the Turkish defeat of Lepante in 978/1571, the island as well as the country dwelled henceforth under Ottoman domination.

In the $11^{th}/17^{th}$ century, two-thirds of the island had been won over by Wahabism. In the $12^{th}/18^{th}$ and $13^{th}/19^{th}$ centuries, the *Nukkariya*s, confined to the eastern zone of the island, progressively converted themselves to Malekism, reinforcing the grip of Tunis as a central power. The system of *'azzaba*s was from the start based on a vision of power upheld by the original initiators, but its development presents a gradual fissure between the two powers. Dynasties of local governors seized transient power for themselves, leaving the *'azzaba*s to deal with justice and teaching.

On the 28th July 1881, French troops occupied the great fortress, the Burj al-Kabir, just as they had occupied the rest of Tunisia. Since Independence, Jerba has returned to being the fascinating, mysterious island it once was, with its blond sandy beaches, filled with sea and sun, dotted with small white and curiously shaped mosques, revealing themselves to those with inquisitive gazes and yet how secret they are!

The fruits of a long local tradition, the buildings of Jerba, are scattered according to the image of spatial occupation held by the Jerbian. Breaking away, in effect, from the classical city which for a long time had flourished near the coast, these islanders, for reasons of security, had surged back further into the island, developing thus a dispersed community. From the Middle Ages onwards, they flocked towards different areas in order to exploit the land agriculturally, assuring their self-sufficiency. In this

ITINERARY XI   *Ibadite Architecture*

Humt Suq

Rural mosque, Jerba.

type of settlement, the mosque occupies an essential place in community life. It is the spiritual centre, even though it is located at the periphery. Sources attribute the island as having 360 mosques, that is nearly a mosque for every day of the year, demonstrating thus the profound piety of its inhabitants as well as their dispersion. These monuments were, successively or at the same time, the preferred place in which to live out the cultural, administrative, military, and indeed political life of the population. They assured the formation of the frameworks necessary to govern the island in an autonomous manner. They thus reflect the moments of strength within the Ibadite epic which enabled the island to be kept in the lap of Islam, despite the pressures that weighed down on her during the centuries of trouble. Whether it be religious or used for economic purposes, the island's architecture is characterised by its sobriety, its minimalism and its functionality. Nothing is superfluous. It is the expression of the egalitarian teachings of a rigorous Islam, believed in by the first initiators of the Ibadite doctrine. Local in origin, most of the monuments described below are built in this mould, as are even the official monuments which were constructed under the orders of the central state, to which the island was more or less attached during various periods of its history.

XI.1 **HUMT SUQ**

XI.1.a **Sidi Zituni Zawiya–The Museum of Popular Arts and Traditions of Jerba**

This can be found at the entrance of Humt Suq, on "avenue Abdelhamid el-Cadi", which runs into the road that crosses the tourist zone.
Entrance fee. Opening times: 09.00–16.00 from 16th September to 31th March, and from 08.00–12.00 and 15.00–19.00 during the rest of the year. Closed Fridays. Parking and toilets available.

ITINERARY XI *Ibadite Architecture*

Humt Suq

Sidi Zituni, dome covered in green glazed tiles, Humt Suq.

The mausoleum which houses the Museum of Popular Arts and Traditions of Jerba was, two decenniums ago, the only religious building in the woodland area that borders the *manzel*s of Humt Taourit. This beautiful monument, surmounted by a green dome, was erected by the Governor of the island, Hamida Ibn 'Ayed, in the 12th–13th/end of the 18th century, to glorify the work of the Shaykh Abu Bakr Zituni, the Malekite magistrate who, thanks to the functions he fulfilled in Jerba, contributed to the reinforcement of Malekism on the island. The green varnished tiles on the outside, the stucco decorations and ceramic tiles surfacing the interior walls, as well as the painted wood ceilings, all distinguish this mausoleum with the official marks that characterise monuments from the Husaynite era. In fact, this monument has evolved from two buildings from different periods. The mausoleum of the 12th/18th century was enlarged later on through the transformation, in the 13th/19th century, of the patio which precedes the Room of the Saint into a large, high-ceilinged room called *fnar* in which another saint was worshipped: Sidi Ameur. The second building, the *Qubba al-Khayal* or the Dome of the Ghost, does not display a date of any kind but looks older. According to popular belief it is associated with the miraculous cure of certain psychic illnesses.

The museum, opened in 1970, has benefited from the beauty of the whole compound, adding value to the display of its exhibits, which demonstrate various aspects of the traditional life of the Jerbian islanders, through a collection of ceremonial costumes in which one can appreciate, above and beyond the apparent unity, a large amount of diversity, the fruits born of the contribution from each locality – each wearer trying to look different from their neighbour through the colour of their clothes or the way in which they are worn, or through the

ITINERARY XI Ibadite Architecture

Humt Suq

shape of the indispensable hat. A collection of enamelled silver jewels recollects the wonderful era when the Jewish craftsmen of the Hara Kabira and of Humt Suq turned Jerba into one of the main centres of Tunisian goldsmithing. The reconstruction of a pottery studio in the old disused cistern shows us a forgotten world in which the potter peacefully crafted a multitude of objects. A gallery in which varnished objects from Guellala are displayed, as well as two courtyards in which containers of different calibres and shapes can be found, concludes the pottery theme. The reconstruction of a traditional kitchen illustrates the use of several items of terracotta crockery. Finally, the group is completed by a collection of woodwork, giving an idea of the kind of furniture in use inside Jerbian homes.

XI.1.b Burj al-Ghazi Mustapha

Rejoin the road on the sea front and turn left towards the port, the entrance of which is marked by the fort.
Entrance fee. Opening times: 09.00–18.00 from the 16th September to 31th March and from 08.00–12.00 and 15.00–19.00 during the rest of the year. Closed Fridays. Parking and toilets available.

Although well protected by the depths of the sea, Jerba can still be attacked through its vulnerable areas. This is why, facing external as well as internal threats, it had to come up with a system of defence that encompassed its whole territory, enabling it to preserve its integrity. This system involves the forts, *burj*, built, at the instigation of the central government, at points of embarkation.

Burj al-Ghazi, Mustapha, entrance and circular crenellated towers, Humt Suq.

285

ITINERARY XI   *Ibadite Architecture*

Humt Suq

Burj al-Ghazi, Mustapha, prayer room surmounted by two domes, Humt Suq.

The *burj* were taken over by surveillance posts in the form of a place of worship, which mark out the entire coastline and are the result of the population's involvement. This first line of defence was doubled in the north-east by a row of fortified mosques; in a further, third layer, neighbourhood mosques endowed with defensive elements completed the ensemble.

The Burj al-Kabir or Burj al-Ghazi Mustapha, situated north of Humt Suq, constituted the jewel in the crown of this system. It is the most important due to its size and to the role it played.

Built in the $8^{th}/14^{th}$ century under the orders of the Hafsid Sultan Abu Fares, the fort, in its present configuration, is the end-product of various restoration works undertaken by the Turkish Governor Ghazi Mustapha, following damage inflicted on the fort in 967/1560 during the great battle that was fought against a Christian European coalition by Ottoman troops commanded by Dragut. It was following this battle that Jerba was placed in submission to the Sultan of Istanbul. The monument's appearance, unique in Jerba in terms of its style, as well as its location, reveals what it was destined for. It shows the characteristics shared by all classical military monuments built since the $1^{st}/7^{th}$ century and which remained unchanged until the Ottoman era. It takes the form of a quadrilateral whose very high external walls have a span averaging a metre in length, and are built of large local blocks of cut stone. The eastern and southern parts are endowed with five round and crenellated towers whereas the northern and western parts hold four quadrangular towers. Ghazi Mustapha added built-in features to the interior which he thought would be useful in terms of living in the place; thus rooms, stables and a mosque, of which nothing remains, were constructed within this space. He finished off his work with the construction of a prayer hall, preceded by a portico and surmounted by two white domes, no doubt with the view of it becoming a mausoleum. The material uncovered during archaeological digs in the 1970s fell into two

ITINERARY XI   *Ibadite Architecture*
Humt Suq

categories: remains from the Roman era which probably came from Meninx or from Girba, and a selection of ceramics from different periods and of diverse origins.

and bustle which ruled there in the past, linked to commercial activities and lodging, has given way to the peacefulness of a single complementary but scaled-down activity.

XI.1.c Funduq al-Zawiya

Return towards the pedestrian streets of Humt Suq. The monument is situated on "rue Moncef Bey" (perpendicular to "rue de Bizerte"), facing the Hotel Marhala.

According to tradition, this *funduq* was built in the $12^{th}/18^{th}$ century by the Bey Husayn Ibn 'Ali at the same time as the Zawiya of Sidi Jomni. Like the classic layout of traditional *funduqs*, this one is square; it is a two-storey building with rooms opening onto galleries that surround the courtyard. The originality of the *funduqs* of Humt Suq lies in their means of access to the upper floor, which is formed by a staircase that is situated in the courtyard, as if the architect wanted to economise on covered space to keep it for more useful requirements. This *funduq* has two staircases which face one another. All the commodity rooms are located on the ground floor: the cistern and the latrines. The ceilings are of local style, constructed as barrel vaults, except for the galleries: those on the ground floor seem to have kept their original ceilings made of palm-tree whilst those on the upper floor are made of wood. They are the result of restorations done at the beginning of the 20th century, and a more recent, badly executed work of restoration which transformed two sides of this gallery by covering it in cement flagstones. Today, the premises on the ground floor are nearly all used as storerooms for merchandise (raw or spun wool) whilst those on the upper floor are occupied by weavers. The intense liveliness

XI.1.d Sidi Jomni Madrasa

From "rue de Bizerte", turn left towards the Café Fatou. The monument is in the small square, level with the taxi rank.

Founded by the Muradites in the $11^{th}-12^{th}/$ end of the 17th century, the Sidi Jomni Madrasa is one of those rare institutions created in Jerba by central government. The purpose of it, within the framework of a

Funduq al-Zawiya, ground-floor passageway, Humt Suq.

ITINERARY XI *Ibadite Architecture*

Humt Suq

Sidi Jomni Madrasa, courtyard, Humt Suq.

political system based on a centralisation of power, was to spread the Malekite cult, the sect to which the majority of the country's population subscribed. This politic was pursued and consolidated during the Husaynite era through the construction of the Mausoleum of Shaykh Ibrahim al-Jomni in 1133/1721, and the various other religious foundations built on his behalf.

A monument more or less urban in look, it comprises a *madrasa* surrounded by all the buildings from which it once gained a revenue: a *hammam*, two bread ovens and three *funduq*s. The *madrasa* opens out onto the south-east and is composed of ground-and first floors. Through a rectangular hallway, one reaches a square courtyard onto which on one side opens the prayer hall, and on the remaining three sides there is a gallery sheltering the entrance doors to the students' rooms. A staircase runs from the courtyard to the gallery on the first floor, where there is another row of rooms. The ceilings of the galleries rest on arcades and pillars, and rainwater-pipe drains are incorporated into the walls. The oratory, square in plan, is modest in size, without a minaret, like the classic Jerbian mosques; a simple external staircase was used, from which to announce the hour of prayer. The interior is covered by four vaults supported by arches and pillars; the wall of the *qibla* consists of two *mihrab*s that bear witness to an extension carried out later.

The Sidi Jomni Mausoleum occupies the north-eastern corner of the building and is marked on the outside by its dome covered in varnished green tiles. The square room, with its eye-pleasing dimensions, is covered by a superb dome built of cylindrical ceram-

ITINERARY XI   *Ibadite Architecture*
Humt Suq

ic shapes; it is supported, thanks to a circular base, by three arches cut from local stone, and the whole rests on four second-hand marble columns surmounted by Corinthian capitals featuring three levels of sculpted and pierced acanthus leaves. The transition from square to circle was made possible with the aid of four corner squinches in the form of fluted scallops, framed by three circumscribed arches made of cut stone. Between every squinch, square windows light the room, each of which is flanked by small columns surmounted by Hafsid capitals. The dome has been carefully decorated with motifs engraved into stucco, representative of cypresses and rosaries. This monument demonstrates the introduction of architectural elements which until then had been foreign to the island – the closed courtyard, the upper floor, as well as the decoration, which was quite sought-after – without excluding, however, the presence of local imprints, visible in the isolation of the prayer hall and in the shape of the arches.

XI.1.e **Tajedit Madrasa** (this monument is not open to visitors)

From Humt Suq, take the road that heads towards Midoune, followed by the track on the left-hand side situated 700 m. after the 3 km. milestone.

A Wahabite Great Mosque and Madrasa; the name Tajedit, or *Jadid* in Arabic, means "new". However, this is an ancient monument, the foundation of which, according to oral accounts, dates back to the $3^{rd}/9^{th}$ century. Indeed, this monument was totally rebuilt, also at a very early date, all whilst preserving a part of the initial construction. The defensive elements it features date back to the $10^{th}/16^{th}$ century at the very least. What is certain is that the *madrasa* existed in the $9^{th}/15^{th}$ century because the Shaykh Yunes Ibn Ta'arit Essidghiani, then leader of the Wahabite Council, had taught there.

Situated in Fatou, to the east of Humt Suq, this *madrasa* is a part of the line of defence that runs parallel to the north-east coast of the island. It is a multifunctional monument although teaching and defence were the main subjects that were taught. It can be seen from afar thanks to the bursting whiteness of its whitewash and its high minaret, which emerges from the ancient forest of olive trees which surrounds it. A rural mosque, it signposts its defensive nature so that it can be noted from a distance; walled in by an enclosure pierced with rectangular loopholes, it opens onto a vast courtyard whitewashed with a thick, oily coat of lime. At the centre of this enclosure, the prayer

Tajedit Madrasa, lantern minaret, Humt Suq.

ITINERARY XI *Ibadite Architecture*

Midoune

hall is isolated from the other buildings which look out onto the courtyard, like the *kuttab* which is surmounted by a large dome, the utility rooms, and the ablutions hall. The square-planned mosque rises up majestically at the centre of the courtyard. Its walls widen towards the base, lending it the appearance of a truncated pyramid. The main facade is turned eastward, and a machicolation built of rubble stone, resting on a support made of olive-tree wood, protects the entrance door; a second machicolation surmounts a second door on the northern facade. The square minaret embraces the general look of the mosque by widening out towards the base, its lantern surmounted by a small dome that rests on arcades and small masonry columns. Two buttresses flank the southern facade, reinforcing the pyramidal appearance of the whole. The facades are surmounted by a defensive wall above the roof; traces of old loopholes, which were later blocked up, still remain to remind one of the role this monument must have played in terms of the island's security.

The visual harmony of the whole resides in the distribution of space within the area, reserved for the occupation of functions that complement one another. One must finally note, in terms of the interior, the decoration sombrely engraved around the niche of the *mihrab*, representing geometric and floral motifs.

XI.2 **MIDOUNE**

XI.2.a **The Oil-Press of Midoune**

This is found at the centre of Midoune, near the roundabout where the roads to Humt Suq and the touristic zone cross.

Oil-press, Midoune.

ITINERARY XI   *Ibadite Architecture*
Midoune

Oil-press, Midoune.

In Jerba, traditional oil-presses or mills were all underground, but certainly not for reasons of security; it seems that the choice of this type of architecture was justified for climatic reasons: these underground constructions created a constant microclimate favourable to the extraction of oil which usually takes place during the cold season. The variety of olives cultivated in Jerba bear fruits whose oil becomes solid at a certain degree of temperature, in winter.

Most oil-presses can only be viewed from the outside as they are entirely dug out of the tender rockface whilst the harder layer is used as a roof. But some of them, like that of Midoune, have more elaborate architecture and a constructed roof. From outside, this oil-press is not distinct for its white dome, preceded by an inclined vault, and flanked by two long barrel vaults, the whole of which is built on ground level.

The interior space having been dug out, one could only descend with the help of a staircase, reaching a corridor onto which opens the small recesses which act as storerooms for the olives. One then reaches a circular room that houses the press at its centre, with the oil-presses placed to the right and to the left. The dome is pierced with square holes that let in a very low level of light, whilst the vaults receive rays of sunlight through rectangular holes pierced into the south-eastern side. The recesses are endowed with circular holes at their summit, which enabled olives to be poured in from outside. The design of the whole orchestrates the space into a circular motion around the central element that is the press, in such a way that one imagines an animal turning under the dome, continuing to animate this space despite his absence. This type of oil-press only stopped functioning a few years ago.

291

THE POTTERY OF JERBA

Aziza Ben Tanfous

Four-handled jar for storing foodstuffs.

For centuries, Jerba was the only production centre for spun pottery in southern Tunisia. For the benefit of its commercial relations with the eastern Mediterranean, Jerba had to know, ever since Antiquity, how to use a potter's wheel. It had to make its own crockery as well as all kinds of containers for storing and transporting its various agricultural products. In the 12th/18th and 13th/19th centuries, the Island paid its natural dues or taxes in terms of containers that were used for the preservation of food destined for the armies of the *bey*. This craft could not have taken root anywhere else but Guellala, a village surrounded by a plateau, full of the layers of clay that are indispensable to this activity.

Using very simple tools and a wheel made of olive-tree wood, the Jerbian potter fashions clay, which has with difficulty been extracted from the entrails of the earth: he either fashions red clay when he mixes it with softwater, or fashions white clay when he kneads it with sea water. Jerba above all specialised in making large calibre pots.

These pot-bellied jars, the making of which necessitated several stages, can hold up to 300 litres. They were exported all around Tunisia, where one would find them furnishing the provisions rooms of traditional houses as well as the fortified lofts in the south of the country, where they constituted one of the conditions of good ensilage of certain agricultural produce, like cereals, dates and olive oil. Some are decorated and used in Jerba instead of a clothes trunk in order to store away wool fabrics or silk.

The technique of glazed pottery, once widespread in Jerba, totally disappeared around half a century ago; present potters no longer know how to mix the oxides that once allowed their fathers to obtain three colours which were used to decorate the pieces they had created. Having fallen into disuse, the base colours composed of lead oxide — to which one would add

Bichrome glazed jar with two handles and large, open rim.

copper to obtain green, antimony to obtain yellow, or manganese to obtain brown – exist only now in the minds of old potters who recall them with feelings of nostalgia. The colour which was most used was green: as well as crockery, it coloured lamps of various sizes that were used to light houses, mosques or oil-presses. One took more care in decorating utensils that were to be used only occasionally, for marriage ceremonies and the like: they included plates and stemmed drinking glasses, certain ones of which could hold up to 15 kg.

Towards the 1950s, there were still nearly 500 potters working in Guellala; now there are only about 40 remaining. Like other centres of pottery that flourished around the Mediterranean, the Master Craftsmen in Guellala are in the process of disappearing, but the pottery traders of Nabeul have multiplied thanks to tourism.

Glazed oil lamp for domestic use.

GLOSSARY

Agha	An officer's rank within the Turkish army.
Amir	Governar, Prince, dignitary.
'Arrush	(Sing. *'Arsh*), tribes.
'Attarin	Merchants of perfume, incense and medicinal plants.
'Auwla	Provisions.
'Azzaba	Council presided over by a *shaykh*.
Bab	Gate.
Bahu	Hall, inner courtyard, in front of the prayer room. By extension an entrance.
Bahussah	Native Jews of al-Kef.
Bala	Scimitar; a large, rounded sabre.
Barrani	A foreigner.
Bayt	Room, in certain cases a house (*Bayt al-Hikma*; tribunal).
Bey	Title held by the sovereign vassals of the sultan (adj. Beylical).
Beylicat	The sovereignty of the *bey*.
Blaghjiya	Babouche maker.
Bled	In North Africa, land, inland region, countryside.
Burj	Small fort or bastion. Used equally as a secondary residence surrounded by gardens; a pleasure palace.
Caliph	From Arabic *Khalifa*, meaning the supreme head of the Muslim community in the line of the Prophet's successors.
Caliphate	The charge or territory under the power of the *caliph*.
Caravanserai	Hostel along main travelling routes to accommodate travellers and safeguard their goods.
Champlevé	A kind of enamel.
Cuerda seca	Ceramic technique using coloured enamel glazes.
Dahliz	Cave.
Dar	House.
Derb	Alley or impasse. By extension a neighbourhood.
Dey	High-ranking officer in the Turkish militia.
Diaf	Guests.
Diwan	A register; an office of government or ministry; royal reception chamber; a collection of poems.
Driba	Initial entrance room.
Duwar	A hamlet.
Ebourrage	To rub vigorously with a pumice-stone or similar implement in the readying of animal skin in the process of parchment making.
Fnar	Lamp, beacon
Ftur	To lunch, to eat.
Funduq	A term particular to North Africa to designate a hostel which can accommodate both animals and people; a shop for merchandise and a commercial centre, analogous to the *caravanserais* or *khans* of the Muslim East.
Futuhat	Muslim conquests: literally "openings".
Ghaba	Forest.

Ghazi	Warrior for the Faith, organised into military ranks within the Ottoman Empire. The word *razzia* is derived from *ghaziya*.
Ghazwa	A military campaign.
Ghorfa	A troglodytic or cave-like cell used as a dwelling or for storing grain.
Gtif	Nomad rug.
Guenariya	A balcony enclosed with open-work wood panels.
Habus	Gift bequeathed in perpetuity, usually by the deceased. See *waqf*.
Hadith	(Lit "sayings"). Tradition related to the acts, sayings and attitudes of the Prophet Muhammad and his companions.
Haj	(Fem. *Haja*) Pilgrimage (to Mecca). One of the five pillars of Islam. By extension it also refers to a man or woman who undertakes this formality.
Hallab	A ceramic or terracotta bowl.
Hammam	Public or private bath house.
Hara	Quarter, often employed in reference to Jewish Quarters.
Harka	Duty, service.
Harsh	Sandstone.
Hawanit	Punic burial (place).
Heml	Rug-blankets.
Heri	Provisions granary.
Hnaya	Aqueduct, arcades.
Hush	Denotes a courtyard within a house, or an entire dwelling place.
Huma	Quarter.
Imam	One who presides over Islamic prayer; a guide, chief, spiritual model or cleric, and sometimes, also, a politician in Muslim society.
Jabal	Mountain or mountainous terrain.
Jabaliya	Mountain dwellers.
Jadid	New.
Jami'	Main mosque where daily prayers and Friday prayers are celebrated.
Jamur	Lantern of the minaret.
Jesser	Barrier, dam, bridge.
Jihad	Striving towards moral and religious perfection. It can lead to fighting "on the path to God" against dissidents or pagans. Holy War undertaken to protect and defend Islamic territories. *Ijtihad* (same etymological root as *jihad*): a personal effort of interpretation of Islamic law.
Kadhal	Limestone used in paving and in the frames of doors and windows.
Kahiya	Military rank. Also designates an administrative position.
Kambut	A large grain container, also known as a *ruyina*.
Kasbah	Fortress, citadel.
Khammala	Hiding-place for precious objects, adjoining the *ghorfa*.
Khan	Designates a stop-over shelter along communication routes, and a depot as well as a hostel (see also *funduq*) within agglomerations of certain importance.
Khawarij	(Literally "the outcasts" / "outsiders"). Muslims who, from the point of view of the Sunnites, have abandoned the true path. Puritanical and highly militant religious Muslim sect that opposed both 'Ali (Cousin and

Glossary

	son-in-law of the Prophet; Umayyad Caliph, r. 35/656–40/661) and Mu'awiya (Umayyad Caliph, r. 41/661–60/680). Kharijite movement.
Khutba	Sermon of the Friday payer.
Kib	A cabin made of olive-tree branches, a shack.
Kitab	Book.
Klim	Kilim, woven rug.
Ksiba	Small *kasbah*, and the name of a neighbourhood in Bizerte.
Kufic	Angular form, stylised, often highly decorated, Arabic script used in early *Qur'an*s and foundation inscriptions supposedly attributed to Kufa in Iraq.
Kulughli	(*kul ughlu*: "son of the servant"), term designating the children of a Turkish father (servant to the Sultan) and a native mother.
Kuttab	Qur'anic school of the neighborhood.
Limes	Roman fortified frontier.
Madrasa	Islamic school of sciences (theology, law, the *Qur'an*, etc.). Lodgings for students during the Mediaeval Age in Morocco; today, a school.
Mahris	*Ribat*.
Makhzen	The government belonging to the Sultan; comes from *makhzen* (grain silo).
Manar	Light, lamp, beacon.
Manzel	House.
Maq'ad	Open rooms without doors, situated on the sides of a patio.
Maqsura	A recess found on one and then on the other end of the central rut of the central sunken floor of a T-shaped room.
Mashrabiyya	Wooden lattice screens made of turned pieces of wood assembled together to form a window grille.
Masjed	A mosque where daily prayers are held with the exception of Friday prayers (lit. "place of prostration").
Massassa	A drinking fountain.
Matmora	Underground room, by extension an underground prison.
Mawla	Master.
Mazru'at	Agricultural cultivation.
Meddeb	A master in a Qur'anic school, a private tutor.
Medina	Town. In North Africa it is the old part of an agglomeration, in opposition to the European-imposed extensions to the towns.
Manzel	A Jerban house.
Mergum	A woven rug.
Mhalla	Caravan in charge of the collection of taxes.
Midha	The hall where ritual ablutions take place, found next to the mosque.
Mihrab	Arched niche, mostly concave but sometimes flat, indicating the direction of Mecca (the *qibla*) and thus of prayer, found at the centre of the back wall in a mosque.
Minbar	Pulpit in a mosque from which the *imam* preaches his sermon (*khutba*) to the faithful.
Mrah	A distance, or a journey.
Muezzin	Religious Muslim administrator, in charge of announcing the five daily prayers from the top of the mosque's minaret.

Muqarnas	Stalactite or honeycomb ornament that adorns cupolas or corbels of a building.
Murabit	(Pl. *murabitun*). A religious Muslim, sanctified by asceticism, whose tomb is a place of pilgrimage (marabout).
Muwashahat	Arabic-style music.
Najd	A fertile crescent.
Naqsh hadida	Sculpted plaster, done with an iron tool.
Naskhi	(Lit. "copied"). The name of one of the most widely used calligraphic (cursive) scripts from the Arabic alphabet.
Nukkar	Denotes "Those who renounce", the singular name given to members of the religious brotherhood of the *Nukkariya*.
Nukkariya	Religious brotherhood.
Qadus	A rudimentary pottery *clepsydre*.
Qal'a	Citadel.
Qallalin	An area in Tunis where Turkish-inspired polychrome pottery was produced.
Qarya	(Pl. *Qura'*) A hamlet.
Qaysariyya	A name used in certain countries to designate *suqs*. Covered markets.
Qbu	The central sunken area belonging to a T-shaped room.
Qdhib	A long, thin ceramic tile that encircles wall panels.
Qibla	The direction which points towards the *Ka'ba* (literally "cube"), the temple of Mecca which has become the centre of the Muslim faith, which Muslims face during prayer.
Qsar	(Pl. *qsur*) Palace.
Qubba	A dome, by extension a monument or chamber built over the grave of a saint. Marabout.
Qumach	Fabric, textile.
Qur'an	(From the root *qr'*, "to recite, to read"). Sacred text of the Islamic revelation, transmitted by the Archangel Gabriel to the Prophet Muhammad.
Raggam	Weaver.
Rahba	Market Place.
Rbat	A suburb.
Reconquest	Reconquest in Spain by the Christians against the Muslims.
Ribat	Fortresses built on the border zones, from where religious warriors who dwelled there went to fight the Holy War. The town name Rabat comes from *Ribat al-Fath*, *Ribat* of the "Conquest".
Rihya	Babouche, slipper.
Rosfa	Limestone layer or ledge.
Rwa	Open-roof entrance found in country houses.
Sabat	Covered passageway
Sabil	Fountain.
Sahn	Courtyard preceding the prayer room of a mosque.
Sakkajin	Name of an area in Tunis where leather was treated.
Seguia	Irrigation canal.
Senia	Gardens in Tunis.
Seniet	Gardens, orchards.

Glossary

Senjak	A standard, a military unit.
Shamma'in	Candlemakers.
Shamsa	Small window above a door, often plaster coated.
Shawachi	*Sheshiya*s maker.
Shawuch	Orderly or notary, an usher, attendant.
Shaykh	Elderly man, respected for his age and knowledge; Tribal chief or leader of a brotherhood.
Sherif	(Pl. *Shorfa*): A descendant of the Prophet Muhammad.
Sheshiya	Headgear in the shape of a skullcap, worn by men.
Shi'a	(hence Shi'ite) A term for a party or faction, not thought of as part of Orthodox Islam: they believe that 'Ali, the Prophet's cousin and son-in-law, is the first legitimate *caliph*.
Simat al-Adham	A main road.
Sofra	Low table.
Sqifa	Entrance to a house, often twisting and turning.
Sta	A master-mason in Sfax.
Suq	Market place.
Sur	Wall, ramparts.
Sura	Chapter of the *Qur'an*.
Taifa	(Lit. "faction", "party"). In particular referring to the independent principalities which were formed from the remains of the Umayyad Caliphate of Cordoba.
Tariqa	Brotherhood.
Turbe	Private burial place, an architectural practice introduced in Tunisia by the Turks.
Uda	Room, barracks.
Udu	Ritual ablutions before prayer.
Ujak	(Lit. "cauldron"). Refers to the smallest grouping (10 persons) of the Janissary Corps of the Turkish army, who feed themselves from the same cauldron.
Umma	Community.
Wadi	Temporary stream of water running through arid regions.
Wakil	Manager.
Wali	Saint.
Waqf	An endowment in perpetuity, usually land or property, from which revenue was reserved for the upkeep of pious foundations.
Wikala	Lodgings, *caravanserai*s. One of many kinds of trading establishments. (See *caravaserai*.)
Wuli	A male saint.
Zawiya	Establishment under the authority of a brotherhood, reserved for religious teaching designed for training *shaykhs*; includes the mausoleum of a saint, built on the site where he lived.
Zlabiya	A scroll-like decoration created in blacksmithing.
Zellij	Small enamelled ceramic tiles used to decorate monuments and interiors.

HISTORICAL PERSONALITIES

'Abd Allah Ibn al-Habhab
Governor of the Maghreb under the Umayyad Caliphate of Damascus. He is attributed with having founded the Great Mosque of Tunis in 113/732.

'Abd al-Mu'min Ibn 'Ali
Almohad Caliph who undertook, from his capital Marrakesh, the Conquest of Ifriqiya during the middle of the $6^{th}/12^{th}$ century, unifying al-Andalus and the entire Maghreb.

'Abd Allah al-Torjman
Originally known as Anselme Turmeda, a Mallorcan monk who arrived in Tunis in 790/1388, he renounced Christianity and died in his adoptive town where one can find his tomb.

Abu Belhassan Chadhli known as Sidi Belhassan (592/1196–656/1258)
Founder of al-Chadhliya brotherhood; he was expelled by the Hafsid Sultan and died in Egypt in 656/1258.

Abu al-'Abbas Mohamed
Aghlabid Amir, who reigned from 226/841 to 241/856. He built the Great Mosque of Sousse in 236/851.

Abu Fares (796/1394–837/1434)
Hafsid Sultan, he erected the Humt Suq Fortress in the $8^{th}/13^{th}$ century.

Abu Ibrahim Ahmad
Aghlabid Amir who reigned from 241/856 to 248/863.

Abu Ishak (677/1279–681/1283)
Hafsid sovereign; a great *Sufi*, he gave his name to a small village situated 30 km. from Sfax. His mausoleum, visible from the main road, is distinguished by its numerous domes.

Abu Sa'id al-Baji or Sidi Bu Sa'id (550 1156–628/1231)
An important saint whose habit it was to go on religious retreats on the headland overlooking the Gulf of Carthage where he was buried in 628/1231. This laid the foundation of the famous village of Sidi-Bou-Saïd.

Abu Samir 'Abid al-Gharyani
Professor who taught for 20 years in the *madrasa* in which he was later buried in 804/1402.

Abu Zakariya al-Hafsi (625/1228–646/1249)
Governor of the Almohad Caliph in Tunis. Founder of the Hafsid Dynasty, he turned Tunis into the capital of the new kingdom after having freed it from the domination of the Moroccan Caliph (626/1229).

Abu Zama'a 'Ubayd Ibn Arqam al-Balawi
A companion of the Prophet who died in 33/654 during an Islamic military campaign in Ifriqiya against the Byzantine army. He was also called "the barber" because he carried with him several of the Prophet's hairs as a relic.

Ahmed Ibn al-Aghlab
Amir of Kairouan, he reigned towards the middle of the $3^{rd}/9^{th}$ century and put Sfax into the history books through the construction of its ramparts and its Great Mosque.

'Ali Pasha
Nephew of the Bey Husayn Ibn 'Ali, he fomented a Revolt and took power from 1152/1740 to 1169/1756.

'Ali Pasha II
Son of Husayin Ibn 'Ali, he reigned from 1172/1759 to 1196/1782.

'Ali Turki
A Greek from Candie (modern-day Crete) who converted to Islam, he settled in al-Kef as Area Commander. Father of Husayn Ibn 'Ali, founder of the Husaynite Dynasty which governed Tunisia for over two and a-half centuries.

'Amor Ibn Salam al-Ayari known as 'Abada
A great *Sufi* who lived in the first half of the $13^{th}/19^{th}$ century; it is he whom we should thank for the Zawiya and the Museum of Sidi 'Amor 'Abada.

Bachir Abu Lubaba al-Ansari
One of the Prophet's companions. His remains are found in the mausoleum in Gabés which carries his name.

Banu Hilal and Banu Soleym
Bedouin tribes of Arab origin who arrived in Ifriqiya in the $5^{th}/11^{th}$ century, after a stay in Upper Egypt.

Banu Khurasan
Dynasty founded by 'Abd al-Haq Ibn Khurasan, an officer of Sanhadjian origin, sent to Tunis as Governor of the Banu Hammads of Algeria.

Shaykh 'Ali al-Nuri (1052/1643–1134/1722)
An educational scholar and a silent partner in commerce, he organised the struggle against the Cavaliers of Malta. He is to this day considered to be the symbol of the Sfaxian Renaissance.

Shaykh Ibrahim al-Jomni (1037/1628–1134/1722)
Born in Joumna (now Kébilie), he studied in Cairo and settled in Jerba where he dedicated himself to teaching.

Shaykh Ibrahim al-Riyahi (1180/1767–1266/1850)
Born in Testour, scholar, poet, *Sufi* and politician.

Al-Baji al-Mas'udi (1224/1810–1309 1892)
Born in Tunis, he studied at the Great Mosque. He ordered the construction of a fortress on the Gulf of Hammamet to protect the Ifriqiyan coasts.

Al-Mahdi
Spiritual leader of the Fatimids, who are descendants of Muhammad via his daughter Fatima. They consider themselves to be the only legitimate *caliph*s.

Al-Mu'izz Ibn Badis (406/1016–454/1062)
Zirid Prince, he was part of the Banu Hilal, "Sons of the crescent moon", Arab nomads who a long time ago had left behind their native Najd, in the peninsula and had in part emigrated to Upper Egypt.

Al-Wazir al-Sarraj (1069/1659–1148/1736)
Born and died in Tunis. A man of letters, a historian and poet from the first Husaynite period.

Hammuda Pasha al-Husayni (1196/1782–1229/1814)
Son of 'Ali Pasha II. Built the Sidi al-Morjani barracks.

Hammuda Pasha al-Muradi
Mohamed, known as Hamuda, son of Murad, a renegade pirate who founded the Muradite Dynasty (1140/1631).

Husayn Ibn 'Ali Turki (1116/1705–1152/1740)
Agha of the *Spahi*s (a rank in the Turkish army), he instituted the Husaynite Dynasty which retained power until the Proclamation of the Republic in 1957.

Ibn Abi Dhiyaf (1218/1804–1290/1874)
Born and died in Tunis. A high-ranking civil servant, he wrote and left to posterity an important book on the history of Tunis.

Ibn Abi Dinar
Man of letters, historian and poet. Born in Kairouan, he lived in the 11th–12th / end of 17th century.

Ibn Khaldun (732/1332–808/1406)
Man of letters, he influenced universal thought and scholarship by formulating the basis of modern sociology.

Kharijite Abu Yazid
Nicknamed "the man on the donkey", he led a Revolt against the Fatimid *Caliph*. He was captured and put to death in 335/947.

Mahrez Ibn Khalaf (339/951–412/1022)
Patron Saint of the Medina of Tunis; called the *Sultan al-Madina*.

Mohamed al-Sadok Bey (1275/1859–1299/1882)
He promulgated a Constitution, *Destur*, in 1277/1861.

Mulay Hassan
Dethroned Hafsid Sultan; he called on Charles Quint for help.

'Uqba Ibn Nafi'
Troop leader during the Arab Conquest, he founded Kairouan in 50/670.

Qacem al-Zelliji
Of Andalusian origin, Abu el-Fadhel Qacem, called Qacem al-Zelliji, lived in Tunis during the 2nd half of the 9th/15th century; he died in 895/1490 and was buried in his *zawiya* where Andalusian immigrants went to comfort themselves and find lodgings.

Sidi 'Ammar al-Ma'rufi
Religious and well-educated, he took part and was killed in the conflict against the troops led by Saint Louis against Tunis.

Yahya Ibn Ghaniya
Almoravid prince who became Master of the Island of Mallorca. He took it upon himself to relieve the Maghreb of Almohad domination.

FURTHER READING

AFRICAIN, L., *Description de l'Afrique*, 2 V., Paris, 1956.

BAKLOUTI, N., *Poteries modelées de Tunisie*, Tunis, 1990.

BAKLOUTI, N., *Tunisie*, "25 siècles de céramique", Paris, 1994, pp. 277-283.

BARRUCAND, M., *Urbanisme princier en Islam*, Paris, 1985.

CHABBOUH, I., *Le manuscrit*, Tunis, 1989.

COMBES, J. L., and LOUIS, A., *Les pottiers de Jerba*, Tunis, 1967.

EL-BEKRI, A., *Description de l'Afrique septentrionale*, translation by de Slane, Paris, 1913.

LALLEMAND, Ch., *La Tunisie*, Paris, 1892.

LÉZINE, A., *Le Ribat de Sousse suivi de notes sur le Ribat de Monastir*, Tunis, 1956.

LÉZINE, A., *Mahdiya*, Tunis, 1968.

LISSE, P., and LOUIS, A., *Les potiers de Nabeul, étude de sociologie tunisienne*, Tunis, 1956.

LOUIS, A., *Tunisie du sud, Ksars et villages de crêtes*, Paris, 1975.

MAOUDOUD, K., *Kairouan*, Tunis, 1991.

MARÇAIS, G., *Manuel d'art musulman*, 2 vols. Paris, 1926-1927.

MARÇAIS, G., *Architecture musulmane d'Occident : Tunisie, Algérie, Maroc Espagne et Sicile*, Paris, 1954.

MARÇAIS, G., and GOLVIN, L., *La Grande Mosquée de Sfax*, Tunis, 1960.

PELLISSIER, E., *Description de la Régence de Tunis*, Tunis, 1980.

REVAULT, J., *Palais et résidences d'été de la région de Tunis*, Paris, 1974.

REVAULT, J., *Palais et demeures de Tunis, XVIe et XVIIe siècles*, 2 Vols., Paris, 1980-1983.

TERRASSE, A., *L'art hispano-mauresque des origines au XIIIe siècle*, Paris, 1932.

TLATLI, S., *Djerba, l'île des lotophages*, Tunis, 1966.

VEUILLIER, G., *la Tunisie*, Tours, 1896.

AUTHORS

Naceur Baklouti
Born in 1946 in Sfax, Mr Baklouti studied Museum Curatorship and then set up several ethnological museums in Tunisia. He has organised a variety of exhibitions and undertaken research in areas of art and popular culture, such as ceramics, architecture and literature.
Mr Baklouti is the author of several works and articles on the aforementioned subjects. Today, he is a Director of the National Institute of Heritage of Sfax.

Aziza Ben Tanfous
Born in 1942 in Tunis, Mrs Ben Tanfous has been involved in various exhibitions on the arts and popular traditions, both in Tunisia and abroad (France, Morocco, the Gulf States, Canada). She has also been a contributor to various published exhibition catalogues and collections of writing, such as "Women's Ceremonial Costumes " edited by the MTE in 1980. Following a period as a curator at the Museum of Popular Arts and Traditions of Jerba, Mrs Ben Tanfous is now a conservationist in the Museum of Popular Arts and Traditions of Tunis.

Jamila Binous
Born in 1939 in Tunis, Mrs Binous studied history and geography at the University of Tunis and urbanism at the University of Tours (France).
Mrs Binous is Consultant Director to the Mayor, President of the Association for the Safeguarding of the Medina of Tunis.
She was also an appointed expert to Unesco (Mission Sanaa "Historical Town") in 1982; a national expert on the UNDP project for the reconstruction of Mediterranean sites of historic value; a member of the International Committee of Historical Towns; and co-author of the International Charter of Historic Towns (ICOMOS-UNESCO).
Mrs Binous has taken part in various international congress meetings and has written several articles and works such as: *Tunis d'un monument à l'autre*, Tunis, 1970; *Tunis*, Tunis, 1985; *Les chefs d'oeuvre de l'artisanat tunisien*, Tunis, 1982.

Mounira Chapoutot-Remadi
Born in 1942 in Tunis, she was Aggregated A Fellow of the University of Paris, she has a State Doctorate in Mediaeval Islamic History (Aix-en-Provence) and is a specialist on the Islamic world of the Middle Ages in Mamluk Egypt and Mamluk Syria (1248-1517).
Mrs Chapoutot was a founding member of the Tunisian Society of University Historians, after which she became its President; she is a guest at the French Institute of Arab Studies in Damascus.
Mrs Chapoutot also organises various international conferences and has published numerous articles and works such as: *Être Mamelouk aux XIIIe et XIVe siècles* (forthcoming, éditions de la Méditerranée); *Vie quotidienne des femmes en Égypte Mamelouk* (forthcoming, Hachette publishing).

Mohamed Kadri Bouteraa
Born in 1932 in Gafsa, he studied at the National College of Administration in Tunis, then studied Arabic heritage, language and civilisation at a Lebanese University (*jami'a lubnaniya*).

In 1966, he began work at the National Institute of Heritage in Tunis where he was Co-Inspector, Inspector and then General Secretary of Historic Monuments.
Mr Bouteraa is involved in the development of an archaeological map of urban sites and monuments, and is the author of several publications, including: *El Mouhamdiya, bilad al-Mouchir*, which was published in 1995 by Dar Carthage Lil Itissal, as well as various articles on adobe construction.

Salah Jabeur

Born in Paris, he studied in Tunis and took his first steps towards a career in photography in France. In 1981, he participated in various exhibitions both in Tunisia and in France, and settled in Tunisia in 1984 where he works as a touristic, industrial and editorial photographer.
Salah Jabeur has published *La mosaïque en Tunisie*, which was issued by Alif publishing in 1995, *La Tunisie vue du ciel* by the same publisher in 1996, and *La blessure de l'âne* published in 1998 by Script publishing.

Mourad Rammah

Born in 1953 in Kairouan, he is a Doctor of Islamic Archaeology and is also Guardian and Curator of Kairouan's Medina. In 1992, he received the Agha Khan prize for architecture. He has published various articles on the history of Mediaeval Islamic archaeology in Tunisia and participated in several different exhibitions on Islamic architecture. From 1982 until 1994, Mr. Rammah was in charge of the Archive Department of the Centre for Arts and Islamic Civilisations. He is also Director of the Centre for Manuscripts of Kairouan.

Ahmed Saadaoui

Born in 1957 in Mahdia, he completed his studies in history at the University of Tunis, and studied Islamic Archaeology at the Sorbonne. He has taken part in various archaeological digs and teaches history and archaeology in the Humanities Faculty of the Manouba (Tunis).

Mohamed Tlili

Born in 1949 in Kef, he studied history and archaeology in Paris and Rome, and has a Diploma from the Centre of Urban Heritage and Architectural Conservation in Belgium. He is a Member of the National Institute of Heritage, he is also Technical Director of the Association for the Safeguarding of the Medina of Kef. Mr. Tlili has published numerous articles on the history and heritage of the site and town of Kef.

Ali Zouari

Born in 1935 in Sfax, he was Director of Research for many years at the National Institute of Heritage. He managed the Museum of Popular Arts and Traditions in the town of Sfax, where he was also curator, as well as being curator at the Museum of Traditional Architecture of Sfax (Kasbah Museum). Mr Zouari is also responsible for the restoration of various monuments within Sfax's *medina*, including the Great Mosque and the ramparts. Previously a National Institute of Heritage Inspector for the south-eastern region of the country, he has published various articles as well as four books on the town of Sfax.

ISLAMIC ART IN THE MEDITERRANEAN

This cycle of Museum With No Frontiers Exhibition Trails permits the discovery of secrets in Islamic Art, its history, construction techniques and religious inspiration.

ALGERIA

LEGACY OF ISLAM IN ALGERIA: The Art and Architecture of Light* introduces the varied and richest forms Islamic art assumed in Central Maghreb (Algeria), an important artistic heritage related to crucial events that marked the country's history, from the rise of dissident religious movements to the influence of great dynasties, and the roles played by trade and pilgrimage routes and by the Ottomans in the Mediterranean cities. The synthesis of Arab and Berber, African, Andalusian and Eastern influences shaped the artistic and architectural models, the purity and harmony of Ibadid architecture, Almoravid mosques, Ziyanid monuments and Ottoman palaces on the Mediterranean shore.

Five itineraries invite you to discover 70 museums, monuments and sites in Biskra, Ghardaia, Bani Isguen, Algiers, Tlemcen, Nedroma and Tamentit (among others).

EGYPT

MAMLUK ART: The Splendour and Magic of the Sultans tells the story of almost three centuries of political security and economic stability achieved by the sultans' successful defence against Mongol and Crusader threats. The intellectual, scientific and artistic currents that flourished then are manifest in Mamluk architecture and decorative arts, almost modern in their elegant and lively simplicity, bearing witness to the vitality of Mamluk trade, to their cultural exuberance and to their military and religious strength.

Eight itineraries invite you to discover 51 museums, monuments and sites in Cairo, Alexandria and the Nile Delta.

ITALY

SICULO-NORMAN ART: Islamic Culture in Medieval Sicily illustrates how the great artistic and cultural heritage of the Arabs who ruled the island in the 10th and 11th centuries was assimilated and reinterpreted during the Norman reign that followed, achieving its acme in the resplendent age of Ruggero II in the 12th century. Spectacular coastal and mountain landscapes provide the backdrop for visits to villages, castles, gardens, churches and Christianised old mosques.

Ten itineraries invite you to discover 91 museums, monuments and sites in Palermo, Monreale, Mazara del Vallo, Salemi, Segesta, Erice, Cefalù and Catania (among others).

JORDAN

THE UMAYYADS: The Rise of Islamic Art presents a journey through the great artistic and cultural flourishing that gave birth to the formative phase of Islamic art during the 7th and 8th centuries. The Umayyads unified the Mediterranean and Persian cultures and developed an innovative artistic synthesis that incorporated and immortalised Classical, Byzantine and Sassanid heritage. The elegant architecture of desert castles and the frescoes, mosaics and masterpieces of figurative and decorative art still evoke the strong sense of realism and the great cultural, artistic and social vitality of the centres of the Umayyad Caliphate.

Five itineraries invite you to discover 43 museums, monuments and sites in Amman, Madaba, Al-Badiya, Jerash, Umm Qays, Aqaba and Humayma (among others).

MOROCCO

ANDALUSIAN MOROCCO: Discovery in Living Art tells the story of the exchanges between the furthest frontier of the Maghreb and Al-Andalus for more than five centuries. Political and social circumstances gave birth to a crossroads of cultures, techniques and artistic styles revealed by the splendour of Idrisid, Almoravid, Almohad and Marinid mosques, minarets and madrasas. The influence of Cordoban architecture and Andalusian decorative models, horseshoe arches, floral and geometric motifs and the use of stucco, wood and polychromatic tiles, display the continuous interchange that made Morocco one of the most brilliant homes of Islamic civilisation.

Eight itineraries invite you to discover 89 museums, monuments and sites in Rabat, Meknès, Fez, Chefchaouen, Tétouan and Tangier (among others).

PALESTINIAN TERRITORIES

PILGRIMAGE, SCIENCE AND SUFISM: Islamic Art in the West Bank and Gaza explores a period during the reigns of the Ayyubid, Mamluk and Ottoman dynasties when numerous pilgrims and scholars from all quarters of the Muslim world came to Palestine. The great dynasties commissioned architectural and artistic masterpieces in the most important religious centres. Attracting the most learned scholars, many centres enjoyed considerable prestige and encouraged the spread of a rarefied art that still fascinates today. The Islamic monuments and architecture of this Exhibition Trail clearly reflect the connections between dynastic patronage, intellectual activity and the rich expression of people's devotion, rooted in this land for centuries.

Nine itineraries invite you to discover 70 museums, monuments and sites in Jerusalem, Jericho, Nablus, Bethlehem, Hebron and Gaza (among others).

PORTUGAL

IN THE LANDS OF THE ENCHANTED MOORISH MAIDEN: Islamic Art in Portugal uncovers five inspired centuries of Islamic civilisation that shaped the people of the former Gharb al-Andalus. From Coimbra to the furthest reaches of the Algarve there are palaces, Christianised mosques, fortifications and urban centres, all of which bear witness to the splendour of a glorious past. This artistic recollection is the expression of a very delicate symbiosis that determined the particularities of vernacular architecture and still permeates the cultural identity of Portugal.

Ten itineraries invite you to discover 76 museums, monuments and sites in Lisbon, Sintra, Coimbra, Evora, Mertola, Faro and Sesimbra (among others).

SPAIN

MUDEJAR ART: Islamic Aesthetics in Christian Art uncovers the fascinating richness of a genuinely Hispanic cultural and artistic symbiosis that became a distinctive element of Christian Spain after the end of Arab rule. Mudejars were Muslims who were allowed to stay in the reconquered territories and Mudejar artists and craftsmen strongly influenced the culture and art of the new Christian kingdoms. Beautifully decorated brick-built churches, monasteries and palaces in Aragona, Castile, Estremadura and Andalusia provide a unique example of the creative preservation of Islamic forms within Christian art in Spain between the 11th and 16th centuries.

Thirteen itineraries invite you to discover 124 museums, monuments and sites in Madrid, Guadalajara, Saragossa, Tordesillas, Toledo, Guadalupe and Seville (among others).

SYRIA

THE AYYUBID ERA: Art and Architecture in Medieval Syria* focuses on the unique artistic and architectural development in 12th–13th century Syria, when Atabeg and Ayyubid military resistance to the Crusaders coincided with a great cultural and artistic revival in the most important Syrian cities. The Ayyubid patrons provided educative, religious and charitable institutions; their intense activity left its mark in the sober elegance of mosques, madrasas, citadels, mausoleums and hospitals, embellished with Eastern architectural and decorative motifs, muqarnas, Kufic inscriptions, carved stucco and wooden minbars, beautifully illuminated manuscripts, pottery, metalwork and textiles.

Eight itineraries invite you to discover 95 museums, monuments and sites in Damascus, Bosra, Homs, Hama, Tartus, Aleppo and Raqqa (among others).

TUNISIA

IFRIQIYA: Thirteen Centuries of Art and Architecture in Tunisia is a voyage through the history of the Islamic architecture of the Maghreb, to uncover a millenary civilisation that made works of art of its most important spaces. The great Islamic dynasties – Abbasids, Aghlabids, Fatimids, Zirids, Almohads, Hafsids, Ottomans – and Islamic religious schools and movements left the mark of their artistic expression over the centuries. Islamic art in Tunisia is a cultural crossroads, widely influenced by local artistic customs, by Andalusian and eastern architectural and decorative elements, by Arab, Roman and Berber traditions and by the variety of its natural landscape.

Eleven itineraries invite you to discover 108 museums, monuments and sites in Tunis, Sidi Bou Saïd, Bizerte, Testour, Al-Kef, Kairouan, Mahdia, Sfax, Tozeur and Gabès (among others).

TURKEY

EARLY OTTOMAN ART: The Legacy of the Emirates presents the artistic and architectural expressions in Western Anatolia and the emergence of the Ottoman dynasty in the 14th and 15th centuries. The Turkish Emirates developed a new stylistic synthesis by blending Central Asian and Seljuq traditions and the legacy of the Greek, Roman and Byzantine past. The architectural schemes of mosques, hammams, hospitals, madrasas, mausoleums and the great religious complexes, columns and domes, floral and calligraphic decoration, ceramics and illumination testify to the richness of styles. The cultural and artistic flourishing that matched the rise of the Ottoman Empire was deeply marked by the distinctive legacy of the Emirates.

Eight itineraries invite you to discover 61 museums, monuments and sites in Milas, Selçuk, Manisa, Bursa, İznik, Karacabey, Çanakkale, Gelibolu and Edirne (among others).

---

* Under preparation.

www.ingramcontent.com/pod-product-compliance
Lightning Source LLC
Chambersburg PA
CBHW071813230426
43670CB00013B/2443